*Marriages from
The Saugerties Telegraph
1846-1870
And
Obituaries, Death
Notices and
Genealogical Gleanings
from
The Ulster Telegraph
1846-1848*

Audrey M. Klinkenberg

HERITAGE BOOKS
2008

HERITAGE BOOKS
AN IMPRINT OF HERITAGE BOOKS, INC.

Books, CDs, and more—Worldwide

For our listing of thousands of titles see our website
at
www.HeritageBooks.com

Published 2008 by
HERITAGE BOOKS, INC.
Publishing Division
100 Railroad Ave. #104
Westminster, Maryland 21157

Copyright © 1998 Audrey M. Klinkenberg

Other books by the author:

Obituaries, Death Notices and Genealogical Gleanings from The Saugerties Telegraph, Volume 1:1848-1852

Obituaries, Death Notices, and Genealogical Gleanings from The Saugerties Telegraph, Volume 2: 1853-1860

Obituaries, Death Notices, and Genealogical Gleanings from The Saugerties Telegraph, Volume 3: 1861-1870

Obituaries, Death Notices & Genealogical Gleanings from the Saugerties Telegraph, Volume 4 1871-1879

Obituaries, Death Notices & Genealogical Gleanings from the Saugerties Telegraph, Volume 5: 1880-1884

CD: *New York: Volume 5, Obituaries, Death Notices and Genealogical Gleanings from The Saugerties Telegraph, Volumes 1-3*

All rights reserved. No part of this book may be reproduced or transmitted in any form or by any means, electronic or mechanical, including photocopying, recording or by any information storage and retrieval system without written permission from the author, except for the inclusion of brief quotations in a review.

International Standard Book Numbers
Paperbound: 978-0-7884-1078-9
Clothbound: 978-0-7884-7068-4

Marriages
The Saugerties Telegraph
1846-1870

and

Obituaries, Death Notices and Genealogical Gleanings
The Ulster Telegraph
1846-1848

Published by S. S. Hommel, Editor and Proprietor
at one dollar and fifty cents per annum, in advance

Ulster (Saugerties) N. Y.
Wednesday, October 28, 1846

We, this day, offer to our readers the first number of the

ULSTER TELEGRAPH

published in the village of Ulster

October 28, 1846 - December 23, 1870 - Marriages
October 28, 1846 - December 23, 1848 - Deaths

Copied and indexed by
Audrey M. Klinkenberg
Saugerties, New York

Marriage announcements - did the editor know the clergymen involved, did the couples themselves stop in the office to give the news, were they taken from the exchange newspapers received in the editorial office? Where ever they originated, these announcements may be the only record of the marriage. Some church records are not available, other churches did not keep records, but these newspapers, carefully saved by persons unknown, have survived and are on microfilm.

Many notices relate the marriage of either a bride or groom who had been a resident of this area. There are many from Greene County as well. It is also surprising to find that not a few were marriages performed by a Justice of the Peace. I have copied the names of the clergy but, in the interest of space, did not include them in the index. It is often possible to determine which Ulster County church by reading through Sylvester's *History of Ulster County*, which incorporates paragraphs about the various churches, usually including a list of past ministers. It is also interesting to note the number of published separations and divorces, allowing one to believe that many more happened without publication.

The bibliography lists all the extra church records used to verify a date or name. Some are unpublished manuscripts, but others are available for sale.

When the first volume of 'Obituaries, Death Notices and Genealogical Gleanings from the Saugerties *Telegraph*' was published there were no known earlier newspapers. Then Bill Jerwann of Saratoga County told me that he had once worked for a Saugerties newspaper establishment and had, in his attic, a volume of newspapers from the '40's. Little did I know that he meant the 1840's! He very kindly gave me the volume and the death notices simply were too valuable to remain unpublished. So, out of order, but untarnished, the obits &c. from 1846 to 1848 are included in this volume.

Heritage Books kindly agreed to publish this collection, for which I am grateful. I hope you are as well.

November 12, 1846 (Thursday)

1. In the news from Europe, the marriage of the Duke de Monpensier and the Infanta of Spain was consummated on the 10th.

2. It is with deep regret that we record the death of Willett Linderman, Esq., Attorney and Counsellor at Law. He expired at his residence in Tuthilltown on the 4th instant, aged about 50 years. Mr. Linderman stood high in his profession, was possessed of fine talents and enjoyed in an eminent degree the confidence of the community. His private character was irreproachable which gained for him the universal esteem of a large circle of acquaintences. <sic> He has left many warm friends to lament his loss.

3. Married on the 20th ult., by the Rev. R. Dederick, Mr. George Teitzel of Kingston, to Miss Mary Teitzel, of Germany.

4. Married on the 26th ult., by the same, Mr. James Dubois of New York to Miss Mahala Jane Schutt of Catskill.

5. Married at Westkill, on the 25th ult., by the Rev. Mr. Barret, Mr. Joseph O. Reed, of West Hurley, to Miss Zipporah M. Curtis of Windham Centre.

6. Married on the 27th ultimo, by the Rev. Dr. Ostrander, Mr. Cornelius P. Brink, to Miss Louisa Myer, daughter of Benjamin Myer, deceased, all of Saugerties.

7. Died in this village, on the 2nd instant, Mary, wife of Peter Decker, aged about 31 years.

8. Died in this village on Sunday, 24th ult., Harriet, daughter of Charles H. and Harriet Bunt, aged four months and two days.

November 28, 1846 (Saturday)

9. Execution of Flynn - Flynn, the murderer of James, was executed at Catskill on the 19th inst. The execution took place inside of the prison: his body was brought to this village and interred on the following day.

10. Died in this village, on the 16th inst., Abram E. Schoonmaker, aged about 50 years. Mr. Schoonmaker was keeper of the Lighthouse at this place at the time of his death.

December 5, 1846 (Saturday)

11. Wreck of the Steamer Atlantic in the Late Gale - Officers and Passengers of the Boat Lost - Captain Dustan of the Atlantic; Dr. Haslin of the Navy; Lieut. Norton of the Army; a clergyman named Armstrong; Mrs. Hilton, stewardess; Sarah Johnson, chambermaid; Sarah Ruby, of Providence, do; Eliza Wacob, servant of Mrs. Lewis; John Walter, Mrs. Jane Walton, and their children, John, James and Eleanor Jane, all one family, from West Newburgh, for Pennsylvania; Robert Vine and Jacob Walton; of the same family, saved. The following are the names of such of the crew lost as we have been able to ascertain: - John Gleason, Thomas Gedney, Michael Dougerty, Charles Ryley, John Macfarlan. The Boston *Traveller*, of Saturday evening, includes in the list of the dead, the names of Mr. Collamore, of Boston, and W. V. Solace, of Bridgeport, Vt. The *Traveller* also adds to the list of the drowned, the names of two of the crew - Warren Smith and Philip Mayhew. The Norwich *Courier* adds to the list of the drowned, Isaac Fitz, of New York. This makes twenty-three, in all, known to have been drowned. Later - The Boston *Atlas* of yesterday morning adds to the melancholy list the names of Orlando Pitts and Charles French, clerks in insurance offices in that city. Dr. Watson, of that city, and Mrs. Thompson and child, of Danvers. The Boston *Post* mentions in addition to those before mentioned, the name of Mr. William Burbank, of Brooklyn N. Y. The name of Mr. Burbank is included in the list of those of whom no account has been previously given and from a similarity of names, we have reason to fear the individual lost was one of the members of our Assembly from Kings county in 1814. The *Advertiser* adds to the list the name of Mr. Kimball, of Brooklyn. The *Times* closes this list with the name of Mrs. Smart; swelling the aggregate to 32, and leaving, we fear, still several to be accounted for. <long story>

12. General Stephen Watts Kearny, lately Colonel of the 1st Regiment of Dragoons, and who commands in New Mexico, was born on the 30th August, 1794, at the family homestead in Newark, N. J., now owned and occupied by the family. He is a descendant of an Irish

family - his great-grandfather, a barrister, was born on his paternal estate, Garrets Town, County of Cork, Ireland, where he married and afterwards came to this country and settled in Perth Amboy, in this state. Gen. Kearney <sic> received the rudments <sic> of his education in Newark Academy - continued his studies in Columbia College in the city of New York, and would have graduated in the summer of 1812, but upon the declaration of War against Great Britain in June, he applied for and received a commission. He was a Lieutenant in the Battle of Queenston, where Col. Christie presented him with his sword on the field of battle for his cool and determined manner in the execution of the command which devolved upon him. He has ever since continued in the army, having been stationed many years in the West, where he married the step-daughter of the distinguished Gen. Merryweather Clarke, of St. Louis.

13. Married in Loyd, on the 19th ult., by the Rev. A. O. Peloubet, Mr. William H. Bush, to Miss Loretta Dobbs, both of Loyd.

14. Married in Poughkeepsie, on the 5th ult., by the Rev. C. Van Loon, Mr. Robert D. Monell of Kingston, to Miss Mary E. Williams of the former place.

15. Married at St. Andrews, Orange Co., on the 18th ult., by the Rev. Mr. Ten Eyck, Mr. Willett Kidd, to Miss Mary Ann Newkirk, all of that place.

16. Died at the residence of her father, John A. Buckhout, in the town of Loyd, Ulster Co, on the 25th ult., Miss Maria P. Buckhout, aged 29 years and six months.

17. Died in New York, on the 22nd ult., Charles E. Heyer, formerly a resident of Kingston, aged about 35 years.

18. Died in New York, on the 24th ult., Edgar, son of Martin Easterly, aged 6 years.

19. Died at Prairie Du Chien, Crawford County, Wisconsin, on the 11th Sept, Mr. Ezra Pelton, aged 39 years.

20. Died at the same place, on the 13th Sept, Mrs. Nancy Pelton, wife of Ezra Pelton, aged 39 years.

21. Died at the same place, on the 13th Sept, Mr. Champion Pelton, aged 43 years.

22. Died at the same place, on the 29th Sept, Mr. James Hendricks, aged 30 years.

23. Died on the 28th ult., Adam France, a soldier of the revolution, aged 83 years, 4 months.

24. Distressing Ravages of Spotted Fever - We learn from the Rev. Mr. Pilch, of the Bethel Church that the family of Abraham Brown, of No. 9, Beach St. in this city, died with fatal effects of putrid fever. His son James, about 12 years old, died on the 1st of October, after much suffering. Samuel, a little brother, aged about 11, died on the 17th. The father was affected with the same malady, and died on the 25th, aged 46 years, and his daughter Lydia, a little girl of 7 years died on the 23rd inst. The family comprised ten members and all the males have been cut off. Newark *Advertiser*.

December 12, 1846 (Saturday)

25. Zadock Pratt was born on the 30th October, 1790, at Stephentown, Rensselaer Co., NY. His family is descended from the noble band of pilgrims, who first broke ground on the shores of New-England-the first persons of the name in this country being Joshua and Phinehas Pratt, who came over in the autumn of 1623. Ephraim, a grandson of Joshua Pratt, lived to the great age of 116 years and died at East Sudbury, Mass., in May, 1804. Phinehas Pratt removed from Plymouth to Charlestown. John, another of the family, came over in 1633, in company with the celebrated Puritan divines, John Cotton and Thomas Hooker; and when the church which had been formed at Newtown, Mass., by the latter, concluded to remove to Connecticut, Mr. Pratt was one of that number. The father of the principle subject of this notice, (Zadock Pratt, senior) was a native of Saybrook, Conn.; was a tanner and a shoemaker; and when the revolutionary war broke out, he shouldered his musket, and repaired to his country's standard. He was engaged in several hard fought battles-was twice taken

prisoner, and suffered much on board the prison ships at New York. After the close of the war, he removed to the state of New York, and died at Lexington, Greene county, in 1829, at the age of 74. Inheriting the patriotic spirit of his father, Mr. Pratt, in 1814, served a tour of military duty on Brooklyn Heights, when is was deemed necessary to provide fo the defence of New York from any possible descent of the enemy. (The complete first page of this issue is devoted to Zadock Pratt.)

26. Married on the 3d instant, at Olive, by Martin Schutt, Esq., Mr. Leonard L. Whitney, of the town of Esopus, to Miss Mary B. Morgan, of the former place.

27. Married by the Rev. Ira Ferris, Mr. John W. Maney, of Neversink, Sullivan county, to Miss Mary Ann Miller, of Wawarsing.

28. Died at the family residence, in the town of Kingston, Mr. Egbert H. Jansen, in the 31st year of his age.

29. Died in the town of Loyd, Ulster County, on 4th inst. after a lingering illness, William Doran, aged about 30 years.

December 19, 1846 (Saturday)

30. Horrible Death! Effects of Rum! Coroner Brink held an inquest, Thursday of this week, on the body of John Munday, a colored man, who was found dead on the morning of that day, near the house of Mr. Coggeshall, in this village. From the evidence before the Coroner's jury, it appeared that the deceased had been employed by Mr. Coggeshall, who paid him some money on Wednesday evening; at the same time cautioning him not to become intoxicated, or he would freeze to death. It appears that after leaving Mr. Coggeshall, he visited a RUM HELL in Partition street, kept by a Mrs. Welch, where he procured some liquor which he took with him in a bottle. On the way home, he crossed the field of Mr. Coggeshall, where he had been accustomed to work; the path led along the top of a steep bank, at the foot of which he was found in the morning, laying on his back in a small brook; one of his ankles dislocated, and his body bruised in several places, the effects no doubt of rolling down the steep declivity. The probability is, that the injuries he received, together with the state

of intoxication he was in, rendered him helpless, and he laid there until the cold ended the work of death. In the morning when found, the body was frozen stiff-an object dreadful to behold. It occurred to our mind, while viewing the awful corpse, that it would be a suitable sign to be placed in an erect position at the door of the house where he procured the fatal poison. The jury rendered a verdict "that the deceased came to his death by exposure to the cold while in a state of intoxication."

December 26, 1846 (Saturday)
31. Married on the 5th instant, by the Rev. Mr. Birch, Mr. Benjamin Artman to Miss Mary C. Burnett, both of this village.

32. Married on the 12th inst., by the Rev. John C. F. Hoes, Mr. William H. Dederick, of Kingston, to Miss Catharine Schoonmaker, of Rochester.

January 2, 1847 (Saturday)
33. An Elopement - Our city has lately been made the theatre of a crim. con. negotiation, in which great forbearance and moderation were displayed. Dr. Paschal B. Brooks, of Manchester, N. H. about a fortnight ago brought to this city from Lowell, and put up with her at different hotels, a Mrs. Harriet L. Davis, wife of E. D. Davis, Printer, of Manchester. By the aid of officer S. Clark, Mr. Davis and some friends of B.'s wife, traced the false pair to a hotel in this city, and on Thursday night Mr. Davis was conducted to the room occupied by them, and where they were asleep together. Nothing rash was said or done, but the parties were aroused from their slumbers, and Dr. Brooks was requested to get up, which he did, and took a seat on another bed in the room. Negotiations were then commenced, the diplomatists being the friends of Mrs. Brooks and Mr. Davis, and some of his friends; the result was that Dr. Brooks shelled out $1000 for the use of his own wife and eight children, and gave Davis $1000, and agreed to flee to parts unknown. Mrs. Davis agreed to go back to Manchester, and board in some respectable place, at the expense of her husband, whom she had never loved, and never expected to love, she said. She fell in love with the doctor on account of the tenderness with which he treated her while she was sick. Boston *Post*.

34. Gen. Erastus Root, died in New York, on Thursday morning, December 24, in the 74th year of his age.

35. Brigadier Gen. Hamar, of Ohio, died at Monterey on the 3d instant. Later From the Army.

36. The funeral of Major Ringgold was solemnized at Baltimore on Tuesday of last week. The procession was very imposing.

37. Married on the 30th ult., by the Rev. R. Dederick, Mr. John H. Mower to Miss Rebecca Snyder, both of Saugerties.

38. Married at Kingston, on the 24th inst., by the Rev. D. Stocking, Mr. Edward Lounsbery to Miss Ann Jane Beatty, both of Marbletown.

39. Married at Loyd, on the 10th inst., by the Rev. A. O. Peloubet, Mr. Lewis H. Coe to Miss Julia Eleanor Deyo.

40. Married at Loyd, on the 11th inst., by the same, Mr. William H. Wildo to Miss Sarah Jane Dimsey.

41. Married at New Paltz, on the 9th inst., by Rev. J. C. Van Dervoort, Mr. Samuel Dubois to Miss Magdalen Dubois, both of New Paltz.

42. Married at New Paltz, on the 26th inst., by the same, Mr. John W. Dubois to Miss Madgalen Dubois, daughter of Mr. Andrew Dubois, both of New Paltz.

43. Married on the 20th inst., by the Rev. Mr. Fields, Mr. Andrew S. Hill to Miss Louisa N. Wolcott, both of Olive.

44. Married at Ellenville, on the 19th inst., by the Rev. Ira Ferris, Mr. Daniel Masten to Miss Eliza Canfield, both of Mamakating.

45. Married on the 23d inst., by Ten Eyck Dewitt, Mr. Charles Davis of Rosendale, to Miss Leah Plough, of Hurley.

46. Died at Kingston on the 27th inst., John C. Van Buren, aged about 45 years.

47. Died in Kingston, on the 29th inst., John Baggs, aged about 40 years.

January 9, 1847 (Saturday)
48. We learn from the *Democratic Journal* that a man by the name of Addison Tyrrel, living in the vicinity of Ellenville, perished by cold, on the night of the 23d of December last, while in a state of intoxication. The unfortunate man purished <sic> within three rods of his own door.

January 16, 1847 (Saturday)
49. Married on the 24th Dec, by the Rev. Mr. Noble, Mr. Daniel Butts to Miss Caroline E. Dodd, daughter of Lewis Dodd, Esq. of New York city.

January 23, 1847 (Saturday)
50. Fatal Accident - Mr. Peter D. Dubois of this village while engaged in pedling at Rosendale in this county, on Saturday last, met with an accident which terminated in his death. It appears that on Saturday evening, after dark, he crossed the Rosendale bridge; at the termination of which he met a one horse waggon, which caused him to step to the side of the road which was icy, when he slipped and fell down the bank, on a rock, a distance of about twenty feet. It being dark, the persons in the waggon did not notice him. His cries for assistance were heard by some persons passing the place, who immediately repaired to his assistance, conveyed him to a house, procured medical assistance and rendered every aid in their power, but the severe injuries the unfortunate man had received placed him beyond the reach of human skill. After much suffering he expired on Monday morning. We deeply sympathise with his highly respectable widow and children who are in the depth of affliction at their sudden and unexpected bereavement.

51. Capt. James Vickers and nine men, the crew of a Baltimore pilot boat, were lost in the Chesapeake bay in the gale of the 17th ult.

52. Married on the 21st inst., by the Rev. C. Van Santvoord, Mr. Horatio A. Snyder to Miss Anna Maria, daughter of Zechariah Snyder, all of Saugerties.

53. Died at Flatbush, in this town, on the 21st instant, Abram Cole, aged about 21 years.

January 30, 1847 (Saturday)
54. Married on the 23d instant, by the Rev. R. Dederick, Mr. Lodowick Shubb, to Miss Harriet Purdy, both of Saugerties.

55. Died at Portland, Chautauque Co., on the 30th Nov, Emily M. Ogden, only daughter of Reuben and Elizabeth Ogden, aged 23 years. Formerly a resident of Palen Ville, Green Co.

February 13, 1847 (Saturday)
56. Died in this village, on the morning of the 8th inst., Mr. Peter B. Schepmoes, aged 27 years.

February 20, 1847 (Saturday)
57. Another Victim - Henry Stone, a man of intemperate habits, was found dead in his bed, at Krow's Hotel, in this village on Tuesday morning last. He had been unwell for a few days, and the evening preceding his death he appeared very sick; the Overseer of the Poor procured lodging for him at Krows' and called a physician, who, supposing him intoxicated, (which we are informed was not the case) defered <sic> administering medicine until morning. He was left alone in his room about eleven o'clock, and in the morning was found dead. An inquest was held, and a verdict of death, by appoplexy, rendered. The corpse was then taken to the burying ground by three men, employed by the Coroner, unaccompanied by any other person. No sympathetic rum seller was present. Their sympathy and friendship for the unfortunate man ceased when they received from him his last three cents.

58. Died at Malden, on the 13th inst., Doctor Zelotus Ford, about 45. .

59. Died in this village, on Thursday morning, George, son of Mr. Stephen Webster, aged about 2 years.

February 27, 1847 (Saturday)
60. Married on the 17th inst., by Rev. John Watson, Mr. Anthony Fries to Miss Margaret A. Burhans, both of Flat Bush, Town of Kingston.

61. Died on Friday evening, the 19th inst., at the residence of her father in the town of Ghent, Columbia Co., Mrs. Caroline Kiersted, wife of John Kiersted, Junr., aged 30 years.

62. Died at Flatbush, Town of Saugerties, on the 21st inst., Mrs. Rebecca Hendricks, widow of the late Peter Hendricks, aged 66 years.

63. Died in this village on the 24th inst., Mrs. Alida Schoonmaker, widow of Peter Schoonmaker, aged about 73 years.

March 13, 1847 (Saturday)

64. The Murder of Lieutenant Ritchie - We find in the New Orleans *Times* and account of the manner of the death of Lieutenant Ritchie: "On Gen. Scott's arrival at the mouth of the Rio Grande, and assuming the chief command, he forthwith sent despatches to Saltillo, addressed to Gen. Taylor the commanding officer there. When the bearer reached that city, Gen. Butler, the officer in command opened the despatches, the result of which was the immediate departure of Gen. Worth and his division for the Rio Grande. The despatches were then resealed, and sent off in charge of Lieut. Ritchie, 5th infantry, to Gen. Taylor, then on his retrograde movement to Monterey from Victoria. Ten men belonging to Kearney's company of the 5th, accompanied Lieut. Ritchie as an escort. They arrived at Monterey in safety, stopped there one night, and proceeded on their route to meet Gen. Taylor the next day. Towards dusk, Ritchie reached the Ville Grande, distant twenty-three miles from Monterey. Meeting, just after his arrival, with an Englishman established in business there, he availed himself of his services to procure refreshments for himself and command. As they were crossing the plaza of Ville Grande, in furtherance of that object, a Mexican on horseback came whisking by them, when he suddenly threw a lasso over Ritchie, put spurs to his animal, and succeeded in dragging him beyond the town, to a small creek in the vicinity. Here he murdered him, and after mutilating his body in a horrid manner made off with the despatches. These are said to be of great consequence, containing a sketch of the plan of the forthcoming campaign, with other important particulars. It seems as if the movements of Ritchie and his party were narrowly watched by the enemy, for during the night they passed at Monterey, the arms of five of his men were stolen from them, necessitating a demand on the

quarter-master for a fresh supply. Lieut. Ritchie, we understand, is a nephew of the venerable editor of the Washington Union."

65. Married on the 11th inst., by the Rev. R. Dederick, Mr. John David Mower to Miss Rachel Schoonmaker, both of Saugerties.

66. Died on Saturday, the 6th inst., at her late residence near Palen Ville, in the Town of Catskill, Widow Drummond at the advanced age of ninety years.

March 20, 1847 (Saturday)

67. The dwelling house of Mr. Caleb Russell in West-Hurley, in this county, was, with all its contents, destroyed by fire on Saturday night last, and horrible to relate, Mr. Russell, while in a state of intoxication, perished in the flames. A grandson, aged 5, survived.

March 27, 1847 (Saturday)

68. Shocking Occurrence, A Mother and Five Children Burned to Death - The dwelling of Mr. Augustus Holdridge, in the village of North Blenheim, in this county, was consumed by fire on Monday night last, and his wife and five children perished in the flames! Mr. Holdridge escaped with his youngest child, a boy about six years of age, and a daughter aged nineteen saved herself, though fright fully burned, by leaping through a door or window. The mother was twice seen outside of the burning building, but the desire to rescue her children it is supposed prompted her to rush back into the flames from which she was unable to return. These making in all nine persons constituted the whole family, and were asleep at the time in the building. The names of those that perished we have been unable to learn. The oldest, however, was a daughter aged about 23 years; the next a son, aged about 21; then three were between the ages of the two children that escaped - 19. The daughter that saved herself, ran shrieking from the burning house to Fink's Tavern, a short distance off, where she now lies. A letter from that place written the day after the occurrence, informs us that she is not expected to recover. The six bodies were taken from the ruins after the fire, but, of course, could not be recognized. They were all buried at 10 o'clock yesterday. At no time, it is said, for a number of years, until a few days previous to the fatal event, had this family been gathered together under the

paternal roof, the older children not residing with their father, and having merely come together for a visit. Postscript - A gentleman direct from North Blenheim, informs us just as we are putting our paper to press, that the fire originated from the stove-pipe. That Mr. Holdridge, who is a very intemperate man, came home much intoxicated late at night, after the family had retired, and made a great fire in the stove, by which he was sitting when the neighbors rushed into the burning house. He told them the family had left the house and were safe, upon which they ran out, taking him with them; Mrs. H. had fled from the house with her little boy, whom she had taken to Fink's Tavern, and returning to the house pushed in to save her other children, when she was caught by the flames and consumed. Schoharie *Patriot*.

69. Sudden Death - We are pained to learn that Abraham Jansen, Esq., of Shawangunk, died suddenly at Newburgh on Sunday morning last, aged about 64 years. He had attended court all week, and after taking breakfast, he went to the office of John W. Brown, Esq. where he was taken ill, and before medical aid could be obtained he expired. Mr. Jansen was one of our most wealthy and respectable citizens. He was a democrat of the old school, and warm and inflexible in support of his political principles. He represented this county with Mr. Russell in the Legislature of 1842. Ulster *Rep.*

April 3, 1847 (Saturday)

70. Latest News, From the Army - Dr. Turner brought a list of 63 officers killed and wounded from the fight which commenced on February 22 and ended on the 23d. I left in such haste that I was unable to obtain a copy, but recollect among the killed Capt. Lincoln, Assistant Adjt. General, U. S. Army; Col. Yell, of the Arkansas cavalry; Capt. Moor; Adjutant Young, and three others not named of the Kentucky cavalry; Capt. Mc Kee, Lieut Col. Clay, son of Henry Clay; Capt. Willis, 2d Kentucky Infantry; Col. Hardin and Major Gorman, of the Illinois brigade. <another section of the same article> Adjutant Lincoln, also of the General's staff, the intrepid young officer who so distinguished himself at Resaca de la Palma, was killed. New Orleans *Picayune* of Tuesday.

April 12, <sic> 1847 (Saturday)

71. Startling rumor, If True - Passengers from the south last evening heard a rumor, altogether questionable, that an express from New Orleans overtook the mail at Montgomery, Alabama, with late news from Vera Cruz. The report was that Gen. Scott had been killed and Gen. Worth seriously injured. It was not credited in Philadelphia. *Sun.*

72. Battle in Santa Fe - Mexicans Completely Routed. Yet another Victory, Pittsburgh, April 6, 1847 - The news of the assassination of Gov. Bent is fully confirmed; twenty five other Americans fell at the same time.

73. Rev. John Newland Maffit was married in Brooklyn, week before last. A disgraceful riot signalized the occasion. A bonfire was kindled in the street, and hundreds of people surrounded the house, and "made night hideous" with unearthly yells and horrid music.

74. A little girl aged about nine years, the oldest child of Mr. David H. Runyan, of Rushville, near Geneva, was so badly burned on the 6th ultimo, by her clothes taking fire, that she lived but about thirty-six hours after the accident.

75. Henry Moore, a brakeman on the Norwich and Worcester Railroad, was killed on Tuesday of last week, at Dansville. He stepped in between the cars, as they were backing, to separate the train, when his feet slipped and he fell lengthwise on the track, and the freight cars passed over his left leg, crushing it to pieces. He resided in Preston, Connecticut.

76. On Thursday morning last week, the body of a little girl, four years old, the daughter of Mr. Charles Mc Cann, of Poughkeepsie, was found in a small pond in the woods at Van Keuren's Point, near Barnegat. She had strayed from home on the afternoon previous, and although searched for by all the neighbors during the night, was not found till seven o'clock in the morning-dead as above described.

77. Married in Schoharie, on the 24th ult., by the Rev. H. Chase, Mr. J. Lawrence Hackstaff, editor of the Prattsville *Advocate*, to Miss Lydia M., daughter of Cyrus Smith, Esq., of the former place.

April 17, 1847 (Saturday)

78. Francis Fitzpatrick had his arm blown off in Albany, on Monday of last week, by the premature discharge of a cannon, while firing a salute in honor of Gen. Taylor's victory. He was so much injured that it was thought he could not survive.

79. Capture of Vera Cruz and the Castle of San Juan D'Ullon - The total loss of the American army, from the day of landing, March 9th, is sixty-five persons killed and wounded. Officers killed, Capt. John R. Vinton, 2d artillery; Capt. Albartis, 2d artillery; Midshipman T. B. Shubrick, wounded; Lt. Col. Dickinson of SC volunteers, severely; Lieut. A. S. Baldwin, navy, slightly; Lieut. Lewis Neill, 2d dragoons, severely. All the wounded are doing well.

80. Later - Among the killed is Gen. Veldez, who had charge of the Rancheros stationed outside of the city, and on which Col. Harney charged and made such dreadful havoc among.

April 24, 1847 (Saturday)

81. Drowning - A colored man named William Pease, was accidentally knocked overboard. and drowned from off the schooner Thomas H. Benton, when opposite Poughkeepsie on Thursday the 15th inst.

82. Sudden Death - At Boston, on Friday, John Mc Gonagel, an intemperate man, fell dead in the street.

83. Intemperance - The Coroner, on Saturday, held an inquest at the 4th ward police station on the body of Mary Kelly, a native of Ireland, aged about 40, of intemperate habits, who was found Friday night at James Slip intoxicated, and being taken to the Station House died at half past 3 o'clock. Verdict, death by congestion of the brain, caused by intemperance. New York *Sun*.

84. Awful - At Toronto on the 14th inst., Nancy Nichols was found by her husband in bed, when he came home to dinner. He left her and

returned to his work, when the house took fire and she was burnt to a cinder.

85. Married on the 14th inst., by the Rev. R. Dederick, Mr. Wm. W. Heath of Hudson to Miss Jane Eliza Hill of Catskill.

May 1, 1847 (Saturday)

86. Intemperance - Charles Mosler, who was executed in Philadelphia for the murder of his wife, in admitting the justice of the sentence, acknowledged that he was partially intoxicated at the time.

87. A Powder Mill at Hobbs' Powder Works, Barre, Mass., exploded on Thursday last, burning 1200 lbs. of powder, and killing one man, George W. Nurse, a native of Clarendom, Vt., 26 years of age. The loss of mill and machinery was $700.

88. The St. Louis *Reveille* of the 21st, says Mr. Alexander Hoy was shot in the thigh, it is supposed, by Mr. Tallis with whom he had a controversy of a domestic character. The wound is reported dangerous.

89. Mrs. Walworth, wife of Chancellor Walworth, died at Saratoga Springs, on Sunday the 25th ult.

90. Died in the village of Kingston on Sunday morning last, Miss Elizabeth De Witt, aged about 70 years.

May 8, 1847 (Saturday)

91. An interesting lad, about six years of age, son of Mr. Charles Hamlin, was drowned in the pond on the south side of the creek, in this village, on Saturday last.

92. From the Brazos - A free colored man by the named of Gladman, belonging to Galveston and by trade a baker, was found murdered in the late near Matamoras, bearing marks of violence. Information brought by the Propeller Trumbull, which sailed from the Brazos on the 18th.

93. Hon. Edward D. White, formerly a Judge, Member of Congress, and Governor of Louisiana, died at New Orleans, on Sunday, the 18th ult.

94. The 4th floor of the large flouring mill in Hacketstown, Warren Co., N. J., belonging to Mr. Clark gave way on Tuesday of last week under the pressure of a heavy weight of kiln dried corn meal, producing serious and fatal consequences. Peter Rice, a respectable citizen of the place, was caught by the crushing mass and buried, being found some ten feet in meal.

95. William Fox, an Englishman, who had for twenty years resided in Lockport, hanged himself on the 22nd ult. Though apparently lifeless when discovered and cut down, he came to and will probably recover. He is deranged.

96. A melancholy and fatal accident happened at Corning, Chemung Co., on the 14th ult. Two persons were killed by being thrown from the cars on the Corning and Blossburg Railroad, and passed over by the wheels of the locomotive. They had jumped upon the cars as they were coming into the place, and by a sudden backward motion of the locomotive were thrown down from their position and killed. Henry Odell was the name of one of the sufferers.

97. At Concord, NH a man named Edward Croghan became so frightened by discovering a train of cars approaching him, whilst walking on the Railroad track, that he did not know where to go, though there was plenty of room either side of the track. The train struck him and passed over his body, mangling him in a shocking manner. He was about sixty years of age.

98. The body of Mr. Peter Merrill, late Postmaster at Alton, Illinois, was found among some driftwood, about twenty yards from the bank of the Mississippi river. The deceased, who manifested strong symptoms of mental derangement about the first of the month, disappeared suddenly on the evening of the 2d.

99. Alexander Stewart, an Irishman, residing in Clinton County, Ohio, in a state of intoxication killed his wife, while asleep in bed, by beating

out her brains with a club, and mangling her body in a most shocking manner.

100. Mrs. Bell, of Spafford, Onondago Co., committed suicide on Tuesday of last week, by hanging herself with a skein of yarn. Domestic troubles are said to have caused it.

May 15, 1847 (Saturday)

101. Battle at Cerro Gordo - Between Gen. Scott and Santa Anna - American Victory! - Gen. La Vega and Thousand Mexicans taken Prisoner - Gen. Shields was mortally wounded while gallantly leading his brigade to storm one of the enemie's <sic> works. The Mexican loss upon the heights was very great, the ground in places being covered with the dead. Among the bodies found was that of Gen. Vasquez and Colonels Orbando and Palacio.

102. A young man named Charles Fuller, met death in a novel and painful manner recently, at Messardis, Maine. He was in the woods, and while standing upon the snow it gave way, letting him down upon the stub of a brush that had been cut about two feet above the ground, which entered his abdomen, and so injured him that he died in consequence.

103. Fatal Accident - On the night of the 22d ult., a man by the name of Reinhart, was instantly killed on the Railroad at Schuylkill Haven. He was crossing the Road between the bridge and Ware House, unconscious of danger, when the locomotive engine Picayune, coming up in the darkness of the night, struck and killed him instantly.

104. Fatal Accident - James Hennessy, a brakeman on the Utica and Schenectady Railroad, fell from the downward train of cars last Tuesday afternoon, and was run over by a portion of the train. He injuries were such that he died before reaching Fonda, his place of residence.

105. A young girl named Elizabeth Brewer, of Bramville, near Newburgh, committed suicide on Thursday week, by hanging herself. She was but fifteen years of age. No cause can be assigned for the rash act.

106. We have, within a few days, noticed a horrid murder of a wife, by her husband, in Clinton Co., Ohio. The murderer, Stewart, after his apprehension, cut his throat, but the doctors sewed it up, and was confined in a dungeon. Here he put his design of self destruction in execution by striking his head, (while chained down) against the floor and wall until his skul <sic> was fractured, and his brains oozed out. When found he was quite dead.

107. Accident at Utica - While one of the congregation of Utica were on Sunday last, engaged in administering the rite of baptism, in the Mohawk river, a bridge adjoining the scene gave way, and some 16 persons were precipitated into the river. One person, Mr. Smith, was killed, and several severely wounded.

108. Married in this village on Tuesday last, by the Rev. David Webster, Mr. John F. Miller, merchant, to Miss Sarah M. Webster, daughter of Mrs. Stephen Webster. The above notice was accompanied with a bountiful slice of rich wedding cake, which with pure water from our well was admirably suited to our palate. We wish the bridegroom and his amiable bride many years of uninterrupted happiness.

109. Died in this village on Sunday last, after a short illness, Mr. Nicholas Redicker, aged about 33 years. His family are supposed to reside in New York City.

110. Stolen - From the premises of the subscriber, on the night of the 27th ult., when myself and family were absent by some one who was seen on the afternoon of that day with the boy that lived with me; the articles stolen was a chain, bags of corn, a whip and other articles, and kidnapped the boy. The villain wore a white hat, dark coat, and light pants - the boy wore a roundabout of dark satinett, a pair of boots, and a velvet cap, he has a freckled face, and is about 12 years old, his name is William Cook. The subscriber forbids all persons to harbor or employ or trade with said boy. Whoever will inform the subscriber where the villain and the boy resort shall be entitled to a liberal reward. Simeon P. Dewitt. Saugerties, May 15th, 1847.

May 22, 1847 (Saturday)

111. In Chancery - Two large estates in England have fallen to American heirs. The Townly estate is claimed by the Lawrence family in right of an ancestor who originally settled at Flushing, Long Island. The other is the estate of William Jennings, who died at an advanced age, a bachelor and intestate. The estate belongs to the heirs of his brother Joshua Jennings who emigrated to the United States and settled in Fairfield, Connecticut. Miss Burnett, now the wife of Mr. Lawrence, becoming one of the heirs of the Townly estate by marriage connection, and her cousin, William J. Burnett, one of the heirs of the Jennings estate by regular descent.

112. Among the killed at the battle of Buena Vista was Lieut. William Price, of Illinois, in the seventy second year of his age. He had left his home of affluence, and ease, with the expressed wish to die in the service of his country.

113. Shot Himself - A young man named Wm. A. Glanton met with a fatal accident at Columbus, Ia. on the 28th ult. He was loading a rifle, which at the time was half cocked. In ramming down the ball, the rod got fast, when he attempted to extract it with his teeth. At this moment the gun slipped and went off, sending the ramrod and the ball through his head, killed him immediately.

114. Indian Chief Dead - Lafontaine, the principal chief of the Miami tribe of Indiana, died lately at Lafayette, Indiana, on his return from the far west, where his tribe has recently emigrated. Lafontaine was rich and civilized, farmed extensively and was a heavy dealer in produce and merchandize.

115. A Murder Case - The Pittsburgh *Chronicle* gives the details of a savage murder on the person of Mr. Ballmeyer of New Lebanon, Ohio. He arrived at Pittsburgh, and took a canal boat for Freeport, his body was found in the canal, upon the forehead were marks of a 'colt' or club, his feet were tied together with a rope and another rope was twisted round his neck. He appeared to have been robbed and thrown into the canal. He was last seen in company with two rough raftsman who are not yet found.

116. A couple of weeks since Mr. James Callan, residing near Yazoo City, Miss., was fatally poisoned, and all his family partially so, by eating pies which were seasoned with peach leaves-the prussic acid contained in the leaves having become concentrated by baking.

117. In Tallapoosa Co., Alabama, week before last, Ann Adelia Moore was tried for the murder of her husband. The jury returned a verdict of "guilty of murder in the first degree" and the sentence is confinement in the penitentiary for life. It appears that while Moore was asleep she fractured his skull with an axe.

118. Three brothers named Whitridge, of the town of New Paris, Preble Co., Ohio, died recently, within a few days of each other. Two of them were physicians - one a merchant and member of the last Legislature of Ohio - all active enterprising business men, and men with families. They died of an acute affection of the lungs; and it is very remarkable that, of such a disease, their deaths should have occurred in such close proximity of time.

119. George W. Hudson, who it will be remembered, ran off with Andrew R. Jones' wife from Hempstead (Long Island) last fall, was, a few days ago, mulcted in $5000 damages, in an action of crim. con. brought by Hudson against him.

120. Died on Wednesday last in the city of New York, Doct. Augustus Van Buren, eldest son of John Van Buren, Esq. of Kingston. The deceased was a young man of fine talents and irreproachable character. His loss will be severely felt by his relatives and a large circle of friends and acquaintances in this county.

May 29, 1847 (Saturday)

121. Died in this village, on Friday last, Mr. James Hurle in the 59th year of his age.

122. Died in this village, on Saturday 22nd inst., Mr. Theodore Barrell, aged 76.

June 5, 1847 (Saturday)

123. Body Found - Mysterious Death - A passenger on the Utica road informs us that last night as some men were fishing in Cuyadutta creek, near Fonda, they discovered the body of a man, whose linen was marked with the name of "Geo. W. Hathaway, Fall River, Mass." He had on his person about $260 in eastern money and was about 35 years of age. He is supposed to have fallen off the cars in the nighttime.

124. Highly Important from Mexico - Latest News - Generals Lemus and Iterburde are dead.

125. Married on the 29th ult., by the Rev. R. Dederick, Mr. Joseph F. Carnright of Catskill, to Miss Cornelia Gardiner of the same place.

126. Died in this town on Sunday morning last, Lucy Maria Decker, aged 9 years and 3 months, daughter of Isaac Decker of Broome, Schoharie Co.

127. Died in this village on Sunday evening last, Mrs. Margaret Bradbury.

128. Died in this town, on Sunday last, Mr. Florence Fitzpatrick, aged 35 years.

June 12, 1847 (Saturday)

129. A High-Minded Duellist - It is said that Gen. Dromgoole, who recently died in Virginia, left all his fortune to the children of Mr. Dugger, whom he killed in a duel ten years ago. We have few such just and generous impulses to record.

130. Died in this town, on Tuesday last, Miss Jane Catharine, daughter of Peter H. Freligh, aged about 4 years and 10 months.

June 19, 1847 (Saturday)

131. Late Duel in the Army - Richmond, June 16, 1847 - A letter received here from the Army in Mexico furnishes an account of the late duel between Lieut. Mumford, of Carrington's Company, and Lieut. Mahan, both of Virginia. They fought with muskets. Both

were wounded at the first fire, Mumford receiving seven buckshot. Mahan's friends have three letters written on the evening of the duel, (21st May) when both were living, but not expected to recover.

132. Daniel O'Connell died at Genoa, May 15th. He has directed his heart to be deposited in Rome, and his body to be buried in Ireland. Latest From Europe.

133. Latest from Europe - Rev. Dr. Chalmers the eminent theologian, died suddenly on the 31st ult.

134. Mr. Williams, of Alexander, New York, cut his throat on Wednesday. Loss of property and the hopeless illness of his wife, overwhelmed his reason. His widow sunk under the blow, and they are occupying one common grave.

135. Miss Mary Watson, of Southwark, Philadelphia lost her life on Saturday evening through an attempt to fill a spirit gas lamp whilst it was lighted. The gas took fire, and she was instantly enveloped in flame, and notwithstanding great effort to save her, she was so burned as to survive but a few hours. Her brother Thomas had his hands so much injured in attempting to save her, that it is feared they will be rendered useless.

136. A dreadful accident happened on the Norwich and Worcester railroad, on Wednesday evening at the moment the cars from Boston to New York were passing the Oxford depot.- A crazy man by the name of Harris, aged about 30, jumped on the track ten feet before the locomotive; danced, and in an instant was struck down by the iron spiked cowcatcher. The train was stopped as soon as possible, but the poor creature had ceased to live. The accident was entirely unavoidable by the engineer.

137. John Parker and Mary Myers have been tried in Butler (Pa.) for the murder of John Myers, the husband of the woman indicted. It was proved that arsenic had been administered to Myers, and the circumstance pointed so strongly to Parker and Mrs. Myers, who have been living in improper intimacy, that the jury brought in a verdict of murder in the first degree.

138. A Boy Gone Over the Falls - An awful accident occurred at Niagara Falls on Sunday, 13th inst. John Murphy, a boy, attempted to cross from the American to the Canada side; he got drawn into the current and jumped out to save himself by swimming but suddenly disappeared from view. It is supposed he was drawn over the cataract. The fragments of the canoe were found below the Falls next morning, but his body could not be found.

139. A blacksmith named Oliver Hulse hung himself near South Middletown, Orange Co., a few days since.

140. Married in this village, on Wednesday last, by the Rev. Mr. Van Santvoord, Mr. Nathan Kellogg of Malden to Miss Helen M. Laflin, of this village. The happy couple did not forget the printer, but sent with the above notice a bountiful slice of delicious cake, for which we tender our acknowledgments in this public manner. The opportunity does not occur every day.

141. Died in this village, on Thursday last, Mr. William Hanna, aged about 60 years.

142. Died in this village, on Thursday last, John Scribner, aged about 18 years.

143. Died in this village, on the 17th inst., Mary Elizabeth, daughter of Thomas and Catharine Walsh, aged 5 years, 7 months and 2 days.

144. Died in this village, on Saturday last, Miss Evilena Van Buskirk, aged 10 years and 2 months.

June 26, 1847 (Saturday)

145. Capt. Canot, a well-known African slave-dealer, and the owner of one of the most extensive slaving establishments on the coast, was arrested on Monday last in the City of New York, where he had been for some days, by officer Smith, a Deputy United States Marshal, for having fitted out at that port, in December last, a vessel for the slave trade, in which he himself went out to Africa as a passenger.

146. Letter from Vera Cruz - We regret extremely to say that Paymaster Bosworth, who sailed from New-Orleans on the 18th ult., sickened and died at Vera Cruz of the vomito. His remains were brought back on the Massachusetts in charge of his brother.

July 3, 1847 (Saturday)

147. Thomas Fowley, alias "Big Thunder" a man of intemperate habits, and who had been intoxicated daily for two or three weeks, committed suicide on Monday last. <no geographic data, ed.>

148. A man who said his name was Davis, about 35 years of age, jumped from a boat near Syracuse, on Thursday last, into the canal and was drowned. It is supposed that his real name was not Davis but that this was assumed to conceal his whereabouts from his friends. He was a member of the convention that nominated John Tyler. He was from Orange county.

149. Benjamin Sweet, indicted at Geneseo, for the murder of his wife, has been acquitted. The Mount Morris *Spectator* says that from the testimony, it appears Mrs. Sweet died in February last, and her body was sent to this city for interment. Here, some suspicions were excited, and a post mortem examination of her body made. It was proved pretty clearly, that her death was occasioned by arsenic, but on account of the entire absence of all testimony to implicate the husband, jury acquitted the accused without leaving their seats.

July 10, 1847 (Saturday)

150. A young man named John Donivan, engaged in firing salutes from a small howitzer, near the Troy, R. R. bridge, was killed by a premature explosion. Fourth of July Accidents.

151. The Daily *Wisconsin* says: - Mr. D. O. Baker, merchant of Johnstown, Rock Co., was struck by lightning on Saturday last while standing in his store door in conversation with a friend. He died instantly. Mr. B. was formerly from the State of New York and aged only 21.

152. Drowned - Coroner Daniel Bodley held an inquest on the 14th June last on the body of John Golenger, who was found in the D. & H.

Canal near Bloomingdale. It appeared that on going to his place of work in the morning he accidentally got into the canal, and was drowned. Verdict accordingly.

153. Shocking Death - A Mr. Willard, citizen of White River village, on the line of the Vermont Central Railroad, was blown up while blasting rocks, on Monday, and killed. His head was literally torn to pieces.

154. Fatal Accident - On Thursday last, a young man, named Goslin, was killed accidentally, near Berlin, Fredrick Co., on the Baltimore and Ohio RR. He was engaged in building of a culvert, when the crane car upset and threw him a considerable height into the air, and he fell to the bottom of the culvert. He lived about 20 minutes.

155. Accidental Drowning - On Saturday afternoon, Charles Higgins, aged 10 years, was drowned in a pond at the head of Patroon street, Albany, whilst bathing. Sunday night about 10 o'clock, Jeremiah Degnon was found drowned in the Little Basin, Albany, He was a laborer residing in the neighborhood.

156. A violent thunder storm, accompanied with torrents of rain, in the vicinity of Putnam, Muskingum Co., Ohio, on Friday week, occasioned a remarkable rise in the streams South and West of that place, carrying away most of the bridges. An aged man named Carlisle, being in his saw mill, which was carried away, was drowned.

157. Married on the 3rd inst., by the Rev. R. Dederick, Mr. Edwin Holden to Miss Catharine Jane Mc Chesney, all of Saugerties.

158. Died in this village, on the 4th instant, Mr. Samuel C. Bradbury, aged about 45 years.

July 17, 1847 (Saturday)

159. Body Found - We understand that on Tuesday evening last the body of the son of Mr. Daniel Wise, of this village, who was drowned last winter while skating, was found floating in the river near this place. The skates were still on the feet and the mittens on the hands. Poughkeepsie *Eagle*.

160. Death by Drowning - On Wednesday last a little boy about eight years old, a son of Mr. Mc Kiean, of this village, was drowned in the Fallkill, near High Street, while bathing. Poughkeepsie *Eagle*.

161. Mr. Joel Akin of Memphis (Tenn.) was instantly killed last week, at a grocery in that city, by an awful wound in the left breast from a bowie knife, in the hands of Nathaniel Ursery, a returned volunteer. Ursery instantly fled, but was pursued and arrested, and confined in the calabouse.

162. Gilbert Wright, of Charlotte, Monroe county, a hand on board the propeller Genesee Chief, was drowned whilst attempting to pass on to the steamer Patchin, in tow, near Manition Island.

163. Died at his residence in Catskill, Greene Co., after a protracted illness, which terminated suddenly on Wednesday evening, the 5th inst., Mackay Croswell, father of the senior editor of the Albany *Argus*.

July 24, 1847 (Saturday)

164. The Newburgh *Courier* states that the body of an unknown man was found in the river opposite that village on Wednesday week. From appearances it had been in the water about six months, and was much mutilated. The deceased was clothed in woollen, and also had on mittens and an oil cloth pea jacket, among other things, was found a silver watch, marked No. 7612, cylinder escapement, four holes jeweled - M. T. Tobias, Liverpool.

165. During a thunderstorm near Centreville, Washington county, (Pa.) on the 5th instant, two young men, brothers-named John and Joseph Wilson-were struck by lightning, whilst standing under a tree, where they had taken shelter from the rain. John was killed instantly, and Joseph dreadfully injured, but is was hoped he would recover.

166. An inquest was held by Coroner Suydam on the 15th, upon the body of Thomas Keegan, aged 21 years, who was accidentally drowned in the Rondout Creek, on that afternoon, by falling from the Steam Dredging machine at work near the new dock. Deceased was a native of Ireland, and his only near relative in this country is a sister at New York. Verdict according to the facts. Rondout *Freeman*.

167. A child of Mr. Charles Chapman, of Danbury, Conn., was poisoned on the 5th inst., by putting a visiting card in its mouth, which its mother had given it to play with. It died in forty-eight hours after. An analysis of a card showed that the enamel or coating was composed of carbonate of lead.

168. Death of an Editor - The Columbia *South Carolinian* announces the death of Col. A. H. Pemberton, the former editor and proprietor of that paper.

169. Suicide in Barnwell Village, SC - This heinous crime was perpetrated on last Friday, by a young man named Samuel Simmons, a resident of that village. The unfortunate wretch had been apprehended, tried and convicted of the offence of vagrancy by Magistrate's Court. He severed his throat to the bone with a razor.

170. Abraham D. Brink, a son of the late John Brink, was drowned while bathing in the Esopus creek, in Marbletown, on the evening of the 8th inst.

171. Joseph C. Neal, author of the 'Charcoal Sketches' and editor of the Saturday *Gazette*, in Philadelphia, died suddenly on the 18th inst.

172. H. D. Huested cut his throat in Poughkeepsie, on Monday of last week. He was 36 years of age, well off, but partially deranged.

173. The remains of Col. Hardin and Lieut. B. R. Houghton reached St. Louis on the evening of the 7th inst., and were escorted to the steamer Defiance, from which they will be debarked at Meredosia, and taken to Jacksonville, Ill., their last resting place. The boat which brought up these remains also brought a large number of the Illinois Volunteers, who were addressed by Mr. Eager of St. Louis. A reply was made by Lieut. Evans of the volunteers.

174. Shocking Accident - The Troy *Daily Telegraph* states that on Sunday last, D. Murray, one of the city milkmen, was thrown from his wagon, his back broke, and his body otherwise seriously injured. The accident was caused by a hoop trundled by a boy in the street, getting between the horse's legs, and at which he took fright. Mr. Murray, if he recovers, will be a cripple for life.

175. Alexander Fish, a lad 12 years of age, on Tuesday last was run over by one of the cars near the railroad bridge, Troy, and instantly killed.

176. The Subscriber will sell at Public Auction on Saturday the 4th day of September next, the House and Lot formerly occupied by Samuel Bradbury, deceased; situate on the south side of Bridge Street, in the Village of Ulster, said sale to take place at 4 o'clock, P. M., at the house of Edward Laverty near the premises. Terms Cash. Jeremiah Russell Saugerties, July 21, 1847.

July 31, 1847 (Saturday)

177. The funeral of the late gallant officers of the Kentucky regiment who fell at Buena Vista, took place at Frankfort on the 20th. The ceremonies are represented as having been grand, solemn and imposing, and to have been participated in by a concourse of 15 to 20,000 persons. Mr. Brekenridge delivered an eloquent and appropriate oration. Mr. Clay with the orphan children of his fallen son, Mrs. Mc Kee, the lady of the deceased Col. and Mrs. Vaughn, widow of the deceased adjutant of the Kentucky Regiment, were among the chief mourners.

178. Fatal Accident - A young man named Anderson, about 21 years of age, lost his life on Monday, in Howard Co., near Fayette, Missouri, by attempting to climb a tree and pull his rifle up after him.

179. Maguire, who had his tongue chewed off in a fight with Rushworth, in Philadelphia, has since died from the effect of the wound. Four men have been arrested, and held in $500 each to answer as aiders and abettors in the brutal act.

180. Mr. Henry G. Gudther, a highly respectable citizen of Bethlehem, Penn., was killed a few days since, and his daughter shockingly, but, it is hoped, not fatally injured by the upsetting of a wagon in which they were riding.

181. Gift for the Washington Monument - A man by the name of Morgan, lately deceased, says the New York *Express*, in that city, has left the sum of fifteen thousand dollars to be expended in the erection of the Washington Monument.

182. Death of Ex-Governor Edwards, of Connecticut - Hon. Mr. Edwards, formerly Governor of Connecticut, died at New Haven on the 22d instant, in the 68th year of his age. He was the son of Judge Pierpont Edwards. Ogden Edwards, also a Judge, was his brother, and Judge H. P. Edwards of New York city, his son. Mr. Edwards had been Governor of Connecticut, Speaker of its house of representatives, and also a member of both branches of the Congress of the United States.

183. On the 5th inst., Elijah Vancleaf committed suicide by hanging himself, at his house near the village of Blue Ball, Monmouth Co., N J, while under the influence of delirium tremens. He was 35 years of age and leaves a wife and several children.

184. Miss Elizabeth R. Lippincott, of Morristown, NJ, a young lady in delicate health, was so much interested in viewing Niagara Falls as to have occasioned by fatigue and exposure, a hemorrhage of the lung with which she died a few hours after returning to the Hotel.

185. Fatal Accident on the Railroad - We learn from the Frederick *Herald* that on Thursday evening last an accident occurred on the railroad, (going west) somewhere between Sikesville and the incline plane, by which a man named Gurley lost his life. He got upon a burthen train somewhere between the points named, and on the route fell and was caught between two cars, breaking his leg and spine and otherwise severely injuring him. He was conveyed to Frederick and submitted to amputation, but died about twelve o'clock of the same day. A part of his family arrived at Frederick in the passenger train, shortly after his own arrival. Baltimore *Sun*.

August 7, 1847 (Saturday)

186. Drowned - Charles Maginnis, aged about 14 or 15 years, was drowned at Glasco in this town, on Sunday morning last, while bathing in company with a number of boys. On Wednesday last his body was found, about two miles below that place on the opposite side of the river.

187. Shot his Wife by Mistake - Dr. J. B. Pierce, of Troy, Pa., shot his wife by mistake, on the evening of the 22d ult. Mistaking her for a robber breaking into his house, he seized his gun and fired. The whole charge entered her breast, and she fell dead on the floor.

188. Killed by Lightning - A young man named Muter was instantly killed by lightning, near Troy, Ohio, last week. He was leaning against the wall of his house near the fire place at the time; the lightning coming down the chimney through the wall and over his head. Mrs. Mc Intire was at the same time in the act of removing a coffee pot from the fire, and was severely shocked, throwing the coffee pot up, the contents came down on her, scalding her very badly.

189. Shocking Accident - On Tuesday night, at half past ten o'clock, in Catherine St., above Third, some young men were preparing for a gunning expedition. One of them had a musket which he was putting a cap upon, when it was accidentally discharged, and wounded four or five persons. James Mc Mullen, residing in Catherine St., who was engaged in putting on the cap, had his whole lower jaw shot away and was dreadfully wounded in the breast. A young man, whom they called Balty, was severely wounded in the left breast and was taken to the hospital. The others were wounded about the limbs, but not dangerously. Phila. *Led.*

190. Poisoned - A little son of Mr. Samuel R. Per Lee, of this village, came near to losing his life on Friday last from the effects of arsenic. The little fellow found in the house a bit of cake nicely sugared as he supposed, which he ate, but unfortunately it proved to be a piece on which the poisonous drug had been sprinkled and laid away for the purpose of destroying rats. Norwich *Journal.*

191. The President has appointed George W. Clinton, of Buffalo, in the office of U. S. District Attorney for the Northern District of New York in place of Wm. F. Allen, elected a Justice of the Supreme Court. Mr. Clinton is the eldest son of the late Governor Dewitt Clinton, and is in every respect qualified for the office.

192. A recruit in the United States service, named Bozeman, cut his throat in a fit of mania a potu, on the 3d inst. in Tallahassee. The weapon was a razor, and the poor fellow died a few minutes after the infliction of the wound.

193. At Independence, Pennsylvania, a few days ago, Mr. Henry Virtue took down his gun-not knowing it was loaded-to shoot a fowl. As it is a foolish custom with many people, he put his mouth to the muzzle to ascertain if there was a load in it, and, by some means, it was accidentally discharged while he was blowing in it. The whole contents of the load passed through his head, killing him instantly.

194. Railway Accident - Yesterday afternoon, as the freight train from Springfield to Albany was near the bridge which crosses the creek at East Albany, an aged man, named Smith, was observed crossing the track, and before he could be apprised of his danger, or the train stopped, he was thrown down, both his legs cut off, and he was otherwise seriously injured. The unfortunate man was dull of sight and of hearing, and to this is to be attributed the melancholy accident. He was carried to his son-in-law's residence, near the scene of the accident, in a state precluding all hope of recovery. Albany *Argus*.

195. Drowned - A young lad, named Truman Underwood was found drowned in the creek, near his father's house in Roxbury, on Saturday last. he had gone to the creek to bathe, and, as it is supposed, getting in beyond his depth, was drowned. Prattsville *Advocate*.

196. An Untimely End - Semmes, the young man who shot Professor Davis, some years ago, at the Virginia University, recently committed suicide at the house of his brother in Washington, Ga. He shot himself with a pistol. the ball entering his left eye, and penetrating the brain and lingered in a state of insensibility about five hours. When his room was entered, he was found in a chair, placed at a table. A pistol was

lying across his lap, and on the table was an open razor. On the table was found an open note, stating, in the form of a certificate, dated July 9th, 1847, that his death was occasioned by himself, and was brought about either by pistol or razor.

197. Married on the 31st ult., by the Rev. Mr. Bloomer, Mr. Andrew J. Brink to Miss Elizabeth Myer, both of Unionville, Saugerties.

198. Sheriff's Sale - Under and by virtue of a writ of Fi. Fa. issued by the Clerk of Ulster Co. and to me directed and delivered against Emanuel Roosa, I will sell at Public Auction on the 25th of September next, at one o'clock, pm, at the Hotel kept by William Krows in Ulster Village, in the Town of Saugerties, all the right, title and interest of the said Emanuel Roosa unto the following described real estate: situated in the town and county aforesaid, bounded on the north by lands of Wm. Rightmyer, east by Adam Moose, south by Nicholas Mower and others and on the west by Nicholas Mower. Dated August 4th, 1847. Charles Brodhead, Shff. James D. Brink, Deputy.

August 14, 1847 (Saturday)

199. Drowned - John P. Winchester, a son of Mr. Abel Winchester of Eddyville, aged 6, on Saturday. He fell through the floor of the Dye Mill into the main flume. When his body was recovered, life was extinct.

200. Killed - We regret to learn that Mr. Wm. L. Dickerson, recently of Monticello, died at South Middletown, Orange Co., on Friday last, in consequence of a wound inflicted by a man named Legrand Warring. Mr. Dickerson and Warring were millwrights. The latter had been employed to build a mill. For not performing his work satisfactorily, he was discharged and Dickerson employed. This enraged Warring to such a degree that he assaulted the deceased with a club, and injured him fatally. Dickerson, we understand, refused to quarrel with Warring, and was leaving him, when his murderer struck him upon the head with a club. Mr. Dickerson was a respectable and industrious man. He has left a young family to mourn his loss. Warring, soon after committing the assault, absconded. The authorities of Orange have not acted as promptly in the matter, as they should have done. Monticello *Watchman*.

201. More of Rum's Doings - On Sunday last between the hours of three and four in the afternoon, might be seen a small row boat leaving our shore freighted with three human beings, who were each heavily loaded with Rum. They passed over to Athens, and like most others in the same situation, thought they had not got enough, when they hauled up to the Athens dock and again drank. After drinking in Athens, they again returned to the boat and rowed into the Athens Channel. This last drink, this finishing stroke from the Athens Rumhole, in connection with what was procured in this city, sent one of their number, a man by the name of Turner, unbidden into the presence of his God. Thus another victim has gone to swell the number in the drunkard's grave!- Yes he has gone to his long home, but let me ask who sent him there? Common sense answers the man or men that made him drunk! Yes the rumsellers in Hudson and the rumsellers in Athens were mainly instrumental; and for what? For a little more of the filthy lucre! Who can analyze and estimate those tears of anguish shed by the widow and six fatherless little ones at the grave? "It shall be ill with him, for the reward of his hands shall be given him." Ye pests of community, when will you cease in your drunkard making business-when will you stop your unholy career? When will your vile fountains cease to emit the streams of death which flow from them. When shall we have a jubilee here over your cessation from you body destroying and soul killing business. Heaven grant it may be soon. Oh! Rumseller, fearful is your guilt-dark is the account which a future day will be unfolded for your adjustment. Why will not stop in your traffic? We envy not the man who has pocketed three cents for the glass that consigned poor Turner to a drunkards grave. Columbia *Washingtonian*.

202. On Tuesday afternoon, a very serious accident happened at Bethlehem, which has cast a gloom over the whole borough. Mr. E. F. Black, teacher of a private school, went with his pupils to bathe in the river Lehigh, when it happened that several of the boys waded across the river, but in returning, two of them, Wm. Schall, from New Orleans, aged 10 years, and Charles Brunner, from Lehigh county, Pa. aged 13 years, got beyond their depth, and although their teacher made the greatest exertions to save them, they were both drowned-the teacher narrowly escaping the same fate. Phil. *Ledger*.

203. Melancholy Accident - Edwin R. Andrews, of Webster, Monroe Co., formerly captain of a lake boat, met with such serious injuries on board a lake boat, at Castleton, on Thursday last, that he died yesterday afternoon. His body will be brought to this city today, and placed in charge of the proper authorities to await the action of his friends. He is an Odd Fellow, about 25 years of age, unmarried, and respectably connected. As soon as the accident happened Andrews was removed to the Hudson River Railroad and Steam Boat Hotel, at Castleton, kept by John C. Dowling, medical aid was procured and every attention and care bestowed upon him, with much sympathy for his suffering and fate. Albany *Argus*, 9th inst.

204. Accident and Death - A stage with a load of passengers, this afternoon, suddenly turning near the corner of River and Fulton streets, in order to avoid the cars that were passing, was upset, and a man named Calvin Manley, an agent for some of the steamboats, who was standing on the steps of the stage at the time, was killed almost instantly, the stage falling with full force upon him. None of the passengers inside were seriously injured. Manley was an old stage driver, formerly from Vermont, aged about 45. We understand he was warned repeatedly by the driver to get off the steps, but did not obey. At the time of this writing the Coroner's jury had not returned a verdict. Troy *Budget*.

205. Lawrence Tearney - The Easton *Argus* says: "Samuel Adams, the Sheriff of our County, last Friday received from governor Shunk, the official warrant for the execution of Lawrence Tearney, for the murder of his wife. He is to be hung in the yard of our County Jail, on Friday, the 1st day of October, between the hours of ten and three o'clock. We understand that when his Counsel visited him and informed him of the fact, he wept violently and seemed much affected, but still declared his innocence-remarking at the same time that he would do so upon the gallows."

206. Fatal Accident - A lad of 13, named Charles Hibbard, came to his death in East Henrietta last week, under the following melancholy circumstances. He was loading hay, and his brother, of about 18, was pitching to him. As he leaned forward to secure a large fork-full of hay, he struck his eye against a prong of his brother's fork, which

penetrated the brain. Notwithstanding every effort to avert it, inflammation speedily ensued, which terminated in death in about a week. Geneseo *Democrat*.

207. Accidental Drowning - Wm. E. Douglass, an aged and respectable resident of Schuylkill, Water street, below Lombard, was accidentally drowned on Sunday afternoon. He had a small skiff, which he advertised for sale, and a few young men who wished to purchase, applying to him on Sunday afternoon, he proceeded with them some distance down the Schuylkill in the boat, in order to show her capacities. In returning up the stream, the tide being contrary, he was pushing the skiff along with a pole, when his foot slipped, and he was precipitated head foremost into the river.

208. Another - Ald. Eyre, of Kensington, yesterday held an inquest on the body of Captain Edward Dunn, who was drowned on Sunday evening at Maiden street wharf, having as is supposed fallen overboard, while stepping from the shore to his boat. He was in charge of a coal barge, and is said to have a family in Albany, N. Y. His body has been placed in ice by B. Cohen, and will be kept until Wednesday. Phil. *Ledger*.

209. John Whiteman, a German, recently cut his throat in a beer house in Philadelphia, and was removed to the hospital in a very critical state. He had lost his money by gambling, and being a stranger in a strange land, attempted to commit suicide in despair.

210. Fatal Accident - We learn that a young man by the name of George Mc Chesney, was killed this morning, in the town of Wilton. He was leading a cow along the highway by a rope and the Whitehall stage coming up, the cow became frightened and ran across the road dragging the unfortunate man under the stage, the wheels of which passed over his head and shoulders, killing him almost instantly. The passengers all concur in entirely exonerating the driver from any blame. Saratoga *Republican*.

211. Suicide - Mr. John N. Lukin, of Damascus, Pa., on Tuesday last, committed suicide by shooting himself thro' the head with a pistol. He had been subject to temporary fits of insanity for several years.

August 21, 1847 (Saturday)

212. Latest from Europe - The steamship Cambria, Capt. Judkins, arrived at Boston on Wednesday evening, having left Liverpool on the 4th instant. In the news brought by the steamship - The remains of Mr. O'Connell were embarked from Birkenhead for Dublin, on Sunday, where they arrived the following day.

213. Latest from Europe - Mr. Walter, the celebrated proprietor, is dead. He was justly considered the wall of the steam press.

214. Singular Affair - Supposed Murder at Melville, West Jersey - The West Jersey *Telegraph*, printed at Bridgton, has the particulars of an occurrence which is singular from its fatal result and the extreme youth of the parties concerned. On Saturday morning last, two lads, one named Polston and the other Dilks, left home together, for the purpose of going out of town, a short distance to gather blackberries. Polston returned home some time during the day, and when questioned as to the whereabouts of Dilks, said that had some dispute, and separated before reaching the blackberry field, and he knew nothing of him afterward. No search was made for the boy until Sunday afternoon, when a number of persons commenced searching and dragging the river, supposing that he had probably been drowned, but finding no tidings of him, they proceeded to search the surrounding country, but did not find the body until Monday evening one and a quarter miles from town, and near where the two boys were seen together. He had been shot - several shot having entered his face and head; he had been otherwise beaten and seriously injured. It would seem almost impossible, from Polston's age (he being only about ten years old) that he should commit the horrible deed, but the evidence is much against him. The deceased was about eight years of age.

215. We regret to announce the death of Marvel Hale, Esq., proprietor and editor of the Elizabethtown *Journal*, at his residence in Elizabethtown. His death was caused by lock-jaw, resulting from the injury received a few days since on the railroad. Mr. H. was a gentleman of exceeding amiability and very considerable talent, but had suffered several severe misfortunes during his life, among which are deafness and the loss of an eye. Albany *Argus*.

216. Melancholy Event - A most deplorable accident occurred on Friday afternoon last in Gloucester Co., NJ, which has suddenly bereaved a most excellent man of two sons, whom he had looked upon as props of his declining years. Two sons of James L. Gibbs, one aged twenty and the other about eleven, proceeding from the residence of their father, below Woodbury, to Mantau Creek, about a mile distant, with a couple of horses, for the purpose of giving them a wash. After accomplishing this, they determined on taking a bath themselves. As the younger brother could not swim, the elder took him upon his back and swam into deep water. It is supposed that the younger brother was seized with the cramp, and clasped the other so tightly about the neck as to render him utterly powerless, and both were drowned together. The body of the young man was recovered, but the other had not on Saturday morning. The father is a man of great respectability, and formerly was Judge of the County Court. Philadelphia *Ledger*.

217. Murder - We learn from the Wayne Co. *Herald* that a man named Harris Bell murdered the wife of Rev. G. Williams, of Scott township, Pa., on Sunday morning, the 1st inst., while she was on her way to attend a Sunday school, about a mile from the residence of her husband. Bell has been arrested, and confessed that he assaulted Mrs. W. for a villainous purpose, and she having threatened to have him hung for it, he choked her to death.

218. A Genuine Wind Fall - We hear that letters were received by the last European steamer, of the death, of a Capt. Lamphere, in England, who has left a large property and some $100,000 in cash to five persons in Lapeer county. The immediate heir in this country was Mrs. Hubbard, of Winsor, Vt., formerly a Lamphere. She died some two years since, leaving four sons by the name of Hubbard, and a daughter, who reside near Lapeer county seat. The daughter was the wife of Dr. Carpenter, of Almont, who will soon visit London on the business. Detroit *Free Press*.

219. Gov. Young had issued his proclamation offering a reward of $500 for the arrest and delivery of Le Grand Warren, late of Montgomery, Orange Co., who, it will be remembered, inflicted a wound upon the person of Wm. L. Dickinson, late of Wallkill, in the

same County, whereof he has since died. Le Grand Warren is a man about 5 feet, 6 inches high, square built, black hair slightly grey, heavy black eyebrows, black eyes, square short face, high cheek bones, cheeks a little sunken in, quite talkative, and is about fifty years of age and a millwright by trade.

220. Capt. A. A. Moberg perished in the sinking of the ship Chenunga, Patten, from Liverpool 13th ult., bound for Boston, 171 others also perished.

221. Two young miners, natives of Pottsville, (Penn.) named Edwards and Williams, recently left home for the western part of the state to be married. Returning with their brides, the railroad train they were on board of, came in collision with another, and both of the men were instantly killed, and one of the women was severely wounded.

222. A man named Michael Jingler, while in a state of intoxication at a grocery in Buffalo on the 8th, was turned out of doors, and fell upon the Tonawanda track just as a locomotive and tender were passing, both of which passed over his legs, cutting them both off near the feet. He was not expected to live.

223. A daughter, five years of age, of Mrs. Alden, of Boston, fell from the Portland stage, near Lewistown Falls, and the hind wheel passed over its body, breaking some of the bones of its back. It lived but a short time. The mother and grandmother of the child were in the stage.

224. Two boys, Smith Phelps and George Henold were drowned on Wednesday last while bathing in the Black River, at Watertown.

225. Horrible - Michael Depre, a young man working in Wolff's foundry, Cincinnati, had one of his feet burned off by molten iron, on Wednesday afternoon. He had on large boots, but by some mishap the liquid metal was poured into one of them.

226. Died at Utica, on the 5th inst., Mrs. Julia Ann Thompson, aged about 48 years, daughter of Tjerk Myer of this village.

227. Died in this village, on Wednesday last, Mrs. Margaret Montross, aged 74 years.

August 28, 1847 (Saturday)

228. William Freeman, who murdered the Van Nest family, in Cayuga county, about a year ago, died in the county jail at Auburn on Saturday morning last. It will be remembered that Freeman was convicted of the murders and that a new trial had been granted.

229. A Lover Caught - A man by the name of Richard Tabner, an Englishman by birth, has been caught in a desperate love-scrape. It seems that Mr. Tabner, forgetting the laws of this country, and not being particular about color, fell desperately <sic> in love with a negro woman belonging to Mr. J. M. Cobb, living in Haywood Co. Tabner believing that Mr. Cobb would not give his consent to their union, prevailed upon his fair damsel to elope with him. Accordingly, on Monday night, the two youthful lovers met, and after calling upon the "silver queen of the night" to bear witness to their vows they set out for a distant land. To avoid detection, or suspicion, our thoughtful hero persuaded his lady-love to put on a full suit of his clothes, which was done, and away they started to the tune of O'er the hills and far away". But before this happy pair 'got out of the woods,' as it were, they were surprised and taken; and on Wednesday morning both were brought into this city, where a painful separation took place. Mr. Cobb taking his negro home and the Sheriff taking Tabner to jail. West Tenn. *Whig*.

230. Old Age - The Hudson *Gazette* says there died in that city, last week, a colored woman named Punch, at the advanced age of one hundred and ten years.

231. Murder - Mr. Phelps, an old resident of Nassau, formerly the keeper of the principal public house, was found murdered in his bed on the morning of Friday last-his head being split open as with an axe. He was in his 79th year, and was alone in the house. A few articles, money and clothing, were taken away by the murderer. Albany *Argus*.

232. The Grand River Rapids (Michigan) *Eagle*, announces the death of an Indian of that village, known as Blackskin. The Eagle says he

lived to be upwards of a hundred years old, and has enacted, at the head of his tribe, many exciting scenes during his life. His hand first applied the torch to the city of Buffalo in the war of 1812. The old man, with remnant of his tribe, has long been on friendly terms with the whites, and his death is a notable event in the history of his tribe.

233. Mr. Samuel D. Wallingford, residing a few miles from Fleming, Ky., was deliberately murdered by one of his slaves as he lay asleep in bed. The fellow, with a single blow of an axe, split his head open from the crown to the lower jaw bone. He then went to the stable and fed the horses, and returned to the house, where he confessed his crime and was secured.

234. Died in this village on Monday last, Mrs. Eliza Coggeshall, wife of Mr. Samuel P. Coggeshall, aged 35 years.

September 4, 1847 (Saturday)

235. Death of Hon. Silas Wright - After our paper was issued on Saturday last we received the unexpected and melancholy intelligence of the death of this esteemed man and eminent statesman. He expired almost instantly in an apopletic fit at his residence in Canton, St. Lawrence county on Friday morning, August 27th in the 53rd year of his age. Ogdensburgh *Rep.* Extra, Aug 27. <very long article>

236. Murder at Prattsville - We learn from the Prattsville Advocate that on Monday morning, 23d ult., Mrs. Lucretia Lewis, a lady about seventy-five years of age, who resided alone in the upper part of that village, was found dead in her bed. At first it was the general opinion that she had died suddenly in a fit, but upon further examination, marks of violence were observed around her neck, as if she had been throttled, and thus murdered. Suspicion at once rested upon an Irishman, named Kelly, who was seen at the old lady's house on Sabbath evening, and subsequently a little after midnight, about three miles from the village. Officers were immediately sent in pursuit, and Kelly was overtaken when about twelve miles on his way to Catskill. His demeanor during his detention was quite indifferent, and he expressed himself quite careless about the matter. A Coroner's inquest was held over the body, and the jury after hearing the testimony of several witnesses returned a verdict that the deceased had been

murdered by John Kelly, after which an examination was had before a Justice, who committed Kelly to the Jail of the County, of Catskill, to await his trial. The old lady murdered was a most inoffensive woman - a friend of all, who maintained herself by selling small-beer, cakes and candy, and who by her industry and economy had saved a small amount of money, probably some ten or fifteen dollars, which undoubtedly led to the perpetration of one of the most revolting murders on record.

237. Latest from Europe - Lt. Monroe, late of the second regiment of Life Guards, was yesterday found guilty of the murder of Col. Faucett, whom he slew in a duel about four years ago. The verdict of the jury has caused considerable excitement and surprise.

238. Sad Accident and Death at Clinton Prison - On Tuesday the 24th inst., Mr. George A. Jenkins, of Auburn (the master mason at Clinton Prison) while directing the hoisting of stone, was struck down by the falling of the tripod or shears, used for that purpose. He survived the blow (which was upon his head) but for a few hours, and died without a return of consciousness. He left a wife and one child, who were dependent upon him for support. The remains of Mr. Jenkins were brought to this village on Thursday, and placed in a tomb. They will be moved to Auburn in a few days, we learn. Plattsburgh *Republican*.

239. Death by Drowning - A melancholy accident occurred about five miles up the lake on Wednesday last, which resulted in the death of two boys - one 14 and the other 10 years of age. They had constructed a sort of raft, and pushed into the lake a short distance for the purpose of fishing. A breeze sprung up suddenly from the west - their frail craft was parted, and through fear of being carried far out into the lake, they leaped into the water, and sank to rise no more. Their bodies were soon after found in six feet of water; and every effort used to resuscitate them but in vain. They were the sons of a Mr. Wood, a widow, upon whom the loss of two promising boys in so sudden and unexpected a manner, fell with uncommon heaviness. Geneva *Gazette*.

240. Melancholy Accident - Wm. H. Jamison, an ice distributor, came to his death on Saturday last by falling out of his wagon, while his

horse was running away. He fell off while endeavoring to regain the reins which he had dropped, and having been caught in the wheels, was so dreadfully bruised that he died in a few minutes. NY *Express.*

241. Fatal Accident - Yesterday, about noon, a fatal accident occurred at Mr. Howland's paper mill in the fifth ward of this city. One of the workmen, an Irishman named John Flannerty, was by some means caught in the belt attached to the main shaft, round which he was whirled some time before discovered. He was found lifeless and horribly mangled. He was a young man - said to be under 20 years of age and unmarried. Troy *Budget.*

242. Died at Glenerie, Saugerties, August 25th, George Percival, son of Fanning and Mary Albert, aged 4 years and 9 months.

243. Died in this village on Tuesday last, Antonio Hoffman, aged 77 years.

September 11, 1847 (Saturday)

244. Awful Murder - At Mount Pleasant, Westchester County, on Sunday, August 29th, between 3 and 4 o'clock in the afternoon, Miss Mary Goodyear, aged 15 years was fatally stabbed by Amos Northrup, a shoemaker by trade. This girl, Northrup professed to love and wished to marry. But she declined and absolutely refused because of his intemperate habits, and his age, which is about 45 years. In one of his drunken fits, he abused the girl and threatened her, and said also to her married sister, "she (Mary) thinks she has got along with it (the refusal to marry him) but she'll find the worst is to come.

They had an interview on Sunday at the house of her sister, at the close of which her sister heard her cry out, "He is murdering me! Jump out of the window." Both of the females then sprang out of the window together, the sister having seen the handle of a knife in his hand, the blade having already been buried in her left breast. Mary was hardly able to move after reaching the ground, and died in a few minutes. The murderer made his escape, but has since been caught, and is now safely secured in jail. He was found secreted in the neighborhood of the murder, and had made an attempt to take his own life by cutting his throat; but the wound is not likely to prove mortal.

245. The family of Mr. William Gorham, of Troy, consisting of himself, wife and child, contracted the ship fever from a family of immigrants whom he received into his house a few days since. Mr. G. was seized with delirium, and supposing his wife to be dead, started out to make arrangements for the burial, and fell dead in the street.

246. Married at Kingston on the 7th instant, Mr. James Kiersted of Saugerties to Miss Sarah Ann, daughter of Egbert Jansen, Esq., of Kingston.

247. Died in this village, Sept. 9th, Gertrude, daughter of F. B. and Mary Porter, aged 1 year and 7 months.

September 18, 1847 (Saturday)

248. Highly Important From Mexico - Terrible but Victorious Battles of Centras and Churubucco - At 7 o'clock on the 18th, Gen Scott arrived at San Augustin. At 10 o'clock Gen. Worth was in full march for the City of Mexico, by the main road. Majors Smith and Turnbull, Capt. Mason and other engineer officers were sent in advance, supported by Capt. Blake's squadron of dragoons, to reconnoitre when a masked battery opened upon them, and killed Capt. Thornton, beside seriously wounded a guide.

249. Died at Binghampton, on the 30th ult., Robert C. Whitmore, publisher of the Binghamton *Democrat*, aged 28 years.

September 25, 1847 (Saturday)

250. Later from Europe - The French steamer Union arrived at New York on Thursday the 10th inst., at one o'clock P. M. with twelve days later intelligence from England. Paris is excited by the murder of the Dutchess of Praslin by her husband, and his suicide in prison. The cause of the murder was reproach of the Duchess with his connection with a governess. The Government is charged with conniving at his suicide. The Duchess was a daughter of Marshal Sebastiana.

251. From the army of Gen. Taylor - The steamer E. A. Ogden, Captain Bowman, arrived yesterday morning from Brazos Santiago, whence she sailed on the 7th inst., making a very fine run. We learn with regret that Brigadier General Hopping died at Mier on the 1st inst.

The General was appointed from the western part of the state of New York, and was a gentleman of ability well known in the politics of the State.

252. John Kelley, who killed Mrs. Lewis in Prattsville on the 22d of August last, has been sentenced to be hung on Thursday the 28th day of October next. Catskill *Recorder*.

253. Yellow Fever in the Gulf Squadron - The Pensacola *Gazette* just received, has a letter from Anton Lizardo dated 27th August, announcing the deaths of Doctors Bache and Kearney, surgeons of the fleet in the Gulf; and a great extension of the yellow fever among the ships of the squadron.

254. The house of Major Samuel George, of Seabrook, NH was recently destroyed by fire, and his house-keeper, widow Jane Dow, perished in the flames. The unfortunate woman passed out of the house after the fire commenced, and returned, as is supposed, for the purpose of saving her money and papers, which were in her chamber. Her bones were found among the ruins of the house.

255. Died on the 22d inst., at West Camp Landing, Mr. John B. Adams, in the eightieth year of his age.

October 2, 1847 (Saturday)

256. From Santa Fe - We learn from a letter from a volunteer that six of the prisoners charged with the murder of Lieut. Brown, James Mc Clenahan and Chas. Quisenberry, were hung on the 3d of August, under the sentence of a drum head court martial. Major Edmondson is bringing home with him the remains of the late Lieuts. B. F. and G. E. Lackland, for interment in St. Louis county. - Capt. Horine has likewise with him the ashes of Charles Quisenbery and James Mc Clenahan. St. Louis *Republican*, Sept. 20.

257. Shipwreck-Eighteen Lives Lost - Long Beach, Sep 25, 1847. The ship Orbit, of New York, Capt. White, from New Orleans came ashore on Long Beach, Barnegat Inlet, on Saturday night last. She has gone to pieces, and the captain, first mate and sixteen others are lost. Very respectfully, Edward Gennings, Wreckmaster.

258. Married in Kingston, on the 19th inst., by the Rev. C. Shook, William H. Griffiths to Miss Rachel Ann Swart, both of Saugerties.

259. Died at his residence in this village on Wednesday the 29th inst., Francis Neelis, aged 62 years, 1 month and 14 days.

October 9, 1847 (Saturday)

260. Capture of the Capital of Mexico - The steamer James L. Day arrived at New Orleans on the 25th ult., with the most important intelligence yet received from the seat of war. The New Orleans Picayune has the following particulars - We lament to hear the loss of Gen. Leon, since dead; that of Col. Balberas, of the valiant Cols. Huerla and Geleati, and of the determined Capt. Mateos, of Puebla. A Mexican letter announces that Riley and his Legion of St. Patrick, seventy in number, were ordered by the court martial to be hung. The sentence was approved by General Scott, and on the 8th of September the whole legion were hung in the presence of the army, as also of the enemy.

261. Capture of the Capital of Mexico - The *Diario del Gobierno* says, "At half-past 4 o'clock in the morning, the Americans attacked the position of the mill of El Rey, close to the fortress of Chapultepec. We lament the death of the gallant Col. John Lucas Baldras, and Gen. Don Antonio De Leon, being wounded."

262. Sad Accident - Mr. John William Benner, a resident of this town, fell from the steamboat Hudson on her way up last Monday night, and was drowned. It appears that he got up in the night and went on deck, and receiving a slip when standing near the gang-way, fell through into the river. His hat was found on deck, which, it is presumed, dropped off when he fell. His cries for help were heard for some time, and every possible effort to save him was in vain. His friends are deeply afflicted by the painful and sudden bereavement. - The accident occurred just this side of Newburgh. Rhinebeck *Gazette*. We understand that at the time of the occurrence of the accident above related, the steamboat was not provided with a small boat, and there being no means of reaching the unfortunate man, the loss of his life was the consequence. Had a small boat been in readiness for use when he was first discovered overboard, he might easily have been saved.

"Every possible effort to save" a drowning man is of little use without the means to accomplish it.

263. Atrocious Murder - We learn that on Sunday night, the shanty of Patrick Loftus, on the Rail Road section of Mr. Morse, at Collaberg, was forcibly entered by five or six Irishmen, armed with muskets, one of whom after demanding to know whether he was a Connaught man, and whether he had arms in his house, shot him through the body, the ball entering his right side, and producing death in a short time. The murderers immediately fled, and have not been pursued, as we have heard. The wife of Loftus was present, and thinks she will be able to recognize the wretch who killed her husband. We can obtain no further particulars of the cause of this diabolical act; but the Coroner, who is to hold an inquest, will perhaps be able to elicit further particulars. The act is supposed to have been perpetrated by some men who had been employed on the Brick yards at that place. Westchester *Herald.*

264. Married on the 2nd inst., by the Rev. R. Dederick, Mr. John C. Knox to Miss Margaret Schutt, both of Saugerties.

265. Married on the 3d inst., by the Rev. R. Dederick, Mr. John Kiener to Miss Matilda Bell, both of Saugerties.

266. Married on the 5th instant, at the residence of Mr. James Brink in this village, by the Rev. Mr. Van Santvoord, Mr. Wm. M. Brink to Miss Ann I. Felter. The Printers acknowledge the receipt of a basket containing a beautiful supply of the richest kind of wedding cake, and unite in wishing the happy Bridegroom and his amiable Bride many years of uninterrupted happiness.

267. Married at Coxsackie, on Wednesday last, Dr. John R. Henshew to Miss Caroline Collyer, both of that place.

268. Died in this village, on Tuesday last, Mr. Albert Dubois, aged 17 years.

October 16, 1847 (Saturday)

269. We like short courtships, and in this Adam acted like a sensible

man - he fell asleep a bachelor, and awoke to find himself a married man. He appears to have popped the question almost immediately after meeting Md'lle Eve, and she, without any flirtation or shyness, gave him a kiss and herself. Of that first kiss in this world we have had, however, our own thoughts, and sometimes in a poetical mode have wished we were the man "Wot did it." But the deed is done - the chance was Adam's and he improved it. We like the notion of getting married in a garden. It is in good taste. We like a private wedding. Adam's was private. No envious beaux were there; no creaking old maids; no chattering aunts and grumbling grandmothers. The birds of heaven were the minstrels and the glad sky flung its light upon the scene. One thing about the first wedding brings queer things to us, in spite of its scriptural truth. Adam and his wife were rather young to be married - some two or three days old, according to the sagest speculations of theologians - mere babies - larger, but not older - without experience, without a house, without a pot or kettle, nothing but love and Eden! *Noah's Weekly Messenger.*

270. Major Edward Wade, an officer of the army who received a severe wound at Monterey, was found dead in his bed, on the morning of the 30th ult., at his lodgings in Cincinnati, at which city he was recruiting. The cause is supposed to have been a paralytic stroke.

271. Died at Otego, Otsego Co., on the 1st instant, very suddenly, Job Gillespy of Montezuma, Cayuga county, in the 66th year of his age.

October 23, 1847 (Saturday)

272. Latest from Mexico - The *Picayune* says Col. Mc Intosh and Cranson, Lieut. Col. Martin Scott, Lieut. Col. Graham of infantry, Lieut. Col. Baxter, New York regiment, and Lieut. Col. Dickinson of the South Carolina regiment are dead. Another account says, Major Twiggs, Captain Van Olinda and Capt. Merrill, were also among the killed.

273. The Death of Lieut. Twiggs - We announce with deep regret the death of Lieut. George Decatur Twiggs, until a few months ago a resident of this city. He was young, gallant and gifted. The late Com. Stephen Decatur was his uncle by his mother's side, and Gen. Twiggs, of the United States Army, his uncle by his father's side. It is only a

short time since that he called at our office to bid us farewell, just as he was about to leave for the seat of the war, to join the staff of his uncle, the veteran General. It appears that Major Lally's command had three separate engagements with the guerillas, in all of which Lieut. Twiggs distinguished himself, and in the last fell gallantly sustaining the reputation of our arms. This brave young officer was a fine scholar, wrote well, and at the time he left was reading law with a distinguished member of our bar. He would have been admitted to practice on his return home, if he had survived the war with Mexico. He was an only son, and his deeply afflicted mother and sisters are residing at our Navy Yard. The citizens of Philadelphia will deeply sympathise with them in their melancholy bereavement. Major Twiggs, the father of Lieut. Twiggs, is with Gen. Scott. Philadelphia *Ledger*.

274. Married on the 21st inst., by the Rev. R. Dederick, Mr. Jacob H. Elmendorf to Miss Anne Elizabeth Kimble, all of Saugerties.

October 29, 1847 (Saturday)

275. Capt. Edward D. Bill, of the 16th infantry, died at sea on the 12th inst., on board the Tampico, of yellow fever. His remains have been brought to New Orleans for interment. From Mexico.

276. Death of Mr. Everett - On the 20th of June, at Canton, the Hon. A. H. Everett, Commissioner from the United States to China, expired. Interment on Dane's Island, Whampoa. <details of the funeral in the item>

277. A terrible riot took place among the firemen at Baltimore, on Friday evening of last week. A young man named Bond was shot in the abdomen, and died before he could be conveyed to his home. <details of the riot in the article>

278. A fatal accident occurred at Hamilton Square yesterday. Two horses attached to one of the ammunition wagons, having been frightened by continued firing, started off at full speed and made a complete circuit of the ground, and knocked down five of the pupils of the Institution for the Deaf and Dumb, one of whom, Morgan Jones, about 13 years of age, son of Mr. David Jones of 9 Monroe St., was almost instantly killed. NY *Express*.

279. Horrible Murder - A Mr. J. Clipfell, a highly respectable old gentleman, of Colon, in this county, has for a long time been living with a son, who was of intemperate habits. At about 4 o'clock on Wednesday morning, the 6th inst., the son called his father out on some pretence, when he struck him with a large iron bar, so severely fracturing the skull that he died in about an hour. After the horrible deed, the report of a gun was heard from an old brewery, distant some few rods from the scene of the murder. On repairing to the place, the wretch was found at the head of the stairs, with his skull blown nearly away - having closed up the bloody drama with the destruction of himself. The frequent expostulations of the old gentleman with his son, on his intemperate course, and some other difficulties of long standing, are the only known causes for these horrible proceedings. The father's age, we believe, was 89 and the son's 51. St. Joseph (Mich.) *Repub.*

280. A letter from Vera Cruz, dated September 10th, announces the death of Lieutenant Murray Winder of Maryland. He was wounded in the engagement with Major Lally's command, at the National Bridge, and died a few days thereafter at Jalapa. "He fought gallantly", says the letter, "and was wounded in the midst of the conflict."

281. George Jacobs, of South Boston, was accidentally shot dead in a boat, while out after geese, in company with his son and another person. Two of them fired upon a flock of geese. The deceased's gun was heavily loaded, and kicked him directly before the muzzle of the other's gun whose charge was lodged in the back of his head.

282. Mr. Tucker, a young man residing in Cincinnati, committed suicide on the 18th instant, by blowing his brains out with a pistol. He died instantly. He had been for some time in a melancholy mood, but none knew the cause of his dejection.

283. Francis Brugman, a druggist in Sandusky City, has been arrested on a charge of murder, by administering poison to Conrad Alder, his partner in business. Poison was found in the dead man's stomach.

284. John Betz, a young man, has been arrested in Centre township, Berk's Co., Pa., on a charge of having murdered his brother. They had

been drinking, quarrelled violently and one was shortly afterwards found dead.

285. Married on Tuesday evening last, by Rev. Dr. Ostrander, Mr. Abraham Wing to Miss Rachel Heermans, all of Saugerties.

286. Married by the Rev. James Burch, Mr. E. L. Crawford of Saugerties to Miss Lanah Smith of Catskill.

287. Married at Kinderhook, on the 26th instant, by the Rev. George Townsend, C. Strong Clay of Kingston to Miss Jane Vallett of the former place.

288. Married on the 20th inst., at Delhi, by Rev. George Waters, Robert F. Macauley of Kingston to Miss Rebecca, daughter of Amasa Parker, Esq., of the former place.

289. Married at Cicero, on the 18th inst., by the Rev. S. J. May, P. H. Agan, Editor of the Onondaga *Standard* to Miss Hannah E., daughter of Hon. John L. Stevens of Cicero.

290. Died in Esopus, on the 6th inst., Mr. Solomon Teerpenning, aged 65 years.

November 6, 1847 (Saturday)

291. Late from Mexico - The steamer James L. Day has arrived at New Orleans, with dates from Vera Cruz, to the 19th ultimo. Richard Bemish and Wm. Miller, soldiers, died on board the steamer Day.

292. Powder Mill Explosion - The Powder Mill of Laflin's Smith and Co., at the High Falls, in the town of Catskill, about eight miles from this village, exploded on Monday morning last, about nine o'clock, instantly killing three persons named John Westgate, Peter Overbagh and Martin Schriver, all of whom were at work in the mill at the time. They were all blown to atoms. Schriver and Overbagh have each left a wife and five or six small children. Westgate has left a wife only. The mill contained from two to three tons of powder. The shock was sensibly felt in this village, and the report was heard at the distance of twenty miles.

293. Another - A serious accident occurred at the Powder Mills of Laflins & Smith in this town, about five miles from this village, on Thursday last. Mr. Samuel Babcock was engaged in charging the mill with dry charcoal and brimstone, which is usually wet, whereby fire was communicated to the powder dust about the mill, which flashed and horribly burnt Mr. Babcock, so much so that he is not expected to recover. Mr. James Mc Donald of this village, who was carting powder from the Mills, was within a few feet of the door of the building at the time and was also badly burnt, but not dangerously.

294. Execution of Kelly - This wretched man suffered the extreme penalty of the law, within the walls of the prison in this village on the 28th ult. Everything had been admirably arranged by our efficient Sheriff, Robert Fulton, Esq., and his prompt Deputies, and at precisely 10 minutes to 1 o'clock, P. M., he was launched into eternity. He met his death with the utmost fortitude, actually carrying with him, rather than being led by, the Deputies on his way from his cell to the gallows. During the night preceding his execution he uniformly expressed himself innocent of the crime of which he was convicted, and at the moment of affixing the fatal cord around his neck, he firmly declared to the Priest attending him and the spectators that he had made no confession of the crime to anyone. Yet strange to say, W. A. Sternbergh, Esq., his counsel, has since his execution, published what purports to be a full confession by him of the crime, but which Kelly at the moment of his execution, solemnly declared, of any such thing should appear, was a forgery, and got up for the purpose of making money, and which we are bound therefore to believe is untrue. His heart ceased to beat in fourteen minutes from the time he was run up. The body was taken to Hunter for interment, by his wife and several other acquaintances. Catskill *Democrat*.

295. Another Explosion at the Powder Mill - At about half past 3 o'clock today (Thursday) while the Sham Fight was being carried on upon Chatterdon's Hill, a large explosion was heard in the direction of the Powder Mills at Hart's Corners one and one half miles below this and soon a dense cloud of smoke was seen rising up over that place. It was the explosion of the press house at that establishment, by which one man, a German, named Benj. Hugle, was instantly killed, and two others badly injured, one of whom has since died and the other is not

expected long to survive. Upon information being given, our Coroner, Dwight Capon, Esq., who was a spectator at the Sham Fight here, immediately repaired to the scene of the calamity, with a Jury, and held an inquest on the body of Hugle - the result being a verdict that he came to his death through the means of the explosion. One of the wounded men, with the body of Hugle, was thrown into the Bronx river by the explosion, and the other was thrown some distance from the press house. *Eastern State Jour.*

296. Andrew Meehan, aged 23 years, whose parents reside at Rondout, was found lying on a sidewalk in Leonard street in New York, yesterday morning (2d inst.) in a dying state. Blood was flowing freely from a wound inflicted apparently by a small knife, just above the collar bone, probably having penetrated the carotid artery. He died before reaching the station house. Oliver Bartol or Bartow, a Frenchman, who worked with Meehan, has been arrested as the supposed murderer. Ulster *Republican.*

297. The Cincinnati *Signal* learns, that on the 17th, as Mr. Sawyer, a young gentleman of high respectability, was riding at a very fast rate, to see a female acquaintance in Dearborn Co., Indiana, he came up against the Telegraph wires, which cut his throat, producing almost instant death. The wires had been lowered for the purpose of making certain repairs on the line.

298. A boy named George F. Shultz, about 7 years old, whose parents reside in Varick street, New York, during their absence, got hold of a bottle of rum, of which he drank, and died in consequence.

299. Married on Saturday evening last, by the Rev. Mr. Crawford, Hon. Jeremiah Russell to Miss Christina Crawford, all of Saugerties.

300. Married on Saturday last, by Rev. Henry Ostrander, Mr. William Dubois, of Kingston to Miss Rachel M. Snyder, daughter of Mr. Tjerk E. Snyder of Saugerties.

November 13, 1847 (Saturday)
301. Fatal Railroad Accident - On Sunday morning, the dead body of James Forbes, a single man, aged 46, was found upon the track of the

Western Railroad near King's Tavern, Westfield, about seven miles from here. One of his legs was cut twice in two; once above and once below the knee; and it is consequently supposed that he lay with that leg in a angular position across the track, and was run over by one of the trains, which passed on Saturday evening. It is not positively known whether it was the passenger train down; or the freight train which went up afterward. The appearance of the blood on the track and the position of the body indicated that it was run over by the former; while the testimony of the neighbors, who heard halloeings about midnight, the time the freight train passed, would seem to prove that it was the latter. There was no other injuries on the body, and he probably lay there till he bled to death, being, as is supposed, intoxicated. A bottle of rum was found in his pocket. Those who heard the noises which are now supposed to have been made by him, thought they came from some boys or others who were having a "spree" at the tavern. Springfield *Republican*, 8th.

302. Vincent H. Gunn was tried last week in the Superior Court at New Haven, for the murder of a man named Avis, in that city, one night last summer, and was found guilty, notwithstanding the fact was established that Avis was in habitual adulterous intercourse with Gunn's wife, and received the fatal blow while in bed with her. Rather a cold-blooded verdict. Robert Channing was also convicted of a rape on a little girl twelve years of age.

303. Married in this village, on Monday evening last, by the Rev. Mr. Bloomer, Mr. Wm. M. Patterson to Miss Matilda Artman.

304. Married in this village on Thursday last, by the Rev. Mr. Van Santvoord, Mr. Joseph W. Kerr to Miss Susan S. Knapp.

305. Married at Marbletown, on the 6th inst., by the Rev. J. C. Cruikshank, John C. Wolven, of Saugerties, to Henrietta E., daughter of Clinton Woolsey.

306. Married by the Rev. Wm. S. Mikels, Nov 4, Mr. Peter Decker of Saugerties to Miss Helen Burgher of Rondout.

307. Married on the 3d inst., by the Rev. Martin L. Schenck, Frederick B. Low of Saugerties, to Rachel Ann Brink of Kingston.

308. Died in this village, on Saturday last, Henry, son of James Russell, aged about 4 years.

309. Whereas my wife Sarah has left me, I hereby notify all persons not to harbor or trust her on my account, as I will not pay any debts of her contracting. Michael Flynn, Saugerties, Nov 4, 1847.

November 20, 1847 (Saturday)

310. Later from Mexico - New Orleans papers announce the arrival of the steamer Galveston, with the Vera Cruz dates to the 3d inst. It is said that Capt. Walker was not killed by a Mexican lance, as heretofore stated, but that he was struck by two balls, one hitting him in the head and the other in the breast.

311. Capt. Walker's body remained unburied for two days. His death creates an unusual sensation throughout the whole army. Two Skirmishes at Puebla, Latest from Mexico.

312. Lieut. Scott died of apoplexy on the passage to Vera Cruz. Two Skirmishes at Puebla, Latest from Mexico.

313. Singular and Fatal Occurrence - On Friday last, about 3 o'clock, the line boat M. Kingman, Capt. Wm. Babcock, and a scow boat, in passing each other near the Amboy bridge, about six miles west of this place, became wedged. Capt. Babcock, we learn, immediately went on board the scow boat, and commenced an assault on the captain, and beat him severely. During the assault, a son of the sufferer, who had been out with his gun, following the boat, came on board, when Capt. Babcock, leaving the father, wrenched the gun, which was loaded, from the boy, and broke the stock in pieces on the deck of the boat. The gun was discharged from the effect of the blow, and the whole charge lodged in the thigh of Capt. B., near the groin, causing his death in an hour and a half! The deceased, we understand, resided at Weedsport, Cayuga county. Onondaga *Standard*.

314. The daughter of Mr. William Chatfield, of Derby, Connecticut, while laboring under an attack of delirium tremens, attacked her father with a fire shovel and fractured his skull, by which his life is endangered.

315. Died in this village, on Wednesday last, suddenly, Miss Nancy Hubbard, aged 33 years, daughter of Moses Hubbard of Greene county.

316. Died in this town, on Monday last, Mr. Samuel Babcock.

November 27, 1847 (Saturday)

317. Benjamin Smith, former Senator of Vermont, died suddenly on the 9th inst., at St. Albans, in that State.

318. The Rev. Charles Van Loon, Pastor of the Baptist Church at Poughkeepsie, died suddenly in that village on Sunday evening last. His death was caused by an apoplectic attack. His age was 29 years. He was one of the ablest advocates of the Temperance cause. A resolution of the Hope Temperance Society is published.

319. Confession of a Murderer - The Plattsburgh *Republican* Extra, of Wednesday, contains the following confession made by the murderer Joseph Levert, who was convicted at that place on the preceding day:- On the 7th of December, 1846, I took my wife to Bushby's, on the south side of the Saranac, near Treadwell's mills, to make a visit; and she was pleased to go. I got the axe in the wagon that day with the intention of killing her, and on my return from Bushby's on the plains, I told her that something about the wagon was out of order, and she got out of the wagon. I told her that a screw was loose, and I wished her to hold the shafts while I fixed it; and at the time I had the axe in my hand and struck her on the right side of the head with the flat of the axe. She was stooping a little at the time. Her hood was then on her head. I then took off the left forward wheel and drew the wagon forward a short distance, and I then came back and gave her another blow, with the flat of the axe, in the same place. I then threw the axe into the bushes, and started for the house of St. Dennis. I thought it was going to snow, and would cover the axe. I found young St. Dennis at the stable door with a span of horses harnessed, and told him

that the left wheel of my wagon had run off, and that my wife had broke her neck or split her head open. I went back on foot, and St. Dennis came up with his horses and wagons as fast as he could. I got back a little the first. I found my wife who tried to talk with me, and I took up the wheel and struck her with it on the forehead once. This deed was done, for the purpose of getting my wife out of the way, that I might marry a girl with whom I had had improper intercourse and save myself from prosecution, and save my money. Joseph Levert. Signed in the presence of Zeph. C. Platt, M. E. Platt, Smith Mead.

320. Izry Roberts, a farmer living eight miles back of Camden, was murdered on Saturday night, while in his wagon returning home from the Philadelphia market. The murder occurred near Cooper's Creek Bridge, and was committed by a young man 18 to 20 years of age. He was shot in the back of the head, and his skull was fractured with some blunt instrument. The murderer escaped over to the city in the ferry boat. The pockets of the murdered man were rifled of all the money he had received at the market, about $10. The murderer drove the wagon some distance containing the body of his victim. $500 reward is offered for the detection of the murderer.

321. Thomas Brady, an Irishman, who keeps a grog shop at West Farms, Westchester Co., poured a pint of liquor down the throat of Stephen Curtis, while the latter was lying on the floor nearly dead drunk. Curtis lived but a short time. Brady is in jail.

322. A young gentleman named Crawford, a son of the late Hon. W. H. Crawford, of Georgia, and a member of the Jefferson Medical School, of Philadelphia, came to his death a short time since in that city, from the effects of a slight puncture received in one of his hands, whilst dissecting.

323. Plain Talk - Mrs. Elizabeth Peters, of Boone Co., Indiana, notices her absconding husband in the following plain terms: Left my bed and board last fall, thereby rendering my expenses lighter, John Peters, without cause or provocation. All the old maids, young girls, widow of all ages and conditions, are hereby forewarned against harboring or trusting him on my account, as I am determined not to be accountable for his debts, or more especially for his conduct, because he is a loafer,

a drunkard, a gambler, a thief, a liar, and above all, a Whig.

324. Two Murders in Madison. On Friday night the 5th inst., a man named Couch, overseer for Mrs. Carroll, on Walnut Bayou, Madison parish, La., was shot by some unknown assassin, and on Saturday the 6th, Rev. Mr. Preston was shot and instantly killed in the same parish while sitting at his dinner, by John Elliott, formerly of Natchez. The murderer, in the latter instance, is said to have been for some weeks partially insane. An Indian, supposed to have been bribed to the deed, is under arrest for the murder of Mr. Couch.

325. Married on the 18th inst., by the Rev. R. Dederick, Mr. Philip A. Genthner, of Saugerties, to Miss Eliza Catharine Lasher, of Catskill.

December 4, 1847 (Saturday)
326. Fatal Accident - On Friday of last week, a daughter of Mr. Broadstreet, of Shandaken, in this county, aged about 18 years, was instantly killed in Middletown, Delaware Co., by being thrown from a one horse wagon while driving a horse, which became frightened and unmanageable.

327. In Tiverton, on the 16th ult., Jerome B., son of Mr. Silas Manchester, about 3 years of age, fell over a chair, bit his tongue, and bled to death. He lived about 24 hours after the accident.

328. A German named Henry Sach, who arrived in New York on Thursday week, accidentally met his brother, from whom he had been some time separated, in a house in Washington street, which caused him such excessive joy and excitement, that he burst a blood vessel in the chest, and died in a few minutes.

329. From the Delaware *Gazette* - Lieut. Gantt, 7th infantry, with a portion of the party, was ordered to cross the ditch on the left of the road, and proceed further to the left of the base of Chapultepec, and by scaling the wall, gain admittance to the body of the work. This gallant officer was shot dead at the head of his men. <in an article about Lieut. Frederick Steele, ed.>

330. A day or two ago we published a deplorable account of a shipwreck, given by the survivors from the wreck of the schooner Caroline, Capt. Wm. Smith, bound from Savannah for Bath. Captain Smith arrived at Boston on Thursday morning, and furnished the following to the editors of the *Traveller*. Captain Smith states that he left Tybee light, mouth of the Savannah river, Oct 24th. On the 26th, took a heavy gale of wind from N. E. and sprung a leak in lat 32,43 long. 77. Laid to all that day. At 7 pm, was thrown on her beam ends, but on cutting away the weather lanyards, she righted. On the 31st spoke to barque Isaac Mead, Brown, from Savannah for New York. The barque laid by us from 7 am to 4 pm but a tremendous sea prevented them from rendering us any assistance. Our provisions and water were all stored on deck, save one barrel of water in the run. By the disaster, both provisions and water were carried overboard, save that below, which it was impossible to get at. Thus we were without food or drink. Henry Hughes, one of the crew went on deck and was probably washed overboard, and never seen afterward. Charles Brown, an Irishman, who had S. D. marked on his arm, was chosen as the person who should suffer death to save the lives of the others. He was eventually killed and his body eaten. <long story, ed.>

331. Horrible Murder - A letter from Auburn, Ala., to the Montgomery *Journal*, dated Nov 23, says: - There is a great excitement here this morning, occasioned by a most outrageous assault committed on the partner of Mr. Davis, of Richmond, Va., who was returning to Virginia from New Orleans, where he had just taken 100 negroes. The assault was committed some five miles beyond this place, at a grocery (the same place where Burks a short time ago stabbed S. Rease so severely.) It appears that the gentleman arrived here in the cars yesterday, and after taking his dinner started in his buggy for home, and arriving at this grocery was attacked by six men who were drinking. They dragged him from his buggy and beat him with clubs, breaking his skull in a shocking manner. I have just seen one piece of his skull as large as a half dollar brought to town by Dr. Mc Ghee. The grocery keeper, by the name of Thornton and two men by the name of Williams are said to have committed the foul deed; and I understand they have fled. Several men have gone in pursuit. The name of the murdered man was Watley.

332. Suicide - Rev. Mr. Bennet, of Woburn, one of the most distinguished Congregational clergymen in Massachusetts, committed suicide last week at his house in Woburn, by cutting his throat with a razor. He had lectured the preceding evening. He had recently shown symptoms of insanity. He has been settled in Woburn upwards of twenty five years. He graduated at Harvard College in 1818. He married a young wife but a short time ago, and was pleasantly situated.

333. Married at Woodstock, on the 23d ult., by the Rev. S. M. Knapp, Mr. Wm. C. Low, of Saugerties, to Miss Ann L. Short, of Woodstock.

December 11, 1847 (Saturday)

334. On Wednesday evening of last week, two sons of Mr. Jacob Bowman, of Palmyra, Lebanon Co., Pa., as they were going to bed, got to wrestling; the elder threw the younger, who never rose again, but expired almost instantly.

335. Married at Saugerties, on the 7th inst., by J. P. Foland, Esq., Peter Cramer to Sarah Latsal, all of Saugerties.

December 18, 1847 (Saturday)

336. Devoted to the President's Message, James K. Polk, Washington, December, 1847.

December 25, 1847 (Saturday)

337. Something Mysterious - By a gentleman from Kortright, in this county, we learn that a Mr. Matthew Mc Clelen, of that town, started from Keeler's store, North Kortright, on horseback, on Wednesday evening last, and the horse returned that evening, without its rider. Search being made, the next morning Mr. Mc Clelen was found in a raceway at the side of the road, about one and half miles from home, dead. Various conjectures are made as to how the deceased came to his death. We have not heard the result of the inquest of the coroner. His age was about 30. Delhi *Voice of the People*.

338. Patrick Carrol, formerly of this town, and who left here about two months ago, committed suicide in Brooklyn a few days since, by hanging himself. Mr. Carrol, had by industry and close attention to his business, acquired considerable property, and left here with the

intention of establishing himself in business in Brooklyn. We have heard no cause assigned for the commission of this rash act, but suppose the unfortunate man to have been insane at the time.

339. Disastrous Wreck and Loss of Life - The brig Falconer, of Belfast, Captain Rollerson Sidney, master, bound for Boston, was wrecked on Ipswich beach, two miles from the lighthouse, in the gale of Friday night last. Of about fifty persons on board, the captain, his wife, two children, 15 passengers and some of the crew, perished before assistance could be rendered. Eighteen of the bodies were picked up on Saturday, and carried to the town of Ipswich.

340. Execution - Lawrence Tearney, was executed at Easton, Pa., on the 10th inst., for the alleged murder of his wife. He was calm and collected, and made this address immediately before the cord was cut: "Gentlemen, as I expect shortly to appear before my God, I can declare before God and man that I am innocent of the crime for which I am to suffer. I forgive all who harmed me-may God have mercy on my soul."

341. At St. Louis, on the 15th, Harrington, of Rockwell & Company's Circus, shot Hiram Franklin, the well known equestrian of the same troupe, and wounded him slightly. Harrington afterwards committed suicide, by shooting himself twice in the head.

342. Hon. Timothy Childs, late member of Congress from the Rochester district in this State, died on the 25th of October last, on his way to St. Croix, for which island he had started in the hope of improving his health.

343. The Hon. James Kent, formerly Chief Justice of the Supreme Court and Chancellor of this State, died in New York on Monday of last week, aged 84 years. He was long distinguished as one of the first jurists and purest men of the age.

January 1, 1848 (Saturday)

344. Death of U. S. Senator Fairfield - Senator Fairfield died suddenly, at Washington, on Friday night of last week. Affected with dropsy in the knee, he submitted to a surgical operation which proved fatal. His

funeral was attended by both houses of Congress, preceded by their officers; members of the cabinet; officers of government and of the army and navy, foreign ministers and citizens. The funeral procession formed at the boarding house of the late Senator, and his body was conveyed thence to the rail-road cars, and delivered in charge of Mr. Clark, Representative from Maine, who, accompanied by the relatives of the deceased, proceeds with his charge to Saco, Maine, where it will be interred in the family burial-ground.

345. Death of Rev. Walter M. Lowrie - The Rev. Walter M. Lowrie, an American missionary at Ningpo, a gentleman of eminent attainments, has been cruelly murdered in the Chinese seas by pirates. The reverend gentleman took his passage in a Chinese boat from Shanghai to Ningpo and during the voyage was attacked by a piratical vessel. At first, it would appear that the pirates only meditated robbery, but fearing that Mr. Lowrie might bring them to justice, they resolved to throw him overboard. Two of the ruffians seized him for that purpose, but not being able to accomplish it, a third joined in the murderous attack, and they succeeded in throwing him into the sea. As the waves ran high, though he was seen two of three times, he soon sank to rise no more. Mr. Sullivan, the English Consul at Ningpo, proffered every aid his official station enabled him to render and steps were taken to recover the remains, if possible. Liverpool Times, Dec 4th. Mr. L. was a son of Hon. Walter Lowrie, for many years Secretary of the U. S. Senate, and a graduate of the Princeton Seminary. He married a daughter of the late Samuel Boyd, Esq., of the N. Y. Board, and went to India in the service of the Presbyterian Board of Missions. Newark *Advertiser*.

346. Capt. James Smith, of the 3d infantry, died at Encerro on the morning of the 4th instant, of congestion of the brain. Later from Mexico.

347. A sailor, named John Arland, who deserted from the U. S. schooner Flirt, and joined a company of dragoons, was arrested and taken back to the Flirt. He attempted to escape again, and was shot by the sentinel posted at the guard-house. Later from Mexico.

348. Distressing Accident - On Monday last, two young men, named Elisha S. Purdy, of Marlborough, Ulster Co., and William Le Roy, of this town, were in a boat near Hampton, shooting ducks. Purdy was in the bow of the boat, Le Roy in the stern, with some cedar boughs between them. The latter saw a flock of ducks, and levelling his gun called out to Purdy to lie still; but just as he fired, Purdy raised up, and received the whole charge in his head-killing him instantly. He was about 20 years of age. Pough. *Telegraph.*

349. A man named Albert Vedder was found near Schenectady, with his neck broken. He was lying on the east side of the Railroad culvert, from which he had probably fallen. He was a resident of Greenville.

350. Heartrending Calamity - It is with feelings of unusual sadness, that we present the following authentic account of a most melancholy casualty, resulting from the recent flood in the Ohio, and of which distressing rumors have been prevailing in town of several days. The extract which we give below is from John O. Wattles, well known in this vicinity, and one of the survivors of the accident. The building spoken of was a large, substantial brick house with thick walls and three stories in height, with a stone foundation. It had been built with care, and was but just finished. It stood near the bank of the river in Clermont county, three miles below Augusta in Kentucky and about forty miles from this place. At the time of its fall, the water, which was still rising, (on last Wednesday) stood ten feet deep on every side. The village spoken of is a small hamlet called Rural. So secure was the building considered that several of the neighbors had left their own houses to seek refuge in it. Dear Brother:- Our fine house has fallen in the flood, and seventeen of those who were within it are either drowned or buried beneath it ruins. The names of the lost are: Moses J. Cornell and wife and both children; our friend James A. Mackinson from Scotland; Mrs. Ransom, Elizabeth Ransom, Henry Ransom, Alonzo Guernsey, Mrs. Hannah Lee, Ann Madison, Charlotte Hemphill, John Hemphill, Charles R. Keenan, J. R. Shoeder, Chas. Lee and Henry Woodson. <long story> Cincinnati *Herald.*

351. Shipwreck and Loss of Life - The schooner Effort, Bartlett master, from Philadelphia, for Newburyport, was run into at midnight, on the 24th ult., off the Isle Shoals, by the schooner Bellona, Allen,

Master, of Boston, for Sedgwick. Henry Stickman and J. H. Brown got on board the Bellona. The Effort sunk shortly after. Captain Bartlett, Gideon Hickman, the mate and John Macar were lost. The Effort was a good and staunch vessel of 87 tons. She was insured in the Neptune Office, Boston, for $2,500.

352. Explosion and Loss of Life - An explosion of a boiler took place at the kitchen of the eating house of Mr. Fox in Baltimore on Monday morning, immediately killing Mrs. Mary Ann Roden and seriously scalding Miss Nancy Quynn and Miss Sarah Healey, also a beggar woman and two colored persons. Miss Healy <sic> is not expected to survive.

353. Judge Hubbard, of the Supreme Judicial Court of Massachusetts, died at his residence in Boston, on Friday morning last.

354. Shocking Accident - On Tuesday evening a young girl, an adopted daughter of Mr. Harvey Borthwick, one of the clerks in the Post-office, while asleep on the chair near the stove, accidentally had her clothes take fire. The pain of burning awoke her, and with her clothes in flames she ran up two pair of stairs and down again before assistance came to her and the flames could be extinguished. As might be expected, the whole of her person from the knees upwards was most dreadfully burned, and no hopes are entertained of her recovery. She is about ten years of age, and is an intelligent, active girl, and much attached to her adopted parents. Albany *Argus*.

355. Married on the 20th ult., by the Rev. R. Dederick, Mr. John A. Meyer, of Claverack, to Miss Lucinda Crawford of Saugerties.

356. Married on the 23d ult., by the Rev. S. M. Knapp, at the Parsonage, in Woodstock, Mr. John S. Everett to Miss Sarah Catharine Brower.

357. Married on the same day, by the same, Mr. William Brower to Miss Amanda Alvira Martin.

358. Married on the same day, by the same, Mr. Seth N. Hubbard to Miss Harriet Brower, all of Hurley.

359. Died in this town, on Wednesday last, Mr. Henry Plough, aged about 33 years.

January 8, 1848 (Saturday)

360. Tragedy in Mississippi - Fearful State of Society - The N. O. *Picayune* relates at length the particulars of a tragedy recently enacted in Hancock county, Miss., which we briefly sum up as follows: An old man, named Brown, had passed a quantity of counterfeit coin on the citizens of the county, and on election day he was seized and taken to jail. In consequence of threats of lynching, he made disclosures, implicating two men, brothers, named Washington and James Bilboa, farmers, and men of substance in the county. A party started for Bilboas' residence headed by Brown and a man named Wages. Near the house they found the implements for casting the counterfeit coin. Surrounding the house, they succeeded in arresting both Washington and James, whom they bore back prisoners to jail. Through the influence of the Bilboas they procured bail, and then preferred a charge against Wages of stealing or branding other people's cattle, the raising of cattle being a common pursuit in Hancock county. Wages having a bad character previous to this, both be and Brown proposed to move out of the county. The Picayune tells the rest of the story as follows: "When it was known that Brown and Wages had gone, the Bilboas' started out after them. The general belief is that they desired to provoke a personal conflict with Wages, they being athletic and powerful men, and each armed with a rifle and knife. Wages, however, was prepared for them. The Bilboas' were upon horseback, accompanied by a friend. They rode struggling along, one after the other, James Bilboa being in advance. In an abrupt turn of the road, he came suddenly upon Wages in the road on foot, and armed with a double barrelled gun. Neither James nor Washington was prepared to shoot at once-the one having a feather in the vent of his rifle, and the other a bit of rag in the pan of his. Not so with Wages. Them moment James Bilboa came in view he deliberately drew up and discharged one barrel of his gun. The charge, consisting of buckshot, took effect in the breast of Bilboa, and he fell from his horse, and expired almost instantly. His brother Washington, immediately hove in sight, when Wages discharged at him the second barrel, but with less accurate aim. The charge took effect in the hip and groin. The thigh bone was shattered close to the socket, and the body so terribly

wounded that, at last account, it was thought impossible for him to survive twelve hours. Wages immediately made his escape. A cart coming along the road a mile behind the Bilboas, reached the scene of the tragedy, and upon it the wounded man was carried back to his family. His recovery is regarded as quite hopeless. Wages was supposed to be lurking in the woods of the vicinity, but he is so desperate a ruffian, and had rid the country of two men whom none regretted. (all believing fully in their guilt in counterfeiting) the inhabitants have taken no measures to arrest him.

361. Married in this village, on Wednesday last, by the Rev. C. Van Santvoord, Rufus Lasher, Esq., Merchant of Coxsackie, Greene County, to Miss Cornelia Hommel, of this village. We are at all times pleased to "Telegraph the news," and chronicle the doings at the altar of Hymen, and particularly so when, as in the present case, we are personally acquainted with the parties. The ways of Providence (and Cupid) are mysterious, and we feel no inclination to find fault with the decrees of either, but much of the pleasure of announcing the above matrimonial connection is allayed by the reflection that the fair bride has left us. We hope they will be as happy in the selection and retention of friends in the place they have chosen for their residence, as they were here, and that they may live to enjoy many years of social happiness.

January 15, 1848 (Saturday)

362. Shocking Accident A Man Burnt to Death! - In the town of Woodstock, about ten miles from this village, Mr. John Lasher was engaged with another man by the name of John Shultis in burning charcoal. The coal pit being situated some distance from the house, Mr. Lasher had erected a temporary shanty, into which he had carried a quantity of straw, a few blankets and a buffalo robe to serve as a bed for them to sleep on. Monday evening being uncommonly cold, they built a large fire in front of the cabin, and retired. About eleven o'clock Mr. Lasher says he was aroused by Shultis, with the exclamation, "We are all on fire." upon which he (Lasher) sprang through the blaze in front with no serious injury, and to his astonishment discovered that Shultis had not followed. He immediately after heard him at the back part of the shanty, calling for help to burst off the boards. Mr. Lasher sprang to his assistance and

succeeded in tearing off two or three boards, when a strong current of air drawing through the shanty and bursting out at the aperture he had made, enveloped him in flames and drove him from the assistance of poor Shultis, who perished without even knowing that his friend had very nearly lost his own life in an effort to save his. Mr. Lasher was so badly burned that it was with great difficulty he succeeded in getting to the nearest house to relate the distressing affair. The body of Mr. Shultis was found near the back part of the cabin, where he was last heard calling for help, in an awful and heart-rending situation; both of his feet, one of his hands and an arm were entirely consumed-the burning mass has lost all appearances of a human body. He has left a wife and three small children to mourn his untimely end. We understand that hopes are entertained of the recovery of Mr. Lasher, although his case is considered quite doubtful.

363. Lost Child - On the 14th of December, a little boy, named Alonzo Adebbut, 3½ years old, the son of William H. Mc Elroy, of Napanock, Ulster Co., NY, is supposed to have been taken away by a stranger who passed through the village on that day. <long story, ed.>

364. Married on Tuesday, the 4th inst., at Rondout, by the Rev. W. S. Michels, Mr. Henry Wells of Kingston, to Miss Catharine A. More, of Rondout.

365. Married on the 30th ult., by the Rev. John C. F. Hoes, Mr. Richard Norton of Lloyd, to Miss Sarah Ann Van Gaasbeck of Kingston.

366. Died in New York, on the 10th inst., John Kearney, eldest child of Michael and Jane Kearney.

367. Died in Kingston, on the 31st ult., of consumption, Mary Delia, eldest daughter of James J. Styles, aged 20 years, 10 months and 23 days.

368. Died in Kingston, on the 4th instant, Mrs. Mary Elizabeth Wetherell, wife of Wm. H. Wetherell, aged 23 years, 10 months and 8 days.

369. Sheriff's sale. By virtue of a writ of Fi. Fa. to me directed and delivered against Robert Laverty and Edward Laverty. I will sell at Public Auction at the Exchange Hotel, kept by A. H. Richmond, in the village of Ulster, in the town of Saugerties, Ulster County, on the fourth day of March next, at 10 o'clock in the forenoon, all the right, title and interest of the said Robert and Edward Laverty, of which they were seized or possessed of on the 15th day of October, 1847, or at any time afterwards in whose hands sover the same may be, of and unto the following lands and tenements, viz:- All and singular that certain part pf a lot formerly owned by Edward Laverty, deceased, situate in the said village of Ulster, in the town and county aforesaid, and is the easterly part of a said lot, which is undivided between the defendants, and is bounded on the north and east by lands of Henry Barclay, on the west by lands of the said Edward Laverty and Robert Laverty, and on the south by lands of the said Robert Laverty. Dated Jan 15th 1847. <sic> Charles Brodhead, Sh'ff. J. D. Brink, Deputy

January 22, 1848 (Saturday)

370. Lost Child Found - We learn from the Kingston *Journal* that Mr. Mc Elroy, of Napanoch, traced his lost child to Syracuse, and found him there, at a boarding house, where he had been placed by the person that took him away.

371. Tragedy in Pleasant Valley - We learn from the Poughkeepsie *American* that on Sunday, 9th inst., the wife of Mr. Benjamin Russell, who lives on the road between the village of Pleasant Valley and Salt Point, in the town of Pleasant Valley, was shot by a man named Wesley Pine who resided in that town. The ball was extracted from Mrs. Russell on Sunday, when the physicians thought she could not recover. But as she was still alive at the last accounts, and was easier, hopes are entertained that she will recover. <long story, ed.>

372. Mysterious Disappearance - On Monday, the 3rd of January last, Mr. James Underhill, of this village, who kept a small market, went over to Newburgh, for the purpose of making purchases of meat and other articles, designing to return on the same day, since which time no tidings whatever have been had of him by his afflicted family and friends. He had with him about $50 in money, and was seen on or near the ferry landing at about 4 o'clock, P. M., in that village, since

which no trace can be had of him. He is of small statue, light hair, blue eyes, sharp features, and about 30 years of age. Any information of him will be gratefully received by his disconsolate family. Papers copying the above may subserve the cause of humanity by affording some clue to his whereabout, though very serious apprehensions are entertained for his safety. He was perfectly temperate and fond of his family. Fishkill *Standard*.

373. Married at Saugerties, on the 15th inst., by Rev. C. Van Santvoord, Mr. Robert Phillips of Fort Plain, Montgomery Co., to Miss Sarah Elizabeth, daughter of Jonas Myer, Esq., of the former place. That the happy couple did not forget the Printers is evident from the bountiful donation of the richest kind of cake sent us. May they be as happy through life as they were generous towards us.

374. Removal of a Pastor. Mr. Editor, We the Roman Catholics of Saugerties, beg, through the medium of your valuable publication, to express our regret and bemoan the loss of our late worthy Pastor, the Rev. M. Maxwell. A loss too heavy to be borne with in silence; a loss which we are forced to complain aloud of to the whole world. We may indeed say, in the language of the Prophet Jeremiah, "All ye that pass by on the highways come and see if your grief be like mine." He had served for seven years in the parishes of Saugerties and Rondout. We now present to him our grateful thanks for all his past kindness and services to us, and may the Almighty and most merciful God still infuse into his heart the same spirit of piety he manifested to us-may grant him length of days and increase of happiness. Signed - Catholics of Saugerties, Jan 14th 1848. <long letter, ed.>

January 29, 1848 (Saturday)

375. Later From Mexico - The bark Afton arrived at New Orleans on the 6th inst., bringing Midshipman Wilson of the Navy as bearer of despatches. Maj. Gen. Lambert Commaur, Commander-in-chief of the British forces on the island of Jamaica, died at Kingston on the 4th inst., aged 66 years. His remains were buried the same day with military honors. The death of Paymaster Lieutenant Minor of the Artillery is confirmed.

376. Marriage in High Life - At Washington, on the 17th inst., Sarah,

daughter of Senator Benton, was married to a young gentleman of St. Louis. There were seven bridesmaids. The happy pair, (with their friends) took passage in the evening cars for Baltimore, whence they will go West. Col. Benton is one of the kindest and best fathers that ever lived; and when he took farewell of his daughter at the depot, he pressed her in his arms, kissed her, and said: "A father's blessing go with you my child." *Herald*.

377. A little girl, seven years of age, daughter of Mr. Daniel Hook, of Philadelphia, died of hydrophobia, a few days ago. She was bitten by a dog in August last, supposed at the time to be rabid, and the usual remedies were resorted to.

378. Hon. John Hornbeck, Whig member of Congress from the Lehigh Districts, Penn., died at his residence in Allentown, on Sunday of last week.

379. Mrs. Eliza Russell, who was shot by John Wesley Pine, at Pleasant Valley on Sunday the 9th inst., died about 2 o'clock pm, on Thursday of last week.

380. Letter in response to the Catholics of Saugerties, from M. Maxwell, dated Jan 26th 1848, Rondout.

381. Married on the 22d inst., by the Rev. R. Dederick, Mr. Nelson Burhans to Miss Sarah E. Dederick, all of Saugerties.

382. Married at Rondout, Dec 23d, by the Rev. Mr. Philips, George Dressel to Miss Mary Ann Dickerson, both of Rondout.

383. Married by the same, on the 5th inst., at Eddyville, Mr. Thomas Merchant to Miss Jane E. Winfield, both of Eddyville.

384. Married on the 20th inst., by the Rev. Davis Stocking, John B. Roe, Esq., to Emeline Hasbrouck, all of Kingston.

385. Died at Flatbush, in the town of Kingston, on the 23d inst., John P. L. Osterhoudt, in the 70th year of his age.

386. Died in the village of Kingston, on the 24th inst., of Consumption, Cornelius P. Cole, son of Alexander Cole, aged 22 years.

February 5, 1848 (Saturday)

387. A young man by the name of Keithley, in Georgetown, Tennessee, in shooting at a mark on the 1st ult., shot his sister, Mary Keithley, through the head, who died immediately. She was sitting in the house, and the gun in her brother's hands went off by accident, while he was walking to the spot from which he intended to shoot. The ball passed through the window, struck her in one temple and went out the other.

388. The Hon. Geo. P. Barker, late Attorney General of the State, died at Buffalo, on Thursday last, in the 40th year of his age.

389. William Buffum was instantly killed by the bursting of a grindstone at the Scythe Factory at Nasonville, in Rhode Island, on Wednesday week.

390. Another Atrocious Murder at Pleasant Valley - Our citizens have not had sufficient time to recover from the shock given by the bold and daring murder of Mrs. Russell, before the intelligence comes of another murder equally atrocious and revolting, in the same town. The facts in relation to this second murder, as far as we can gather them, are as follows: On Tuesday, the 18th inst., a colored man by the name of John Yates, residing in the western part of the town of Pleasant Valley, and his wife, took their child, nineteen months old, and placed it upon a hot stove and there burned it to death! They then beat its head until they broke its skull, and buried it. As an excuse for the act it is alleged by the fiend who did the deed, that the child had the rickets. <long story, ed.> Poughkeepsie *Eagle*.

391. Col. Taney, brother of Chief Justice Roger Taney, died at Washington Co., Missouri, on the 20th ult.

392. Married on the 22d inst., by the Rev. R. Dederick, Mr. Nelson Burhans to Miss Sarah E. Dederick, all of Saugerties.

393. Married at Rondout, Dec 23d, by the Rev. Mr. Philips, George Dressel to Miss Mary Ann Dickerson, both of Rondout.

394. Married by the same, on the 5th inst., at Eddyville, Mr. Thomas Merchant to Miss Jane E. Winfield, both of Eddyville.

395. Married on the 20th inst., by the Rev. Davis Stocking, John E. Roe, Esq., to Emeline Hasbrouck, all of Kingston.

396. Sheriff's Sale. By the virtue of a writ of Execution, issued by the County Clerk of Ulster County, and to me directed and delivered, against Robert Carter, I will sell at Public Auction, at the Phoenix Hotel, kept by Henry Turck, in the village of Ulster, in the town of Saugerties, Ulster County, on the 25th day of April next, at 2 o'clock in the afternoon, all the right, title and interest of the said Robert Carter, of which he was seized or possessed of on the tenth day of April, 1847, or at any time afterwards in whose hands soever the same may be, of an unto the following lands and tenements:- All and singular that certain house and lot of land situate in the said village of Ulster in the town and county aforesaid, and is bounded Northerly by the street, running from Partition street to Barclay's Dock, Easterly by Ripley street, Southerly by lands of Jeremiah Russell and Westerly by the lands of Joseph O'Farrell. Dated Feb 4, 1838, <sic> Charles Brodhead, Sh'ff. J. D. Brink, Deputy.

February 12, 1848 (Saturday)

397. Murder and Suicide. The Rochester *Daily Advertiser* contains the particulars of the murder of an infant child by its mother. Mrs. Barnard, wife of Mr. Alanson Barnard, committed this double crime, on Sunday, in a paroxysm of insanity, caused, it is supposed, by child-birth fever.

398. Arrival of the Remains of Col. Ransom, and Others - Yesterday forenoon, the ship Windsor Castle, from New Orleans - in command of Capt. Patterson - arrived in our harbor, bringing the dead bodies of Col. Truman B. Ransom of Connecticut, commander of the ninth regiment; Capt. Martin Scott, of the regular army, and Capt. Thompson of Maine, also, we believe, of the regular army. The Columbian Artillery discharged one hundred minute guns, upon the

arrival of the ship. The remains of Col. Ransom will be taken at once to Connecticut, we understand, and the bodies of the others be delivered immediately to their friends for interment, it being desired that no parade will be made. General Pierce who is now in town, will supervise the removal of Col. Ransom's body to Connecticut, where he resided for about 20 years. Boston *Times*.

399. A man named John Gorden, of North Blenheim, Schoharie Co., died a few days since, in consequence of merely knocking the skin off one his knuckles, by striking it against a knife in the hands of a fellow workman. He continued at work as usual throughout the day, but on the following morning his hand began to swell, and became very painful. He died in the evening in great agony. He was engaged in currying Spanish hides.

400. Married at Hurley, on the 3d inst., by the Rev. J. C. Cruikshank, William J. Scott, of Napanock, to Maria V., daughter of Benjamin G. Newkirk.

401. Married on the 27th ult., in the town of Olive, by Martin Schutt, Esq., Horatio G. Davis to Catharine North, both of Olive.

402. Married on the 5th inst., by the Rev. A. Fort, John H. Kipp, of Rhinebeck, to Miss Celia H. Post, of Esopus.

403. Died at Malden, on Wednesday last, Henry Reuben, infant son of Henry Dick.

404. Died in the village of Kingston, on the 9th inst., of Pulmonary Consumption, Jane, wife of Mr. Joseph Chipp, aged about 35 years.

405. Died in Esopus, on the evening of the 5th instant, Peter Sluyter, aged about 66 years.

406. Died in Windham, Greene Co., on the 7th inst., Blandina, daughter of the late John C. De Witt.

407. Died in Hurley, on the 8th inst., Mynard, youngest son of John M. and Sally Myer, aged 11 years.

February 19, 1848 (Saturday)

408. Thomas Cole, the distinguished landscape painter, died on Saturday at his residence near Catskill. He leaves a wife and numerous family to mourn his loss, a sorrow in which a large circle of devoted friends will share. To Art his death is a great calamity.

409. Fatal Accident - On Tuesday morning last, Andrew S. Wood, a son of Aurt Wood, of Rosendale, whilst hauling stone for building a slope wall on the canal, near Coxing bridge, was killed by a stone thrown from a blast from Button's point. The stone weighed 22 pounds and was thrown about 400 yards, striking his right arm and breaking his back, producing almost instant death. Mr. Wood was about 35 years of age, an estimable citizen and leaves a wife and six children to deplore his loss. Rondout *Courier*.

410. Frozen to Death - Jacob Countryman, a farm laborer and single man of middle age, was frozen to death on Saturday night, the 5th instant, in the town of Hurley. He was at a bee in the afternoon, and started for his employer's in the evening, quite intoxicated. Cries were heard in the night, but this being common in the neighborhood, no attention was paid to them. On Sunday morning his stiffened corpse was found in a small brook by the roadside. Rondout *Courier*.

411. Mrs. Lanman, widow of the late J. G. Lanman, and mother of Park Benjamin, was burned to death at Norwich, Conn., on Friday last, by her clothes taking fire. She was 70 years old.

412. Married in the city of New York, on the 15th instant, Prosper P. Shaw, of Kingston, to Miss Caroline Johnson, of the former place.

413. Married at Rondout, on the 9th instant, by the Rev. H. Lounsbery, Elias Coleman to Miss Eliza Parker, of that place.

414. Married on the 27th ult., by the Rev. W. Emerick, Mr. Wesley Lewis of Saugerties, to Amelia G. Mount, eldest daughter of Joseph Mount, Esq., of Hurley.

415. Married on the 20th ult., by the Rev. J. C. Van Dervoort, Niel Tounsley Mc Ewen, M. D., to Sarah Elizabeth Dubois, of Rosendale.

416. Married at Port Byron, on the 9th inst., by the Rev. Wm. Theodore Van Doren, Mr. Thomas W. Smith, of that place, to Miss Maria S., daughter of Herman M. Romeyn, of Kingston.

417. Died in this village, on Wednesday last, Charles Ody, son of James Swart, aged 10 months and 26 days.

418. Died in Prattsville, on Thursday evening, 10th inst., Mr. Hart C. Sage, aged 36 years.

419. Died in the village of Kingston, on the 15th inst., James Chipp, aged 67 years.

February 26, 1848 (Saturday)

420. Suicide - On Sunday night last, the wife of James R. Goodwin of West Hurley, jumped into a well in which there was about six feet of water, and was drowned. Mrs. G. had for some time manifested an aberration of mind. Rondout *Courier*.

421. A Murder in our County - On Tuesday night last, a man named John Whispell, formerly of Shandaken, was killed at Mill Hook, a locality in the town of Rochester. Whispell was in a grocery kept by a widow. One John Bush came to the door and was refused admittance. He used threats and Whispell came out of the house. Bush had an axe in his hands, which Whispell wrenched from his grasp, and then struck Bush with the helve. Bush recovered the weapon and struck Whispell twice with the blade; the first blow cleaving the shoulder of the unfortunate man, and the second splitting his head. Whispell fell and instantly expired. Bush is in the County jail. Another statement says that after wrenching the axe from Whispell's hands, Bush threw it down, and ran a short distance to obtain his own axe which was a much sharper weapon, and with this committed the fatal act. Bush is a married man and has children, Whispell was unmarried. Rondout *Courier*.

422. Arrival of the Germantown - The U. S. ship Germantown, arrived at Philadelphia on Thursday night week, from the Gulf of Mexico via Havana, having on board the remains of a number of our gallant countrymen who perished in Mexico. Among them those of Col.

Watson and Major Twiggs, of the marine corps; Lieutenant Chancy, Dr. Kearney, Smith, Bates and Midshipman Carmichael, of the navy; Lieutenants Morris and Rogers, of the army.

423. Mr. Samuel Francis Davis, aged 23 years, eldest son of the Hon. J. W. Davis of Indiana, who was about to depart on his mission to China, was instantly killed at Carlisle, Indiana, by being accidentally struck on the head by a piece of timber, at the launching of a flat boat.

424. Terrible Railroad Accident - On Friday evening, about 10 o'clock, a shocking accident occurred to a train on the Reading Railroad, a short distance this side of Schuylkill Haven, which resulted in the death of four men. Mr. John Leoser of this city, the conductor, was one of the latter. He was removed to Pottsville, where he died about 4 o'clock on Saturday afternoon. Mr. John Mackinson, of Kingsessing, Philadelphia, who was on his way to Reading, was one of those whose sufferings were terminated by death before he could be released. His remains were taken to Philadelphia on Sunday last. He was an unmarried man, in the 26th year of his age. John Schecance, another victim of this disastrous event, was taken to Philadelphia on Sunday; he resided in Kensington. He leaves a wife and family. E. B. Johnson, the fourth victim, was brought to this city, and taken to the residence of his widowed mother. Henry Christian was also seriously injured, and another whose name we could not ascertain. <details of the accident not copied, ed.> Reading, Pa. *Legion*.

425. Killed by an Ox - Mr. Samuel W. Whittlesey, of Saybrook, was killed on Thursday, at Lyme Ferry, by an enraged ox. He had purchased a pair of young cattle, and was getting them on board of the ferry boat at that place, to cross the river, when the animals turned, ran against him and injured Mr. W. so badly, that he survived but about three quarters of an hour. He was one of the oldest inhabitants of Saybrook, being between eighty and ninety years of age, and was greatly beloved and respected by all who knew him. New Haven *Register*.

426. Died in the town of Catskill, on Tuesday last, Mr. Abram Post, in the 79th year of his age.

March 4, 1848 (Saturday)

427. Death of John Q. Adams - After our paper of last week was issued, we received the melancholy, though expected intelligence of the death of a venerable Ex-President Adams. He expired on Wednesday evening in the Speaker's room in the Capitol; to which place he was conveyed upon his first attack on Monday, the particulars of which we gave last week. John Quincy Adams was born in Braintree, Mass., on Saturday, July 11th 1767. <long biography, ed.>

428. He's to be Pitied - Tobias Lower of Ramapo, by a notice in the Rockland Messenger, forbids all persons trusting his wife Sarah on his account - she having left him for the sixth time. If Sarah has thus acted "without cause" she ought not to be allowed to reduce Tobias Lower by running him in debt.

429. Justin Hoyt, a prisoner in the penitentiary in St. Johns, New Brunswick, was shot in attempting to escape - he died the next morning.

430. Destructive Fire - Loss of Life - The alarm of fire was given last night about half past 12 o'clock. It proceeded from a frame building No. 84 Quay street, occupied as a grocery and boarding house, by Patrick O'Toole. The flames had made considerable progress before they were discovered. They spread with such rapidity that a woman in the building where the fire originated was very badly burned before she escaped, and a lad employed by O'Toole was burned with the building. When discovered this morning, his legs and head were severed from his body. The woman cannot, it is feared, recover. Richard Gillespie, a young man who has been for four years employed in the Journal office was also killed. He was engaged in assisting Engine Co. 2, when the walls of Mr. Shepard's store on Quay st. fell in and crushed the wooden building where he stood, burying him beneath the ruins. He was found this morning about 8 o'clock, much mutilated but not very badly burned. His features were somewhat blackened bloody and swollen. From his position - a large beam lying across his hips, and the rubbish lying compactly around him - his death must have been almost instantaneous. Richard was about 21 years of age - quiet, industrious and attentive to his business. He had no near relatives in the city - both of his parents being dead. He has a sister living in Bridgport,

who has been sent for, and also one in New York. His death will be sincerely mourned by all who knew him; for his general deportment was such as to secure the respect and esteem of his associates. The buildings on Broadway and on Quay street very nearly joined in the rear, and the flames spread with such fury that it was impossible to stop their progress until some eighteen or twenty buildings were destroyed. The total loss is estimated between $60,000 and &70,000. Albany Eve. *Journal*.

431. A Fatal Duel - Burlington, NJ, Feb 23, 1848 - Dear sirs, We have just received authentic accounts of the duel between Joshua Wallace Collet and Alexander Wilkin, Captains in the 10th regiment of Infantry, on the morning of the 21st of January last, at Camargo; which resulted in the death of Capt. Collet by the first shot, the ball passing entirely through the body. He lived three hours and died on the spot where he had fallen, a temporary tent having been placed over his body. He was perfectly calm and resigned to his fate, and gave directions about his affairs. Capt. Collet was a native of this place, and under thirty years of age. He entered the army in the winter of 1847. He had been a lawyer before joining the army, having read law with Daniel Haines, the present Governor of this State; and also with Garret D. Wall. Yours. &c. J. H. S. Phila. *Enquirer*. The survivor of this fatal duel, a son of the Hon. Mr. Wilkin, of our Senate, is a young man of excellent character and amiable deportment. His principles, education and habits were such as ought to have exempted him from a conflict so repugnant to his feelings. But in the army, there is no escape from this false code of honor. Capt. Wilkin received two challenges, both of which he accepted. The first terminated fatally, and the second was prevented by the arrest of the parties.

432. A funeral instead of a bridal ceremony - Miss Nancy Bailey, of Merrimac, formerly employed in the factories here, visited Nashua last week, for the purchase of her wedding dress, bonnet, and bridal cake, &c. preparatory for her marriage on Wednesday next. She had completed her purchases, and was on her way the depot, Saturday evening, when the cars left. She therefore returned to the house of a friend, Mr. Mitchell, on Canal street, near the Jackson Corporation. About half past three on Sunday afternoon, as she sat at the window, she threw up both hands, exclaiming, "Why there is Mr. Drew!" (the

name of the young man to whom she was to be married and who is a resident of Concord, Vt.) Mrs. M. went to another window, but no one was in sight. At this moment a crash of glass called her attention to Miss Bailey, who had fallen forward against the window. Help was instantly called, and she was placed upon the bed, but with two grasps <sic> she lay a corpse. And when the bridegroom comes it will be to lay her in the grave, whom he had hoped so soon to call wife. Miss Bailey was about 26 years of age and latterly had not been in perfect health. Nashua *Oasis*.

433. A Terrible Tragedy occurred at Mobile on the evening of the 18th instant, which is related in the *Herald* of that city as follows: "A man named Francis Conklin, an engineer, in a fit of anger, caught his wife by the head, while she was seated in a chair sewing, and forced her back, made a deadly wound in her throat with a razor. Ir is scarcely possible, we hear, for her to survive. He then made an attempt to kill three other women who were present - one of whom was his wife's mother. They fortunately made their escape from him. He afterwards very deliberately cut his own throat, and falling on his face expired immediately. It is supposed that he was actuated by jealousy.

434. Rum and Death - Two brothers, by the name of Thomas and Charles Laffaday, of west Sparta, while intoxicated on the 12th inst., had a dispute in relation to some trivial matter, and there brains being maddened with rum, resorted to hoes to settle the dispute. Thomas inflicted two severe wounds on the head of Charles, one with the back and one with the edge of his hoe, from the effects of which he died on Friday last. Our informant stated that no arrest had been made. Livingston Co. *Union*.

435. George Travis, son of Stephen Travis, was recently drowned at Peekskill; he left home with his father to draw up their fish nets and fell thro the ice. His father who was a short distance behind, fell through several times, and was unable to render him any assistance. The body was found.

436. Sheriff's Sale, By virtue of two writs of Execution, lands of John V. H. Van Dyke.

March 11, 1848 (Saturday)

437. Benjamin Heermance, of the village of Kingston, was found dead in the street one morning last week - the result of exposure from intemperance. His age was about 50 years.

438. Mrs. Louisa Catherine Adams is the relict of the late John Quincey Adams and has been granted the franking privilege for life.

439. Dreadful Accident - As Mrs. Abram Ostown, of Fitchburg, Mass., and her daughter, Mrs. Tolman, wife of Jacob Tolman, of West Sterling, were crossing, on Thursday last, the track of the Vermont and Massachusetts Railroad in a sleigh, the horse becoming frightened at the locomotive, backed upon the crossing, and threw the ladies under the wheels of the engine. Both were instantly killed. Mrs. Tolman leaves a number of children.

440. We regret to learn that a man named James Sanders lost his life in this city the day before yesterday. He had some little difficulty with some one, and had placed his knife open in his pocket. Falling from his wagon, into which he was climbing, the knife penetrated his thigh, and although medical aid was soon called in, he died from flow of blood, in the course of some 8 or 10 hours. Augusta, Ga. *Republic*.

441. Homicide - In Indianapolis, on the 19th of February, Eleazar Luce, an apprentice to H. and E. Gaston, coachmakers, was killed by Hiram Gaston, one of the firm. The apprentice was trying to fit a plate of iron to a carriage, and not making a good job of it. Mr. Gaston told him to leave it - that he would do it himself. The young man refused and Gaston laid hold of the iron to take it from him. A scuffle ensued, in the heat of which Gaston caught up a hammer and struck Luse <sic> on the neck. The blow was fatal in a few minutes. Mr. Gaston was held to bail on the charge of manslaughter. His distress at the fatal result was painful to behold. So much for flying into a passion.

442. Mrs. Hannah Kitty Chase, widow of the late distinguished Judge Samuel Chase, of Maryland, died on Thursday, at her residence in Baltimore. She was 97, and previous to her death, one of the three surviving widows of the signers of the memorable Declaration of July 4th, 1776.

443. Married at Albany, on the 24th ult., by John Miles, Chaplain of the Bethel, Mr. John Elmendorf, Jr., to Miss Caroline M. Burgess, both of Albany. <actually printed as Eemendorf, ed.>

444. Married on the 24th ult., at Washington, Dutchess Co., Alfred Higbie, of Rondout, to Miss Ann Andrews, of the former place.

445. Married at Marbletown, on the 2d inst., by the Rev. J. C. Cruickshank, Mr. Ten Eyck Veeder, formerly of Schenectady, to Miss Jemima F., daughter of Clinton Woolsey.

446. Married on 2d inst., by the Rev. Abm. Fort, Mr. Van Gasbeck Du Mont to Miss Henrietta Mosier, all of Esopus.

447. Married in Lexington, on the 26th Feb., by the Rev. H. Petit, Mr. J. A. Simpson, of the firm of Newkerk & Simpson, to Miss Julia Longyear, all of Shandaken.

448. Died in this town, on the 6th inst., Peter D. Myer, in the 56th year of his age.

449. Died in Olive, on the 20th inst., Joseph Fish, a soldier of the Revolution, aged 87 yrs and 6 months.

450. Died in Olive, on the 2d inst., Emma, daughter of Lewis and Jane Hollister, aged 4 months and 5 days.

451. Died in New Paltz, on the 18th ult., Edward Upton, aged 75 years, a member of the Society of Friends.

452. Died in Brooklyn, on the 2nd of March, aged 37 yrs, Lydia, wife of Moses E. De Witt.

March 18, 1848 (Saturday)

453. Death of the Hon. Ambrose Spencer - This distinguished jurist died at his residence in the village of Lyons, Wayne Co., on Monday last at the advanced age of eighty-three years. His remains were brought to Albany for interment.

454. The Lost Child - We rejoice to learn that the child of Mr. Mc Elroy, of Napanoch in this county, kidnapped in Dec. last, has been recovered in Canada and is now on its way to its parents. The thief, for whose apprehension Gov. Young offered a reward of $500, has been arrested and in charge of an officer is on his way to this county.

455. Powder Mill Explosion - The Powder Mill of Laflin and Smith, in this town, blew up on Monday afternoon, between one and two o'clock, instantly killing one man and injuring another so severely that his recovery is considered doubtful. The name of the person killed was John Frederick, that of the other is Herman Henry, both Germans and single men. The quantity of powder in the mill at the time of the explosion was about six hundred pounds. The loss of property is about four hundred dollars. We understand that the accident was the result of the ignorance or carelessness, or perhaps both, of the unfortunate men before mentioned. Instead of removing the powder before cleaning the mill, as they had been instructed to do, they put it in barrels and left it uncovered in the mill, and with a copper spud undertook to remove the powder adhering to the iron wheels. This operation produced fire and consequently the explosion. The mill was not running at the time.

456. Lieut. Henderson and four Georgia volunteers were killed in a separate fight between Briscoe's command and the guerillas at Mittigoras. From Mexico.

457. From Santa Fe - Mr. Mc Knight has arrived at St. Louis, from Santa Fe, which place he left on 5th February. Don Francisco Riben committed suicide while coming down the river. Insanity is supposed to have been the cause. He had a large amount of money in his keeping.

458. There was an alarm of fire in Baltimore on Sunday last, which was the occasion of a dreadful riot among several fire companies. The Independent Watchman joined against the New Market and United, and from one to two thousand men were engaged in the fight, which occurred at the corner of cathedral and Madison streets. A man named Anthony Hughes was shot dead.

459. Mrs. O'Tool, a lady of exemplary character, who was badly burned at the late fire in Albany, died on Friday last. Her death was caused in heroically rescuing her children from the flames; having contracted from the devouring element bodily and mental afflictions, whose certain and rapid advances admitted no hope of recovery; the stamp of death was so firmly fixed upon her that all human efforts proved unavailing.

460. Mr. Marshall Johnson, a highly respectable citizen of Rappahannock Co., Va. was accidentally shot about three weeks since. Being dressed in a thick coat, he was mistaken for a bear, and fired upon by Mr. Madison Fletcher.

461. Married on the 16th inst., at the parsonage in Westcamp, by the Rev. R. Dederick, Mr. Jacob Richlie Lewis to Miss Anna Magee, all of Saugerties.

462. Died in this village, on Monday last, Lucy, daughter of Major Egleston, aged four years.

463. Supreme Court in Equity - Jeremiah Russell, Plaintiff, vs. Frances Schoonmaker & others, Defendants. J. L. Bookstaver, Solicitor for Pl'ff. Under and by virtue of decree made by this court in the above cause, bearing date the 7th of March, 1848, I will sell at Public Auction, to the highest bidder, at Krow's Exchange Hotel, kept by A. H. Richmond, in the village of Ulster, Town of Saugerties, on the 29th day of April, next, at 10 o'clock in the forenoon, the following lands and real estate described in said decree as follows:- All that certain lot, piece or parcel of land situate, lying and being in the village of Ulster, in the town of Saugerties, and bounded as follows - beginning at a stake at the north east corner and running in a southerly direction along the east line of land sold to Hannibal Condgon, ninety seven feet to a lane or road, thence along said road in an easterly direction fifty two feet, to lands formerly the property of Robert L. Livingston, thence running along said lands of said Livingston in a northerly direction ninety seven feet to the lands of William Post, thence along the line of the said Williams Post's Land in a westerly direction fifty two feet to the place of beginning. Dated the 11th day of March, 1848 Charles Brodhead, Sheriff, Joel T. Persons, Deputy.

464. Sheriff's Sale - Under and by virtue of a writ of Fieri Facias, issued by the County Clerk of Ulster County and to me directed and delivered, against the goods, chattels, lands and tenements of Andrew Hommel, in my baliwick, I will sell at Public Auction at Krow's Exchange Hotel, in the village of Ulster, town of Saugerties, in the said county, on the 23d day of May next, at 10 o'clock A. M. of that day, all the right, title and interest which the said Andrew Hommel had on the thirtieth day of April, 1841, or at any time afterwards, of and unto the following described lands and premises:- All that certain piece or parcel of Land situate lying and being in the said town of Saugerties, in the said county, bounded on the east by lands of Peter Snyder, on the south by lands of James Kiersted, on the west by lands of Jonas Myer and on the north by lands of Jeremiah Snyder and others. Dated March 15th 1848. Charles Brodhead, Sheriff Joel T. Persons, Deputy.

March 25, 1848 (Saturday)

465. Abdication of Louis Phillippe of Paris in favor of the Count de Paris.

466. A young man named Isaac Ogden, from Kinderhook, NY, was drowned in Billington Sea, Plymouth, on Saturday, the 4th inst. He slid upon an air hole but slightly frozen over, and sunk before assistance could arrive.

467. The Hon. J. M. Holley, member of Congress from the 27th District of New York, died at Jacksonville, Florida, on the 9th inst.

468. Died at the residence of Henry Barclay, Esq., on the 17th inst., Catherine Barclay, infant daughter of Catherine B. and Cornelius Battelle; and on the 19th inst., aged 26 years, Catherine Barclay, wife of Cornelius Battelle, and daughter of John W. Kearney, Esq.

April 1, 1848 (Saturday)

469. A Mr. Rademacher, vender of Homeoepathic medicines, in Fourth street, above Arch, Philadelphia, was found, March 23d, in his bed-room, stabbed and cut in twenty places, nearly dead, and his wife hacked to death. A German shoemaker named Sangfeld has been arrested as the murderer.

470. A terrible fire occurred at Watertown, Jefferson Co., on Tuesday of last week. It raged four hours, destroying property valued at $55,000. Two men, named Lemuel Wright and Levi Palmer, were burned to death.

471. Sudden and Mournful Death - On Monday afternoon, Charles Peterson, a native of Norway, a shipwright of this place, but who has been doing a winter's work in New York, was brought on board the Norwich by a comrade, suffering under a severe attack of rheumatism, of five days standing. Mr. P. was almost helpless, and turned into a berth as soon as he came on board. During the evening he appeared to suffer much, but it was regarded as only the result of his painful though not usually dangerous complaint. On Tuesday morning a fellow passenger discovered Mr. Peterson seated on a settee, his head thrown back into his berth and his head resting on the edge. On taking Peterson's hand he found it to be cold, and further investigation only showed that he had probably been dead some time. An inquest was held on the body, by B. Hendricks, Justice, acting Coroner, and the Jury, resting upon the opinion of Dr. Wales, came to the conclusion that he died of Pulmonary Apoplexy, couching their verdict in the usual formula, 'died by visitation of God.' Rondout *Cour.*

April 8, 1848 (Saturday)

472. A vinegar manufacturer, named Richards, and a negro man, were suffocated in one of the vats of an establishment in Philadelphia, by inhaling a noxious gas, on Monday last.

473. Wm. Betchell, of Philadelphia, killed his wife on Saturday night, by cutting her throat with a razor. He subsequently made an ineffectual attempt to take his own life with the same instrument.

474. Death of John Jacob Astor - This celebrated millionaire, the wealthiest man in the United States, died in New York, on Wednesday of last week,, at the advanced age of eight-five years. His property is variously estimated at from twenty to forth millions of dollars. Son, Wm. B. Astor is the great residuary legatee. <long story>

475. Fatal Accident - On Monday last, Mr. Stephen Carman, of the town of Olive, was accidentally killed in this village. He was coming

from Rondout with a two horse wagon, and just upon entering the village he engaged in racing with another team, and by some accident he was thrown our of his wagon, the wheels of which passed over his body. He was immediately taken up, and every effort was made to relieve him, but he lived only about fifteen minutes after the accident. Ulster *Republican.*

476. An explosion, furnishing another warning to all who use spirit gas, lately occurred in the village of Le Roy. Three children were burned to death in the family of a Mr. Bacon.

477. Horrible Discovery - It will be recollected that a Doctor Goss, of Seneca Co., very mysteriously disappeared some months since, and that the most thorough searches, in that county and elsewhere, proved entirely fruitless. There was great excitement at the time in reference to the matter, but the long time that has elapsed in a measure dissipated this feeling, and all hope of discovering him had been given up. We learn that a man was discovered in Geneva a few days since, having in his possession a note which it was known belonged to Dr. Goss at the time of his disappearance. He was immediately arrested, and is said to have made a full confession of the manner in which Dr. Goss was murdered. The substance of it is, that himself and Featherly, who is in jail at Canandaigua, for the brutal fight at Geneva, some time since, murdered Dr. Goss, supposing him to be the collector of Waterloo; that they afterwards burnt his body in a lime kiln, and that some of the bones which were not entirely consumed, were buried; and these have been found in the spot indicated by the man who made the confession. thus the perpetrators of a most foul murder are suddenly and unexpectedly exposed, at a moment when they supposed themselves most secure. The mysterious case in this city may possibly be thus suddenly, by some unlooked for circumstance, unravelled, and the murderers brought to justice. Rochester *Democrat.*

478. Dreadful Accident - A horrid railroad accident happened yesterday about four o'clock, at the corner of Ninth and Wallace streets, Spring Garden. As three cars loaded with lime were being pushed by hand in to the lime yard of Cox & Company, an intelligent lad of about 16 years of age, son of Mr. James Aarrigues, an officer in the Bank of the Northern Liberties, jumped upon the foremost car to

ride, and fell off. Tow of the cars passed over his legs, and crushed them in the most horrid manner. The limbs were both amputated near the groin, but it was thought that the sufferer could not survive. Phila. *Bulletin*.

479. Melancholy Occurrence - On Sunday evening last, Mrs. Fanny Chase, wife of Mr. Gilbert Chase, engineer of the ferry boat plying between this village and Newburgh, and living at the extremity of the Long Wharf, committed suicide by throwing herself into the river, while in a state of mental aberration, to which we understand she has for some time past been subject. She was neat, prudent, and economical in her household, a kind and affectionate parent, leaving four young children, and a kind indulgent husband to mourn their irreparable loss. Fishkill *Standard*.

480. Ben Johnson, Esq., an eminent lawyer, died at his residence in Ithaca, on Sunday the 19th inst. On the Monday preceding he was stricken with paralysis, and was almost entirely unconscious and insensible until his death. He was distinguished as a lawyer, and was highly respected and beloved wherever he was known. Last spring he was one of the whig candidates for Justice of the Supreme Court. Chenengo *Union*.

481. Died in Flatbush, on Wednesday night last, Mrs. Ann Turck, widow of Jacob Turck, aged 83 years.

482. Died in Glasco, on Sunday night last, Mrs. Dubois, wife of Mr. Richard Dubois, aged about 38 years.

483. Died in Hamden, Delaware Co., on the 17th ult., Mr. Teunis Swart, a Revolutionary soldier, in the 85th year of his age, formerly from Kingston, Ulster Co.

484. Died in Rondout, on the 28th ult., Mr. Castle Betts, about 60.

485. Died in this village, on the 29th ult., Henry De Witt, son of Hezekiah H. Wynkoop, aged 2 years and 8 months.

April 15, 1848 (Saturday)

486. Col. Nicholas Van Rensselaer, a soldier of the Revolution, expired at Greenbush on the 30th ult., aged 94 years. He was with Montgomery at the storming of Quebec, at Ticonderoga, Fort Miller, Fort Ann, and at Bemis' Heights, and was deputed to convey to Albany the intelligence of the surrender of Burgoyne.

487. A Family Burned to Death - A family residing in Mount Prospect, NJ, by the name of Stur, were burned to death, on the night of the 10th inst., Mr. S. alone escaped by jumping from the second story. He requesting his wife to follow him, but for some reason she was unable to do so, and remained with her three children, the eldest being 17 years of age.

488. From England - Queen Victoria was safely delivered of a Princess on March 18. A few minutes after the birth the Royal infant was shown to the Ministers and Great Officers of the State and Household in the ante-room, when the usual formalities and ceremonies on the birth of a Prince and Princess were gone through. From Europe.

489. Rum and Murder - A man killed by his father - On the 10th of March an altercation took place in Hebron, in this county, between Titus Foster and his son, Titus Foster, Jr., which terminated in the death of the latter on the 25th. The circumstances are in brief these. It appears that the old man had long been addicted to the vice of intemperance, and while under the influence of liquor was in the habit of abusing his wife, who, as she alleges, was afraid to remain with him, and requested her son, the deceased, to come and take her to his home. He went to the residence of his father for the purpose of complying with the request of his mother. Some dispute arose as to the manner in which the old lady should leave, and a scuffle ensued between the father and son, in which the former was thrown down, but not injured. The son then left the house, and was followed by the old man, with a knife in his hand, with which he made frequent attempts to stab his son, and when about seven rods from the house accomplished his purpose. The knife entered the left breast and penetrated the lobe of the lung, from which wound he died on the 25th. Russell W. Platt, Esq., coroner, held an inquest on the body of the deceased on the 27th ult., and the jury returned a verdict of wilful murder; and the prisoner

was conveyed to the county jail, on his way to which he met the funeral procession, on their return from the burial of his son. The prisoner in seventy-four years old, and is a wealthy farmer. Sandy Hill *Herald*.

490. Miss Caroline E. Field, a young lady of Westfield, about 25 years old, committed suicide at the house of the father of her intended husband in Southampton, by taking arsenic, on Monday, the 3d inst. Miss Field had always maintained an excellent character, but for a short time past had, either from mental derangement or some other cause, manifested a distrust of her lover's fidelity. In a frenzy of excitement she repaired to his house on Monday, and in the evening committed the desperate act which speedily terminated her life. Springfield *Gazette*, Saturday.

491. Horrible Affair at Grafton, NH, Arrest of a Baptist Clergyman for the Murder of his Wife - Correspondence of the Boston *Mail*, Canaan, N. H., April 8, 1848. The quiet community of this charming inland town has been thrown into a feverish state of excitement by the arrival here yesterday of the Rev. Enos Dudley, a Baptist clergyman of some note in these parts, in charge of an officer, to undergo an examination for the murder of his wife, in the neighboring town of Grafton, about five weeks since. The facts connected with this horrible charge, as I have been able to collect them are these: - About the middle of March, Rev. Mr. Dudley took his wife out to ride, and after an absence of a couple of hours he returned to his house, bringing back the lady a corpse. In explanation of the tragedy he told his family that the sleigh upset, and his wife was violently thrown against a stump, causing her death upon the spot. He at once proceeded to make a coffin with his own hands, and, with as little assistance as possible, placed the body in it. The funeral was conducted with haste, and marked by a total absence of all decent preparation and display. The version he gave of the manner of his wife's death, appears at first to have been credited; but the manner of her burial, and something peculiar in the conduct of the husband, after the funeral aroused suspicions of foul play. At the suggestion of several of the deceased's friends, the body was disintered in the early part of this week, and a council of physicians held a post mortem examination upon it. The result was a unanimous opinion among the medical men, that the deceased was strangled! The

announcement caused an immense excitement in Grafton, where the accused was well known, and aside from some peculiar leaning towards to doctrine of Millerism, much esteemed and respected. He was immediately arrested and conveyed to this place, where the affair is now being investigated. What adds still more to the mystery of this tragical affair and the apparent guilt of the accused, is the fact which has come out during the examination, and of his corresponding, for some time previous to the death of Mrs. Dudley, with a young woman, a school teacher in this town; and it is rumored that his intimacy with her has partaken of a far more criminal character than mere letter writing. In justice to the young lady, however, against whose character nothing has heretofore been said, I will state that the latter charges are based upon mere rumor. She was called as a witness against the prisoner, and is now being questioned before the Justice. A son and daughter of the accused have also been upon the stand, and their testimony, as well as that of the school mistress, is represented as bearing fearfully upon the guilt of the accused. The examination I hardly think will be concluded before Monday or Tuesday. The most intense excitement prevails in this village, which is filled with people from Grafton and the adjoining towns. I am told that Rev. Mr. Dudley has for some time back preached the Millerite doctrine in Grafton, and that he recently predicted his wife would soon die - the Lord having, as he said, divulged that event to him in advance.

492. Died at Flatbush, on Thursday last, Mary, widow of Peter I. Osterhoudt, aged about 70 years.

493. Died also at Flatbush, on the same day, Abby Catherine, daughter of James Burhans, aged about 3 years.

494. Died in the village of Kingston, on the 9th instant, after a lingering illness, Jacob B. Elting, aged 52 years.

April 22, 1848 (Saturday)

495. A Murderer Executed - Thomas Nash, who had been convicted of murdering a female near Waynesburg, North Carolina, some two of three years ago, paid the penalty denounced by the law against his awful crime, on Friday last. He was hung at Troy. The rope by which he was first suspended, broke, and he fell to the ground. He requested

the handkerchief to be removed from his eyes, which was done, and he sat up and conversed with the bystanders until another rope was procured, and he was then hung. Verily, "the way of the transgressor is hard."

496. Suicide - James Ervin, Esq., a grandson of Mr. Clay, shot himself at the St. Charles, New Orleans, on the morning of the 3d instant. He was perfectly dead when discovered. No cause is assigned for the act. Mr. Ervin had arrived a few weeks previous, from Kentucky, for the purpose of challenging S. S. Prentiss for imputations against his father, contained in a speech of Mr. Prentiss. The challenge had been accepted, but the affair was arranged by mutual friends.

497. Murder of Midshipman Mc Lanahan - Late accounts from California bring the sad intelligence that Midshipman T. Mc Lanahan, of Baltimore, has been murdered by a band of Guerillas.

498. Shocking - Last Saturday evening, says the Worcester *Journal*, the Rev. Erastus Hopkins, of Northampton, lost a fine little boy, about three years old, under the most distressing circumstance. Previous to putting him to bed, the girl having charge of the nursery put a quantity of boiling water in the bathing tub, preparatory to the accustomed ablution of the children, and left the room without qualifying its temperature. The little naked boy, supposing the water ready for his use, jumped into the tub, and was immersed in the scalding water! He died on Sunday morning.

499. Death of Chapman - Joseph Chapman, the well-known crowing politician in Indiana, we see it stated, died recently in Mexico.

500. From New Granada - Horrible Steamboat Explosion - The fine bark Bogota, Captain Thomas, arrived from Santa Marta, after a quick run of twenty days. A most unfortunate occurrence happened at Baranca, on the Magdalene river, on the 25th of February. It was the explosion of the boiler of the steamboat Magdalena, with the loss of 12 lives, among them Captain Henry Beekman, the commander, who is well known in New York, and has commanded vessels between there and Carthagenia for many years; his loss in this untimely manner will be a severe blow to his family, who are in this country.

501. Accidents - Two of the locomotives on the Reading Railroad Company ran together at the crossing of the Mine Hill and Reading railroad, on Wednesday week, and killed Martin Kowan, Jr., a young man about 18 years of age. The locomotives were both destroyed.

502. At the launch of the schooner Emblem, at Wilson, Niagara Co., on the 8th instant, Mr. Knowlton Harrington was run over by the schooner in its course to the water, and instantly crushed to death. He was 48 years of age. Rochester *Democrat*.

503. As Mr. Bigelow, of East Abington, was in the act of stepping from the platform into a car, while the train was waiting at the Neponsent depot, his foot slipped upon the track, and, the cars starting at the time, the wheels passed over one of his feet, cutting it completely off. The boot, and foot were cut as though by the blow of an axe. Boston *Courier*.

504. A son of the Hon. David Wilmot, some 13 years of age, died on Monday, at Athens, Pa., of the poisonous effects of eating wild parsnip. The melancholy intelligence was sent to Mr. W. at Washington, the next morning by telegraph.

505. The Lost Child Found - The mystery hanging over the fate of the child of Mr. Mc Elroy, of Napanoch, whose disappearance and supposed abduction awakened so much sympathy, is at last dispelled. On Tuesday its body was found in the Rondout Creek, a little below Port Benjamin, three miles from Napanoch. The body, owing to the coldness and purity of the stream, was very little decomposed. It was buried on Wednesday. Thus an end has been put to the wearing anxiety of the parents, and which has brought the mother almost to the grave. Rondout *Courier*.

506. More Anti-Rent Outrages! A Deputy Sheriff Shot! - A short time since, John H. Smith, one of the Deputies of the Sheriff of this County, had placed in his hands an execution against Geo. I. Finkle, issued on a judgement obtained against him, a few weeks since, by Geo. Weeks, in the Justices Court in this city, for damages done said Weeks by having his harness and farming implements destroyed last season. On Saturday last, the day of sale, Smith proceeded to Finkle's place, but

finding no bidders for the property, he adjourned it to a future day. From thence he proceeded to summon one of the jurors drawn for the next Court (Philip B. Miller) who, by the way, is said to be under an indictment for participation in previous outrages. From thence Mr. Smith proceeded homewards, and when nearly a mile from Finkle's he was fired upon from the side of the road, by two persons with rifles, standing about fifty feet distant. Both balls took effect, one passing into the fleshy part of the thigh, taking a course slanting downwards, and the other striking him directly in the breast passing through his lungs, and now remains in his body somewhere near the shoulders. The first ball has been extracted, and the wound in the breast probed to the depth of six or eight inches. Immediately on being shot he fell forward in his wagon, where he remained a short time when Mr. Ambrose S. Russell, who was riding in the same direction, came along, and conveyed him home. This took place, as we understand, late in the afternoon. We understand that the chances of his recovery are very slight indeed. To show that the villains intended to make sure work, and commit downright murder, they did not even take the trouble to disguise their faces. The officer knew them perfectly, that their names have been handed over to the proper authorities. Only a week or ten days since, we understand a house was pulled down in the town of Tagkanic by a gang of desperadoes, and it is looked upon as quite a remarkable coincidence, that the day on which that outrage was committed, as well as that of last Saturday, that Mr. George I. Finkle should be in this city making himself as conspicuous as possible. We can hardly suffer ourself to comment upon this cold-blooded attempt (most probably a successful one) to commit murder on the public highway in open day. The heart recoils from such atrocities. We trust the authorities have acted promptly and vigorously in this matter, and that the perpetrators, as well as those who planned the deed, will be brought to speedy justice. Columbia *Republican*.

507. Gov. Young has offered a reward of $1000 or the arrest of John Mosher, under indictment by the Grand Jury of Columbia Co., for the crimes of burglary, arson and conspiracy, also $1000 each for the arrest of John Miller and Conrad C. Wheeler, who attempted the murder of Deputy Sheriff Smith, in the same county.

508. The *Austian* (Texas) newspaper announces the death at that city, on the 18th ult. of the Hon. Richard Bache. Mr. Bache was a native of Philadelphia, and was the father-in-law of Robert J. Walker, Secretary of the Treasury, brother-in-law of George M. Dallas, Vice President of the United States; also connected by marriage to John Sergeant of Philadelphia, and was the grandson of Benjamin Franklin. He was the oldest member of the Senate, and was one of the framers of the constitution of Texas. He was formerly Postmaster of Philadelphia.

509. Verdict and Sentence - Wesley Pine charged with the murder of Mrs. Russell at Pleasant Valley, was tried at the Dutchess Circuit last week, Judge Barculo presiding, and found guilty. Pine was sentenced to be hung on the 26th of May next.

510. Murder - The proprietor of a porter house at the corner of Fourth-avenue and Thirty first St., in NYC, by the name of Patrick Cogan, was killed last Monday evening, by being struck a blow on the head with a heavy club by a pedlar known as Dutch Jake. According to the information obtained it appears that as Jake and some of his friends were passing the house of Cogan with a large dog, the latter was attacked by another dog belonging to a person then at Cogan's house, and on Jake's attempting to separate the two dogs he was knocked down by one of Cogan's acquaintances or customers, whereupon Jake and his companions, after providing themselves with clubs at an engine-house, repaired to the house of Cogan, and on being refused admission to find the person who had knocked one of Jake's friends, Jake struck Cogan a severe blow on the head which caused Cogan's death in about two hours after the occurrence.

511. Married in Kingston, on the 12th inst., by the Rev. D. Stocking, Levi Snyder to Rosina Keator, all of that village.

512. Died in this village, on the 19th inst., Charles Emery, son of Rev. R. H. Bloomer, aged 2 years and 8 months.

513. Died in Kingston, on the 15th ult., Martha, aged 5 years, daughter of Frederick Lockwood.

514. Died on the 11th inst., Frederick Lockwood, aged 31 years.

515. Died on Monday last, at Jersey City, Henry W. Brundige, formerly of this village and a compositor in this office, in the 22d year of his age. The deceased was a young man of exemplary deportment and was much esteemed by those acquainted with him.

April 29, 1848 (Saturday)

516. Later - A violent emeute took place at Madrid on the evening of the 26th. The people and the soldiers fought in the streets from 7 in the evening until 3 or 4 in the morning, and a considerable number were slain on both sides. Mr. Whitwell, an English engineer, was killed.

517. The *Union* publishes an official note from Com. Perry, announcing the death of Commander James B. Wilson, of the U. S. steamer Spitfire. He died on board the Spitfire in the Alvarado River, on the 13th ult.

518. Hon. Asa Clapp, father of the Member of Congress from the Portland District, father-in-law to Judge Woodbury, for many years an enterprising merchant, and at the time of his death the richest man in Maine, died at his residence in Portland on Monday, after a long illness, at the age of 86.

519. Death by Accident - On Monday, the 10th inst., Mr. Gilbert R. Holmes, of Columbus, in this County, was struck on his head by a limb of a tree as he was chopping in the woods. He was carried home, and expired in about two hours. On examination, his skull was found to be fractured in several places. He was 40 years of age, and has left a wife and six children to mourn his loss. Chenango *Union*.

520. On the same day, a Mr. Havens, of New Berlin, fell into a stream of water not more than two or three feet deep, and was drowned. He was in the water only three or four minutes, but when taken out life was extinct, and all efforts to resuscitate him proved unavailing. He was an intemperate man, and was probably intoxicated when the accident occurred. Chenango *Union*.

521. Married in this village on the 20th instant, by the Rev. Mr. Bloomer, Mr. William H. Barber, to Miss Louisa Van Etten.

522. Married on Thursday evening last, by the Rev. C. Van Santvoord, James Hansen, Esq, "Body and Wagon Maker," to Miss Catherine Van Debogert, all of this village.

523. Married in Kingston, on the 19th inst., by John C. F. Hoes, Henry W. Goodrich, of Port Dixon, Cayuga Co., to Lavina Wheeler, of the former place.

524. Married on the 22d inst., by the Rev. M. L. Schenck, Mr. Charles Dederick, of Catskill, to Mrs. Helen Snyder, widow of the late Charles Snyder, of Kingston.

525. Died at Utica, on the 17th instant, suddenly of an apoplectic fit, John T. Romeyn, Esq., of Kingston, Attorney and Counsellor at Law, in the 48th year of his age.

526. Died in Kingston, on the 20th inst., of consumption, Anna Maria, daughter of Cornelius Beekman, aged 15 years.

527. Died in Kingston, on the 11th inst., Joseph, son of Henry Van Buren, aged 2 months and 2 days.

528. Died in Rondout, on the 15th inst., of consumption, Lucy, wife of John Colvill, formerly of Hudson, aged 68 years and 11 months.

May 6, 1848 (Saturday)

529. Mrs. Julia Webster Appleton, wife of Samuel Appleton, Esq., and only daughter of Daniel Webster, died in Boston on Friday evening. The bark Chief, from Vera Cruz, arrived on Monday afternoon with the mortal remains of his son Edward from Mexico.

530. The Michigan *Telegraph* announces the death of Dr. Lewis F. Starkey, in Kalamazoo on the 19th. He has represented Kalamazoo Co. in the State Senate, and edited with eminent ability The Gazette, of that village, a leading democratic organ. Dr. Starkey was formerly connected professionally at Detroit with the celebrated Dr. Theller, who acted such a conspicuous part in the Canadian border difficulties.

531. Another Sad Case of Hydrophobia - A daughter of Mr. Jacob Brown, of South Easton, Pa., aged about six years, died in that place, on Sunday last, under all the symptoms of a decided case of hydrophobia. She was bitten by a dog supposed to have been rabid, about five weeks since. The wound was under the left eye, and healed up in a short time. The first symptoms of the disease were discovered the day preceding her death.

532. Railroad Accident and Loss of Life - Mr. William Smith, of Herkimer, and Mr. Welch, of Utica, were instantly killed. One of them had his face and head crushed, and the other both legs of taken off. Mr. Bennet of Albany, 33 Hamilton St. had both legs broken at the thigh, and there is little hope of his recovery. Mr. Crittenden, the father of the conductor, was in the baggage car, and had his head cut in two of three places and was scalded by the water from the engine which was thrown back. He was taken to Utica. We further learn that Mr. Howland, of Jefferson Co., who was standing on the platform at the time of the collision, died on Monday morning. Mr. Bennett is still living, but in a very precarious state. The accident took place on the Utica and Schenectady Railroad, at a point a mile and a half west of Herkimer on Sunday last. <long story, ed.> Albany *Atlas*.

533. Massacre of an Entire Family - The Paulding (Mi.) *Clarion*, of the 15th ult., contains an account of the murder of Dr. James Longgon, Jr. of Garlandsville, Jasper Co., his wife, Mrs. Ann Longgon, and their infant child, some nine months old. An older daughter, about 3 years old, was also dreadfully mutilated, so that her life was despaired of. A negro girl named Seciley, who was hired in the family, first gave information of the murders, stating that five individuals had come to the house, and killed her master, mistress, and their infant. The girl was afterwards arrested, and the proof is almost positive that she was the perpetrator of the awful deed. The Clarion says: The people residing in the neighborhood immediately collected and proceeded to the house, and found Mrs. Longgon lying dead some yards from the house, with a gash on her head which had penetrated the skull and entered the brain. A broad axe was then discovered lying near the house, covered with blood. The party then proceeded into the house, where they found Doctor Longgon lying on a bed with his head entirely dissevered from his body, with two long gashes on his head,

both of which had entered the brain. His eldest daughter was found lying close to his breast strangling in his blood, with large wounds inflicted on her right arm, and other marks of violence on her person. She is still living, and some hopes are entertained of her ultimate recovery. The infant child was lying on the same bed, with its face so awfully mutilated that it died in a few hours afterwards. It is generally believed that the negro girl, Secilley, committed the murders - unparalleled as they are in blood and atrocity. Her tracks were discovered in the blood of her murdered victims, and when arrested, the purse of Dr. L. was found in her possession.

534. Arrest for Murder - E. Greenwood, late of the brig Col. A. A. Taylor, just arrived from St. Jago de Cuba, was arrested in New York on Monday last, on a charge of having murdered William Coibyle, a seaman on board the Taylor. It is alleged that Greenwood killed Coibyle by a blow with the ship's axe; also that he tried to induce the murdered man and the steward to aid him in killing the captain and running away with the vessel.

535. Fatal Railway Accident - A locomotive exploded on Monday last on the Reading railway. Nagle, the engineer, and Gaffney, one of the fireman, killed. Four others badly wounded.

536. Rum on a Railroad Track - James G. Gregg, a man of 45 years old, laid himself down yesterday afternoon, with his skin full of rum and a bottle of the same in his pocket, between the rails on the Medford Branch Railroad. He was discovered in his perilous position, and though the engine was reversed and the brakes set, it was too late to save him. The down train passed over the sleepy inebriate, and crushed him to death. Boston *Mail*.

537. Warren W. Scudder - At the Court of Oyer and Terminer held at this place last week, this individual was arraigned on an indictment for the murder of O. N. Steel, in August, 1845, and by his attorney N. K. Wheeler, Esq., plead not guilty and intimated his readiness for trial. The District Attorney, A. J. Ten Broeck, Esq., moved that his case should be put over to the next Circuit, when the presiding officer, Hon. E. Morehouse recommended the District Attorney to take the case under advisement. Delaware Co. *Voice of People*.

538. Summary Process - Since the killing of Davis, at Charlestown, in Indiana, by Vanover, noticed by us some two or three weeks ago, the Citizens of Charlestown, held a meeting on the public square, and passed a resolution, requesting the keeper of the grocery in which the murder was committed to close his house and refrain from farther sale of spirituous liquors. He refused to comply with the request of the meeting, when the citizens entered the house, removed the liquor to the street, and emptied it upon the ground, agreeing to pay all damages that might be sustained by the vendor, and passed a series of resolutions declaring that no liquor should be sold within the limits of the town. New Alb. *Bulletin*.

539. Morals of Boston - Mysterious - Five dead bodies have been picked up in this city within a week, viz:- Mrs. Bullard, Joshua Marshal, a man unknown, (near the Lowell Railroad) James Murray, near the State Prison, and Adams, the volunteer, in Charlestown. In no case has the certain cause of death been ascertained. In addition, the bodies of several infants have either been buried surreptitiously or found floating in the water. These are melancholy comments on the morals of our city, and the fact that they produce so little effect on the public mind, is the most alarming circumstance. Boston *Traveller*.

540. Death of Gen. Ashley - Hon. Chester Ashley, one of the Senators from Arkansas and Chairman of the Judiciary Committee, is dead, after a severe illness of two days. His complaint was inflamation <sic> of the bowels; and its sudden and unexpected termination with the life of the sufferer has cast a shadow of gloom even over the heart of the stranger who saw the deceased by as if it were yesterday, in the full energy of health, and strength, debating for hours at a time, the Supreme Court bill, before the Senate. Gen. Ashley was some fifty years old, and three days ago he bore in his appearance the promise of thirty years to come. Cor. N. Y. *Herald*.

541. A petition to the Governor is in circulation, at Poughkeepsie, asking that the sentence of Wesley Pine may be commuted to imprisonment for life, on condition that he shall never be pardoned. The American says it is numerously signed.

542. Unnatural Murder - We learn from the Petersburg Republican

that on Saturday, the 15th inst., Grief Nunnally was shot by his own daughter, a Mrs. Moody, in the public road in Dinwiddie, and survived only three days. Mrs. M. is now in custody. No reason is assigned for the revolting deed. Nunnally is described as having been an industrious and thrifty man, but at time intemperate, when he was cruel in his family and turbulent in his neighborhood.

543. Married on Thursday last, in this village, by the Rev. Mr. Bloomer, Mr. John Philips to Miss Catherine Gillespy, both of Marbletown.

544. Married in Kingston, by the Rev. C. Shook, on Thursday, the 27th ult., Mr. Jacob Rider, to Miss Sarah Schepmoes, both of that village.

545. Died on the 29th ult., Mary Ann, wife of W. Ten Broeck Sharp, and daughter of Henry and Maria Myer, aged 27 years, 10 months and 23 days. Death seldom invades a family when his stroke is more keenly felt than in the present instance. Independent of the peculiar circumstances attending her departure, aged parents were leaning on her as their only earthly support in declining years. Cut down in the summer of life, a large circle of relatives are suddenly bereft on one to whom they were dearly attached, and called to deck themselves in the garments of mourning. Possessed of a native sweetness of temper, and an amiability of disposition, she was known only to be loved. Although she had never made a public profession of religion, still her expiring hours were of a character calculated to administer consolation to the afflicted and bereaved. Resigned to the will of Providence, and even anxious to depart, she called her weeping friends around her dying bed, and calmly gave to each her parting salutation, while she bade them not to mourn, for Jesus, her Saviour called her. "Just as I am-thou wilt receive, Wilt welcome, pardon, cleanse, relieve, Because thy promise I believe - O Lamb of God, I come!" *Com.*

546. Died in this town, on the 25th April, Mrs. Elizabeth Albert, aged 81 years. Brooklyn papers please copy.

547. Died in Flatbush, on Thursday, Mrs. Gertrude Osterhoudt, widow of John P. Osterhoudt, aged 75 years. Her friends and relatives are invited to attend the funeral Saturday afternoon, at 2 o'clock, pm.

548. Died in Plattekill, town of Saugerties, on the 27th ult., Jane A. Dumond, wife of Cornelius I. Longendyck, in the 44th year of her age.

549. Died at the Steep Rocks, town of Kingston, on the 26th ult., William Masten, aged about 45 years.

550. Died at Rondout, on the 15th ult., Lucy, wife of John Colvill, formerly of Hudson, aged 68 years and 11 months.

551. Died at Lexington, Greene Co., on the 25th ult., of dropsy in the chest, Ogden E. Edwards, late of the City of New York, aged about 45 years.

552. Died on Sunday, 23d ult., near Libertyville, Mr. Wilhelmus Dubois, in the 64th year of his age.

553. Died at Wexford, Canada West, Mr. Daniel Aiken, aged 120 years. He had, during his life, contracted 7 marriages, and had 570 grand children and great-grand children - 300 boys and 270 girls.

May 13, 1848 (Saturday)

554. Explosion and Loss of Life - On Saturday night last an explosion of powder took place in one of the shanties on the line of the Hudson River Railway, at St. Anthony's Nose, in the Highlands. The powder it is supposed was fired by an incendiary and at the time of the explosion there were, says the Peekskill Republican, 265 kegs of powder in the shanty. It is not stated whether the whole of the powder exploded, but the building and several others near it were blown to atoms. The Republican says: "We have seen a gentleman who visited the spot the next day. One man, Mr. Stephen Garrison, was killed, some seven or eight others were seriously injured - some, it was believed, beyond the hope of recovery, and numbers more were in some respects hurt. Two horses, one ox and a cow were killed; the blackness and darkness was upon every surrounding object."

555. Fearful Casualty - Death of Mathew Reed, Esq. - A very sad accident resulting in the death of an esteemed citizen, Mathew Reed, Esq., late President of the Tradesmen's Bank, and formerly one of the Aldermen of the Sixth Ward. Mr. Reed, about 10 o'clock yesterday

morning while in the act of assisting in the removal of a bale of leather, from one of the upper lofts of the store of Armstrong & Co., No. 8 Ferry street, in consequence of the slings slipping, while in the act of lowering the same, fell through the hatchway to the floor below, breaking his neck and fracturing several ribs. He died almost instantly, and Coroner Walters being called to hold an inquest, a verdict was returned in accordance with the above facts. Mr. Reed was elected in 1824, Alderman of the Sixth Ward, and continued to represent that Ward until 1826. He was a man universally esteemed, and at the age of 62, has died much lamented. N. Y. *Globe*.

556. Died on Tuesday, 9th inst., in this village, Joseph O'Farrel, aged 38 years.

557. Died on Sunday last, Mrs. Alida Hardenburgh, wife of John D. Hardenburgh, aged 49 years.

May 20, 1848 (Saturday)

558. Horrible and Fatal Accident - A frightful accident, terminating fatally in a few hours, occurred at the Iron Rolling Mill, in this village, on Wednesday last. Francis Rhind, aged about sixteen years, son of Widow Rhind of this village, while engaged at one of the small rollers, was struck by a piece of hoop iron in a red-hot state, entering his clothes near the hip and extending upward, his clothes keeping it close to his body, until it penetrated between the ribs. A physician was immediately called, and every assistance possible, rendered the unfortunate lad, but he expired in about six hours. It was one of those accidents that the greatest care cannot guard against, resulting neither from his own carelessness not that of any one connected with the Mill.

559. Tragical Occurrence - The report of a very tragical affair which occurred near Natchez a few days ago, from the N. Orleans *Delta* - "Mr. Charles Jones, who has practised law in La. and who was originally from Red River, was shot at his residence on Black River, near Natchez, by a highly respectable lady, said to be a relative of his. The lady drove in a carriage to Jones' dwelling and called him out. As he approached the carriage she fired a revolver at him, the ball taking effect in his abdomen. As he bent down, under the effect of the wound, she fired two barrels, the balls of which took effect upon his

head. At the last accounts Jones was lying in a hopeless condition but not quite dead."

560. Suicide - A Mr. Relyea, of Clintonville, New Paltz, committed suicide, a few days since, by hanging himself in the woods. He was about 30 years of age, and leaves a wife and three children.

561. A Blood Chilling Tale - In Edgecomb, Me., on the 10th inst., a man named Pinkham, a ship carpenter, cut off the heads of his wife and four children! - two boys and two girls, the oldest twelve years of age, - and then cut his own throat with a razor! The deed was not discovered until Friday morning. Pinkham's own mother was the first who discovered it. A paper was found, signed by both father and mother, stating they had become tired of life, and mutually agreed on the destruction of themselves and children. Both had been subjects of the Miller delusion.

562. Death of the Hon. George Gardiner, of Chemung - The death of this venerable gentleman occurred at his residence in Bigflat, Chemung Co., on the 3d inst., at the age of seventy-eight.

563. Married in this village, on Monday evening last, by the Rev. Mr. Bloomer, Mr. Henry M. Freleigh to Miss Eliza Catharine Van Steinberg, all of this village.

564. Died in the village of Kingston, on the 17th instant, Mr. Tobias Hasbrouck, one of the oldest and most respectable citizens of that village, aged 75 years.

May 27, 1848 (Saturday)

565. Wesley Pine, convicted of murder, was executed at Poughkeepsie yesterday. The execution was conducted in one of the cells of the prison, in the presence of about thirty individuals.

566. Still Another Murder in Pleasant Valley - Another revolting tragedy occurred at Pleasant Valley on Thursday morning last. A man named Richard Wall, in the employ of Mr. John H. Newcomb, was at work at a fence on some property, which was in dispute between Newcomb and Dr. Joel Divine. An altercation is supposed to have

taken place between the former and Divine, who insisted that the road should not be built, and who accordingly got a loaded gun and shot Wall in the head. The ball and several shot took effect over the left eye. He was taken to the residence of Mr. Newcomb and expired in about 45 minutes. A coroner's jury was immediately summoned, and after due deliberation rendered a verdict that the "deceased came to his death by wilful murder at the hand of Joel Divine." Divine was immediately arrested, and after an examination, committed to the jail in this village. Poughkeepsie *American*.

567. Indian War in Oregon - Louisvill, May 21 - By the arrival of Major Meek, from the west, we have late and most important news from Oregon, where all is confusion and bloodshed between the whites and Indians. Four powerful tribes have united, and commenced a deadly war. On the 29th of November, a most horrid and brutal massacre was committed by the Cayuse Indians, at the Presbyterian mission, at the Wallah-Wallah Valley. Dr. White, his man, and wife, with eighteen others, were killed, and sixty or seventy taken prisoner. The houses of the missionaries and their neighbors were burned to the ground. The unfortunate prisoners were subsequently ransomed, through the agency of Peter Sken Ogden, chief factor of the Hudson Bay Company.

568. Death of A Venerable Divine - The Rev. Ashbel Green, D. D., died Friday morning, at his residence in Philadelphia. The Philadelphia *North American* of Saturday morning truly remarks that he was one of the patriarchs of that city - a venerable, much beloved, and highly distinguished citizen. He was first appointed to the chaplaincy of Congress, was formerly professor in Princeton College, and presided over the deliberations of the Presbyterian Church at its early organization in this country. The funeral of Dr. Green took place Saturday, at Princeton, NJ.

569. Death of the Rev. Robert Emory - The Rev. Robert Emory, president of Dickinson College, died at Baltimore, on Thursday evening of last week, of consumption.

570. Heart Rending Calamity - We learn from the Ogdensburgh Sentinel that three children of a Mr. Campbell, of Hermon, St.

Lawrence Co., were poisoned on the 6th inst., by eating poke-root, which they mistook for sweet-flag. There were from 3 to 10 years of age, and the last of them died within 23 minutes after eating the poisonous root. They were the only children of their parents.

571. Another Revolutionary Octogenarian Gone - Judge James M. Marshall, son of Col. Thomas Marshall, commander of the 3d Virginia regiment in the war of independence, and eldest surviving brother of Chief Justice Marshall, died at his residence in Fauquier Co., Va., on the 26th ult., aged 85 years.

572. Charles Langfeldt is Guilty - The jury in the case of Charles Langfeldt, after having been out deliberating about fifteen hours, returned into the court of Oyer and Terminer, yesterday morning at 9 1/2 o'clock, and rendered a verdict of the murder of Mrs. Catharine Rademacher, in the First Degree. The Court room was densely crowded, while an immense number of people had surrounded the Court house, anxious to catch a glimpse of the murderer. His fate is sealed - he must be hanged by the neck until dead - so the judge will pronounce it. <long story, ed.> *Pennsylvanian*.

573. Drowned - James Rightmire, from the town of Caroline, Tompkins Co., was drowned in the Cayuka lake, on the 4th inst., the skiff in which he and three other men were proceeding to the bridge on a fishing voyage, being run over by the steamboat Simeon De Witt.

574. Benefits of Advertising - A man named John Derby advertised for a wife, and received seventy-five applications. Some of the applicants pressed their claims with such vigor, that poor John, to get out of the scrape, placed a rope around his neck and hung himself!

575. Murder - Thomas Hays, cooper, residing at 5 Walnut street, killed his wife, Elizabeth, last week, it is charged, by nearly chopping her head off with a cooper's axe. She appears to have been lying on her left side, as the print of the axe extended from about the centre to the back of the neck, along the right side of the neck to near the corner of the mouth. Hays is in custody. No third party was present at the time. It is said they lived unhappily together, and were at one time separated. N. Y. *Express*.

576. Fatal Accident - A man named Devine was instantly killed yesterday, under the following circumstances: While engaged in chopping the bark from saw-logs, which lay one over the other, opposite Mr. Barhydt's boat yard, one of them slipped from its place and crushed him to death as he sat below. He leaves a family to mourn his loss. Utica *Gazette*.

577. The Little Lovers! - Married, at Temple, Me., Adam Mott to Aunt Tuttle, of Freeman. The entire weight is said to be 580 pounds, the gentleman weighing 340 and the lady 240 pounds.

578. Married in Kingston, on the 23d inst., by the Rev. D. Stocking, Mr. Thomas H. Carson to Susan Dewey, all of that village.

579. Married in Kingston, on the 16th inst., by the Rev. D. Stocking, Mr. Atkinson Hunt to Miss Louisa Porter, both of Saugerties.

June 3, 1848 (Saturday)

580. Strange Suicide - A week or two since, a man named Bruce, living near Cincinnati, committed suicide in the following manner. He went to the church yard and dug his grave beside his wife, who had been buried some sixteen months before. Having procured a coffin under some pretence, he conveyed it to its destination unobserved. He then took off his clothes, except his shirt, put on a night cap, and laid himself in the coffin which he had previously placed in the newly made grave, with a loaded pistol in it. He now drew on the cover of the coffin, and then placing the pistol to his right temple fired it. It is supposed he died instantly. There was no doubt that Bruce was crazy.

581. Mr. James Hurley, a subtractor and foreman of the tunnel on the Hudson river railroad at Breakneck Hill, was instantly killed on the 6th instant, by the premature explosion of a blast. He was aged twenty-five years, and a native of the county of Tiperary, Ireland. A brother named Thomas, who was also a foreman on the works, was somewhat injured. They were both distinguished for their efficiency on the works.

582. A man who gave his name as Kelly, and said he was from Dubuque, Iowa, attempted to murder a man named Mull, in Albany,

on Sunday afternoon, and it is feared has succeeded. Kelly, it seems, had insulted a man and woman who were in a wagon, and when moving off was seized by Mull, at whom he discharged a pistol. Mull then closed with Kelly, who stabbed him severely, and probably fatally, with a bowie knife. Kelly is said to be crazy.

583. Suicide - Judge Dunn, for many years an associate Judge, in Green Co., Pa., committed suicide on Wednesday, the 17th inst., at his residence, a few miles below Enon, by hanging; cause unknown.

584. Married in Rondout, on the 22d inst., by the Rev. B. T. Phillips, William Ball to Miss Mary Ann Mc Millan, all of Rondout.

585. Died in Glasco, on Saturday last, Harmon Osterhoudt, aged about 50 years.

586. Died in Rondout, of consumption, on the 22d instant, George C. Metcalf, aged 27 years.

June 10, 1848 (Saturday)

587. Distressing and Fatal Occurrence - Mr. John Hendricks, of Flatbush, in this town, aged about 33 years, was burned to death, on Wednesday last, in the most shocking manner. Mr. Hendricks had been subject to fits almost from boyhood, and so much so that of late years the family have rarely left him alone. On that day while part of the family were absent, and the young lady in whose care he was left was engaged in the door-yard, it is supposed he was seized with a fit while sitting before the fire and falling forward into it was burned to death before he was discovered. The young lady on entering the room found him lying in the fire and succeeded in removing him from it, but he had already expired. He was an amiable man and devoted christian, and his death, under the painful circumstances, has cast a gloom over the neighborhood. We deeply sympathise with the family at this unexpected affliction.

588. Drowned - Coroner Hays, on the 27th ult., we learn from the Rondout *Courier*, held an inquest on the body of James Brooks, a native of Ireland, who fell off a canal boat in the Rondout creek, about a mile above Eddyville. Verdict of the jury, "accidental drowning."

Deceased was about 23 years of age, and had been in this country but a short time.

589. Also on the 29th, an inquest was had on the body of Pilsbury S. Haskell, who, in jumping from a small boat to a rope attached to the schooner Ruby, from Maine, slipped his hold and was precipitated into the creek, and not being able to swim, sunk without rising to the surface. Verdict "accidental drowning." He was about 18 years of age and a native of Maine.

590. Also, the 31st ult., an inquest was had resulting in a verdict of accidental drowning, on the body of James O'Hara, aged about 30, who accidentally walked off the dock, about 10 o'clock on the night of the 30th ult. Persons heard the splash and saw the man struggling in the water, but had not the means to render assistance promptly enough to save the unfortunate.

591. Jacob Schmidt, a German, aged about 25, fell from a canal boat into the creek, June 2d, and was drowned. Rondout *Courier*.

592. Murder - We learn from the Delaware *Gazette* that a Mrs. Beckwith, about 80 years of age, was killed in Franklin on Saturday afternoon last. It is said, that she and her husband, who is about 85, have been in the habit of drinking to excess, and on that day or the one previous, had brought home some whiskey, which they divided. During Saturday afternoon the old man was gone out an hour or two, and he says while he was gone, the old woman hid his whiskey - that they had a quarrel, and he struck her. There were five pretty severe wounds on the head, apparently inflicted by some instrument with sharp corners, although none could be found except the whiskey jug. A Coroner's inquest was held on Monday afternoon, which rendered a verdict that she came to her death by wounds inflicted by him.

593. Stabbed - We learn that on Friday of last week, a Mr. John L. Milligan, a collector of school taxes in the town of Canajoharie, being resisted in the discharge of his duties by Mr. Elijah Dunckel, drew a knife and stabbed him. Milligan applied to Dunckel for his tax who wanted him to wait until he could go to "Muttonville" to procure it. Milligan refused, and proceeded to levy upon some of the property of

Dunckel, when a quarrel ensued which resulted in the latter's being stabbed in the side - the knife penetrating to the kidneys. Dunckel is said to be in a critical state. Canajoharie *Radii*.

594. A man named Barnes was recently shot at New Bremen, Ohio, by a Mr. Speckman, on account of having made infamous proposals to his wife. Mr. Speckman was examined and discharged by the authorities.

595. The Stolen Child - On Thursday last an advertisement appeared in the Philadelphia Ledger, in which the advertiser, John Dawson, a young man, desired to learn something of his relatives from whom he had bee separated eighteen or twenty years, under the following circumstances. In the year 1829, when about four years of age, he was stolen from his parents, then living in Philadelphia, by a man named Charles Ingelfritz, who took him on board of a vessel bound to New Bedford, and subsequently carried the child with him on various voyages to all quarters of the globe. The boy, though conscious of having been stolen from his parents, had no knowledge of his real name or place of birth, and no clue could he obtain, until one day Ingelfritz happened to be intoxicated, when he said that he had taken him from Philadelphia. Like another Japhet, he started in search of his father, and after an unsuccessful quest, he determined to advertise. This had the desired result, and he has found his father in the person of Daniel Brosnan, residing in Mc Coy's Court, South Front street, Philadelphia. The father identified him as his long lost son by certain marks upon his person. The meeting took place on Saturday, and the joy on the part of both is said to have been indescribable. The father, and a brother and a sister, were all that survived to rejoice over him, his poor mother having become deranged in consequence of the fiendish act of the monster that stole him, and died years ago. Ingelfritz was in New York when the hero of this sketch separated from him. We should like to record his arrest and conviction. *True Sun*.

596. Distressing Occurrence - Edward Wisely, a blacksmith, and his sister, Margaret Wisely, were burned in the most shocking manner, by the accidental ignition and explosion of some powder and other materials, which they were using in the manufacture of fireworks, on Wednesday, in the rear premises of No. 136 Mulberry street. The

explosion tore out the whole side of the building and set fire to the premises. The policemen of the 6th ward were promptly on the spot, rescued the before named persons, and conveyed them on biers to the City Hospital, where but very slight hopes are entertained of their recovery. By the exertions of the firemen, the flames were prevented from spreading. On examining the premises two kegs of powder were found stored away in the basement, which, had the fire communicated to them, might have caused a serious loss of life. NY *Sun*.

597. The Honesdale (Pa.) *Herald* says that Harris Bell, convicted of the murder of Mrs. Eliza Williams, of that county, is to be hung on the 29th day of September next.

598. Died at Poughkeepsie, on the 30th ult., Mrs. Elizabeth Heermance, wife of Simon P. Heermance, printer, formerly of this place, aged 33 years and 23 days.

June 17, 1848 (Saturday)

599. A Fatal Accident - On Monday afternoon, says the Herkimer Co. Democrat, as a train of cars used to carry gravel, &c., was backing into this place from the West, Mr. John Lepper, resident of this place, was standing or walking in a state of intoxication, between the track and wood-house. The track was very narrow, and the cars were passing slowly by him, he staggered between the second and third cars, was struck down, and the wheels of one of the cars passed over both of his legs, crushing them in pieces. He was immediately carried to his residence, and survived but two or three hours. He leaves a wife and seven children. We understand no blame can be attached to any one connected with the train.

600. Horrid Affair - We learn by a gentleman from Belleville, that on Monday last, David Cooper, about seventeen years of age killed his uncle, Samuel Cooper. These persons belonged to an emigrating party from Tennessee, on their way to Arkansas; the young man's father had whipped his mother, and the uncle said he would beat her to death. Some altercation took place between the parties, the boy taking the part of his mother. The boy attempted to get out of his way, but the uncle pursued him - and young Cooper seized a rail, struck the old man a blow over the head, and killed him. The young man delivered

himself into custody at Belleville. St. Louis *Republican*, of 7th.

601. Died in Brooklyn, on the 8th inst., suddenly, Col. Edward Clark, formerly of this town, aged 65 years.

June 24, 1848 (Saturday)

602. Shocking Occurrence - Mr. I. A. Blakeslee, says the New Haven *Courier*, well known in this community as an upright Christian man, was yesterday pitched head first from the top of the church, now being erected in College street, falling more than forty feet into a pile of stones, and instantly killed. It seemed that he had gone up at the request of some of the workmen, where they were erecting the steeple, and passing out on the edge of a plank, it tipped, letting him fall backward. He struck on his head and shoulders, badly bruising his head and breaking his limbs.

603. Suicide - We learn from the Sullivan *Whig* that a man by the name of Hamilton Brown, 80 years of age, hung himself in the eastern portion of the town of Liberty on Saturday last. He was an Irishman, but had long been a resident of that town.

604. Railroad Accident - A freight train coming west over the Boston railroad, on Saturday afternoon, when near Chatham Four Corners, run off the track. One of the breakmen, Henry Van Buren, was killed.

605. Latest From Mexico - Dates to the 13th have been received. Lieut. Bedford, of the 17th Infantry, died on board during the passage of the steamer Portland.

606. Mysterious Circumstance - Monday morning, about 5 o'clock, the neighborhood of Leonard street was thrown into a considerable state of excitement, on account of a man named Thomas Powell being found in the entry of house No. 134 Leonard street, occupied by J. Ferral as a porter house, lying dead, with a large wound on the left side of his head, supposed to have been inflicted with a heavy club. Capt. Magnes, of the sixth Ward, accompanied by Officer Barber, immediately used every exertion to sift the matter, but without success. Coroner Walters held an inquest on the body, and from the evidence adduced in the examination, it appeared that the deceased

was a man of intemperate habits, and had fallen down and injured his head while in a state of intoxication, and had died from loss of blood. But though strong suspicions are entertained that the deceased met with foul play, the jury were unable to determine in what manner the wound was inflicted, and returned a verdict accordingly. NY *True Sun*.

607. Awful Tragedy - We learn from the Hagerstown *News*, that on Friday morning a man named Alexander Redman, residing a couple of miles distant from that place, laboring under a deep depression of spirits, first murdering his child, a boy about three years of age, by cutting his head almost entirely off, and afterwards committed suicide by cutting his own throat. He took him to a neighboring thicket for the commission of the deed. A neighbor passing soon after, he hailed him and informed him that he had just killed his son. When asked the reason for so doing, he replied that he feared he might some day come to want - that he had made way with him, and intended also to make way with himself. He then went into the house, deliberately took down the looking glass and cut his own throat. Redman had formerly been an intemperate man, but not for a year or so past. Balt. *Sun*.

608. Murder - We learn from a gentleman who arrived here yesterday from Memphis, that a murder was committed at Evansville on the evening of the 9th inst., on board the General Scott, which was lying at the wharf. The circumstances are about these: The boat-hands were at supper, and two of them, named Joseph Curry and Joseph Brown, got into a quarrel about some slight matter. Hard words passed between them, and Brown, seizing the carving-knife, seized Curry with his left hand and plunged the knife into him, severing the heart. Brown was immediately arrested and committed for trial. Curry was an Irishman, who made his home in this city, where he has a sister. Both were hands on the Scott. Cincinnati *Herald*.

609. Fatal Leap over the Genesee Falls - A daring and foolhardy young man, named Hosea Hollenbrook, who was ambitious to become another Sam Patch, leaped over Genesee Falls at Rochester on the evening of the 15th inst. Up to the last accounts his body had not been found. He had made an arrangement with some of his shopmates to help him out of the water below the Falls, as he could not swim, and

made the leap for the mere purpose of showing his courage, in the belief, if successful, he would make a speculation on the 4th of July.

610. Fatal Accident - When the steamboat-train for Stonington had got a few miles from this city last evening, they missed one of the brakemen. Reversing the engine, they came back and found him with his head smashed near one of the bridges. He was taken up and the train returned to the city and left his body. His name was Nathan Davis of Woonsocket. Providence *Journal*, Saturday.

611. A dreadful explosion took place in the fireworks manufactory of S. W. Jackson, Shippen street, Philadelphia, on Monday afternoon. A lad named Edward Bowman and a young woman named Mary Jenkins were engaged in making rockets in the place at the time. The lad was not dangerously injured, but the poor girl was so shockingly burned that she died the same evening. The explosion was supposed to have been caused by friction.

612. Married in Kingston, on the 24th ult., by the Rev. Davis Stocking, Mr. William Oliver, of Catskill, to Miss Ann M. Jennings, of Kingston.

613. Married in Rondout, on the 15th inst., by the Rev. H. Lounsberry, Benjamin Ketcham to Miss Angeline Tompkins, all of that place.

614. Died in this village, on Sunday evening last, Miss Elizabeth Mains, aged 63 years.

615. Died in Shawangunk, on the 18th instant, the Hon. Joseph Jansen, aged 72 years.

616. Died at his residence in Peekskill, on the 13th inst., Gen. Pierre Van Cortland, aged 86.

617. Died at Rondout, on the 14th inst., of consumption, Mrs. Phebe Ann Maybee, aged about 30.

July 1, 1848 (Saturday)

618. Death of Thomas Snowden - We perform a most painful duty this afternoon in announcing the sudden death of Thomas Snowden, one of

the oldest and most respectable printers in the city. Mr. Snowden has been for many years the overseeing director of the business affairs of the *Courier & Enquirer*, and was perhaps as widely known and esteemed as any member of his profession in the city. He was one of the oldest members of the typographical society, and was renowned for his friendly conduct towards the brothers of the craft. We can but briefly allude to this melancholy event of the day. N. Y. *Mirror*.

619. Powder Mill Struck by Lightning - The pulverising Mill connected with the Powder Works of Mr. S. M. Hopps, of Barre, was struck by lightning on the afternoon of Friday last, and completely ruined. A man named Nathan Mallot, who was in the mill at the time, was thrown some fifteen rods, and breathed but a moment after he was found. The loss of powder was quite small. This is the third mill, we believe which has been destroyed on the same spot within five years. Boston *Jour*.

620. Judge Archer, Chief Justice of Maryland, died at Baltimore on Sunday night.

621. Fatal Occurrence - Mr. James Dubois, of Jamaica, L. I., while climbing up some rocks near that town, on Sunday morning last, was precipitated to the ground from a height of some thirty feet, in consequence of a bush to which he had clung, giving way. A stone which was detached at the same moment, fell upon him, crushing one of his legs, and he died the same evening under the amputating knife, or within a short time after the limb had been taken off.

622. Another Mercer Tragedy - At Reading on Sunday evening, a music master by the name of Hooper, shot a Mr. Norris, and dangerously wounded him. Hooper says that Norris had seduced his sister, and that this was the cause of his committing the deed.

623. Married on the 22d inst., by the Rev. B. T. Philips, William Mc Cullough, of Rondout, to Miss Jane Duncan, of New York.

624. Married at Marlborough, on the 18th inst., by Rev. Mr. Hawley, John Hepworth, to Miss Ann Eliza Hohnes, all of that place.

625. Died at Jersey City, on the 22d inst., of disease of the heart, Samuel Freligh, aged 67 years, formerly of this village.

626. Died in the village of Kingston, on the 16th inst., Maria, daughter of Wm. Vredenburgh, aged 19 years and 6 months.

627. Died in the town of Kingston, on the 22d inst., Hiram O. Henion, aged 29 years.

July 8, 1848 (Saturday)

628. Accidents on the Fourth - In the City of New York, a little girl, daughter of Montgomery G. Gillen, 215 Bleecker street, was run over by one of the Knickerbocker stages and instantly killed.

629. As the Williamsburg ferry boat "Wallabout" was nearing her berth at Peck slip, between 3 and 4 o'clock in the morning, she was struck immediately forward of the wheel-house, by one of the Fulton ferry boats, which had but a little before left the New York side on her way to Brooklyn. By the collision the whole forward part of the ladies' cabin of the Wallabout was stove in and the timbers connected with it destroyed. Two gentlemen, who were passengers at the time, coming to the city with a view of passing the 4th of July, were struck, and seriously, if not fatally, injured. One of them, a nephew of Judge Leayenft, had one of his legs broken in two places - and the other, a Mr. Hanson, keeper of a hat store, was dangerously hurt in the back, and it has been stated that he is since dead.

630. Terrible Accident - We learn, just as we go to press, says the Troy *Commercial Advertiser*, that Lewis Fellows, Alderman of the Sixth Ward met a terrible, and it is feared, fatal accident. He was sawing a short block of wood with a buzz saw, and as the block passed through the saw it was caught by the reverse motion, and struck the top of his head with great violence, inflicting a horrible wound, from which it is hardly possible for him to recover.

631. Lynching - The Indian who killed Tornell and Mackelray, near the falls of the St. Croix river, was lately hung at that place, in compliance with the sentence of a Lynch court. A white man, who had something to do with the murder, was warned to leave the country in thirty hours.

632. Horrid Murders - Noah Smith and his wife, both of 70 years of age, were murdered at Petersburgh on Saturday night. Mr. Smith was a farmer, an old resident of the town - a very quiet, inoffensive, man - and was known to have quite a sum of money in his house, generally supposed to be from $1000 to $1500, and that much of it was in specie. They lived about a mile and a half east of the village of Petersburgh, on the Williamston road. Mrs. Smith was a sister of the father of the Hon. Gideon Reynolds, present member of Congress from this district. Mr. Smith was a citizen of high character, and enjoyed the confidence and respect of that community. The occurrence produced the most profound sensation and highest excitement in that section of the county; and as the news spread like electricity, thousands assembled yesterday at the scene of the horrid tragedy. <long story> Troy *Commercial Advertiser*, Monday.

633. Suicide - Information was received on Thursday, we learn from the Boston *Transcript*, that Mr. Edward Bromfield Phillips, a graduate of Harvard University in the class of 1845, and about twenty-two or twenty-three years of age, shot himself in his room, at the water-cure establishment in Brattleboro, Vt., on Tuesday last. He was a son of the late Edward Phillips of Boston, and had recently come into possession of property estimated at upwards of half a million of dollars. An affair of the heart is said to have been the cause of the act. The mother and sister of the deceased reside at Cambridge port.

634. Awful Calamity by Lightning - During the severe thunder storm which passed over our city yesterday, about 5 o'clock, P. M., Messrs. Carey and Ryan, Brothers of the Order of Presentation of the Catholic Church, were returning to their residence near Birmingham, after teaching at the Sunday School, and were just ascending the hill in front of the house, when they were both struck by a flash of lightning and instantly killed. - Mr. Carey had his clothes torn into more than a hundred pieces, and scattered in the road. What is most remarkable is, that another person, one of the junior members of the order, who was walking between Mr. Carey and Mr. Ryan, escaped unhurt. Mr. Carey was principle teacher of the Free School of St. Paul's Church, and was beloved by all who knew him. Pittsburgh *Gazette*, July 3.

635. Horrid Murder - The corner of Ann and Nassau Sts., was the scene of a bloody tragedy last night about half-past six o'clock. Mr. P. D. Bremoud, of the firm of Savage & Company, the well known Gold Pen Manufacturers, was found murdered in his room, over the book-store of Talbot Watts. The brother-in-law of the murdered man, calling on him at that hour, found the door locked, which led him to suspect that all was not right. Procuring aid from persons about the house, the room was forced open, when the shocking spectacle was revealed. Mr. Bremoud, in the agonies of death, lay upon the floor, while a female, named Mary Ann Stewart, who was known to be of notoriously bad character, held his head in her lap and appeared to be trying to restore him to consciousness. His head was shockingly bruised, the skull being fractured in several places. Marks of blood were visible about the room and two heavy pitchers, broken and stained with blood with which the wounds had evidently been inflicted, lay on the floor. The woman, on being questioned, stated that he had fallen down stairs, but from the circumstances of several gold pencils being found on her person, as well as the disorder manifest among the articles, it is supposed that she attempted stealing them, and upon his resisting, committed the horrid deed. She was taken to the Second Ward Station House, for the night, where she persisted in denying the crime, but raved frantically about the deceased for a long time. The coroner's inquest will be held this morning. NY *Tribune*, of Thursday.

636. Fatal and Heart-Rending Accident - Messrs. Minor & Horton of this village, have recently put up in their foundry an engine of considerable power, to drive their blowers, saws and other machinery. To this engine, Frederick Minor, a noble and intelligent boy about 14 years of age, acted as tender; and on Friday afternoon last, he was, it is supposed, caught by the fly-wheel, and thrown twice around the shaft; he then fell against the bar by which the machinery attached to the blowers are put in motion, thereby starting it, when he was caught between the cogs and crushed, and mangled most horribly. He breathed but once after he was taken out. Peekskill *Republican*.

637. Married at Kingston, June 29th, by Rev. Dr. Gosman, of Hudson, David Anderson, of Rondout, to Miss Phebe, daughter of Jas. Russell, of Kingston.

638. Married June 28th, by Rev. B. F. Philips, John Summer, to Miss Mary Sapetch, all of Rondout.

639. Married at Hurley, by the Rev. J. C. Cruikshank, on the 28th ult., Cornelius Robinson to Sally Ann, daughter of David Slayter.

640. Died at Rondout, on the 26th ult., Sophia Weed, daughter of Lewis and Elizabeth Smith, aged 2 years and 9 months.

641. Died at Kingston, on the 4th inst., Mr. Abraham Schoonmaker, aged 36 years, late of Orange Co.

642. Died at Morristown, New Jersey, on the 21st ult., Mrs. Sarah Blauvelt, aged 39 years, wife of Isaac A. Blauvelt, Esq., former principal of Kingston Academy.

July 15, 1848 (Saturday)

643. Shooting an Elephant - The great elephant Rajah was shot at the Zoological Gardens, Liverpool, just before the Caledonia left. He had destroyed his keeper, Richard Howard, by stamping upon him with one of his enormous feet. It appears that Howard struck the animal a savage blow on one of its tusks, with a broom, whereupon the elephant killed the man and then ate the broom. Two ounces of Prussic acid, and 25 grains of aconite were given to the creature, in beans and molasses, but the poison only made him a little sick for a few moments! Twenty four rifle balls were then fired into him, when he reeled and fell dead, one of the bullets having passed into his chest.

644. Death of a Venerable Lady - A letter received in this city yesterday announces the decease of a distinguished matron, a relic of the era of the Revolution, Mrs. Julia Rush, widow of the distinguished Dr. Benjamin Rush, and mother of Hon. Richard Rush, now Minister of the United States to France. She died on Friday night last, in the ninetieth year of her age, at Sydenham, near Philadelphia, (the residence of her son.) She was the sister of the late Hon. Richard Stockton, of New Jersey, and grandmother, therefore, of Com. R. F. Stockton, U. S. Navy. She was venerable not only for her age, but for her valuable qualities; and has left many relatives and friends to bear testimony to the excellence of her life. *National Intelligencer.*

645. Shot Herself for Love - A young girl named Caroline Hall shot herself, at Evansville, Ga., last week, and died soon afterwards. The refusal of her parents to allow her to marry a young man in the army was the cause.

646. The Late Captain Van Olinda - The funeral honors paid to the remains of this brave officer, at Albany, on Friday last, are described as being highly impressive and appropriate. The weather cloudy, but not rainy. A very large number of people came in from the adjoining county to attend the solemn rites.

647. Casualties and Death by Lightning - The Wilkinson (Miss.) *Whig* says that on the 14th ult., during a severe thunder storm, John Embree was killed by lightning, on the plantation of Dr. Patrick. He was in the open field, no trees or objects near. The heat was so intense as to fuse his watch and other metal about his person.

648. During a thunderstorm on Wednesday week, a son of Deacon David Clark, of Westfield, Mass. was instantly killed. There were no marks upon his body, indicating the cause of his death (says the *Standard*) nor did the building appear to have been touched by the fluid, and no traces of its course could be discovered upon the house or upon the ground about it. The boy was standing upon a stoop or open shed, leaning over the railing, which was elevated some distance from the ground, and immediately below him stood a large iron kettle.

649. Mr. Austin Pierpont, of East Farms, near Waterbury, Ct., was killed by lightning on Friday week, under the following circumstances, as related by the Waterbury American: - The family were all seated, Mr. P. on the left hand side of the fire-place, near the mantle piece - one of his sons, a young man, a few feet on his right, a young lad living in the family, in front of the fire place, and Mrs. P. on the right, but several feet back from the range of the chimney. The fatal bolt came - all were stunned, but none were thrown to the floor - and Mr. P. though killed outright, never moved, but remained in the same upright position as when last observed by those who had recovered from the shock. The floor was literally strewed with fragments and dust, and it was some minutes before any one fully recovered from their sudden bewilderment. It was some time before the son came to

consciousness. Mrs. P. and the other young man were more fortunate. It is almost a miracle that any one of the little circle escaped - for the space occupied by the four was not over 6 or 8 feet square.

650. Accident and Death - On Friday last, as Mrs. H. E. Riell, Mrs. Fowler and her child, were riding in a carriage near Rossville, Staten Island, it was accidentally overturned, the child instantly killed, and both Mrs. Riell and Mrs. Fowler very seriously injured.

651. Murder and Suicide - We learn from Harrisonville that a man by the name of Ison, of Van Buren Co., in the early part of last week, was found dead in his door-yard, and his wife a corpse near him. Both were shot, and it is supposed that he first killed his wife, and then put an end to his own existence with the same gun. Lex (Mo.) *Express*.

652. Augustus Dutee Convicted - The trial of this man before the Supreme Judicial Court at Boston, for the murder of Ellen Oakes, whom he pistolled because she refused to marry him, has resulted in a verdict of guilty.

653. Longevity - Mrs. Mary Bacon, aged one hundred and eight years, died in Providence, RI, on Monday afternoon last.

654. Abortion and Death - Dr. Calvin Batchelder of Lowell, charged with procuring abortion by means of an instrument or otherwise, upon the person of Mrs. Eunice King, a widow lady, formerly a resident of Stow, resulting in the death of Mrs. King, was bound over on Saturday in the sum of $5,000 for his appearance at the higher Court, to be held in October in that city, and for the want thereof was committed.

655. The Lowell *Courier* also gives another case, as follows: Mrs. Mc Cann, on Adam-St. died on Friday night by the means used, as is stated, to procure abortion. On Wednesday she was well, and called upon one Mrs. Curtfs, <sic> a pretender of an 'Indian Doctor.' She was immediately taken sick, and could scarcely get home. Mrs. Curtis called on her professionally, several times, and assured her but an hour or two before her death, that she was recovering and would get well soon.

656. Drowned - On Saturday last a man named Stephen Welsh, employed by the Peoples' Line of Steamboats, at Albany, in collecting ashes from the furnaces of the boats, was drowned near the Hamilton street bridge. Mr. W. was coming to the dock with his boat, standing up at the time, when his boat suddenly struck the stern of a canal boat, and he was thrown into the river by the shock. He was not seen to rise; his body was recovered about half and hour afterwards. Mr. Welsh was a single man, and had been in the country about a year.

657. A Good Man Departed - We learn that the Rev. Oliver William Bourne Peabody, pastor of the Unitarian congregation at Burlington, Vt., died in that place on Wednesday. Mr. Peabody graduated at Harvard University in 1846. He was a brother of Mrs. Alexander H. Everett, and a twin brother of the late Rev. W. B. O. Peabody of Springfield. Mr. Peabody has been an able contributor to the North American Review, and was for a time connected with the editorial department of the Daily Advertiser of Boston. He was a good writer, and accomplished scholar, a pure minded, upright and most estimable man. He was engaged upon a memoir of his brother, (whose poetical writings will have a lasting place in American literature) when the summons came for his own departure.

658. Married on the 12th inst., by the Rev. Josiah Leonard, Mr. Jacob Shaffer of Clermont, Columbia Co., to Miss Susan Ann Gardiner, of Saugerties.

659. Married in the village of Kingston, on the 5th instant, by the Rev. John C. F. Hoes, Mr. Lewis W. Winley to Miss Phebe Jane Woolsey, both of Kingston.

660. Married in the town of Olive, on the 7th of July inst., by Martin Schutt, Esq., John S. Bell to Nancy Bell, all of Olive.

661. Married in the village of Kingston on the 11th inst., by the Rev. John C. F. Hoes, Mr. Theodore Elmendorf, Commander of the Steamer Santa Claus, to Miss Cordelia King, of Kingston.

662. Married in Poughkeepsie, on the morning of the 6th inst., by the Rev. S. Van Duesen, Mr. Isaac V. Lake, of Poughkeepsie, to Miss

Mary Davis, of Lloyd, Ulster Co.

663. Died on the 8th inst., at Malden, Mrs. Flora, wife of Mr. Charles Isham, in the 51st year of her age.

664. Died in this village, on Sunday last, Cornelia Jones, wife of J. Warren Rogers, and daughter of the late Tobias L. Stoutenburgh. Her remains were interred at Hyde Park.

665. Died in the town of Kingston, on Tuesday evening last, Mr. Wilhelmus France, a soldier of the Revolution, aged 94 years.

666. Died on Friday evening, July 7th, at Poughkeepsie, of Scarlet Fever, Russel Scouten Heermance, aged 8 years, 10 months and 2 days, son of Simon P. Heermance.

667. Died July 4th, at New York, Charles G. Ferris, late M. C., aged 56 years.

July 22, 1848 (Saturday)

668. Frightful Case of Hanging - On Saturday, two persons passing through a very secluded spot between the Wissahicon and Roxborough, were attracted by a dog to the remains of a man suspended from the limb of a spruce tree about ten feet from the ground, with a rope around his neck. The body had gone far into a state of decomposition; the flesh having dropped from the bones, and the skeleton remaining in his clothing, presenting altogether one of the most frightful and melancholy sights imaginable. From his dress and other circumstances he was recognized as Charles Holland, a German, about forty-five years of age, formerly a workman in one of the factories at Manayunk, where he has left a wife and two children living. The deceased had been missing sine the 21st of May, and it is supposed that he had been hanging there since that time. When last seen he was perfectly sane. It could not be ascertained or determined by the jury how or in what manner the deed was perpetrated. *Phil. N. American.*

669. The Petersburg Murder - Andreas Hall, was on Saturday, after an examination which lasted all the week, committed on the charge of the

murder of Noah and Amy Smith, on the night of the 1st of July. Hall is about twenty-five years of age, is umarred, <sic> and has for some months past had a home at his brother-in-law's in Green Island, opposite this city. The next Circuit held in this city, will be in October. A special term for his trial prior to that time may be ordered. Troy *Com. Adv.*

670. Died at Clovesville, Delaware Co., on the 8th instant, of consumption, Adaline, daughter of Robert Humphrey, Esq., in the 18th year of her age, and late a pupil of the State Normal School.

July 29, 1848 (Saturday)

671. The funeral of the late celebrated Tom Steel has taken place in Dublin, with every testimony of respect. The Lord Mayor and the greater part of the Corporation were present; and the Messrs. O'Connell acted as mourners. In accordance with Mr. Steele's last wish his body was deposited near the remains of his deceased friend and leader. News from Ireland.

672. News from Bohemia - Count Von der Lippe, Governor of the fortress of Ulm, has put an end to his life by shooting himself.

673. Melancholy Accident - On Monday afternoon, Messrs. A. Ten Eyck and Chas. H. Adams, of Albany, two sons of Dr. Henry Adams, and two sons of Cuyler Adams, of Coxsackie, were fishing in the river opposite Coxsackie; the boat in which they were seated was upset, and Egbert Adams, aged 15, a son of Dr. Henry Adams, was drowned. The party had a narrow escape from drowning.

674. Ex-Governor Shunk, of Pennsylvania, died at his residence at Harrisburgh, on Thursday week. Few public men enjoyed a more unspotted reputation, or had a stronger hold upon the confidence of the people.

675. Horrible Death - A son of Daniel Raredon, aged seven years, residing near Wilbur was bitten by a rabid dog about two months since, and on Wednesday last died of that most horrible of all diseases, hydrophobia. Rondout *Courier*.

676. Horrible Death - A lad about eighteen years of age, named Patrick Mullen, died while being conveyed to the Pennsylvania Hospital, on Friday evening, from injuries received in the vicinity of Spring Mill. He was upon a horse upon the towing path of the canal, and the animal taking fright from a locomotive on the rail-road, ran off, and the lad getting entangled in the gearing, was dragged for nearly half a mile, and bruised and mangled in a shocking manner. Phila. *N. Am.*, Monday.

677. A fatal accident occurred on the Troy and Schenectady RR on Thursday, Miss Clure, of Niskayuna, was run over near the station house, and almost instantly killed. The young lady was deaf. Troy *Budget*.

678. Lightning - We learn that the house of Benjamin Simpson, in Groton, near West Rumney village, was struck by lightning on the afternoon of the 14th inst., instantly killing his wife, and injuring other persons. Several narrowly escaped with life. *Granite State Whig.*

679. Murder - On Saturday last, at a fandango near the steamboat landing, Sergeant Smoot, belonging to the 3d dragoons, was stabbed to death by one or more Mexicans. It seems that hatred had been engendered between the parties about a woman, when the dragoons were stationed here last fall, and on their return down the river, the unfortunate subject of this notice was recognized, and followed a short distance from fandango as he was wending his way homeward, and brutally murdered. His murderers have not been arrested. Matamoras *Flag*, June 28.

680. Married on the 22d instant, at the residence of Mr. Hull, by the Rev. N. H. Cornell, Mr. Philip F. Koons, of Redhook, to Miss Charlotte A. Hull of Saugerties. The gordion knot! first tied in Eden's bower, Mid humming streams and fragrance breathing flowers, Thou art mid light and gloom, thro' good and ill, Youth's goal, and man's chief blessing still.

681. Married on the 27th, by the Rev. N. H. Cornell, Mr. John Braidy to Miss Elizabeth Landt, all of Saugerties.

682. Died in this village, on Thursday last, Mrs. Irena Purdy, aged about 74 years.

August 5, 1848 (Saturday)

683. The mortality from yellow fever in Vera Cruz, has of late been very great, and was rather on the increase when the N. Orleans left. Among the recent deaths there we regret to announce that of Capt. Gleason, Assistant Quartermaster. He died of yellow fever, on the 16th inst. Lieut. Martin of the 3d dragoons, died at the National Bridge, of the same disease, on the 12th inst. From Mexico.

684. Affray in South Troy - On Saturday evening a number of men entered the grocery of a man named Daniel Wynn, in South Troy, for the purpose, as we understand, of a row, intending to drive him from the premises. Wynn was aware of their intentions, and as soon as they commenced operations, which was by abusing his wife, he ordered them to leave, which they refused to do. Wynn, who is a powerful man, then proceeded to apply the force necessary to carry out his request, and in doing so, injured one of the men, named Roger Ryan, so severely that he is not expected to live. One of the rioters was arrested and committed the same evening. Wynn was arrested yesterday. When arrested, he snapped a pistol at the man who accompanied the officer to assist in the arrest. The pistol was found to be loaded to the muzzle, but fortunately missed fire. Ryan was struck, on the head, either by Wynn or some one else, by a fire shovel, and a stone beer bottle. The Coroner's inquest to-day will probably develop the facts. Troy *Com. Adv.*

685. The Nassau Murder - The Troy *Commercial Advertiser* of Saturday says that officer Philips of that city and Deputy Sheriff Waterbury, of Nassau, arrived at Troy on Saturday morning by the steamer Troy, with their prisoner O'Donnell. They also brought with them the organ and cap belonging to the murdered man, Ratto. O'Donnell has rather a bright look and shows considerable cunning in evading questions put to him in relation to the murder. He will be taken to Nassau, where an examination will be held before the coroner.

686. A woman named Dorn, residing near Ogdensburgh, recently destroyed the life of her son, aged about 16 years, and a cripple. She was insane at the time, and while the boy was engaged in plucking a fowl, she seized an axe, and, by a single blow, nearly severed his head from his body.

687. Lieut. Tilden, recently convicted of robbery and murder in Mexico, and sentenced to be hung, was, previous to the breaking out of the war, a resident of Sackett's Harbor, where his young wife now lives, to whom he was married the evening before leaving for the south. He graduated from West Point in 1840.

688. The Buffalo papers announce the death of Judge Wilkeson, of that city. He died at Kingston, Roane Co., Tennessee. He was one of the first Mayors of Buffalo - formerly a member of the Legislature, and identified with the history and growth of Western New York.

689. The St. Louis *Union* had advices of the death of Maj. Spaulding, Paymaster U. S. Army, at Chihuahua.

690. Died July 24th, at Tivoli, after a short and severe illness, Frederic W. Moore, in the 27th year of his age.

August 12, 1848 (Saturday)

691. Dr. H. C. Flood, a physician attached to a detachment of returned volunteers, committed suicide at New Orleans, on the 26th, by cutting his throat. He was nephew to the former Charge to Texas.

692. Another Revolutionary Patriot Gone - Died at Petersburgh, on Thursday, 27th inst., in the 85th year of his age, Budd Steward, a soldier of the Revolutionary Army, and Pensioner, and the last of that veteran and gallant band in Petersburgh. Mr. Steward served nine months under Col. Marinus Willett and arrived at Schoharie a few hours after the village was burned. He was in several battles that Willet fought with the Indians, along the valley of the Mohawk.

693. Fatal Accident on the Eastern Railroad - On Saturday forenoon, a boy named James C. Dunn, aged 12 years, son of Owen Dunn, was standing between the tracks of the eastern railroad, near the depot at

East Boston, and near one of the crossings. He was looking at a train upon one track, and as he stepped upon the other did not notice that an engine was approaching upon it. He was struck by the train, run over, and killed instantly, his body being literally hacked to pieces.

694. Death by Shooting - A young man named Fox, of the firm of Foster & Company, of Worcester, was shot near Sandwich on Saturday by the careless use of fire arms. He had been stopping on the South Shore a short time for his health, and was about to return, in a wagon, to take the cars for Boston, when a companion who was to come on with him, attempted to enter the wagon with a loaded gun, which he struck against a wheel, by which it was discharged, and the contents entered into the breast of young Fox, who exclaimed, "I am a dead man." and almost immediately expired. He was a young man of excellent character and most respectable family. Boston *Courier*.

695. Life Insurance - Mr. D. W. Gihon, whose sudden death by lightning was recorded in the Philadelphia papers last week, had, a few days before, insured his life for $25,000. The amount was promptly paid over to his administrators by the Company.

696. Drowned - Coroner Chapman held an inquest this morning on the body of a man named Payn, who fell into the canal near the weigh lock on Saturday night last and was drowned. He belonged to the canal boat Palo Alto, of Pine Valley, Capt. A. Shear. It is said he has a brother in Rochester. His effects are at the Coroner's, No. 50 Chapel street. *Eve. Jour.*

697. Married at Malden, on the 10th inst., by the Rev. Mr. Leonard, Mr. L. M. Murray, of Charleston, S. C., to Miss Sarah Ann Calkins, daughter of Judson H. Calkins of Malden. Cake received.

698. Died on the 9th inst., Anna Elizabeth, daughter of Tjerck Schoonmaker, aged eleven months and two days.

699. Died at Glenerie, Saugerties, July 29th, of dysentery, Frank, youngest son of Fanning and Mary Albert, aged 3 years and 2 months. Brooklyn papers please copy.

700. Died August 1, in New York, Helen Lispenard, wife of Col. James Watson Webb, and daughter of the late A. L. Stewart, Esq., of that city.

August 19, 1848 (Saturday)

701. Loss of Life - We regret to learn that several lives were lost (in the conflagration in Albany on Thursday afternoon). Two men were drowned in the Basin, near the foot of Maiden Lane. They were floating on a raft, and in the midst of the conflagration, fell off and sank. The owner of the steamboat William Seymour, Benj. Wakeman is missing. A man named Hardely, an Irishman, died from over exertion. A man named Johnson, and several others are missing.

702. Information Wanted - William Cooke, an inhabitant of Catskill, unsound in mind, wandered away a few days ago, and no tidings of him have yet been received by his friends. He is from 45 to 50 years of age, about 5 feet, 3 inches high, had on a dark colored sack coat of Kentucky Jean, dark pantaloons, and old wool hat, and a pair of shoes much worn. He is naturally retiring and inoffensive, and talks much to himself. Whoever will return him to Catskill, and apply to J. R. Sylvester, at the office of the Catskill Recorder, shall be paid all reasonably <sic> expenses. Papers in neighboring counties will confer a very great favor by giving this notice one or two insertions. Catskill, August 16, 1848. Catskill *Recorder*.

703. The California *Star* of April 1, mentions the deaths, in the NY regiment of volunteers, of 1st Lieut. W. C. Tremmels and 2d Lieut. Charles C. Anderson. From California.

704. Died in this village, on Thursday last, Mrs. Catharine David, aged about 84 years.

705. Died at Newburgh, on the 15th inst., of consumption, Elizabeth, wife of E. Pitts, editor of the Newburgh *Telegraph*, daughter of John and Mary Jamison, in the 30th year of her age.

706. Died on the 4th inst., William Andrew, son of Philip and Catharine Van Buren, aged 3 years, 8 months, and 22 days.

707. Died, also on the same day, Christina, daughter of the above, aged 1 year, 9 months and 17 days, both of Kingston.

August 26, 1848 (Saturday)

708. Coroner's Inquest - A Coroner's Inquest was held on Monday upon the body of Walter P. Lawrence, who died at the Western House, in this village, on the morning of the 21st inst. The particulars of the case are briefly these: Deceased resided in New York City and had been visiting some of his relations, in the town of Woodstock. He left Woodstock on Saturday afternoon last, and, at Chapman's tavern, took passage in the stage for this place. He was quite intoxicated when he arrived here, and he continued drinking very freely during the evening. In the course of the night he was seen intoxicated by a number of our citizens, in various places in the village. Between the hours of twelve and three o'clock, he went to the Western Hotel, demanded lodging for the night, and was shown to a room. About 10 A. M. of Sunday last, the landlord went to his room, and found him apparently in a fit, insensible. A physician was called in, but he was beyond the reach of medical aid. He lingered in the same state until Monday about noon, when he expired. The verdict of the coroner's jury was - that his death was occasioned by a rush of blood to his head, caused by intemperance and exposure. Kingston *Journal*.

709. Drowned - Coroner Hayes was called on Monday morning last, (says the Rondout *Courier* of Saturday) to hold an inquest on the body of John Sullivan, of Wilbur, aged 20 years, who fell from the top of his canal boat cabin into the Rondout creek on Sunday night previously, while asleep. Deceased was an industrious, hard working man, but would occasionally get intoxicated, and it was shown on the inquest that he had been drinking rather freely during the afternoon of Sunday. The Jury brought in a verdict of "accidental drowning."

710. Died in this village, on Monday last, Egbert, son of Abram F. and Frances J. Post, aged seven months and 20 days.

September 2, 1848 (Saturday)

711. The European Times notices the death at Langham, Norfolk, (England) of Capt. Marryatt, of the British Navy, the author of "Peter Simple" and many other naval stories.

712. Married on Sabbath last, by the Rev. V. M. Hulbert, Mr. Daniel Cogserll to Mrs. Rachel Bourne, both of Glasco.

713. Died at Kingston, on Saturday last, Sarah Elizabeth, daughter of James S. and Sarah M. Pine, aged about 8 months.

September 9, 1848 (Saturday)

714. William, a son of Samuel Beyea, near Goshen, was killed by the accidental discharge of his gun while hunting, in company, with several other boys, Saturday before last. He was a promising lad of about 15 years of age.

715. A. son E. L. Dibble, Esq. of Batavia, aged three years, was accidently drowned in a cistern on Saturday last. He had been missed but a few minutes, when a search was commenced, but some half and hour elapsed before the body was discovered. His father had but just started in the cars for Buffalo, with stock to exhibit at the state fair, when the accident occurred.

716. Casualties - The Batavia *Spirit of the Times* states that Mr. John Bean, a respectable citizen of that town, was instantly killed by a thrashing machine on Wednesday week. He was standing on a barrel feeding a thrashing machine, cylinder being uncovered - by some means he lost his balance on the barrel, and falling head foremost into the machine, his right arm and the back part of his head was torn off, producing instant death. He was a single man, about 35 years of age.

717. Foreign Missionary Intelligence - The news of the death of Mrs. Walker, wife of the Missionary to Western Africa has just been communicated.

718. Death From the Explosion of a Spirit Lamp - The Springfield *Republican* states that Mr. Calvin Barrett, Jr. of that town, was filling a lighted spirit lamp (Porter's fluid) with the assistance of his wife on Thursday evening, when the flame communicated to the contents of the lamp, causing the whole to explode. The head and upper part of the body of Mr. B. were enveloped with flame, and the resulting injuries were so severe that he died the next day. His age was 32.

September 16, 1848 (Saturday)

719. Destructive Fire in Brooklyn - Many fatal accidents occurred. Mr. Edward Crowley, of New York Engine, No. 20, was almost instantly killed by the engine, which ran over his head, breaking his skull. Mr. Kirby, a baker, and member of the Brooklyn Hose Co. No. 14, was so seriously injured by the falling of a wall, that he has since died. The fire started on Saturday night. <long story, ed.>

720. Death of Com. Mackenzie - Alexander Slidell Mackenzie is no more. He died at Sing Sing on Wednesday from an affection of the heart. He was attacked while riding upon his horse in that village. He succeeded in getting his feet out of the stirrups, and immediately fell to the ground upon his head; was taken up and carried into a house by two persons who witnessed the fall, and breathed but twice afterwards. Rev. Dr. Creighton was in the village at the time and carried the news to the family of the deceased. His remains were removed in the afternoon to his residence, about two miles below the village.

721. Acquittal of Louisa Bremond - The trial of this woman for the murder of Pierre D. Bremond, at his business office in Nassau St., in July, resulted in her acquittal last night. Little additional evidence to that published at the time of the murder was given. The prisoner, it was proved, was married to the deceased; letters addressed by him to her in that character and the certificate, being produced in Court. NY *Com. Advertiser.*

722. Simon Willard, "The Massachusetts Clockmaker," died in Boston on the 30th ult, aged 95 years and 5 months.

723. Married at Albany, on Tuesday last, by Rev. Dr. Wycoff, Mr. Paul Francis, of Chatauque Co. to Miss Margaret Snyder, of this village.

724. Died in this town on the 8th inst., Rachel Myer, widow of the late William Myer, aged 84 years, 5 months and 2 days.

725. Died at the residence of his father in Shandaken, on the 8th inst., Riley Lane, in the 31st year of his age. The deceased enlisted in Capt. Wilkins's company and served as an officer during the Mexican war.

September 23, 1848 (Saturday)

726. Death of Judge Cushman - The Hon. John P. Cushman, of Troy, died on Saturday afternoon, in the 65th year of his age. Judge Cushman established himself in the Practice of the Law, at Troy, about forty years ago, since which time he has been closely identified with all the interests and enterprises, whether of a business, political, literary or religious character, of that city. He was a member of Congress in 1846, and succeeded the late Judge Vanderpool as Judge of the 3d District, in which office he was succeeded by Judge Parker, upon arriving at the age of 60. Judge Cushman was a man of decided talent. He was honest and independent in the discharge of his public duties; upright in all his private dealings; and virtuous and amiable in all his social relations. Evening *Journal*.

727. Collision of Railroad Trains - Two Men Killed - A collision took place about 1 o'clock on Monday morning, on the Baltimore Railroad, near Wilmington, between the up and down trains, by which Michael Mc Dermott, brakesman, and Mr. Mc Chickering, a machinist, were crushed through the door of the baggage car. Their injuries were of the most serious nature, and terminated fatally. Mc Dermott died in about an hour, and Chickering about 4 o'clock. <details of the accident not copied, ed.>

728. Four Children at a Birth - The Hartford *Courant* states that on Friday night last an Irish woman in Wells street, named Banin, gave birth to four children - two girls and two boys. The mother and one of the children survived but a short time after the event. The united weight of the children was twenty-eight lbs., or an average of seven lbs. each. The woman had had twins twice, and within the space of ten years and eight months had become the mother of fifteen children.

729. Death of a Murderer - John Slaight who shot his wife Mary Slaight, about ten days ago, died in the City Prison about half past 4 o'clock yesterday afternoon. Since he was taken into custody, a week ago yesterday, he has not taken a particle of sustenance, having resisted every effort that has been made to accomplish that object, until noon yesterday, when he was induced to drink a little milk punch. He was quite conscious to the last moment, and entreated that he might be permitted to die quietly, being fully aware as he expressed

himself, that there was no hope for him to escape an ignominious death on the gallows. During his confinement, Dr. Covell, in addition to his own personal attention, assigned two individuals to attend him, and render him as comfortable as circumstance would admit. *True Sun*.

730. Fatal Accident - An Irishman named William Mc Quinn, about 26 years old, was on Tuesday, while blasting rocks near Fort Washington struck by a piece of rock from the blast, and killed on the spot.

731. Fatal Accident - On Saturday last, at a Democratic meeting held at Peningtonville, Chester Co., Pa., a party were engaged in firing a canon, <sic> when a man named James Parke, residing at Parksville, accidentally got before the gun just before the match was being applied. - The piece was discharged before the unfortunate man could be warned of his danger and he was killed instantly.

732. Married on the 21st inst., at the city of Brooklyn, by the Rev. John Gosman, D. D., Henry D. Van Orden, Esq., of Saugerties, Ulster Co., to Miss Mary Jane, daughter of the late John Gaul, of Hudson.

733. Married in this village, on the 16th inst., by the Rev. Dr. Westbrook, John Kugleman to Sarah Plas, daughter of Jacob Plas, of the town of Hurley, N. Y.

September 30, 1848 (Saturday)

734. Hon. Michael Hoffman, Naval Officer for the Port of New York, died on Wednesday evening last, in Brooklyn, aged 60 years. Mr. Hoffman was from Herkimer Co., which he has represented in the State Legislature, in Congress, and in the Convention, which framed our present State Constitution. He was a man of strict integrity and respected by all who knew him.

735. Hon. J. W. Graves of Kentucky, one of the whig electors of that State, died on the 27th inst. Mr. Graves while a Member of Congress, a few years ago, it will be recollected, killed Mr. Cilley of Maine in a duel. He was long a member of Congress from his district.

736. Accidental Death of a Child - A son of Peter Foland of Dunnsville, Albany Co., aged between two and three years was

accidentally killed on the 13th inst. by being rode over with a load of rye. He expired almost immediately.

737. Information Wanted - Elijah Davis, of Saugerties, N. Y., left home on the 23d of August last for New York City, intending, as he stated to his family, to return in two or three days. On the following day he called upon a relative of Washington Market, New York City, and stated that he had some business in Brooklyn, to which place he was then going and would return next day in time to dine with him at his residence in Jane street, and that he would leave the city for home at 5 o'clock in the Manhattan. He did not return next day, nor has he yet been heard from by his family who have made diligent search for him. Mr. Davis is a little over six feet in height, slim built, of light complexion, light brown hair, and wears whiskers. On the left side of his forehead, where his hair parts, is a mark of darkish color and about the size of a five cent piece. He wore when he left home, and when last seen, black cloth coat and pantaloons, black satin vest and a white hat. Editors of New York city and Brooklyn papers by giving this an insertion, or stating its main particulars will confer the greatest favor upon his disconsolate wife.

October 7, 1848 (Saturday)

738. Painful Accident - A little daughter of Mr. M. H. Anthony, of this village, aged four years, fell into a tub of hot water, on the 17th inst., and was so badly scalded that she expired after about seventeen hours of dreadful suffering. The tub was overturned, and the mother who was standing near, was also considerably scalded. Plattsburgh *Republican*.

739. Horrible - A young man, named Beach, was shot about three miles from Auburn a few nights since. He with a companion, both under the influence of liquor, went to the house of a man named Christian Geilfus, who has a couple of daughters, suspected to be of easy virtue. They asked for admittance, but were refused, when they attempted to enter the house, Geilfus warning them to desist. Yet they did not, but forced upon the door, when he fired a gun, the charge of which took effect upon Beach, causing his death in a few minutes. Geilfus had been much annoyed by persons about his house, and took counsel respecting what it was lawful for him to do to rid himself of

the nuisance. Pursuant to that, he armed himself and the above tragic event followed. After committing it he underwent an examination, and was discharged.

740. Married in Flatbush, on the 3d inst., by the Rev. Mr. Hulburt, Mr. Joel Burhans, to Miss Eliza C. Wynkoop.

October 14, 1848 (Saturday)

741. Fatal Leap - A young man by the name of Munn jumped off the bank of the Genesee river, at Mt. Morris, on Sunday morning, and was instantly dashed to pieces. The precipice, at the point from which he leaped, is about 500 feet high. The young man had been slightly insane for two or three years, and for several weeks past had been noticed to be worse than usual, but no one apprehended so rash an act. Rochester *American*.

742. Melancholy Accident - A boat from Boston, with three persons, was capsized near Nantasket, on Sunday night, and two persons drowned. Mr. Leach, blacksmith, and Mr. Vanvormer, carpenter, both of Boston. The name of the survivor was Pierce, a seaman.

743. Fatal Accident - The Po'keepsie *Telegraph* says: A melancholy accident occurred at the tunnel for the Hudson River Railroad at New-Hamburgh, on the 29th ult., by which a laborer, named James Sollins, was killed. It seems that a large box is used for hoisting the stone and dirt through an opening at the top, and on the day mentioned the tackle gave way and let down the box, which contained about a ton of stone, and S. standing directly under it, was killed instantly. He leaves a wife and children.

744. Horrible Murder - We learn from the Troy *Commercial Advertiser* that Peter Turner, captain of the Toronto, one of Col. Hooker's canal boats, was killed at lock No. 11 of the "sixteen locks," on Friday last, by James Whaling, under the following circumstances: Whaling was steersman of the boat Oregon. The two boats were advancing to enter the lock, when the towing line of the Oregon was cut, whereupon Whaling remarked that it was the last towline the captain of the Toronto would ever cut. As the Toronto rose to the top of the lock, Whaling, who had on a heavy pair of coarse boots, kicked

Captain T., inflicting a horrid wound, throwing him some 20 feet across the deck into the canal, from which Capt. Turner was taken out dead. Whaling is in jail at Albany.

745. Horrible Case of Stabbing - At about 3 o'clock this morning, a boy named Edward Kavanagh, aged 16 years, an apprentice in Davis & Nickerson's soap manufactory, at Cambridge, was stabbed in the abdomen by Patrick Delaney, and so severe a wound inflicted that it is feared the boy will not recover. Kavanagh and Delaney were crossing Cambridge bridge together, having been in company during the day, when a dispute arose, and the parties agreed to step aside and fight it out. Another person of the company, who made the proposition, stood by to see fair play. The parties had just come together when Kavanagh fell, and on going to him it was discovered that he had been cut on the ribs and in the abdomen, a wound more than three inches long. Delaney immediately fled and has not yet been arrested, but the police are on his track and it is thought will secure him. Boston *Times*, of Monday.

746. Mournful Accident - An unfortunate Irish laborer named Thomas Douglass was killed yesterday morning on the Harlem Railroad, by the train from Croton Falls. It is stated that he was asleep on one of the timbers of the bridge across the Bronx. (about 8 miles on the New York side of White Plains.) when the locomotive struck him, and no human effort could have arrested its progress in time to save him. The poor fellow lifted up his head just in time to see that death was rushing upon him, but, stupefied by fear, made no effort to escape it. We learn that Douglas has a sister and a mother in this city. He survived his injuries but a few moments. *True Sun.*

747. Serious if Not Fatal Accident - On Wednesday of this week, Mr. John Green, a very worthy respectable farmer of Somers, Westchester Co., and for many years a justice of the peace in that town, met with an accident which came near depriving him instantly of life. He was engaged in some farming operation that occasioned the use of a lever, which by some means was thrown with great violence, striking Mr. Green across the lower jaw, and under the ear breaking the jaw and rendering him insensible, in which state he still remains, with little prospect of recovery.

748. Shocking Casualty - We learn by the Burlington (Vt.) *Courier* that a house occupied by Mr. Palmer, in Jericho, was burnt to the ground on Tuesday evening, 26th ult. and two little children of Mr. P.'s - four and six years of age - perished in the flames.

October 21, 1848 (Saturday)

749. A Good Old Age - The Newport *News* says, the funeral of Mrs. Martha Taber took place on Tuesday afternoon. The age of the deceased was one hundred and four years and six months! She had a sister at the funeral whose age in ninety-three years, and a niece aged seventy-eight years. The combined ages of these three females in two hundred and seventy-five years.

750. Death on the Prairie - The Chicago *Democrat* gives an account of the death of Dr. Daniel Duck, of Athens, of Naperville, an Englishman, aged 70 years, who was returning from a sick call on Thursday week last, and had been piloted half way home from the house of Peter Warden, in Du Page, when last heard from. He was found within a mile of his own house on the prairie, lying on the grass with his overcoat under him. His horses were found within four rods of the body, the wagon in a slough and the horses under the wagon dead and considerably eaten by the wolves.

751. Bloody Affair - Yesterday afternoon Mr. Robert Ewing, a young man of very highly respectable family in this city, rode to the house of Mr. Wm. H. Kelly, called him out, and for some alleged grievance, struck him with a whip. Mr. Kelly seized his assailant by the collar, whereupon the latter drew a pistol, and shot him, the ball entering near the left ear, breaking both jaws, entirely severing the tongue near the roots, and lodging, as the surgeon supposed, near the right ear. Mr. Kelly was alive last night, but it was not thought that he could live long. Mr. Ewing after shooting Mr. Kelly, remounted his horse and rode off. The marshal informed us last evening that he had heard of him four miles from the city on the Salt River road, and sent two police officers in pursuit of him. Louisville *Jour.*, Oct 10.

752. Horrible Murder - The wife of Mr. Henry Wade, druggist, at Roscoe, Ohio, was murdered in the most horrible manner, a few days since. He head was cut almost entirely off, and her body thrown into

the cistern, where it was found by her husband. J. Thomas Cathart, the hostler of the tavern at which they were boarding, has been arrested on suspicion, blood having been found on his clothes. He had also been sent into the room where she was shortly before.

753. We understand that a young man by the name of Manly, about 24 years of age, a son of Gov. Manly, of North Carolina, died at the United States Marine Hospital, Providence, on Tuesday. He had been in Mexico, as a Lieutenant in the North Carolina Regiment, and more recently seaman on board a vessel, lately arrived in Providence.

754. Melancholy Shipwreck and Loss of Life - The ship Mobile, Capt. Long, sailed from New Bedford on the 7th ult. bound to the Pacific Ocean, on a whaling voyage, having been fitted out for three years. On the 23d ult., when in about latitude 30 deg. N., longitude 62 deg. W., she encountered a severe gale, during which a tremendous sea broke on board, Capt. Long and Mr. Stewart, the chief mate, the carpenter, a boat steerer and seven seamen perished. <long story, ed.> Boston *Post* of Saturday.

755. Terrible Death on a Railroad - Yesterday morning between 1 and 2 o'clock, the mangled body of a man was found on the track of the Reading railroad, near Richmond, which was recognised as that of Francis Smith, one of the employees of the company at the switches. Both of his legs were cut off, and also one of his arms. He was undoubtedly run over by a train of cars during the night, but in what manner or at what precise time was not known. One leg was cut off between the hip joint and the knee, and the other at the knee. His arm was severed from the body just below the shoulder. The deceased was 25 years of age, and lived at Richmond. The coroner held an inquest on the body, and the jury rendered a verdict that he came to his death from the injuries, though the precise manner in which they were received, or the time when could not be ascertained. Philadelphia *Ledger*.

756. Railroad Accident and Death - We are informed that a Mr. Miller was crushed by the cars at Tonawanda, on Saturday last. He was standing by the side of the station house when the train was backed by it for some purpose, and was caught between the cars. He survived

the injury only about five hours. Niagara *Dem.*

757. Murder at Sea - A vessel called the St. Louis, left Vera Cruz for New York on the 21st ult. She had a crew of eight hands before the mast, two of whom were Spaniards, named Antonio Chapedor and Pedro Vantema. Shortly after leaving port, a steamboat came along side, and delivered on board a box of money for a Mr. Chappell, a passenger. On the voyage, two or three nights after being out, the two Spaniards above named, came aft, complained that the crew threatened to throw them overboard, and asked to remain aft. Their request was granted. The Captain and mate were then lying asleep upon a mattress. Soon after, supposing the Mate and Captain to be dozing, Chapedor jumped up, gave Mr. Chappell a fatal stab, and rushed upon the Captain and Mate. They however escaped, though the former received a thrust in the breast, the knife going to the shoulder blade. The crew were called, the two Spaniards secured, and put in irons. Mr. Chappell lived but 20 minutes. On being stabbed he exclaimed, "My God, what have I done that they should murder me!" The money for which this homicide was committed, and other murders attempted, was only $400 in silver, Mexican coin. It was thought to be much more. Chapedo and Vantema are now in prison in New York to answer. <Chapedor and Chapedo both used, ed.>

758. Decapitated by the Halter - The Niagara *Chronicle* of the 5th inst. says "Pursuant to his sentence, Thomas Brennen was hanged in front of the jail yesterday forenoon. The hangman gave him less than the usual fall - about ten feet; but strange to say, this jerk actually severed his head from his body, and both fell to the ground. We do not remember having heard or read of a similar occurrence. The rope used on this occasion was of the ordinary thickness, and the decapitation in all probability was the consequence of disease. When on the scaffold the miserable man denied his guilt. Since his conviction he has told different stories - varying so much that no faith could be placed in what he said."

759. Fatal Accident - On Monday last a span of horses, attached to a wagon, ran away with Mr. Henry Martin, about 60, of New Scotland, and one of the wheels of the wagon passed over him, in such a manner as to cause his death in a few hours after the accident.

October 28, 1848 (Saturday)

760. The trial of Dr. Joel Divine for the murder of Richard Wall took place at the Circuit Court of Poughkeepsie, Judge Edmonds presiding, last week. The trial commenced on Monday and the case was given to the jury on Friday morning. On Monday morning the jury were discharged, being unable to agree upon a verdict. At the time of their discharge they stood 5 for conviction, 5 for acquittal, and 2 for a verdict of manslaughter. Another trial will be ordered.

761. Death of Dixon H. Lewis - Hon. Dixon H. Lewis, a member of the United States Senate from Alabama died in the city of New York on Wednesday. He arrived in that city about two weeks ago on a visit and was shortly afterwards attacked with the disease which terminated fatally. Mr. Lewis was an able man and had attained a great popularity in his state, and in fact throughout the Union. In his death the nation has lost one of its ablest men and the United States Senate one of its most accomplished members.

762. Death of Joseph T. Lee, Esq. - On Saturday last, Joseph T. Lee, Esq., District Attorney of Dutchess Co., died very suddenly at Poughkeepsie. He died of a disease of the heart, with which he had been afflicted for three years past. His age was about 35 years. He was a man of considerable ability, and had discharged the duties of District Attorney, with satisfaction.

763. Ireland - The trial of Smith O'Brien has been concluded. This ardent patriot and self sacrificing man has been found guilty and sentenced to be hung by the neck until he is dead and them beheaded and quartered and his head placed at the disposal of Her Majesty!. Foreign News.

764. England - The Earl of Carlisle is dead, and the consequent elevation of Lord Morpeth to the House of Peers, creates a vacancy in the representation of the West Riding of Yorkshire. Foreign News.

765. Ulster Circuit Court - Jeremiah Pells vs Ext's of Abraham De Witt, dec'd. This was the most singular case of the calendar. The facts were as follows: Jeremiah Pells and wife, of Dutchess Co., from diversity of temper found the marriage yoke uneasy. Somewhere

about 1823 they separated, executing formal articles separating their interests. Pells went to Michigan, the wife came to Saugerties, and entered the service of Abraham De Witt, an ancient widower. About 1835 De Witt and Mrs. Pells were married by the Rev. Dr. Ostrander. Pells, we believe, having previously contracted a marriage in Michigan. De Witt died about 1845, and passed over his nominal wife in his will. She sued for the recovery of her dower as his wife, and was defeated by proof that Pells, the original husband, was alive. The present action was another suit instituted in the name of Jeremiah Pells to recover compensation for services, and the value of property carried into the family. The Jury found for Plaintiff, $868, being about one-third of the claim.

766. Lingfeldt, the murderer, was executed in the yard of the Philadelphia Jail yesterday about 2 o'clock, P. M. Yesterday forenoon he continued in conversation with a number of ministers of the gospel, and finally united with them in prayer. The Sheriff, about half-past 1 o'clock entered his cell and prepared him for the execution. He conversed freely with various clergymen on Thursday, and having become convinced that no hope of escape remained, his stoical indifference gave away to fear and anxiety. He ascended the scaffold with a firm step, still manifesting considerable indifference. After a short speech, which was interpreted by the Rev. Mr. Fleichman, of the German Baptist Church, he asserted his innocence of the murder, and still insisted that the fifteen witnesses swore falsely against him. He forgave all - the judges, the jury, the witnesses, and every body. Finally, he shook hands with the sheriff and the clergy, who were on the scaffold and at ten minutes before 2 o'clock the drop fell, and the doomed man, was launched into eternity. *True Sun.*

767. Married on the evening of the 17th inst., at the house of Mrs. Trumpbor, by Rev. N. H. Cornell, Mr. Egbert Cooper to Miss Caroline Trumpbour, all of this place. "The world was sad, the garden was a wild, And man, the hermit, sighed till woman smiled."

768. Married in this village, Oct 26th, by Rev. C. Shook, Mr. Stephen B. Chambers, of Marbletown, to Miss Amelia Post, of this village.

769. Married at the same place, and time, by the same, Mr. Henry Hagell, of New York City, to Miss Melissa Post, of this village. Cake received and excellent.

770. Run Away from the subscriber, Mary Ann Murry, an indented apprentice. All persons are hereby forbid harboring or trusting her on my account, as I will pay no debts of her contracting. Saugerties, Oct 24, 1848, Jonas Myer.

November 4, 1848 (Saturday)

771. Death of General Kearney - A telegraphic despatch from St. Louis, announces the death of Brigadier General Stephen W. Kearney, on Wednesday morning. No officer of the army stood higher in the estimation of his fellow soldiers or of the country generally. General Kearney was born in Newark, New Jersey, about the year 1793, and was thus in the 55th year of his age at the time of his death. He entered the army, as Lieut. in 1812; fought at Queenston and served through the war with credit. He was a Major in 1824, a Lieut. Col. in 1833, a full Colonel in 1836, and a full Brigadier General in 1846. His abilities as a tactician were acknowledged to be very superior, and have been frequently made use of by our government in drilling and improving the cavalry arm of the service. Our readers may perhaps not generally know that he was a brother of John W. Kearney, Esq. of this village. <more on General Kearney in the November 11 edition, including the fact that "he left a widow and several children, and died on the 31st of October.">

772. Fearful Shipwreck - The Schooner Sea Belle, of New Haven, sailed from Attakapas for New York on the 26th of September. On the night of the 13th of October, she was thrown on her beam ends, during a heavy gale, and three of her crew were drowned. The remaining four clung to the vessel, but one of them, Capt. Peterson, was so injured that he died on the following Sunday. The survivors, three in number, were on the 17th taken off the wreck by Captain Smith, of the barque I. Welsh, of New York and they speak in terms of great gratitude of the kindness of Captain Welsh and his crew.

773. Harrison G. Otis died on Saturday last, at Boston, aged 81 years. He was one of the early statesman of the Republic.

774. Married at Saugerties, on the 1st inst., by the Rev. Sherwood, of Hyde Park, H. B. Lathrop, to Charlotte, daughter of the late Thomas Barrell.

775. Married on the 28th ult., by the Rev. N. H. Cornell, Mr. Peter Mower, to Miss Elizabeth Lasher, all of Saugerties.

776. Died on the 31st October, Mr. James Cockburn, a highly respected citizen of this town, aged 74 years and 2 months.

November 11, 1848 (Saturday)

777. Shocking Accident - Mr. Calvin Symmes was instantly killed in a most shocking manner, in the Cotton Factory on Mount Ida, on Saturday the 4th inst. He had charge of one of the rooms, and wishing to make an alteration in his machinery staid <sic> at noon for the purpose, while the factory was stopped and the hands out to dinner. While he was in the act of putting on the belt to start up, he caught his hand in it and was carried round until he was crushed and torn horribly, one leg and arm being severed from his body. Troy *Post*.

778. Death of Col. James Johnson - We are called upon to announce the death of Col. James Johnson, of Liverpool, one of the oldest residents of this county, and within up to a few days of his death actively engaged in business. He was distinguished throughout his life for strict probity, great industry and perseverance. On Monday he was attacked with bilious cholic, which disease, in spite of the best medical remedies terminated his life yesterday morning. *Argus*.

779. Railroad Accident - A frightful railroad collision occurred on Thursday night of last week, about twelve o'clock, between Lynn and Salem, Mass. The persons killed or injured were in the train from Marblehead. It was not as large as the other and probably was not going at as great speed. The following is a list of the killed and wounded: Samuel Manningy, Jr., 25 years of age - shoe manufacturer; Nathaniel W. Roundy, John G. Stevens, John Cross, 15 years of age, son of a widow lady; Henry Trefry, 20 years of age, son of the cashiar <sic> of the Marblehead Bank, and a lad named --- Russell - all of Marblehead. Among the wounded are Benjamin Brown, son of Capt. B. Brown, who had both legs badly crushed, probably rendering

amputation necessary, Moses Hill, Esq., and a man named --- Gardiner, the latter dangerously; Mr. --- Drummer, Tilit Perkins, and several others, who were comparatively slightly bruised. <details of the accident not copied. ed.>

780. Drowned - On the evening of the 24th of October, John P. Clark, tender of Lock No. 12, at Cohoes, fell into the Lock and was drowned. A jury was called by J. Hastings, Coroner; and it appeared by the evidence given, that a boat, on its downward passage. was let into the Lock, and when the water was nearly drawn off, Mr. Clark, either fell from the side of the Lock or from the plank on the balance beam a distance of ten to twelve feet, into the water. A hand on the boat attempted to catch him as he fell but only caught his hat. The night was very dark, and his body was not recovered till the level was drawn off. The hands on the boat, when they found Mr. Clark was drowned - not to their credit for humanity - opened the gates and passed on, leaving the other Lock tender alone to raise help and get his companion out, as best he might. The jury found a verdict of accidental drowning. West Troy *Advocate*.

781. Horrible - The Alabama *State Guard* of the 24th ult, contains an account of the killing of a little boy in the neighborhood of Sullacoffa. Talapega Co. by his own father in a fit of partial derangement. The man named Rhodum, had been partially deranged for some time on the Biblical offerings. In one of those fits he killed his son and then piling rails and other wood upon ths body, he set fire to the whole. The wife found out what had been done, sent for the neighbors. When afterwards asked why he did so, he said that he was making an offering of the lamb. The body was considerably burnt before it was taken from under the pile, Rhodum is confined for the present in jail.

782. Breach of Promise - A case was tried a few days ago in the Circuit Court at Buffalo. The plaintiff was Mary Ann Cambell, and the defendant, Charles Jones. Courtship commenced in 1834. Defendant went West, and plaintive heard he had married another woman. On his return he offered to marry her, but she postponed the nuptials to learn whether he had in fact married as reported. Defendant then went west again and married another person. The jury punished him to the amount of $500. Rochester *American*.

783. Married on the 4th inst., by J. P. Foland, Esq., Mr. Joseph Herzog, of Saugerties to Miss Jeanette Midas, of the city of New York.

784. Died in the village of Poughkeepsie, on the 6th inst., William A. Ostrander, son of Philip Ostrander, deceased, aged 24 years. His sufferings were borne with christian fortitude, and his death was that of the righteous.

November 18, 1848 (Saturday)

785. Missionary Calamities - The English *Church and State Gazette* says: - We regret to learn from the public papers that Dr. Bettleheim and his family have been murdered at the capital of Loo Choo under the auspices of the Bishop of London, who promised we believe, to ordain him after a specified time of service, in the Loo Choo Mission, was a native of Hungary, was originally of the Jewish persuasion, and was educated for the surgical profession, but afterward joined the Church of England. He was a young man of much talent, and of no inconsiderable experience. His wife was a native of London, and we believe that they had two children. The disastrous fate which has fallen upon them is said to have visited the Roman Missionaries also.

786. Married at Coeymans, Albany Co., on the 11th inst., by Rev. C. Van Santvord, Peter Carknerd, to Sarah Vanderbilt, both of the former place.

November 25, 1848 (Saturday)

787. Awful and Fatal Accident - About 3 o'clock on Thursday afternoon last, Novatus Blish, Esq., a highly esteemed and respected citizen of Stamford, in the county, ascended a ladder and stepped upon a scaffold of an out building near his store, where is son was painting. The scaffolding appearing rather weak he turned and was about stepping upon the ladder to descend, when the scaffolding gave way, and Mr. Blish fell upon the end of the ladder, which had been broken off, and which entered the lower part of his body penetrating some twelve inches. As he fell his son drew him from the ladder, when he was taken to the house, where he lingered in great agony until Friday evening, when death ended his sufferings. We believe Mr. Blish was a native of this county and about 52 years of age. He had accumulated a

comfortable property, and has left a worthy family and many friends to deplore his awful and sudden death. Delaware *Gazette*.

788. Died in this town on Monday last, Helen Mariah, wife of Alexander Burhans, aged about 25 years.

December 2, 1848 (Saturday)

789. Suicide - We learn from the Poughkeepsie *Telegraph* that Doct. Joel Divine, on whose late trial for the murder of Richard Wall the jury were unable to agree, and who was in prison waiting for a second trial, committed suicide on Sunday morning last, by opening the jugular vein in his neck, which caused him to bleed to death. - He had made the incision with a surgical instrument called the scalpel. The cut was about two inches long. Both the vein and the artery were severed, showing that he meant to make sure work of self-destruction. The deceased was about 38 years of age.

790. Murder and Robbery - We learn through the St. Joseph (Missouri) *Gazette* of the 10th inst. the following horrid account of the murder of Paymaster Major Singer and his family: Just as we were going to press, we received information that Major Singer, Paymaster of the U. S. Army, was murdered and robbed in Saline Co. a few days since. He had in his possession $160,000, and was on his way to the upper part of this State, to pay the volunteers their three months' extra pay. His wife and sister-in-law were in company with him, who were also murdered. It is supposed they were murdered by the soldiers who were acting as an escort.

791. Lamentable and Fatal Accident - The New York *Tribune* states that James Planter, Esq., the sheriff elect of Otsego Co., was thrown from a wagon in the upper part of the city of New York, on Sunday, and fatally injured. 'He was taken up in a state in insensibility (says the *Tribune*) and conveyed to the Jefferson County House in the Third-Avenue. Doctors Bumstead and Parker were immediately sent for, when it was discovered that Mr. P.'s neck was broken, and although alive at the last account, no hopes were entertained of his recovery.'

792. An afflicted father would be grateful to receive information where he can find his son, named Urial Springstein, aged about 28, who left his home in Windsor, Broome Co., NY, on the 6th of November inst., deranged, and has not since been heard of. Any person who will return him to the subscriber, will be reasonably rewarded, and receive the thanks of his parents. Information may be sent to Windsor P. O., Broome Co., NY Uriah Springstein, November 22, 1848. Exchanges will confer a favor by copying the above.

793. The Barnstable *Patriot* states that Miss Betsey I. Knowles has been appointed Postmaster at Orleans, in place of Matthew Kingman, Esq., deceased.

794. Matthew A. Black, the barkeeper of the steamer Atlantic of Pittsburg, who shot Charles Saunders, a negro, in that city on the 22d instant, has been bailed out in the sum of $5000, the evidence showing that the act was committed upon strong provocation.

795. Death of an Old Jersey Woman - Sarah Long, a native of New Brunswick, died recently at her house in Madison street, NY, at the age of 109 years! She was a lady of fine spirits and good memory, and could walk about within three months of her death.

796. Fatal Accident - One of the newsboys, James Hays, 14 years of age, was run over this morning by the cars, and almost instantly killed. As the company very properly preclude boys from the depot, they are <not> usually able to get inside the cars until they pass outside the enclosure. They then jump on and ride a short distance, and jump off before the trains acquire great speed. This James designed to do this morning, but he did not attempt to get off until the train had reached the engine-house, and was moving with considerable rapidity; and when he attempted to get off, he jumped the wrong way, and held on the prevent himself from falling. In an instant his body was swung beneath the wheels of the car, and two of them ran over him. He was horribly mutilated, and died in half an hour. Alb. *Eve. Journal.*

797. Died in this village, on Sunday last, John C. Burhans. He was a member of the Ulster Lodge, I. O. of O. F. The funeral was attenned <sic> by the brotherhood.

December 9, 1848 (Saturday)

798. Died in this village, on the 30th ult. (at the residence of her brother John Field) after a long and painful illness Maria Field, daughter of O. Field, deceased, formerly of Sing Sing, Westchester Co., NY where the remains were taken for interment.

December 16, 1848 (Saturday)

799. Married in this village on the 10th inst., by the Rev. Mr. Oakley, Mr. Samuel Merclean, to Miss Julia Houghtaling, all of this village.

800. Married in this village on the 1st inst. at the house of Hon. J. Russell, by Rev. N. H. Cornell, Mr. Benjamin Winne, to Miss Nelly Cath. Cole, all of Saugerties.

801. Married at West Camp Landing, on the 9th inst., by the same, Mr. Claudius Lepareux, of Bristol, to Miss Hannah Conklin, of the former place.

802. For California - As I am about arranging my business preparatory to leaving for California I hereby call on all persons indebted to me to pay up on or before the first day of January next. All debts due me remaining unpaid at that time will be collected as soon as the law will permit. James Russell, Saugerties, Dec 16, 1848.

December 23, 1848 (Saturday)

Passage to California We have received many letters asking for information in regard to the best route to California, cost, distance, &c. The shortest passage, of course, can be made by the mail steamers from this port via Charges. <sic> The distance of the route to San Francisco is about 5,500 miles, and it is believed that the journey may be performed in 30 to 35 days. The cost to Chagres, in saloon, is $125 to $150; in a lower cabin, $100 to $120. The transit across the Isthmus is made partly in canoes and partly on mules. The journey is performed in two days, and costs $15 to $20. From Panama the costs are as follows:

Panama to Realejo, 700 miles in state rooms $64
   "   Acapulco. 1,500   125
   "   San Blas, or
   "   Mazatlin, 2,000   "   "   175

"	San Diego, 3,000	"	"	225
"	San Francisco, 3,500"	"		250

Passage in the lower cabin at a deduction of one fifth from the above rates. Passage in the forward cabin from Panama to either of the above named ports $100, including only the same rations as are furnished to the crew. Passengers in the after cabin are furnished bedding, but no wines and liquors, and will be allowed space for personal baggage, free to the extent of three hundred pounds. Freight on exces <sic> and all other goods $50 per ton, and one per cent on specie. Packages should not exceed 150 lbs. weight, for mule carriage. <long article, many more details>
N. Y. *Tribune*.

803. Hydrophobia - Mr. Abraham Decker of Bath, opposite Albany, died recently of hydrophobia. He was bitten in the lip, several weeks since, by a dog supposed to be mad. Frequently recurring symptoms of the disease were noticed, but attributed to another cause. He died, manifesting the usual evidences of this horrible disease. He was 39 years of age.

804. Murder of the Rev. Daniel Baker - Rev. W. Hill, of this city, received a letter conveying the sad intelligence, that Rev. Daniel Baker, who has been laboring as a missionary, under the care of the Presbyterian Board of Missions for some months past in Texas, was murdered in cold blood by the Camanche Indians while on his way from San Antonio de Bexar to Victoria. He was also scalped by the savages. The same band had killed about twenty persons in the vicinity a few days previous to his death. He was one of the most extensively known, laborious, useful and generally beloved ministers of the Presbyterian Church. Having labored in protracted meetings in nearly all the States and territories of the Union. He was for a number of years pastor of a flourishing church in Washington city, whence he removed to Frankfort, Ky., to take charge of the church there. From that place he was called to Holly Spring, Mass., where he remained until he went to Texas. Louisville *Courier*.

805. Arson and Suicide at Palmyra - We learn from the Rochester *Advertiser*, that on Monday last the barn of Mr. Samuel Wilbur, of Palmyra, was burned, together with a span of horses and other property. Some time after, Mr. B. Allen, father-in-law of Mr. W., was found hanging in another barn near by, which had also been fired, but did not burn. Mr. A. was a cattle buyer, and had been involved in a pecuniary controversy with his son-in-law that had led to a great bitterness of feeling. It is supposed that he fired the two barns and then hung himself expecting to be burned. Utica *Gazette*.

806. Coroner's Hays Inquest - On Monday last, on the body of Patrick Brady, an Irish laborer, at Rondout. From circumstances and testimony elicited on the inquest, it was believed that he came to his death by violence. Edward Cannon and James Davi were accused of committing the same. The Coroner issued warrants, and Cannon was arrested. The other is still at large. Kingston *Journal*.

January 27, 1849

807. Jan 14, Saugerties, Mr. Montgomery Landt to Mrs. Matilda Landt, both of Saugerties, by Rev. N.H. Cornell.

808. Jan 13, Rondout, Martin Stevenson to Hannah Jane Henderson, both of Eddyville, by Rev. B. T. Philips.

809. Jan 17, Eddyville, Coe F. Young, merchant, of Barryville, Sullivan Co., to Mary A., daughter of Peter Cornell, Esq., of Rosendale, by Rev. W. S. Mikels.

810. Jan 10, Mechanictown, Nathaniel C. Woolley of New Paltz to Cornelia Miller of Middletown, Orange Co., by Rev. H. Lounsbery.

February 17, 1849

811. Feb 7, Saugerties, Mr. Augustus W. Hunter to Miss Angelica Griffin, both of Catskill, by Rev. B. C. Crandall.

812. Feb 10, Bristol, at the home of Mr. David Volk, Alexander Lepareux to Miss Mary Underhill, both of Bristol, by Rev. N.H. Cornell.

February 24, 1849

813. Feb 2, Kingston, Mr. Abm. D. Whitaker to Miss Sarah Maria Yates, both of Flatbush, by Rev. C. Shook.

814. Feb 15, Kingston, Mr. William Cockburn to Miss Elizabeth, daughter of Tobias Van Buren, Esq., both of Kingston, by Rev. J. C. F. Hoes.

815. Feb 15, Kingston, Mr. Eli Morkee to Miss Francis Miller, both of Kingston, by Rev. J. C. F. Hoes.

816. Feb 8, Marbletown, Mr. Abraham W. Smedes of Hurley to Miss Belinda Davis of Marbletown, by Rev. W. Bloomer.

March 10, 1849

817. Mar 7, West Camp, Mr. John H. Morterstock to Miss Nelly Bear, both of West Camp, by Rev. N. H. Cornell.

818. Mar 8, Mr. George Alvin Ben to Miss Margaret Bear, both of West Camp, by Rev. N. H. Cornell.

March 17, 1849

819. Mar 4, Hurley, Mr. Hiram A. Cramer of Kingston to Miss Jerusha C. Nash of Hurley, by Rev. H. Wheeler.

March 31, 1849

820. Mar 19, Woodstock, Richard France to Julia Hoovenburg, both of Saugerties, by Rev. Alexander Gulick.

821. Mar 19, Rondout, Christian Charles Farney to Mrs. Barbara Kasper, both of High Falls, by Rev. C. H. Siebke.

April 14, 1849

822. Undated, Thomas S. Thompson of Saugerties to Louisa Weaver of Hudson, by Rev. Mr. Gosman.

April 21, 1849

823. Whereas by wife, Jane, has left my bed and board, without any cause or provocation, this therefore is to forbid all persons to harbor

her or to trust her on my account as I am determined not to pay any debts of her contracting. Signed William Post, Apr 6, 1849, Saugerties.

April 28, 1849

824. Apr 7, Flatbush, Mr. John H. Grassfield to Miss Lucinda Lasher, both of Saugerties, by Rev. J. M. Hulbert.

825. Apr 14, Flatbush, Mr. Thomas V. L. Whitaker of Kingston to Miss Nelly Ann Osterhout of Saugerties, by Rev. J. M. Hulbert.

826. Apr 26, Rondout, Mr. Henry Soule to Miss Catharine M. Burnette, by Rev. Mr. Still.

827. Apr 18, Kingston, Alonzo Nichols to Philis, daughter of William Mc George, by Rev. C. Shook.

May 5, 1849

828. May 2, at the house of Mrs. Trumpbour, Mr. Stephen Wolven to Miss Clarissa Hommel, both of the Town of Saugerties, by Rev. N. H. Cornell.

829. Apr 25, Flatbush, Robert Whitaker to Miss Estha Eliza Olivitt, both of Kingston, by Rev. Mr. Hulbert.

830. Apr 22, Rondout, John M. Castle to Catharine Myers, by Rev. Mr. Mikels.

May 12, 1849

831. May 6, Saugerties, Mr. Chancy M. Swart to Miss Catherine Lasher, both of Saugerties, by Rev. N. H. Cornell.

832. May 3, Ellenville, Mr. Charles Roves to Miss Amelia A. Snyder, both of Port Benjamin, Wawarsing, by Rev. S. B. Ayers.

May 19, 1849

833. May 12, Mr. Abram J. Myer to Miss Amanda M. Turner, both of Saugerties, by Rev. N. H. Cornell.

834. May 10, Rondout, Simon P. Morris to Mrs. Permelia Palmer, both of Dashville, Esopus, by Rev. W. S. Mikels.

May 26, 1849
835. May 13, Burlington, Vt., Mr. Robert S. Styles, printer, of Kingston to Miss Philura Adeline, only daughter of Mr. Warren Hatch of Burlington, by Rev. J. K. Converse.

836. May 16, South Rondout, Mr. Jefferson Mc Causland of Rondout to Miss Margaret, daughter of Robert Rouse of South Rondout, by Rev. B. T. Phillips.

837. May 17, Shandaken, Hiram W. Shultis to Miss Elizabeth Yerry, both of Woodstock, by William Risely.

June 2, 1849
838. May 26, Mr. John H. Stratten to Miss Wyan Hauver, both of Rondout, by Rev. B. T. Philips.

839. May 17, George Gifford, formerly of New Paltz, to Miss Eleanor C. Van Ramst, both of New York, by Rev. Dr. Lansing.

June 9, 1849
840. Jun 7, Mr. Benjamin Bronk to Miss Margaret Mower, by J. P. Foland, Esq.

June 16, 1849
841. Jun 2, Saugerties, Alexander Middaugh to Miss Susan Dier, both of Saugerties, by Rev. P. C. Oakley.

842. Jun 2, Saugerties, Peter Dier to Miss Margaret Parker, both of Saugerties, by Rev. P. C. Oakley.

843. Jun 6, Town of Lloyd, Mr. Edwin Cornell of Plattekilll to Miss Nancy E. Pratt of Lloyd Township, by Otis Church, Esq.

844. Mar 23, New Brunswick, New Jersey, Rev. Charles H. Still, pastor of the R. E. Church of New Paltz to Miss Margaret Acken of New Brunswick, by Rev. Geo. Schenck.

845. Jun 6, Albany, NY, at St. Mary's Cathedral, William F. Shufeldt of New York to Erina A., youngest daughter of the late Col. James R. Mullany, by Rev. Bishop Mc Closky.

June 23, 1849

846. Jun 15, Saugerties, Ira A. Shattuck of NYC to Rachel Baker of Hudson, by Rev. C. Van Santvoord.

847. Jun 7, Olive, Christopher S. Lockwood to Catharine Dubois, both of Olive, by Martin Schutt, Esq.

848. Jun 9, Olive, Isaac D. Eckert, Jr. to Sarah Ann Dubois, both of Olive, by Martin Schutt.

June 30, 1849

849. Jun 21, Henry Yerry to Mary Happy, both of Woodstock, by Rev. Alexander Gulick.

July 7, 1849

850. Jul 4, Saugerties, Nelson H. Burhans to Miss Cornelia Turck, both of Flatbush, by Rev. P. C. Oakley.

851. Jun 28, Rosendale, S. P. Keator to Miss Hannah Coutant, both of Rosendale, by Rev. Mr. Strong.

852. Jun 24, Rondout, John G. Laandan to Miss Martina Egger, both of High Falls, by Rev. C.H. Siebke.

July 14, 1849

853. Jun 25, Ellenville, John Lute to Catherine Sage, both of Sholem, by Milton Shelden, Esq.

July 21, 1849

854. Jul 4, Mr. William Rosa to Miss Ann Marie Brink, both of Kingston, by Rev. Mr. Hulbert.

855. Jul 12, Woodstock, Manassah Longyear of Kingston to Miss Elizabeth Hudler of Woodstock, by Rev. H. Wheeler.

856. Jul 15, Kingston, Abm. V. Wiest to Miss Wealthy A. Blake, both of Kingston, by Rev. C. Shook.

857. Jul 14, Moses E. Bishop to Miss Elizabeth Ann Short, both of Shandaken, by Martin Schutt, Esq.

858. Jul 3, New York City, Capt. John T. Roosa of Kingston to Miss Jane Rhodes of Hempstead, LI, by Rev. Mr. Wood.

859. Jun 30, Isaac Terwilliger to Miss H. Dubois, both of New Paltz, by Rev. B. F. Wile.

August 4, 1849
860. Jul 26, George Sparling to Miss Maria Krum, both of Saugerties, by Rev. H. Ostrander, D. D.

861. Jul 23, Saugerties, Reuben Burnet of Rondout to Miss Josephine Lewis of Saugerties, by Rev. Mr. Oakley.

August 11, 1849
862. Aug 5, Edwin D. Gay of Ellenville to Miss Maria Goetschius of Kingston, by Rev. Jno. C. F. Hoes.

863. Jul 4, Salem, Alfred Sluyter, merchant, to Miss Martha Ellen Richey, daughter of James Richey, Esq., all of Salem, by Rev. H. N. Wilbur.

864. Jul 15, Rondout, Charles August Heingmann to Miss Catharine Elizabeth Kuhaupt, both of Rondout, by Rev. C. H. Siebkie.

865. Aug 1, Adam Braman to Miss Jane A. Meeham, both of Esopus, by Rev. A. Fort.

866. Jul 2, Poughkeepsie, Eli Bingle to Miss Rosina Dunwoodie, both of Kingston, by Rev. S. D. Cochran.

August 25, 1849
867. Aug 19, Glasco, Daniel B. Stow, 3rd to Miss Emily B. Delanoy, both of Rondout, by Rev. P. C. Oakley.

868. Aug 19, Kingston, Robert Fairchild of West Point to Miss Sarah M. Place of Kingston, by Rev. C. Shook.

869. Aug 12, Rondout, Daniel Spindler to Louisa Rembaldt, both of Kingston, by Rev. C. H. Siebke.

870. Aug 14, Rondout, Emanuel Fuehs to Catherine Mecking, both of Rondout, by Rev. C. H. Siebke.

871. Jul 12, Milton, Henry Conklin to Mary E. Carpenter, both of Milton, by Rev. Mr. Hall.

September 1, 1849

872. Aug 29, Town of Saugerties, Mr. Tjerck Joy of Kingston to Miss Betsy Adaline Valck of Town of Saugerties, by Rev. Mr. Redford.

873. Aug 30, Mr. Elias Snyder of Unionville to Miss Eliza Lasher of Saugerties, by Rev. N. H. Cornell.

874. Aug 19, Shandaken, Daniel D. Decker to Miss Lucretia Rogers, both of Shandaken, by William Risley, Esq.

875. Aug 23, Rochester, Jacob Osterhoudt to Miss Maria Rider, both of Rochester, by Rev. C. L. Van Dyck.

876. Aug 27, Marbletown, Cornelius Schoonmaker to Miss Ann Eliza Bennet, both of Rochester, by Rev. C. L. Van Dyck.

877. Aug 19, Rondout, Louis Weister to Miss Theresa Honk, both of High Falls, by Rev. W. S. Mikels.

September 8, 1849

878. Sep 4, Saugerties, Mr. Samuel P. Coggeshall to Miss Martha Knapp, both of Saugerties, by Rev. C. Van Santvoord.

879. Sep 1, at the home of Mrs. Trumpbour, Mr. John Acker to Miss Rachel Vroman of West Camp, by Rev. N.H. Cornell.

880. Sep 3, James Crawley to Mary Ann Mc Graw, by J. P. Foland, Esq.

September 15, 1849

881. Aug 30, Mr. James Welch to Miss Elizabeth Delanoy, both of the Town of Saugerties, by Rev. V. M. Hulbert.

882. Sep 9, Mr. John Henry Mickle to Miss Catherine Ann Brink, both of the Town of Saugerties, by Rev. V. M. Hulbert.

883. Sep 13, Saugerties, Mr. Augustus Myer to Miss Hermina Herzog, both of Saugerties, by J. P. Foland, Esq.

September 22, 1849

884. Sep 19, Saugerties, Mr. Henry L. Finger to Miss Ann Christina Snyder, both of Saugerties, by Rev. P.C. Oakley.

885. Sep 19, Saugerties, Mr. George Cunningham, a printer, to Miss Mary Elizabeth Miner, both of Saugerties, by Rev. B. C. Crandall.

886. Sep 13, Mr. Abraham Hommel to Miss Catherine Mower, both of Saugerties, by Rev. Mr. Beers.

887. Sep 15, Saugerties, Mr. Henry Kline to Miss Elizabeth Keener, both of Saugerties, by Rev. P. C. Oakley.

September 29, 1849

888. Sep 22, Saugerties, Mr. Edmund O'Brien to Miss Jane Ann Fiero, by Rev. C. Van Santvoord.

889. Sep 22, Saugerties, Mr. Jesse Middaugh to Miss Elmira Hardenburgh, both of Saugerties, by Rev. P. C. Oakley.

890. Sep 25, Mr. William Rhind to Miss Susan Preston, both of Saugerties, by Rev. H. Ostrander, D. D.

891. Sep 17, Mr. James Williamson to Miss Jane Powell, both of Saugerties, by Rev. H. Ostrander, D. D.

892. Sep 26, Mr. James J. Van Der Beck to Miss Mary Elizabeth, daughter of Christian Fiero, deceased, all of the Town of Saugerties, by Rev. H. Ostrander, D. D.

893. Sep 20, Olive, John Swartwart to Mary E. Ketch, both of Olive, by Martin Schutt, Esq.

October 6, 1849

894. Sep 29, Mr. William Carle to Miss Matilda Rosa, both of Saugerties, by Rev. N. H. Cornell.

October 13, 1849

895. Oct 9, Saugerties, Gaston Wilbur to Maria, daughter of Mr. Peter D. Schoonmaker, both of Saugerties, by Rev. C. Van Santvoord.

896. Oct 9, Kingston, Mr. Jansen Hasbrouck to Miss Charlotte, daughter of J. D. Ostrander, Esq., by Rev. J. C. F. Hoes.

October 20, 1849

897. Oct 3, Greenfield, Wawarsing, Mr. William Birchall to Miss Sarah Powell, by Rev. Thomas Newman.

898. Oct 4, Oak Ridge, Wawarsing, Charles Williams to Almira Slater, by H. B. Taylor, Esq.

899. Oct 9, Martin C. Hotaling to Ann Lee, both of Rondout, by Rev. Mr. Phillips.

900. Oct 11, Isaac Houghtailing of Esopus to Eleanor Martin of Lloyd, by Rev. A. Fort.

901. Oct 4, Augustus Lewis to Hannah Rich, both of Woodstock, by Rev. Alex. Gulick.

902. Sep 29, Jacob Smith of High Falls to Hannah De Puy of Marbletown, by Rev. E. De Puy.

903. Oct 19, Apollas Decker to Jane Westbrook, both of Rochester, by Rev. E. De Puy.

904. Oct 6, Rosendale, Richard Freer to Charlott Schoonmaker, both of Rosendale, by Rev. C. L. Van Dyck.

905. Oct 10, Marbletown, William P. Cole of Hurley to Margaret B. Oliver of Marbletown, by Rev. C. L. Van Dyck.

October 27, 1849

906. Oct 25, Saugerties, Charles S. English to Ellen D., daughter of the late Franklin Miller, by Rev. Dr. Ostrander.

907. Oct 25, Saugerties, John E. Fenwick to Elizabeth, daughter of Captain John Field, by Rev. C. Van Santvoord.

908. Oct 15, Quarryville, Mr. Christian C. Fiero to Miss Sarah J. Maxwell, both of Quarryville, by Rev. B. Redford.

909. Oct 18, Mr. William Yerry to Miss Irena Shultis, both of Woodstock, by Rev. H. Wheeler.

910. Oct 18, Woodstock, Mr. James Smith of Wilbur to Miss Matilda Shultis of Woodstock, by Rev. H. Wheeler.

November 10, 1849

911. Oct 28, Saugerties, John H. Vandenbergh to Miss Sophia Burnett, both of Saugerties, by Rev. P. C. Oakley.

912. Nov 3, on the steamboat Robert L. Stevens, Abraham F. Valck to Miss Maria Hommel, both of Saugerties, by Rev. H. Ostrander, D. D.

913. Nov 8, Saugerties, Henry Fuller to Miss Margaret, daughter of Peter Van Vlierden, all of Saugerties, by Rev. C. Van Santvoord.

November 17, 1849

914. Nov 6, Ellenville, Mr. John H. Elting to Miss Sarah Carling, by Rev. Thomas Newman.

915. Nov 4, Woodstock, Joel Green to Miss Harriet A. Furman, both of West Hurley, by Rev. Mr. Voorhees.

916. Nov 8, Thomas Fowler to Ann Heustis, both of Rondout, by Rev. T. B. Phillips.

917. Nov 7, Kingston, Matthew P. Dewitt of Hurley to Blandina Elting of Kingston, by Rev. J. C. Cruickshank.

November 24, 1849

918. Nov 4, Alfred F. Quinlan, printer, of Binghampton to Miss Henrietta Amelia, daughter of Jos. Huntington, Esq., of Thompson, Sullivan Co., NY, by Rev. Mr. Bloomer.

December 1, 1849

919. Nov 29, Saugerties, Robert A. Hempstead to Miss Sarah C., daughter of Mr. George Gleason, all of Saugerties, by Rev. C. Van Santvoord.

920. Nov 6, Mr. Jacob Snyder of Saugerties to Miss Christina C. Brink of Kingston, by Rev. V. M. Hulbert.

921. Nov 7, James E. Wolven of Woodstock to Miss Nelly Hendricks of Saugerties, by Rev. M. L. Schenck.

922. Nov 24, Abraham Van Houvenburgh to Miss Elizabeth Sparling, both of Saugerties, by Rev. M. L. Schenck.

December 8, 1849

923. Dec 3, George Colmitz to Margaret Stouse, both of Saugerties, by J. P. Foland, Esq.

924. Nov 18, Town of Saugerties, Mr. George C. Zeidder to Miss Hannah Jones, by Rev. John Hendricks.

925. Nov 16, Saugerties, Mr. John H. Coon to Mrs. Ella Cook.

December 15, 1849

926. Dec 1, Andrew Vedder to Miss Eliza Brower, both of Kingston, by Rev. M. Schenck.

927. Dec 8, Levi Carle of Kingston to Miss Lydia C. Wicks of Saugerties, by Rev. M. Schenck.

928. Dec 6, Mr. Jacob Wolven to Miss Lavinia Lasher, both of Saugerties, by Rev. N. H. Cornell.

December 22, 1849

929. Dec 13, Rochester, Mr. Nelson Krom to Miss Elizabeth Davis, both of Rochester, by Rev. Cornelius Wyckoff.

930. Dec 5, John J. Mc Lain to Miss Harriet C. Ackert, both of Esopus, by Rev. Sherman Hoyt.

931. Dec 8, Ellenville, Mr. George Miller to Miss Mary Connelly, both of Ellenville, by R. B. Taylor, Esq.

932. Dec 11, Ellenville, Mr. John E. Sherwood to Miss Mary Ann Maclins, both of Kingston, by Rev. S. B. Ayres.

January 19, 1850

933. Jan 1, Town of Saugerties, Ira T. Smith to Ann E., daughter of Jacob C. Barringer, Esq., all of Catskill, by Rev. D. Lyman.

934. Jan 10, Town of Saugerties, Cornelius I. Elmendorf of Saugerties to Catherine Dedrick of Catskill, by Rev. D. Lyman.

935. Jan 12, Town of Saugerties, Joseph T. Gardiner to Eliza Moon, both of Catskill, by Rev. D. Lyman.

January 26, 1850

936. Dec 25, Saugerties, Frederick Muller to Miss Adaline Maioff, both of Saugerties, by Rev. P. C. Oakley.

937. Dec 16, Saugerties, Alexander Clum to Miss Jane M. Freligh, both of Saugerties, by Rev. P. C. Oakley.

February 2, 1850

938. Jan 23, Kingston, Cornelius S. Stilwell of New York to Miss Amelia, daughter of John H. Schryver, by Rev. H. W. Smuller.

939. Jan 24, Shokan, Wm. Stewart of Marbletown to Miss Eliza Breakey of Olive, by Rev. J. N. Voorhis.

February 9, 1850

940. Jan 26, Kingston, Mr. William Lasher to Miss Isabella Spielman, both of Woodstock, by Rev. J. C. F. Hoes.

941. Jan 30, Kingston, Mr. James Van Vliet to Miss Lucy A. Dubois, both of Kingston, by Rev. J. C. F. Hoes.

942. Jan 30, Catskill, Almon Canfield, Esq. of Malden to Miss Elizabeth Smith of Freehold, by Rev. Dr. Porter.

February 16, 1850

943. Feb 14, Saugerties, John Jay Underhill to Miss Mary E. Schoonmaker, both of Saugerties, by Rev. P. C. Oakley.

944. Jan 27, Saugerties, Mr. Jacob Lumis to Miss Margaret Ann Cook, both of Saugerties, by Rev. H. Wheeler.

945. Feb 4, Kingston, Daniel Eckert to Miss Rebecca Dumont, both of Kingston, by Rev. P. P. Sandford, D. D.

946. Feb 7, Olive, Cornelius Elmendorf to Charlotte Bogart, both of Olive, by Martin Schutt, Esq.

947. Feb 7, Olive, Herman Darkley of Schoharie Co., NY to Sarah Jane Palen of the Town of Olive, by Martin Schutt, Esq.

948. Feb 9, Hurley, Jacob Crips to Lydia Sluyter, by Ten Eyck Dewitt, Esq.

February 23, 1850

949. Feb 7, Kingston, Calvin Schoonmaker to Miss Charlotte Basten, both of Marbletown, by Rev. C. L. Van Dyck.

950. Feb 14, Marbletown, Mr. William Smith of Esopus to Miss Sarah Jane Terwilliger of Marbletown, by Rev. C. L. Van Dyck.

March 2, 1850

951. Feb 23, Town of Saugerties, Mr. Hiram Van Hoovenberg to Miss Sarah A. Stilling, both of the Town of Saugerties, by Rev. N. H. Cornell.

952. Feb 20, Kingston, George Southwick of Rondout to Miss Cecilia A. Myer of Kingston, by Rev. C. Shook.

March 16, 1850

953. Mar 8, at the home of Jacob Mussier, Esq., Mr. John I. Warters of Quarryville to Miss Sarah Mussier of West Camp, by Rev. N. H. Cornell. <further research shows that the groom's name was Waters, ed.>

954. Mar 6, Kingston, J. R. Styles to Miss Rosina Pardee, both of Kingston, by Rev. C. Shook.

March 23, 1850

955. Mar 20, Mr. Solomon Day to Miss Louisa Amy, both of Cairo, by Rev. N. H. Cornell.

April 6, 1850

956. Apr 4, Mr. John Hillas to Miss Isabella Williamson, both of Saugerties, by Rev. H. Ostrander.

April 13, 1850

957. Mar 30, Saugerties, Mr. Anthony Jarver to Miss Rachel Jane Middaugh, both of Saugerties, by Rev. P. C. Oakley.

958. Apr 6, Saugerties, Mr. Edwin Ryne to Miss Jane Mc Linden, both of Saugerties, by Rev. Robert Fisher.

April 20, 1850

959. Apr 6, Mr. Barnet A. Lewis of Woodstock to Miss Mary Smith of Catskill, by Rev. Mr. Lyman.

960. Apr 14, F. B. Purdy of Plattsburgh, NY to Miss Mary A. Hibbard of Fayetteville, Onondago Co., NY, by Rev. C. Shook.

May 4, 1850

961. Apr 30, Matthew T. Trumpbour of Kingston to Miss Arietta Swart of Saugerties, by Rev. M. L. Schenck.

962. Apr 25, Mr. Ranson Prout of Durham, Middlesex Co., Conn. to Mary A. Eckler of Catskill, by Rev. D. Lyman.

963. Apr 18, James A. Jansen of Olive to Miss Catherine Koons of Rochester, by Rev. E. De Puy.

May 11, 1850

964. May 4, Saugerties, Stephen J. France of Kingston to Catherine C. Vanhovenburgh of Saugerties, by Rev. P. C. Oakley.

965. May 1, Mr. Horace W. Montross of Ellenville to Miss Sarah E. Dutcher of Cairo, by Rev. D. Lyman.

966. May 4, Mr. Jacob J. Guilfuss of Hunter to Miss Sally More of Hurley, by Rev. Alexander Gulick.

967. May 8, Saugerties, Henry W. Van Buskirk of Rondout to Martha N. Ryan of Coeymans, by Rev. C. Van Santvoord.

May 25, 1850

968. May 4, Martin Roosa to Miss Catharine Hasbrouck, both of Woodstock, by Rev. M. L. Schenck.

969. May 4, Louis Cashdollar of Kingston to Miss Margaret Van Aken of Saugerties, by Rev. M. L. Schenck.

970. May 16, Calvin D. Davis to Miss Amelia Holmes, both of West Hurley, by Rev. M. L. Schenck.

971. May 19, Woodstock, Mr. George Rick to Miss Harriet Roosa, both of Woodstock, by J. S. Ostrom, Esq.

972. May 14, Thomas Rowland to Jane Finley, both of Rondout, by Rev. B. T. Philips.

973. May 12, Rondout, Alanson Snook of Columbus Point to Catherine Barry of Rondout, by Rev. Mr. Martin.

974. Apr 16, John Kraft of Kingston to Altanah Minnerly of Wilbur, by Rev. H. W. Smuller.

975. May 11, Henry Myer of Rosendale to Elizabeth Mc Cool of Kingston, by Rev. H. W. Smuller.

976. May 16, William Roosa to Effe Maria Wager, both of Marbletown, by Rev. C. L. Van Dyck.

977. May 18, James Hill to Hannah Eckert, both of Olive, by Martin Schutt, Esq.

June 1, 1850

978. May 22, Mr. Jacobus Longyear to Miss Mariah Catherine Newkirk, both of Woodstock, by Rev. Alexander Gulick.

979. May 22, Kingston, by her father, Hannah Van Wyck, daughter of Rev. Dr. Westbrook to Charles W. Darrett, Esq., of Portland, Maine.

980. May 22, Poughkeepsie, at St. Paul's Church, Hon. Charles H. Ruggles to Mary C. Livingston, widow of Edward P. Livingston, by Rev. A. D. Traver.

981. May 20, Milford, Pa., John D. La Forge, Esq. to Catharine H. Burnett, formerly of Kingston, by Rev. T. Wilmer.

982. May 16, Philip Shults to Mary Ann Smith, both of Wilbur, by Rev. J. F. C. Hoes.

983. May 23, Henry Short of Shandaken to Susan Ann Short of Woodstock, by Rev. Jacob N. Voorhis.

984. May 23, Cyrus Elmendorf of West Hurley to Mary Wilder of Olive, by Rev. Jacob N. Voorhis.

June 8, 1850

985. Jun 4, Ulster, at the home of Mr. William T. Beach, Mr. Silas H. Buttrick (of the firm Lombard and Buttrick, NY) to Miss Harriet Bradbury of Portland, Maine, by Rev. Edwin A. Nicholas, Rector of Trinity Church.

986. Jun 1, Saugerties, John A. Ellinger to Sarah Christina Schutt, both of Saugerties, by Rev. C. Van Santvoord.

987. May 27, New Paltz, Floyd Smith Mc Kinistrey of Shawangunk to Gertrude M., daughter of R. Eltinge of New Paltz, by Rev. C. H. Still.

988. May 30, John W. Du Bois to Sarah, daughter of E. Deyo of New Paltz, by Rev. C. H. Still.

989. May 23, Poughkeepsie, Robert Mitchell, Esq. to Sarah M. Finley, by Rev. Mr. Buel.

990. May 25, Rondout, John Allcorn to Mrs. Elizabeth Snelling, both of Rondout, by Rev. B. T. Phillips.

991. May 29, Tivoli, Andrew D. W. Hardenbergh of Eddyville to Mrs. Rachel Schepmoes of Kingston, by Rev. David Morris.

992. May 27, Preston, Conn., Mr. John P. Ross of South Dover to Miss Esther A. Bryan of Preston, Conn., by Rev. Mr. Scott.

June 15, 1850

993. Jun 5, Poughkeepsie, Hiram Oakley to Miss Catharine W. Bush of Kingston, by Rev. L. M. Vincent.

994. Jun 6, Town of Saugerties, Clark Bradley of Norwalk, Conn. to Miss Rosina Swart of Saugerties, by Rev. J. C. F. Hoes.

995. Jun 6, Town of Saugerties, Jacob Plough, Jr. of Kingston to Miss Helena C. Swart of the Town of Saugerties, by Rev. J. C. F. Hoes.

996. Jun 5, Eddyville, Richard G. Townsend of New York to Miss Francis M. Secor of Eddyville, by Rev. B. T. Philips.

997. Jun 2, Hendrick Knoch of Saxonburg, Butler Co., Pa. to Miss Louisa Diechloof of High Falls.

998. Jun 6, Eddyville, Benson F. Ackerman to Miss Mary Elizabeth Carmichael, both of High Falls, by Rev. E. De Puy.

June 22, 1850

999. Jun 18, Catskill, Mr. John V. Sutphin of New Brunswick to Miss Josephine Chalett of Catskill, by Rev. John L. See.

1000. Jun 11, Baltimore, John Bigelow of New York to Jane Tunis, daughter of the late Evan Poultney of Baltimore, by Rev. Mr. Backus.

1001. Jun 12, at the home of James Cole, Jacob R. Ostrander to Jane Van Vliet, both of Hurley, by Rev. J. F. C. Hoes.

June 29, 1850

1002. Jun 22, Saugerties, Jacob Carn to Rachel Maria, daughter of Mr. Simeon P. Myer, all of Saugerties, by Rev. C. Van Santvoord.

1003. Jun 22, Saugerties, Don Albert French to Mary Margaret, daughter of Emanuel Roosa, both of Saugerties, by Rev. Henry Ostrander, D. D.

1004. Undated, in New York City, Mr. Edward Brink of Kingston to Miss Anna R. Whiting of New York City, by Rev. Eli Lathrop.

July 6, 1850

1005. Jun 4, Saugerties, Mr. John Teistler of Samsonville to Hannah Caroline Townsend of Saugerties, by Rev. Mr. Fisher.

1006. Jun 26, Kingston, James S. Evans, cashier of the Ulster Co. Bank, to Mary, daughter of Jacob H. Dewitt of Kingston, by Rev. Thomas Dewitt, D. D. of New York.

1007. Jun 20, New Paltz Landing, John W. Allen to Rebecca J. Dilks, by Rev. M. F. Lebenan.

July 13, 1850

1008. Jul 6, Saugerties, at the Exchange Hotel, Oscar Philips to Miss Jane Laman, both of Kingston, by Rev. R. A. Chalker.

1009. Jun 25, Whitmore Baxter to Mary J. Terwilliger of Marlborough, by Rev. L. M. Vincent of Poughkeepsie.

July 20, 1850

1010. Jul 18, Saugerties, Mr. Andrew Warner to Elizabeth Jack, both of Plattekill, at the house of Francis Haber, by Rev. N. H. Cornell.

1011. Jul 18, Saugerties, Mr. Frederick Weisner to Miss Elizabeth Miller, both of Plattekill, by Rev. N. H. Cornell.

1012. Jul 18, Saugerties, Mr. Michael Spahn to Miss Catherine Egent, both of Plattekill, by Rev. N. H. Cornell.

July 27, 1850

1013. Jul 24, William H. Garrison to Elizabeth Bois, both of the Town of Saugerties, by J. P. Foland, Esq.

1014. Jun 26, Flatbush, Mr. John Young to Miss Sarah Young, both of Glasco, by Rev. V. M. Hulbert.

1015. Jul 11, Shocan, Mr. Martin H. Crispell to Miss Sarah A. Eckert, both of Olive, by Rev. Mr. Harlow.

August 24, 1850

1016. Aug 1, Freehold, Jason Stevens, Esq. of Cairo to Miss Rebecca C. Zieliff of Freehold, by Rev. Edward Hopper.

1017. Aug 5, Poughkeepsie, Mr. Andrew Dewitt of Kingston to Miss Charlotte Griffin of Poughkeepsie, by Rev. Mr. Kettell.

August 31, 1850

1018. Aug 28, Mr. James Reed to Miss Elizabeth Fox, both of Saugerties, by Rev. R. A. Chalker.

1019. Aug 19, Saugerties, Van Keuren Green to Elizabeth Gibbs, both of Kingston, by Rev. C. Van Sanvord.

1020. Aug 15, Shawangunk, George Knapp of New York City to Miss Margaret, daughter of Richard Hardenberg, by Rev. John B. Alliger.

September 7, 1850

1021. Sep 3, Saugerties, Mr. John Van Valkenberg of Courtland Co., NY to Miss Marietta Forrow of Hillsdale, Columbia Co., by Rev. R. A. Chalker.

1022. Sep 5, Saugerties, Elijah Wells of Cairo to Miss Eliza Trumpbour of Saugerties, by Rev. R. A. Chalker.

September 14, 1850

1023. Sep 8, Saugerties, Mr. George B. Matthews to Miss Mary A. Henry, both of Saugerties, by Rev. E. A. Nichols.

1024. Sep 11, Town of Saugerties, Mr. John Fiero to Geneva, NY to Miss Martha, daughter of John Gillespy, Esq. of Saugerties, by Rev. C. Van Sanvord.

September 21, 1850

1025. Sep 12, Saugerties, Mr. Daniel S. Warner of Rondout to Miss Nancy Ryan of Coeymans, by Rev. R. A. Chalker.

September 28, 1850

1026. Sep 23, NYC, Mr. J. G. Glenney of the firm of Coggeshall & Glenney of Milwaukie to Maria L., daughter of the Hon. Charles H. Pond of Milford, Conn.

1027. Sep 21, Saugerties, Mr. Wm. H. Simmons to Miss Charlotte A. M. France, both of Saugerties, by Rev. R. A. Chalker.

1028. Sep 19, Flatbush, Mr. Abram Vredenbergh of Glasco to Miss Eliza Ann Hendricks of Flatbush, by Rev. V. M. Hulbert.

1029. Sep 19, Flatbush, Mr. Charles Burhans of Flatbush to Miss Emeline Lewis of New York City, by Rev. V. M. Hulbert.

1030. Sep 26, Flatbush, Mr. Martin Hendricks to Miss Harriet Ann Wynkoop, both of Flatbush, by Rev. V. M. Hulbert.

October 5, 1850

1031. Oct 1, Fallsburg, Sullivan Co., John Kiersted, Jr. of Saugerties to Maria A., daughter of the late Thomas S. Lockwood of Fallsburg, by Rev. C. Van Sanvord.

1032. Sep 25, Mr. Peter Reynolds to Miss Eliza Elting, both of Woodstock, by Rev. Alexander Gulick.

1033. Sep 26, Theodore Duboise of Olive to Nelly Ann Britt of Beaverkill, by Rev. Alexander Gulick.

1034. Oct 1, Mr. Abram Martin to Miss Sarah Ann Myer, by Rev. M. L. Schenck.

1035. Sep 28, Mr. Joshua Emerick to Rachel Christina Van Aken, by Rev. M. L. Schenck.

October 12, 1850

1036. Oct 9, Mr. William Wynkoop to Miss Susan Mariah Snyder, both of Saugerties, by Rev. N. H. Cornell.

1037. Oct 2, New York, George Merwin Atwater to Harriet Romeyn, daughter of Rev. Dr. Brodhead, all of Brooklyn, by Rev. J. Brodhead at North Dutch Church.

October 19, 1850

1038. Oct 8, John B. Post of Rondout to Elon Mc Eny of Wilbur, by Rev. Jno. C. F. Hoes.

1039. Oct 10, St. Andrew's, Orange Co., Dr. J. V. Holt to Esopus to Miss Dickerson of St. Andrew's, by Rev. Mr. Slingerland.

1040. Oct 12, Sylvester Evertson to Miss Jane Elizabeth Benson of Saugerties, by Rev. Dr. Wyckoff.

October 26, 1850

1041. Sep 24, Saugerties, Mr. Joseph Kingsland to Miss Margaret Ellen Stewart, both of Saugerties, by Rev. Mr. Nichols.

1042. Sep 22, Fishkill, Mr. John A. Turck of Saugerties to Miss Mary, daughter of Mr. John Ter Bush of Fishkill, by Rev. B. M. Genung.

1043. Sep 12, Kingston, Joseph B. Anderson to Miss Jane Emeline Rykert, both of Kingston, by Rev. Daniel Smith.

1044. Sep 6, Shokan, Aaron Scudder of Roxbury, Delaware Co. to Mary E. Ennist of Olive, by Rev. S. Harlow.

1045. Sep 10, Shokan, John Boice to Mary Ann Crispell, both of Olive, by Rev. S. Harlow.

1046. Sep 14, Newburgh, E. Pitts, Esq., Editor of the Poughkeepsie *American* to Margaret A. Whited of Newburgh, by Rev. J. Scott.

November 9, 1850

1047. Nov 3, Saugerties, Mr. George W. Dunn of Rondout to Miss Hannah Foland of Saugerties, by Rev. Mr. Chalker.

1048. Nov 6, Saugerties, Thomas S. Dawes, MD to Miss Elizabeth, daughter of the Hon. Jeremiah Russell, by Rev. Mr. Chalker.

1049. Oct 31, Mr. Moses Shultis of Woodstock to Miss Sarah Eliza Sax of Hurley, by Rev. Alexander Gulick.

1050. Oct 26, Mr. William Turck to Miss Lucinda Porter, by Rev. V. M. Hulbert.

1051. Oct 29, Silas Kiser of Newburgh to Evelina Houghtailing of Kingston, by Rev. J. C. F. Hoes.

1052. Oct 30, John Codington of Hurley to Judith M. Dubois of Kingston, by Rev. J. C. F. Hoes.

1053. Oct 26, Mr. Morgan L. Sparling to Miss Ann Roosa, both of Marbletown, by Rev. C. L. Van Dyke.

1054. Oct 30, Mr. Joseph K. Hornbeck to Miss Hilah Wood, both of Rochester, by Rev. C. L. Van Dyke.

1055. Oct 31, Mr. Daniel Maxson to Miss Elizabeth Ann Dumond, both of Hurley, by Rev. C. L. Van Dyke.

November 16, 1850
1056. Nov 9, Mr. Moses F. Dewitt to Miss Mary E. Martin, both of Saugerties, by Rev. R. A. Chalker.

November 23, 1850
1057. Nov 13, Maple Grove, Kansas, C. Byron Bostwick of New York to Annetta Cockburn, daughter of the late John Cockburn of Kingston, by Rev. Dr. Muhlenberg of New York.

1058. Nov 13, Rondout, James Rose of Wurtsboro to Emily Hotchkiss of Rondout, by Rev. C. F. Pelton.

November 30, 1850
1059. Nov 24, Saugerties, Mr. Lorenzo R. Blanchard, printer, of New York City, to Miss Sarah Pultz of Saugerties, by Rev. Robert Fisher.

1060. Nov 28, Saugerties, Mr. Cornelius Van Buren to Miss Saloma Roe, both of Kingston, by Rev. R. A. Chalker.

1061. Nov 14, Kingston, Andrew J. Snyder to Catherine Snyder, both of Rosendale, by Rev. C. L. Van Dyke.

1062. Nov 21, Peter Van Etten of Kingston to Sally Ann Wolfin of Saugerties, by Rev. Alexander Gulick.

1063. Nov 16, Olive, Thomas Jansen, Jr. of Woodstock to Marilla G. Morehouse of Olive, by Martin Schutt.

December 28, 1850

1064. Dec 25, Saugerties, Mr. Charles E. Cornwell of Utica to Miss Jane Ann Williams of Saugerties, by Rev. Robert Fisher.

1065. Dec 7, M. Hackison to Eve Jennins, both of Shawangunk, by Rev. Dr. Johnson.

February 1, 1851

1066. Jan 22, Coxsackie, Mr. Justus A. Wright of Sacramento, Calif. to Miss Susan Backus of Coxsackie, by Rev. J. Searle.

1067. Jan 22, Albany, Gilbert Lusk, Esq. of Coxsackie to Miss Elizabeth Truesdall of Albany.

February 15, 1851

1068. Feb 13, Mr. James Putney of Kingston to Miss Elizabeth C. France of Saugerties, by Rev. R. A. Chalker.

March 1, 1851

1069. Feb 25, Saugerties, Mr. Henry Beeker to Mrs. Eve Tenbrouck, both of Saugerties, by Rev. Robert Fisher.

1070. Feb 26, Saugerties, Mr. Morgan Gray of Olive to Miss Rachel Freligh of the Town of Saugerties, by Rev. C. Van Santvoord.

1071. Feb 11, Flatbush, Mr. Peter Dubois of Kingston to Miss Sarah Amelia Burhans of Kingston, by Rev. V. M. Hulbert.

March 8, 1851

1072. Mar 4, John W. Davis to Miss Cornelia C., daughter of John Cooper, Esq., both of Saugerties, by Rev. C. Van Santvord.

1073. Feb 23, Middle Hadam, Conn., John M. Burchardt of Coxsackie to Kate M., daughter of Rev. T. B. Woodward, by Rev. Dr. Woodward, of Christ Church.

March 15, 1851

1074. Feb 13, Saugerties, Rev. N. H. Cornell of Middleburgh, Schoharie Co., NY to Maria, daughter of Mr. Adam Finger of Saugerties, by Rev. C. Van Santvoord.

1075. Feb 22, Mr. James O'Bryan to Miss Lavina C. Teetsel, both of the Town of Saugerties, by Rev. Josiah Leonard.

1076. Mar 8, Mr. Judson C. Fiero to Miss Rachel C. Kimball, both of the Town of Saugerties by Rev. Josiah Leonard.

1077. Mar 10, Mr. J. A. Waterbury to Miss Mary C. Newkirk, both of the Town of Saugerties, by Rev. Mr. Bancroft.

March 22, 1851

1078. Mar 20, Saugerties, Mr. Benjamin Harmony of New York to Miss Henrietta Lewis of Saugerties, by Rev. R. A. Chalker.

April 5, 1851

1079. Apr 3, Saugerties, Mr. Isaac L. Griffiths to Miss Margaret Fulmer, both of Saugerties, by Rev. R. A. Chalker.

1080. Mar 16, Plattekill, Mr. Peter H. Brink to Miss Martha Wolven, by Rev. B. F. Snyder.

1081. Mar 22, Abram Wood to Mary Quick, both of Rondout, by Rev. D. Taylor.

1082. Mar 27, Anthony Cooley to Miss Burden, both of Rondout, by Rev. D. Taylor.

1083. Mar 15, Rondout, Joseph Mennany to Mary Ann Mellany, both of Rondout, by Rev. B. T. Phillips.

April 19, 1851

1084. Apr 16, Saugerties, Mr. William Fredenbergh of Kingston to Miss Matilda, daughter of Mr. Alanson Walter of Saugerties, by Rev. C. Van Santvoord.

April 26, 1851

1085. Apr 15, Hudson, Gerrit Van Keuren of Kingston to Catharine Gardner of Hudson, by Rev. Leroy Church.

1086. Apr 22, Kingston, John L. Strutzer of Albany to Louiza M. Cook of Kingston, by Rev. J. C. F. Hoes.

May 3, 1851

1087. Apr 26, Mr. Cornelius Longendyck of Plattekill to Mrs. Jane Schoonmaker of Saugerties, by Rev. F. A. Chalker.

1088. Apr 10, Wm. Carl Chalk to Miss Jane Ann Schoonmaker, both of Saugerties, by Rev. Geo. C. Bancroft.

1089. Apr 28 West Camp, at the home of Wm. Adams, Mr. Talmadge N. Lawrence to Miss Catharine A. Myer, both of Catskill, by Rev. Geo. C. Bancroft.

1090. Apr 23, Brooklyn, Howard Chipp of Kingston to Agnes W., daughter of Thomas Thompson of Brooklyn, by Rev. E. Lathrop.

1091. Apr 25, Richard Dubois to Polly Robinson, both of Glasco, by Edward Davison, Esq.

May 10, 1851

1092. May 9, Saugerties, Mr. Tobias Post to Miss Jane E. Schoonmaker, both of Saugerties, by Rev. Dr. Ostrander.

1093. Apr 30, Chancey Houghtaling of Kingston to Margaret Ann Lee of Woodstock, by Rev. Alexander Gulick.

May 17, 1851

1094. May 1, Bloominggrove, Rev. Anson Dubois of the Reformed Dutch Church Mission at Thousand Isles to Miss Mary Ann, only daughter of Hon. Geo. W. Tuthill of Bloominggrove, Orange Co., NY, by Rev. Luther Halsey, D. D.

1095. May 1, Buffalo, NY, Alexander Rogers of Buffalo to Julia Antoinette, daughter of T. I. Houghtaling, Esq., of Kingston, by Rev. John C. Lord, D. D.

1096. May 11, Mr. Robert Courtney of Albany to Miss Elvira, daughter of Capt. F. G. M. Deming, formerly of Coxsackie Landing, by Rev. Mr. Smithed.

1097. Apr 30, Kingston, Mr. Albert C. Fisher to Miss Augusta Reed, by Rev. Geo. Waters.

1098. May 2, New Paltz, Rev. Henry Ecked to Catharine Hermance, both of Rosendale, by Rev. Mr. Stitt.

1099. May 3, William Burke to Miss Elizabeth De Puy, both of Marbletown, by Rev. E. De Puy.

May 24, 1851

1100. Apr 24, Norwich, Conn., Mr. Francis Parson of Norwich to Miss Caroline Schoonmaker, formerly of Saugerties, by Rev. Mr. Carpenter.

May 31, 1851

1101. May 26, Kingston, William Smith to Catharine Rich, both of Kingston, by Rev. R. M. S. Pease.

June 7, 1851

1102. Jun 4, Saugerties, Mr. James Tanner to Miss Rachel Ann Hommel, both of the Town of Saugerties, by Rev. V. M. Hulbert.

1103. May 31, Palenville, Mr. Peter L. Newkirk to Miss Nancy Steward, both of Saugerties, by Rev. Geo. C. Bancroft.

1104. May 29, Laurenkill, R. B. Taylor, Esq., editor of the Ellenville *Journal* to Miss R. A. Broadhead of Ellenville, by Rev. S. A. Ayers.

1105. May 10, William H. Weeks of Matteawan, Dutchess Co., to Jane E. Philips of Plattekill, by Rev. P. C. Oakley.

June 14, 1851

1106. May 30, Rondout, John Henry Brow of New York to Miss Mary Eliza Cogswel of Rondout, by Rev. M. Van Dusen.

1107. Jun 4, Mr. Alexander Burhans to Kingston to Miss Julia Lewis of West Hurley, by Rev. C. E. Van Dyck.

1108. Jun 5, Stephen Shultis of Hurley to Eve Mariah Van Gaasbeek of Kingston, by Rev. Alexander Gulick.

June 21, 1851

1109. Jun 19, Town of Saugerties, Tobias Wynkoop, Esq. of Saugerties to Mrs. Elizabeth Steenbergh of Catskill, by Rev. H. Ostrander, D. D.

1110. Jun 21, Plattekill, Mr. Peter Snyder to Miss Sarah Osterhoudt, both of Town of Saugerties, by Rev. M. L. Schenck.

1111. Jun 15, Rondout at the Mansion House, George N. Van Dusen of Kingston to Miss Emily H. Brown of Rondout, by Rev. B. F. Philips.

1112. Jun 11, Mr. William B. Dingey to Miss Rachel M. Miller, both of Rochester, by Rev. C. L. Van Dyck.

1113. Jun 19, New Hamburgh, Mr. Frances Bates of Kingston to Miss Catharine L., daughter of William Bennet of New Hamburgh, by Rev. F. T. Williams.

1114. Jun 5, Valatie, Mr. Conrad Cook of Albany to Miss Jane R. Reynolds of Valatie, by Rev. Mr. Niles.

1115. Jun 5, Kingston, Mr. Samuel R. Howard of New York to Miss Mary L. Kimball of Kingston, by Rev. J. C. F. Hoes.

1116. Jun 19, High Falls, Mr. Dubois Hasbrouck, MD, of New Prospect, New Jersey to Miss Mary, daughter of Calvin Hasbrouck, Esq., of High Falls, by Rev. E. De Puy.

June 28, 1851

1117. Jun 24, Pittsfield, Mass., Solomon A. Smith, Esq., of the firm of Laflins and Smith of Saugerties, to Mari L., daughter of Walter Laflin, Esq. of Pittsfield, by Rev. D. Todd.

July 5, 1851

1118. Jun 23, Mr. Peter Emerick to Miss Elizabeth Bouck of Schoharie Co., by Rev. W. I. Cutter.

July 12, 1851

1119. Jul 3, Conrad Hommel to Miss Ann Rightmyer, both of Saugerties, by Rev. Alexander Gulick.

1120. Jul 3, Henry Wood of Woodstock to Sarah Louisa Cary of Shandaken, by Rev. Alexander Gulick.

1121. Jul 2, George W. Landphier to Miss Jane E. Burhans, both of Saugerties by Rev. H. Lonnsbery

1122. Jul 4, Benjamin Edmonds to Miss Martha Crowther, both of Saugerties, by Rev. H. Lonnsbery.

July 19, 1851

1123. Jun 29, Flatbush, Mr. David Vrooman of West Camp to Miss Margaret Whitaker of Flatbush.

1124. Jul 6, Catskill, Mr. Stephen Tyson of New York City to Miss Caroline Wolford of Catskill, by Rev. E. F. Platt.

July 26, 1851

1125. Jul 12, Jacob S. M. De Witt of Elizabeth Henderson, both of Rochester, by Rev. C. L. Van Dyck.

1126. Jul 13, Louis D. Brodhead to Eliza Ann Davis, both of Rochester, by Rev. C. L. Van Dyck.

1127. Jul 4, Rochester, James H. Bishop of Ellenville to Phebe Ann Hoornbeek of Alligerville, by Rev. C. Wycoff.

August 2, 1851
1128. Jul 24, Truman J. Preston of Eddyville to Debora Wiest of Rondout, by Rev. B. T. Phillips.

1129. Jul 12, Shokan, Abram C. Dubois of Olive to Jane D. Dubois of Rochester, by Rev. S. Harlow.

August 9, 1851
1130. Aug 6, Mr. George Walker of Hurley to Miss Charlotte Britt of Woodstock, by Rev. Alexander Gulick.

August 16, 1851
1131. Aug 5, Mr. Thomas E. Slater of Glasco to Miss Lucy M. Stephens of Malden, by Rev. V. M. Hulbert.

August 23, 1851
1132. Jul 14, Edwin Rogers of Shandaken to Mary Cole of Middletown, by Wm. Riseley, Esq.

1133. Aug 16, John Ellifisin of Esopus to Adelia Thompson of Kingston, by Rev. J. C. F. Hoes.

September 13, 1851
1134. Aug 21, Saugerties, William H. Simmons to Mrs. Jane M. Felter, both of Saugerties, by Rev. Mr. Schenck.

1135. Aug 28, Saugerties, Edward Hornbeck to Miss Sally Ann Swart, both of Saugerties, by Rev. Mr. Schenck.

1136. Aug 6, Saugerties, Semon P. Longendyke to Lucinda H. Felter, both of Saugerties, by Rev. Mr. Schenck.

September 20, 1851
1137. Sep 11, Rondout, David Thorp of Rondout to Elizabeth and Thomas Youngman of Kingston to Mary, daughters of P. M. G. Decker of Rondout, by Rev. B. T. Phillips.

1138. Sep 11, Kingston, Charles A. Vandemark to Emeline Osterhoudt, both of Flatbush, by Rev. Jno. C. F. Hoes.

1139. Sep 11, Kingston, Thomas Cooley of Muddy Brook to Hannah Jansen of Kingston, by Rev. Jno. F. C. Hoes.

1140. Sep 8, Kingston, Thomas Melony to Catharine Gahain, both of Hyde Park, by Rev. Jno. F. C. Hoes.

1141. Sep 10, New Paltz Landing, Mr. Reuben D. Hasbrouck to Miss Mary A. Deyo, daughter of Reuben Deyo, Esq., all of New Paltz Landing.

1142. Sep 11, Town of Olive, Francis Hull to Eliza Elliot, both of Olive, by Martin Schutt, Esq.

1143. Sep 18, Hurley, William Shearman to Ann Cronk, both of Rosendale, by C. Newkirk, Esq.

1144. Sep 7, Peter Plough of Woodstock to Miss Margaret Winne of Saugerties, by Rev. A. Gulick.

1145. Sep 10, Thomas Johnson of Woodstock to Adaline Ranson of Saugerties, by Rev. A. Gulick.

1146. Sep 11, Mr. David Griffin to Miss Mary Lawrence, by Rev. V. M. Hulbert.

September 27, 1851

1147. Sep 25, Saugerties, Mr. Fordyce L. Laflin to Miss Helen M., daughter of William Burtt, Esq., all of Saugerties, by Rev. V. M. Hulbert.

1148. Sep 20, Saugerties, Mr. Williamson to Miss Mary Bonner, both of Saugerties, by Rev. John Gilligan.

October 4, 1851

1149. Sep 30, Saugerties, Mr. David V. N. Hotaling to Miss Sarah I. Schoonmaker, both of Saugerties, by Rev. C. S. Van Santvoord.

October 11, 1851

1150. Oct 9, Quarryville, Mr. Osbon Traver of Durham to Miss Nancy H. Jones of Quarryville, by Rev. Geo. C. Bancroft.

1151. Sep 28, Kingston, James Frasier of New York to Mary A. Post of Kingston, by Rev. D. Smith.

1152. Oct 1, Kingston, Peter Van Buren to Adaline Pardee, both of Kingston, by Rev. D. Smith.

1153. Oct 1, Olive, Jacob H. Baldwin of Bradford, Conn. to Harriet Schutt of Olive, by Rev. J. N. Vorhis.

1154. Oct 1, Olive, William Still to Cornelia Taylor, both of Rondout, by Rev. B. T. Phillips.

October 18, 1851

1155. Oct 8, Orchard St. Church, Mr. John Rutgus Suydam to Miss Elizabeth, eldest daughter of Samuel Schoonmaker, Esq., both of New York City, by Rev. C. H. Fay.

1156. Oct 15, Mr. Philip A. Deyo of New York to Miss Louise B. Stilwell of New Paltz, by Rev. V. M. Hulbert.

1157. Oct 9, Poughkeepsie, Mr. Edward S. Wells, printer, of Kingston, to Miss Susan Mary, daughter of Rev. E. Fay of the Layfayette St. Baptist Chapel, by Rev. E. Fay.

1158. Oct 7, Albany at North Dutch Church, Mr. Samuel W. Shaw, editor of the Cooperstown *Journal* to Miss Jane, daughter of Thomas Mc Elroy, Esq., of that city, by Rev. Dr. Kenendy.

October 25, 1851

1159. Oct 21, Mr. William E. Kipp to Miss Nelly Hommel, both of Saugerties, by Rev. N. Cline.

1160. Oct 15, Hurley, Mr. Frances Myer of Saugerties to Miss Margaret Ann, daughter of Benjamin G. Newkirk, Esq., of Hurley, by Rev. B. C. Lippincott.

1161. Oct 1, Mr. Joseph T. Cassel to Miss Ann Catharine Burhans, both of Glasco, by Rev. M. Hulbert.

1162. Oct 9, Mr. Uriah Van Etten of Woodstock to Miss Margaret Osterhoudt of Kingston, by Rev. M. Hulbert.

1163. Oct 15, Plattekill, Mr. P. Carle to Miss R. A Whitaker, both of the Town of Saugerties, by Rev. M. L. Schenck.

1164. Sep 27, Mr. John W. Hutton of New York to Miss Elizabeth Witherwack of Glasco, by Dr. Ostrander.

1165. Oct 11, Mr. William Dederick of the Town of Catskill to Miss Maria Moose of Saugerties, by Dr. Ostrander.

1166. Oct 16, Mr. Philip Henry Lasher to Miss Sarah Catharine Dederick, both of Saugerties, by Dr. Ostrander.

1167. Oct 19, Coxsackie, Mr. Nathaniel W. Wood to Miss Margaret Lamphere, both of Coxsackie, by Rev. Mr. Woodbridge.

November 1, 1851

1168. Oct 25, High Falls, Mr. George Lane of Saugerties to Miss Amanda Jane Gardiner of the Town of Catskill, by Rev. George C. Bancroft.

1169. Oct 26, Mr. Wm. R. Chapman of Saugerties to Miss Harriett K. Van Denbergh of Coxsackie, by Rev. Mr. Woodbridge.

1170. Oct 22, Kingston, Mr. N. T. Curtiss of New York to Miss Mary E., daughter of Dr. L. Wells of Kingston, by Rev. E. Fay of Poughkeepsie.

1171. Notice - Whereas my wife Rachel Ann, having left my bed and board, without any cause of provocation, I hereby forbid all persons harboring or trusting her on my account, or giving her any employment as I will pay no debts of her contraction. Signed - Alexander Souser.

November 8, 1851
1172. Nov 3, Mr. Cyrus Swart of Kingston to Miss Catharine Thompson of Hunter by Rev. V. M. Hulbert.

1173. Nov 3, Mr. William H. Whitaker to Miss Jane C. Simmons of Saugerties, by Rev. B. M. Hulbert.

November 15, 1851
1174. Nov 8, Quarryville, Peter Fiero to Margaret M. Kimble, both of Saugerties, by Rev. David Kline.

November 22, 1851
1175. Nov 20, Flatbush, Theodore B. Gates, Esq. to Miss Maria V. L., daughter of J. V. L. Overbaugh, Esq., both of Saugerties, by Rev. V. M. Hulbert.

1176. Joshua Abberfield to Miss Elizabeth Harris, both of Kingston, by Daniel L. Decker, Esq.

November 29, 1851
1177. Nov 23, Kingston, Mr. John Williams of Woodstock to Miss Harriet Van Gaasbeek of Kingston, by Rev. John C. F. Hoes.

1178. Nov 18, Joseph H. Middaugh, formerly of Rondout, to Miss Catharine D. Abrams of Rochester, by Rev. Mr. Depuy.

1179. Nov 20, Ambrose Shook to Miss Eliza Post, all of Rondout, by Rev. B. T. Phillips.

1180. Nov 23, Saugerties, Benjamin Myer to Miss Van Steenbergh, by Rev. Mr. Lounsberry, at the Exchange House.

December 6, 1851
1181. Nov 29, Mr. John B. Cole to Miss Eliza Catharine Osterhoudt of Saugerties, by Rev. V. M. Hulbert.

1182. Nov 22, Ellenville, Mr. Archibald Hendren to Miss Mary Budd, both of Ellenville, by Rev. James Birch.

1183. Nov 27, Kingston, Derick W. Roosa to Jane C. Ackley, both of Kingston, by Rev. D. Smith.

December 13, 1851
1184. Nov 22, Hudson, Altamont J. Dorman, Esq., of Coxsackie, to Miss Mary Winters of Athens, by Rev. Mr. Scarritt.

December 27, 1851
1185. Dec 17, Town of Saugerties, Ira Leonard Harrick to Ann, daughter of Joel Wolven, both of the Town of Woodstock, by Rev. Thomas Lape.

1186. Dec 14, Saugerties, Mr. James Maybe of Goshen, Orange Co. to Miss Lavina Lounsberry of Le Roy, Genessee Co., NY, by Rev. H. Lounsberry.

January 3, 1852
1187. Dec 27, Mr. Matthew Bird to Miss Elizabeth Williamson, both of Saugerties, by Rev. Dr. Ostrander.

1188. Dec 30, Mr. Samuel Haswell of Bethlehem, Albany Co. to Miss Amelia Ann, daughter of Peter Hovenberg of Saugerties, by Rev. Dr. Ostrander.

January 10, 1852
1189. Jan 1, Thomas Post to Miss Frances Mc Kinney, both of Saugerties, by Rev. G. C. Bancroft.

1190. Jan 1, Kingston, Wm. H. Low to Parmelia Rider, both of Kingston, by Rev. H. W. Smuller.

1191. Dec 29, Wm. Peters to Miss Sarah A. Martin, both of Kingston, by Rev. Mr. Smuller.

1192. Jan 1, Kingston, John J. Baisden to Mary E. Schoonmaker, both of Kingston, by Rev. H. W. Smuller.

1193. Jan 1, Shokan, George N. Vandermark to Miss Mary Ann Myers of Sampsonville, by Rev. Samuel Harlow.

1194. Dec 15, Schoonmaker's Hotel, Zachariah Palen to Miss Phoebe Ann Boice, both of Sampsonville, by Squire Odell.

January 17, 1852

1195. Jan 11, Hudson, Mr. Bryan Finger of Saugerties to Miss Caroline M. Lamphere of Athens, by Rev. Mr. Church.

1196. Jan 10, West Camp, John Friar, Esq. to Miss Helen Wright, both of Saugerties.

1197. Jan 8, Kingston, Mr. Jno. Van Gaasbeek to Miss Sarah Taylor, both of Kingston, by Rev. J. C. P. Hoes.

January 31, 1852

1198. Jan 27, Coxsackie, Mr. John E. Lasher of Coxsackie, formerly of Saugerties, to Miss Elizabeth Wilson of Coxsackie, by Rev. Mr. Woodbridge.

1199. Jan 22, Kingston, Richard Finley of Rondout to Margaret Finley of Kingston, by Rev. J. C. F. Hoes.

1200. Jan 25, Kingston, Wm. Thomas to Sarah M. Decker, both of Kingston, by Rev. J. C. F. Hoes.

1201. Jan 21, Stone Ridge, Herman Best of Kingston to Jane E. Bodley of Stone Ridge, by Rev. Mr. Oldrin.

1202. Jan 15, Rosendale, George Sammons to Miss Elizabeth C. Carter, both of Rosendale, by Rev. J. N. Hope.

February 7, 1852

1203. Jan 14, Saugerties, George Burhans to Miss Hepsabeth Ann Shears, both of Saugerties, by Rev. Mr. Lounsberry.

February 14, 1852

1204. Jan 24, Malden, V. R. Woodward to Miss Rachel Ann Staats, both of the Town of Saugerties, by Rev. Josiah Leonard.

1205. Jan 10, Kingston, William Townsend to Rebecca A., eldest daughter of Jacob I. Signer, all of Kingston, by Rev. J. C. F. Hoes.

1206. Notice - As my wife, Nelly has left my bed and board without any cause or provocation, I hereby forbid all persons harboring or trusting her on my account as I will pa no debts of her contracting.. Signed - John I. Whitaker, Feb 2, 1852, Saugerties.

March 20, 1852

1207. Mar 14, Saugerties, Mr. James Crump to Miss Elizabeth Lewis, both of Saugerties, by Rev. J. I. Jordan.

May 22, 1852

1208. May 17, Saugerties, Jesse F. Bookstaver, Esq. to Miss Elizabeth Marshal, both of Saugerties, by Rev. E. A. Nichols.

1209. May 10, Kingston, Henry Hartwig to Miss Olive Hayes, by Rev. D. Smith.

1210. May 10, Kingston, William Dedrick to Miss Clarissa Hayes, by Rev. D. Smith.

1211. May 19, Blue Mountain, Adam Sax to Harriet Ann, daughter of Henry Teel, by Rev. A. C. Hillman.

May 29 1852

1212. May 26, Saugerties, Mr. William Lane of Olive to Miss Jane E. Slusher of Shandaken, by Rev. C. Van Santvoord.

June 5, 1852

1213. May 27, Catskill, Mr. Elijah Smith to Susan A. Van Golden, by Rev. W. Kline.

June 19, 1852

1214. Jun 15, Saugerties, Benjamin M. Freligh, Esq. to Miss Elizabeth, eldest daughter of John G. Mynderse, by Rev. C. Van Santvoord.

1215. May 26, Mr. Levi Swart of Hancock, New York to Miss Catharine E. Turck of Flatbush, by Rev. V. M. Hulbert.

1216. May 13, Catskill, William W. Banks, Esq. to Miss Lorinda Snyder, both of Catskill, by Rev. D. Kline.

July 10, 1852

1217. Jul 3, Esopus, Mr. Dubois Van Dermark to Miss Mary Ophelia Acker, both of Kingston, by Rev. A. Fort.

July 17, 1852

1218. Jul 5, Town of Saugerties, Mr. Abram Rightmyer to Catherine Plough, both of High Falls, Town of Saugerties, by Rev. Alexander C. Hillman.

1219. Jul 10, Saugerties, Isaac Van Valkenburgh to Mariah Crossburn, by Rev. C. Van Santvoord.

August 7, 1852

1220. Aug 5, Saugerties, Mr. Alexander H. Elwyn to Miss Melissa Bundy, both of Woodstock, by Rev. J. R. Johnson.

August 14, 1852

1221. Aug 5, Kingston, Anson E. Nodine of Yonkers to Mary B. Hart, Principal of Golden Hill Female Seminary, Kingston, by Rev. H. W. Smuller.

September 18, 1852

1222. Sep 13, Mr. Lemuel S. Wright of Malden to Miss Mary Ann Cole of Saugerties, by Rev. Alonzo F. Selleck.

1223. Sep 12, Mr. John A. Coon of Athens to Miss Ellen Smith of Catskill, grand-daughter of Mr. Aaron Smith of the Town of Saugerties, by Christopher Fiero, Esq.

September 25, 1852

1224. Aug 26, Mr. Henry Fries of Arcadia to Miss Jane Burhans of the Town of Kingston, by Rev. V. M. Hulbert.

1225. Sep 19, Glasco, Mr. Henry L. Sutton of New Brunswick, New Jersey to Miss Ellen Burean of Paterson, New Jersey, by Rev. V. M. Hulbert.

October 2, 1852

1226. Sep 30, Saugerties, Mr. John Mattoon of San Francisco, Calif. to Sarah S. Stranahan of Saugerties, by Rev. C. Van Santvoord.

1227. Sep 20, West Camp, Mr. Jacob Overbaugh to Miss Judith N. Overbaugh, both of Catskill, by Rev. D. Kline.

1228. Sep 21, West Camp, Mr. Zachariah S. Smith, Esq. of Saugerties to Miss Sarah Perse of Catskill, by Rev. D. Kline.

1229. Sep 22, Kingston, at St. John's Church, Mr. James W. Davis of Otsego to Miss Catherine Jones, daughter of the late Hon. John Sudam, by Rev. Dr. Sherwood of Hyde Park.

1230. Sep 21, Mongaup, Sullivan Co., NY, Mr. Wynkoop Kiersted to Miss Jane A. Swan, both of Mongaup.

1231. Sep 22, Coxsackie, Mr. Alexander Reed to Miss Henrietta, daughter of Charles Backus, Esq., all of Coxsackie, by Rev. Mr. Woodbridge.

1232. Undated, New York City, Mr. A. G. Smith, formerly of Coxsackie to Miss Euphemia Angevine of New York City.

October 16, 1852

1233. Oct 10, William Myers to Miss Mary Hobleman, both of Saugerties, by Rev. A. F. Selleck.

January 1, 1853

1234. Dec 23, Plattekill, at the residence of Peter P. Felter, Mr. Christopher Snyder of Saugerties to Anna M. Felter of Kingston, by Rev. M. L. Schenck.

1235. Dec 27, Saugerties, James A. Morris, formerly of Saugerties to Mary C., daughter of Hiram Smith of Saugerties, by Rev. Mr. Selleck.

1236. Dec 23, Saugerties, Mr. Benjamin Langley to Miss Anna Williams, both of Saugerties, by Rev. J. R. Johnson.

1237. Dec 30, Glasco, Mr. Christopher Hutton to Miss Malinda Crumb, both of Glasco, by Rev. J. R. Johnson.

1238. Dec 25, Saugerties, Mr. Robert H. Brink to Miss Alida Gardner, both of Catskill, by Rev. A. F. Selleck.

1239. Dec 30, Glasco, Mr. Isaac H. Snyder of Saugerties to Miss Rachel Ann Carle of Glasco, by Rev. A. F. Selleck

January 8, 1853

1240. Jan 2, Kingston, Thomas Rush to Catharine Quinn, both of Saugerties, by Rev. M. Waters.

1241. Jan 1, Saugerties, Alfred Pultz of New York to Cornelia Ann Burger of Saugerties.

1242. Dec 30, Kingston, James Van Ostrand to Elizabeth L. Dubois, both of High Falls, by Rev. H. W. Smuller.

1243. Jan 1, Kingston, Joseph C. Fox to Harriet Bloodgood, both of West Hurley, by Rev. H. W. Smuller.

1244. Jan 1, at the home of J. H. Schryver, Abram J. Steen to Judith A. Van Wagenen and James Elmendorf to Elizabeth Terwilliger, all of Rochester, by Rev. H. W. Smuller.

1245. Dec 30, James Kipp to Clarrissa Freer, both of Kingston, by Rev. Mr. Griffin.

1246. Jan 1, George H. Bradshow to Hannah Vanderbogert, both of Woodstock, by Rev. Mr. Griffin.

1247. Sep 8, Kingston, Joseph Hen to Catharine Brackle, both of Kingston, by Rev. M. L. Schenck.

1248. Dec 30, Charles Phillip Zimmerman to Mary Eva Brackle, both of Kingston, by Rev. M. L. Schenck.

1249. Dec 30, Alfred J. Evory to Miss Julia E. Bond, both of Saugerties, by Rev. M. L. Schenck.

1250. Jan 1, Jacob Sam to Miss Dorotha Walchen, by Rev. M. L. Schenck.

1251. Jan 5, Blue Mountain, George W. Waters to Sarah, daughter of Henry Teel, by Rev. Alexander C. Hillman.

January 15, 1853

1252. Dec 28, Monson, Hampden Co., Mass., Theodore G. Chamberlain of Ellenville to Martha L. Holmes of Monson, by Rev. C. B. Cittredge.

1253. Dec 25, Napanoch, James Atkins to Sarah E. Thorp, both of Napanoch, by Rev. Thomas B. Smith.

1254. Dec 30, William Parks of Sullivan Co. to Cyntha J. Gillet of the former place, by Rev. Dr. Ostrander.

1255. Dec 30, James Beers to Lavinia Jansen, both of Sullivan, by Rev. Dr. Ostrander.

1256. Jan 12, Isaac Ellsworth to Carrie Rouse, both of Rondout, by Rev. B. T. Phillips.

1257. Dec 13, Henry I. Barber to Emma C. Rosa, both of Shandaken, by Rev. John Hammond.

1258. Dec 30, James H. Fairchild to Sarah C. Winne, of Shandaken, by Rev. John Hammond.

January 22, 1853

1259. Dec 29, Andrew J. Conway to Eliza Ann Deitz, both of Rosendale, by Rev. C. L. Van Dyck.

1260. Jan 1, Henry Wells to Lydia Ann Drum, both of Marbletown, by Rev. C. L. Van Dyck.

1261. Jan 15, James Coutant of Esopus to Jemima K. Christiana of Stone Ridge, by Rev. C. L. Van Dyck.

1262. Jan 15, Stone Ridge, Martin T. Schoonmaker to Dinah M. Freer, both of South Rondout, by Rev. S. M. Knapp.

January 29, 1853

1263. Jan 27, Kingston, Mr. Isaac W. Davis to Miss Emeline Teeple, both of Kingston, by Rev. Mr. Smith.

1264. Jan 13, Kingston, B. E. Roe to Jane M. Walker, both of Kingston, by Rev. H. W. Smuller.

1265. Jan 16, Kingston, Elias G. Coutant to Elmira Terwilliger, both of Marbletown, by Rev. H. W. Smuller.

1266. Jan 20, Kingston, John H. Post of Poughkeepsie to Anna Berger of Esopus, by Rev. Dr. Hoes.

1267. Jan 12, Esopus, Johannes K. Osterhousen to Prudence Styles, both of Esopus, by Wm. Smith, Esq.

1268. Jan 13, Esopus, Amos Smith to Rachel Bedford, both of Esopus, by Wm. Smith, Esq.

1269. Jan 13, Samsonville, John J. Springsteen of Owego, Tioga Co., NY to Susan M. H. Tripp of Samsonville, by Rev. W. Taylor.

1270. Jan 19, Andrew S. Weller to John H. Hornbeck, both of Ellenville, by Rev. S. B. Ayers.

1271. Jan 13, John A. Mc Kinney to Elizabeth Sears, both of Homowack.

1272. Jan 20, Kingston, Philip Henry Dietz of New York to Frances Fisk of Kingston, by Rev. Mr. Van Deusen.

1273. Jan 1, Rosendale, James Dumond to Cynthia Parson, both of Kingston, by Rev. H. Eckle.

February 5, 1853

1274. Jan 29, Saugerties, Mark Devlin to Ann Catherine Roosa, both of Saugerties, by Rev. C. Van Santvoord.

1275. Jan 29, Saugerties, Mr. Jacob Cole to Miss Mary Decker, both of Saugerties, by Rev. A. F. Selleck.

1276. Jan 26, Middletown, Orange Co., NY, Capt. L. Elting of New Paltz Landing to Miss Sarah E., daughter of H. Watkins of Middletown, by Rev. J. Selden Spencer.

1277. Dec 15, Kingston, Mr. John Shop to Miss Ellen Brower, both of Kingston, by Rev. Mr. Griffen.

1278. Jan 29, Rosendale, Simon S. Westbrook of Kingston to Miss Lillis Grant of Rosendale, by Rev. H. W. Smuller.

1279. Jan 29, at the parsonage of the 2nd Reformed Church of Kingston, Mattaew <sic> Kros to Matilda Ulrich, both of Kingston, by Rev. H. W. Smuller.

1280. Jan 26, Mr. David Knapp of Walden to Miss Ellen, daughter of Dr. G. G. Graham of Shawangunk, by Rev. Mr. Stewart.

1281. Jan 13, Samsonville, John J. Stringstler of Owego, Tioga Co., NY to Susan M. S. Tripp of Samsonville, by Rev. W. Taylor.

February 12, 1853

1282. Jan 10, Mr. Jacob Rosalaam of Jerley, Greene Co., Wisc. to Anna Jane Pfester of the Canton of Berne, Switzerland, by Rev. M. L. Schenck.

1283. Jan 22, Egbert Van Buren of Kingston to Mary Catharine Longendike of Saugerties, by Rev. M. L. Schenck.

1284. Jan 31, Marx Cahart to Catharine Sheets, both of Kingston, by Rev. M. L. Schenck.

1285. Jan 19, Rochester, Nathan Schoonmaker to Rachel Jannsen, both of Rochester, by Rev. E. Du Puy.

1286. Feb 3, Poughkeepsie, George Krum of West Hurley to Almira Broas of Poughkeepsie, by Rev. L. F. Waldo.

1287. Jan 22, David S. Manchester of Catskill to Eliza Ann Terry of Kingston, by Rev. Mr. Van Deusen.

1288. Feb 1, Esopus, Christopher Brink of Kingston to Sarah Ann Eckert of South Rondout, by Rev. A. Fort.

February 19, 1853

1289. Feb 2, Howard Hasbrouck of Rochester to Mary C. Ladenbergh of Marbletown, by Rev. C. L. Van Dyck.

1290. Jan 29, Shokan, John Palen to Jane Davis, both of Marbletown, by Rev. Samuel Harlow.

1291. Feb 5, Olive, Joseph Mc Elvy to Mrs. Elizabeth Brink, both of Sampsonville, by Rev. Samuel Harlow.

1292. Feb 10, Kingston, William Hopper of Poughkeepsie to Miss Susan Ann Castle of Kingston, by Rev. Dr. Griffen.

February 26, 1853

1293. Feb 15, Hartwick Seminary, Rev. John D. English of Ghent, Columbia Co., NY, to Miss Adeline, daughter of George B. Miller, D. D., by George B. Miller, D. D.

1294. Feb 23, Frederick Eckert to Maria Wassiman, both of Saugerties, by Wm. S. Burhans, Esq.

1295. Feb 15, David Moulton to Margaret Mc Creary, both of Delaware Co., by Rev. Mr. Griffen.

1296. Feb 12, Rondout, Horace A. Elliott of Kingston to Hannah Terwilliger of Rondout, by Rev. Mr. Van Deusen.

1297. Feb 10, Wurtsboro, Ambrose C. Miller to Jane Ann Kuykendall, both of Wurtsboro, by Rev. S. B. Ayers.

March 5, 1853

1298. Feb 23, Kingston, Morris Hoffman to Eliza J. Wheeler, both of Rosendale, by Rev. Dr. Hoes.

1299. Feb 24, Kingston, Hiram Van Steenburgh of Wawarsing to Catharine S., daughter of Thomas Jansen, Esq. of Kingston, by Rev. Dr. Hoes.

1300. Feb 22, Olive, Lovejoy Benjamin of Oneida Lake to Melissa Davis of Shandaken, by Rev. John W. Hammond.

1301. Feb 9, Shandaken, Wm. V. Giles of Shandaken to Elmira Carman of Olive, by Wm. Risely, Esq.

1302. Feb 9, Palenville, Charles Brant of Catskill to Mrs. Jane C. Overbaugh of Saugerties, by Rev. Ira Ferris.

1303. Feb 19, Palenville, Lewis Bemis to Mrs. Catharine Schwart, both of the Town of Saugerties, by Rev. Ira Ferris.

1304. Feb 24, Esopus, Solomon Sahler of Rochester to Caroline Winfield of Esopus, by Rev. Abraham Fort.

1305. Feb 2, Solomon E. Bush to Mary Jane Fish, both of Olive, by Martin Schutt, Esq.

1306. Feb 17, Edward W. Evans to Harriet Eliza Gardner, both of Fallsburgh, by Rev. C. D. Eltinge.

March 12, 1853

1307. Mar 5, Henry Myer to Mrs. Maria Brink, both of Saugerties, by Rev. C. Van Santvoord.

1308. Feb 24, Ellenville, Abraham Osterhoudt to Wealthy Ann Terwilliger, both of Marbletown, by Rev. S. B. Ayers.

1309. Feb 26, Kingston, Gilbert Van Steenburgh to Nancy Moore, both of Malden, by Rev. H. W. Smuller

1310. Mar 3, Wm. H. De Puy to Eliza C. Wager, both of Marbletown, by Rev. C. L. Van Dyck.

1311. Mar 3, Kingston, George Elmendorf to Kate Churchill of Poughkeepsie, by Rev. J. C. F. Hoes.

1312. Feb 3, James Hixon to Elizabeth Graham, both of Shawangunk, by Rev. G. N. Jansen of Guilford.

1313. Mar 3, Jonas F. Atkins to Cornedia M. Slater, both of New Paltz, by Rev. G. N. Jansen of Guilford.

March 19, 1853

1314. Mar 6, Kingston, George Wood to Louisa Dinger, by Samuel Barlow, Esq.

1315. Feb 23, Windham, Greene Co., Francis M. De Witt to Ruth Jones, both of Windham.

1316. Mar 9, Hurley Roberts to Louisa Wilka, both of Kingston, by Rev. J. C. F. Hoes, D. D.

March 26, 1853

1317. Feb 17, Henry Luther Moose to Ann Catharine Bear, both of the Town of Saugerties, by Rev. Thomas Lape.

1318. Mar 15, Wawarsing, Richard Davis to Sarah Jane Jackson, by Rev. James B. Lente.

1319. Mar 12, Rondout, John H. C. Patterson to Lydia C. Hall, by Rev. M. Van Deusen.

1320. Mar 19, Kingston, William H. Carpenter to Margaret Ann Couhoudt, by Ten Eyck De Witt, Esq.

April 2, 1853

1321. Mar 24, Marbletown, Mr. John Bush to Miss Litty C. Mayse, by Rev. C. L. Van Dyck.

1322. Mar 19, Sing Sing, Mr. David M. Wygant of Plattekill to Miss Mary E. Vail of Yorktown, Westchester Co., NY, by J. Urmy, Esq.

April 9, 1853

1323. Apr 2, Peter Wolven, Jr. to Mary Jane Van Kleek, both of Saugerties, by Rev. C. Van Santvoord.

1324. Mar 24, Shokan, William Krum of West Hurley to Eliza Ann Akley of Marbletown, by Rev. J. W. Hammond.

1325. Apr 2, Rondout, Thomas Mulchay to Johanna Mannan, both of Kingston, by Rev. Mr. Madden.

April 16, 1853

1326. Apr 12, Abram J. Suderley to Elizabeth C. Post, both of Saugerties, by Rev. Thomas Lape.

1327. Mar 29, Horatio P. Ballinger to Eliza L. Slighter, both of Kingston, by Rev. H. W. Smuller.

1328. Apr 6, Charles S. Eldridge of Kingston to Harriet Stoutenburgh of West Hurley, by Rev. H. W. Smuller.

1329. Mar 31, Jno. Wilson to Matilda Hutton, both of Rondout, by Rev. B. T. Phillips.

1330. Apr 6, Edward J. Bailey to Lurenna Besemer, both of Ellenville, by Rev. S. B. Ayers.

1331. Apr 8, John Mc Comb to Cordelia Furman, both of Lackawack, by Rev. S. B. Ayers.

1332. Mar 31, Solomon Jones to Sarah Decker, both of the Town of Lloyd, by Philip S. Hasbrouck, Esq.

1333. Apr 1, Brooklyn, James M. Cooper of Kingston to T. Jane Ketchum of Stone Ridge, by Rev. S. S. Bell.

1334. Mar 7, Josiah Vandevoort to Maria Bennet, both of Lloyd, by John A. Bodley, Esq.

1335. Mar 28, William Desch to Henrietta Badgley, both of Olive, by A. W. Benson, Esq.

April 23, 1853

1336. Apr 17, Minden, Montgomery Co., William Hull, Esq. of Saugerties to Miss Elizabeth, daughter of Levi B. Skinner, MD, of Minden, by Rev. M. W. Empie.

1337. Apr 10, Isaac Decker, Jr. to Catharine Helms, both of Ellenville, by Rev. S. B. Ayers.

1338. Apr 6, R. Harrison Anderson to Catharine J. Milligen, daughter of Marcus Millken <sic>, all of Mamakating, by S. M. Wills.

1339. Apr 14, Abraham H. Scutt to Leah C. Van Steenburgh, both of Eddyville, by Rev. H. W. Smuller.

April 30, 1853

1340. Apr 18, New York, Gilbert M. Gillet, late of Kingston to Hannah Hallet of New York City, by Rev. Dr. Hardenburg.

May 7, 1853

1341. Apr 30, Saugerties, Frederick Chaler to Miss Sibella Margaret Fouth, both of Kingston, by Rev. A. F. Selleck.

1342. Apr 25, J. B. Wells of Ellenville to Mary J. Hook of High Falls, by Rev. S. B. Ayers.

1343. Apr 26, Moses H. Davis of Fallsburgh to Marietta Pleu of Kingston, by Rev. S. B. Ayers.

1344. Apr 30, Kingston, George Davis to Nelly Freer, both of Whiteport, by Rev. H. W. Smuller.

1345. May 1, Kingston, Hiram Miller of Woodstock to Jane Whitney of Shandaken, by Rev. Dr. Hoes.

1346. Apr 28, Poughkeepsie, William H. Broas to Alice, daughter of Wm. Mc George, by Rev. Mr. Hageman.

1347. Apr 23, Charles E. Enoe of Cairo to Phebe A., daughter of Cornelius T. Jones of Hurley, by Rev. Mr. Compton.

May 14, 1853

1348. May 2, James Andrews of Schodack, Rensselaer Co. to Nancy Sheffer of Catskill, by Rev. David Kline.

1349. May 4, Esopus, Augustus W. Hale of Glasco Landing to Jane Eliza Eckert of Esopus, by Rev. J. N. Shaffer.

1350. May 8, Stephen D. Mills of Brooklyn to Ann Van Steenberg of Kingston, by Rev. Jno. C. F. Hoes, D. D.

1351. May 5, Cornelius Longyear to Eleanor Shultis, both of Shandaken, by William Risely, Esq.

1352. May 4, Israel Burger to Henrietta Marshall, both of Esopus, by Rev. W. Taylor.

1353. Apr 21, Mr. Anthony L. Schoonmaker to Elizabeth Markle, both of Marbletown, by Rev. C. L. Van Dyck.

1354. May 5, Isaac Mc Kee of Marbletown to Margaret Jane Hudler of Fallsburg, Sullivan Co., by Rev. C. L. Van Dyck.

1355. May 5, Martin W. Sheldon to Rozilla Van Kleek, both of Olive, by Martin Schutt, Esq.

May 21, 1853

1356. May 14, Saugerties, Samuel W. Davis to Sarah M. Underhill, both of Saugerties, by Rev. A. F. Selleck.

1357. May 7, Saugerties, Simon P. Lyons to Miss Rachel Schoonmaker, both of Marbletown, by Rev. C. Van Santvoord.

1358. May 4, Athens, Peter E. Post of Saugerties to Marietta Coon of Athens, by Rev. Geo. Lyle.

1359. May 11, William H. Conklin to Rachel C., daughter of Philip Hendricks, all of Kingston, by Rev. J. C. F. Hoes.

1360. May 12, William Van Keuren to Eliza J. Keogens, both of Grahamsville, by Rev. S. B. Ayers.

1361. May 10, Lewis D. Hornbeck to Margaret Schoonmaker, both of Rochester, by Rev. E. De Puy.

1362. Undated, Olive, Hugh Locks to Margaret Gray, both of Olive, by Rev. S. Harlow.

May 28, 1853

1363. May 15, John Bush of Rochester to Sarah Munkson of Olive, by John Shurter, Esq.

1364. May 2, Rondout, Heinrich Buegel to Mrs. Catharina Werth of Kingston, by Rev. C. H. Siebke.

1365. May 16, Rondout, Ludwig Schwab to Elizabeth Baebel, both of Plattekill, by Rev. C. H. Siebke.

1366. May 16, Rondout, George R. Shick of New York to Barbara Weber of Rondout, by Rev. C. H. Siebke.

June 4, 1853

1367. May 27, Peter Mickle of Glasco to Christina, daughter of Mr. Abram Low of Glasco, by Rev. Dr. Ostrander.

1368. May 26, Kingston, William H. Coutant of Esopus to Aurelia Sanford of Kingston, by Rev. Dr. Hoes.

1369. May 28, Kingston, Wilhelmus Van Gaasbeek to Catharine Bradshaw, both of Kingston, by Rev. Dr. Hoes.

1370. May 23, Kingston, William H. Hacker to Esther P. Guion, both of Pine Plains, by Rev. S. S. Relyea.

1371. May 23, Napanoch, John V. Patterson of Napanoch to Mary A. Martin of Shawangunk, by Rev. Thomas B. Smith.

June 11, 1853

1372. Jun 4, William Fiero to Ann M. Post, both of the Town of Saugerties, by Rev. D. Kline.

1373. Jun 5, Jeremiah Castle to Mary Ann Morris, both of West Hurley, by Rev. A. Gulick.

1374. Jun 1, Charles M. King to Miss A. Frazier, both of Rondout, by Rev. Mr. Fitch.

June 18, 1853

1375. Jun 12, George B. Snyder of New York to Mary A. Rhinehart of Kingston, by Rev. Jno. C. F. Hoes, D. D.

1376. Jun 11, Abraham L. Freer of Rosendale to Harriet A. Haines of Marbletown, by Rev. H. W. Smuller.

1377. Jun 8, William H. Trelease to Ann Mitchell, both of Rondout, by Rev. Silas Fitch.

1378. Jun 6, Greenbush, Capt. A. Matson, of the steamer James Madison of Rondout, to Theresa Wiltsie of Greenbush.

June 25, 1853

1379. Jun 20, Ephraim E. Musier to Mary C. Magee, both of Catskill, by Rev. David Kline.

1380. Jun 21, Lucas E. Schoonmaker to Aurelia Davis, both of Kingston, by Rev. H. W. Smuller.

1381. Jun 17, Kingston, James T. Beers to Cornelia Bostwick, both of Saugerties, by Rev. J. C. F. Hoes, D. D.

July 2, 1853

1382. Jun 9, Saugerties, William R. Marten to Ann Eliza Whitaker, both of Glasco, by Rev. A. F. Selleck.

1383. Jun 9, Saugerties, Abram P. Burhans to Jannette Myers, both of Glasco, by Rev. A. F. Selleck.

1384. Jun 21, Ellenville, Jeremiah Green to Miss Sarah C. Townsend, both of Rochester, by Rev. S. B. Ayers.

1385. Jun 21, Kingston, Jas. Mc Gavy to Catharine Narvy, both of Kingston, by Rev. Dr. Hoes.

1386. Jun 23, West Hurley, John W. Lockwood to Sarah Mariah Dunigan, both of Shandaken, by Martin Schutt, Esq.

1387. Jun 15, New Paltz, Abram W. Lefever to Margaret D. B., daughter of Derrick W. Elting, Esq., all of New Paltz, by Rev. Charles H. Stitt.

July 9, 1853

1388. Jun 28, Saugerties, Mr. Orange Webster to Miss Margaret Craft, both of Saugerties, by Rev. Mr. Johnson.

1389. May 31, Saugerties, Hoyt Weeks to Eliza M. Burhans, both of Glasco, by Rev. A. F. Selleck.

1390. Jul 2, Palenville, Mr. Norman H. Perkins of Saugerties to Miss Celia A. Bonesteel of Catskill, by Rev. I. Ferris.

1391. Jun 29, North Esopus, Nicholas Brinckerhoff of New York City to Catharine D. Crook of North Esopus, by Rev. Wesley Taylor.

1392. Jun 29, North Esopus, Daniel Hardenburgh of New York City to Miss Almira E. Crook of North Esopus, by Rev. Wesley Taylor.

1393. Jun 25, Rosendale, Gabert Miller to Ekee Maria Smith, by James A. Coutant, Esq.

1394. Jun 25, Rosendale, Burket Dawald to Margaret Miller, both of Rosendale, by James A. Coutant, Esq.

1395. Jun 26, Rondout, at the Methodist Episcopal Church, Mr. George Thompson to Miss E. Smith, both of Rondout, by Rev. Silas Fitch.

1396. Jun 30, Lloyd, John W. Smith to Hannah Smith, both of Marbletown, by Silas Saxton, Esq.

July 16, 1853

1397. Jul 4, at the California Hotel, John F. Delamater to Miss Lydia Rachel Rose, both of Marbletown, by Silas Saxton, Esq.

1398. Jul 6, Egbert Hill to Miss Elthea Keator, both of Olive, by Rev. J. W. Hammond.

1399. Jul 3, Victor S. Sickler of Hurley to Jane Lewis of Saugerties, by Rev. Silas Fitch.

1400. Jun 22, Samsonville, Peter Wynkoop of Rochester to Maria Jane Embree of Olive, by John Shurter, Esq.

1401. Jul 4, Ellenville, Robert Terwilliger to Jane Besmer, both of Ellenville, by Rev. S. B. Ayres.

1402. Jul 4, at the Cape, John Teller to Maria E. Morse, both of Ellenville, by Rev. S. B. Ayres.

1403. Jun 28, Methodist Episcopal Church, Alfred Nutting to Miss Eigith M. Green, both of Kingston, by Rev. Mr. Griffin.

July 23, 1853

1404. Jul 12, Peter A. Carle of Saugerties to Adeline Van Etten of Kingston, by Rev. Dr. Hoes.

1405. Jul 14, Kingston, William Burns to Anne Johnson, by Rev. Geo. Waters.

1406. Jun 30, Kingston, John Carrol to Catharine Fosten, by Rev. Geo. Waters.

July 30, 1853

1407. Jul 4, Honk Hill, Charles Conklin to Sarah E. Mosher, by Rev. C. Shook.

1408. Jun 21, Marlborough, John P. Palmateer of Lloyd to Grace Smith of Marlborough, by John Woolsey, Esq.

1409. Jul 6, Shandaken, Peter W. Shultis to Libby Lennard, both of Shandaken, by William Riseley, Esq.

August 6, 1853

1410. Jul 31, Saugerties, John Mohler to Caroline Myer, both of Saugerties, by Rev. A. F. Selleck.

1411. Jul 26, Kingston, Hugh Hackett to Elizabeth Crozier, both of Kingston, by Rev. B. Griffen.

1412. Jul 27, Marcus C. Coggswell of Rondout to Sarah A. Felts of Rhinebeck, by Rev. Silas Fitch.

1413. Jul 25, Poughkeepsie, Henry Frank of New York to Hester J. Jaycox of Eddyville, by Rev. Mr. Buck.

1414. Jul 24, Marlborough, James H. Legroodt to Lydia A. Nichols, both of Lloyd, by Rev. Samuel Hawksley.

1415. Jul 21, Milton, at the home of Benj. Townsend, A. J. Madison Smith to Phebe Jane Elting, both of Lloyd, by Rev. S. Hawksley.

August 13, 1853

1416. Aug 7, Town of Saugerties, Nelson Finger of New York to Eliza Lasher of Ulster Co., by Rev. Josiah Leonard.

1417. Jul 26, John Litts to Julia A. Evans, both of Ellenville, by Rev. T. B. Smith.

1418. Jul 26, Kingston, Orlando Humphrey of Kingston to Nelly Ann Hill of High Falls, by Rev. H. W. Smuller.

1419. Aug 4, Thomas E. Low to Angeline Kelts, both of Kingston, by Rev. H. W. Smuller.

1420. Aug 8, Kingston, Benager Garretson to Harriet Wiltsie, both of Kingston, by Rev. H. W. Smuller.

1421. Jul 31, Olive, Michael Dunnegan to Martha L. Sloat, both of Samsonville, by Rev. Samuel Harlow.

1422. Aug 2, Shandaken, David Ingraham to Miss Hannah Knickerbocker, both of Rochester, Ulster Co., by William Risely, Esq.

August 20, 1853

1423. Aug 14, Saugerties, Charles Bearnheart of New York to Catharine E. Yogt of Saugerties, by Rev. A. F. Selleck.

1424. Aug 10, William J. Leigh to Nancy E. Green, both of Catskill, by Rev. C. Van Santvoord.

1425. Aug 8, Marbletown, Mr. Thomas Sheeley to Miss Mary Ann Davis, by Rev. C. L. Van Dyck.

1426. Jul 23, John C. Brannen to Miss Hannah C. Bush, both of Olive, by John Shurter, Esq.

August 27, 1853

1427. Jul 25, Rondout, Michael Schneider of Greenkill to Anna Jane York of Esopus, by Rev. C. H. Siebke.

1428. Aug 14, Rondout, Christian Buell of South Rondout to Christine Meier, by Rev. C. H. Siebke.

1429. Aug 15, Rondout, Franklin Ritter to Elizabeth Muller, both of Rondout, by Rev. C. H. Siebke.

September 3, 1853

1430. Aug 31, Saugerties, Moses Decker to Cornelia Emeline Dyle, both of Saugerties, by Rev. A. F. Selleck.

1431. Aug 27, Charles W. Newman of Milford, Pa. to Miss Sarah L. Thompson of Kingston, by Rev. Mr. Waters.

1432. Aug 21, Thomas Renison to Miss Mary Ann Guil More, by Rev. Mr. Waters.

1433. Aug 21, Francis Underwood to Phebe Carr, both of Marlborough, by Thomas Bingham, Esq.

1434. Aug 11, Samsonville, Uriah Smith to Emeline Bell, both of Olive, by John Shurter, Esq.

September 10, 1853

1435. Aug 22, Ellenville, Mathias Cooper to Miss Elizabeth Ann Sharp, both of Lackawack, by Samuel Barlow, Esq.

1436. Aug 22, Ellenville, William Sharp of Lackawack to Miss Maria Evarls of Neversink, Sullivan Co., by Samuel Barlow, Esq.

1437. Sep 4, Esopus, Rev. Wesley Taylor, pastor of the Reformed Dutch Church of Esopus, to Melissa, daughter of Cornelius Houghtaling of Esopus, by Rev. A. Fort.

1438. Sep 5, Mr. John Pettit to Miss Amanda Richardson, both of Kingston, by Rev. Geo. Waters.

1439. Aug 3, Jacob Rick to Nelly Rick, both of Woodstock, by J. S. Ostrum, Esq.

1440. Aug 28, New Paltz, Washington Krum to Mary Elizabeth Burk, both of New Paltz, by P. S. Hasbrouck, Esq.

1441. Aug 28, Catskill, William H. Roosa of Kingston to Margaret A. Bogardus of Catskill, by Rev. L. L. Noble.

September 17, 1853

1442. Sep 1, Niles, Mich., at Trinity Church, Mr. Cornelius H. Penrose to Miss Harriet E. Adams, daughter of the Clergyman, by Rev. H. Adams.

1443. Sep 8, Blue Mountain, Frederick W. Cunyes to Alida, daughter of Peter Van Vlierden, by Rev. A. C. Hillman.

1444. Sep 7, Hyde Park, Henry Dwight Laflin of Chicago to Josephine Banker of Hyde Park, by Rev. A. M. Mann.

1445. Sep 4, George Joseph Everitt of New York to Miss Sarah Houghtaling of Esopus, by Rev. A. Fort.

1446. Sep 3, Mr. Squire Spencer Jones to Miss Mary Jane Beaully, both of Marbletown, by Rev. John W. Hammond.

1447. Sep 10, Marbletown, Mr. Nelson Hendricks to Miss Elizabeth Wagoner, both of Rochester, by Rev. C. L. Van Dyck.

1448. Sep 10, Ashokan, Jonathan Gray to Miss Nancy F. Rappleyea, both of Rochester, by Rev. Samuel Harlow.

1449. Aug 27, Edward Steward to Eliza Houghtaling, both of Rochester, by Rev. S. Fitch.

September 24, 1853

1450. Sep 22, Saugerties, at the Reformed Dutch Church, Mr. Christian O. Rightmyer to Miss Matilda Schoonmaker, both of Saugerties, by Rev. C. Van Santvoord.

1451. Sep 18, Mr. Robert I. Anderson of New York City to Miss Mary E. Reightmyer of Malden, by Rev. Ira Ferris of Palenville.

1452. Sep 15, Kingston, at St. James Methodist Episcopal Church, Rev. G. S. Gilbert of New Haven, Conn. to Miss Mary G., daughter of Wm. P. Cole, Jr., Esq. of Kingston, by Rev. Nathan Bangs, D. D. of New York City.

1453. Sep 20, Peter Dumont, Jr. to Sarah H., daughter of Oliver Halsey, Esq., all of Saugerties, by Rev. Mr. Griffin.

1454. Sep 1, Guilford parsonage, William Deyo to Sarah C. Snyder, both of New Paltz, by Rev. John N. Jansen.

1455. Sep 8, Guilford parsonage, Timothy Traphagen of Gardiner to Ann Eliza Acker of Newburgh, by Rev. John J. Jansen.

1456. Sep 17, Marbletown, Mr. David B. Hopper of High Falls to Miss Hannah Goslin of Gardiner, by Rev. C. L. Van Dyck.

October 1, 1853

1457. Sep 28, Saugerties, Mr. Edward Ten Eyck to Miss Sarah A. Simmerman, both of Kingston, by Rev. A. F. Selleck.

1458. Sep 28, Kingston, Mr. Thomas Beekman to Miss Catherine Van Keuren, both of Kingston, by Rev. J. C. F. Hoes.

1459. Sep 14, Mr. Frederick W. Pool to Miss Ellen Gibbs, both of Kingston, by Rev. Geo. Waters.

1460. Sep 21, Nathan Williams to Sarah C. Requa, both of New Paltz, by Rev. A. M. Mann.

1461. Sep 7, Rochester, Mr. Daniel Hasbrouck of Marbletown to Miss Jemima Krom of Rochester, by Rev. H. N. Bangs.

1462. Sep 19, Kingston, Sylvester Near to Adelia C. Vredenburgh, both of Kingston, by Rev. H. W. Smuller.

1463. Sep 12, Kingston, James Middagh to Susan Ennis, both of Olive, by Rev. H. W. Smuller.

October 8, 1853

1464. Sep 29, Blue Mountain, Henry Plum to Anna M., daughter of William Groaber, by Rev. A. C. Hillman.

1465. Oct 1, Blue Mountain, Peter A. Schoonmaker to Sally, daughter of Abram Wolven, by Rev. A. C. Hillman.

1466. Sep 22, Honk Hill, Mr. Peter Irwin to Miss Annis A. Knickerbocker, by Rev. Cyrus Shook.

October 15, 1853

1467. Oct 1, Rochester, Abraham Wynkoop to Catharine Elizabeth Barrett, both of Rochester, by John J. Snyder, Esq.

1468. Oct 8, Olive, Francis Brown to Sarah Ann Elmendorf, both of Olive, by Martin Schutt, Esq.

1469. Oct 9, Flatbush, Mr. William Overbaugh of New York to Miss Jane E. Hummel of Saugerties, by Rev. Dr. Gosman.

October 22, 1853

1470. Oct 18, Saugerties, Francis Van Steenburgh to Catharine Smith, both of Saugerties, by Rev. A. F. Selleck.

1471. Oct 16, Unionville, Nicholas P. Clute of Waterford to Mary Wells of Troy, by Rev. C. Van Santvoord.

1472. Oct 12, Marbletown, Lewis Wilson Ackert to Miss Mary Jane Enest, both of Marbletown, by Rev. C. L. Van Dyck.

1473. Oct 12, Kingston, Mr. Jacob Mills to Miss Emmeline Sparling, both of Saugerties, by Rev. George Waters.

1474. Oct 12, Kingston, Elisha M. Brigham to Isabella Nichols, both of Kingston, by Rev. S. S. Relyea.

October 29, 1853

1475. Oct 26, Saugerties, at the home of Hon. J. Russell, J. P. Russell, Esq. to Miss Christina Crawford, both of Saugerties, by Rev. D. Kline.

1476. Oct 26, West Camp, J. F. Dumont, Esq. of Flemington, New Jersey, to Miss Ann, daughter of Rev. D. Kline of West Camp, by Rev. Dr. Pohlman of Albany.

1477. Oct 22, Blue Mountain, Jacob Mart to Catherine, daughter of John Arnst, by Rev. A. C. Hillman.

1478. Sep 26, West Camp, David Bear to Catharine S. Winchell of this town, by Rev. Thomas Lape.

1479. Oct 25, Saugerties, Hezekiah Wynkoop of Catskill to Louisa, daughter of Mr. Henry Huyck of Saugerties, by Rev. C. Van Santvoord.

1480. Oct 25, Saugerties, Peter Hotaling of New Baltimore to Eleanor Vandenburg of Saugerties, by Rev. C. Van Santvoord.

1481. Oct 11, Fishkill Village, Philip Buckley of Kingston to Miss Bridget Knox of Glenham, by Norris Baxter, Esq.

1482. Oct 12, Ellenville, John B. Mance to Rachael Ann Terwilliger, both of Ellenville, by Rev. J. N. Robinson.

1483. Oct 10, New Paltz, Abner H. Fuller to Anna Wallace, both of New Paltz, by Rev. Chas. H. Stitt.

November 5, 1853

1484. Oct 27, George W. Newkirk to Elthea Corl, both of Kingston, by Rev. Dr. Hoes.

1485. Oct 20, Rondout, Sylvester Viele of Sleightburg to Anna Gaskine of Port Ewen, by Rev. S. Fitch.

1486. Oct 23, Samsonville, John A. Prindle to Rachel Smith, both of Marbletown, by John Shurter, Esq.

1487. Oct 29, Alfred Winne of Shandaken to Nelly Catharine Short, by Rev. Alexander Gulick.

November 12, 1853

1488. Nov 10, Mr. John Van Valkenburgh to Miss Mary Craft, both of Saugerties, by Rev. J. R. Johnson.

1489. Nov 3, Golden Hill, Kingston, Mr. Martin C. White of Pike Co., Pa. to Miss Jane M. Robinson of Golden Hill, by D. L. Decker, Esq.

1490. Nov 2, John Minders to Lydia Smedis, both of West Hurley, by Rev. Alexander Gulick.

1491. Nov 3, Edward Weed of Cairo to Catharine Smedis, of West Hurley, by Rev. Alexander Gulick.

1492. Oct 29, Rondout, Mr. George Gasking to Miss Nellie Houghtaling, both of Port Ewen, by Rev. S. Fitch.

November 19, 1853

1493. Nov 7, David Eble to Serena Witherwacks, both of Saugerties, by Rev. Dr. Ostrander.

1494. Nov 7, Hurley, John Plough to Mrs. Susan Wheeler, both of Hurley, by Ten Eyck De Witt, Esq.

1495. Nov 27 <sic> Port Ewen, William B. Shaw to Hester C. Boughton, by Rev. Wesley Taylor.

1496. Nov 7, Kingston, Rensselaer Houghtaling to Sarah Van Buren, both of Kingston, by Rev. H. W. Smuller.

1497. Nov 16, Blue Mountain, Louis Axahelm to Miss Theressa, daughter of Charles Kaufman, by Rev. A. C. Hillman.

November 26, 1853

1498. Aug 20, Plattekill at the Reformed Dutch Church, Mr. Harman San to Miss Maria Relyea, both of Glasco, by Rev. M. L. Schenck. <Daniel Hammel to Maria Rilyea, widow of --- Whitaker, records of the Plattekill, Mt. Marion Reformed Church, ed.>

1499. Aug 20, Kingston, Mr. Lucius Lawson of West Hurley to Mrs. Arietta Brink of Saugerties, by Rev. M. L. Schenck.

1500. Sep 18, Fort Plain, Mr. Elijah Jones of Cherry Valley to Miss Mary C. Melick of Sharon, by Rev. M. L. Schenck.

1501. Oct 3, Fort Plain, Mr. Horatio W. Stocker of New York City to Miss Ada B. Birge of Fort Plain, by Rev. M. L. Schenck.

1502. Nov 9, Fort Plain, Mr. J. W. Harrison Havens of Pen Yan to Miss Louisa W. Wagner of Fort Plain, by Rev. M. L. Schenck.

1503. Nov 5, Isaac Craig to Mary J. Bush, both of Rosendale, by Rev. H. Eckel.

1504. Nov 12, Marbletown, George Freer of New Paltz to Catharine Dubois of Gardiner, by Rev. C. L. Van Dyck.

1505. Nov 14, James Grimes to Elizabeth Morrison, both of Rondout, by Rev. B. T. Phillips.

1506. Nov 14, Robert Gaddess to Deborah Ann Deming, both of Eddyville, by Rev. B. T. Phillips.

1507. Nov 22, Capt. Robert S. Van Wagner of Rondout to Miss Margaret, daughter of Mr. Pierce Catlin of Kingston, by Rev. Mr. Grigen.

December 3, 1853

1508. Nov 26, Tivoli, Mr. John Jay Low to Miss Sarah A. Bingham, daughter of J. B. Bingham, Esq., of Tivoli, by Rev. Mr. Edwards.

1509. Nov 19, Rosendale, Mr. Moses Keator to Miss Jane Bodley, both of Rosendale, by Rev. C. L. Van Dyck.

1510. Nov 24, Rosendale, Mr. Henry Johnson of Gardiner to Miss Rebecca Low of Rosendale, by Rev. C. L. Van Dyck.

December 10, 1853

1511. Dec 3, Brunswick, Rensselaer Co., Mr. Joseph S. Bulson to Mrs. Mary C. File, widow of Adam File, by Rev. David Cline.

1512. Dec 1, Kingston, Mr. E. H. Webster of Cairo to Miss Sarah Ann, daughter of David Kipp of Kingston, by Rev. Mr. Griffin.

1513. Dec 1, Marenus W. Griffen to Mary C. Burhans, both of Kingston, by Rev. Dr. Hoes.

1514. Nov 30, Middletown, Orange Co., John C. Perry, Esq. of Kingston to Hannah J. Mc Quoid of Middletown, by Elder G. Beebe.

December 17, 1853

1515. Dec 13, Saugerties, James Maines to Margaret Derby, both of Saugerties, by Rev. A. F. Selleck.

1516. Dec 15, Saugerties, Harmon Jay Ten Brook of Hudson to Mary C. Foulks of Saugerties, by Rev. A. F. Selleck.

1517. Dec 4, Kingston, Mr. Charles Hathaway to Miss Sophronia Davison, by Rev. George Waters.

1518. Dec 6, Charles W. Young to Mary M. Hine, both of Wawarsing, by Rev. Thos. B. Smith.

1519. My wife, Sally Ann Lewis, having left my bed and board, without caus or provocation, all persons are hereby forbid harboring her on my account, as I will pay no debts of her contraction. William M. Lewis, Nov 24, 1853, Saugerties.

December 24, 1853

1520. Dec 20, Mr. William Rose to Miss Margaret A. Smith, both of Kingston, by Samuel Merclean, Esq.

1521. Dec 3, Mr. Abram J. Tompkins to Martha J., youngest daughter of Stephen Vandover, all of Denning, by Heman Depew, Esq.

1522. Dec 14, Esopus, Garritt Freer to Miss Sarah Ann, daughter of Chas. Brodhead Elting, by Rev. Abm. Fort.

1523. Dec 3, Bloomingdale, Alexander Evans to Miss Catharine Hull, by Rev. B. F. Snyder.

1524. Dec 8, Poughkeepsie, Robert Monell of Hudson to Catharine Broome of Poughkeepsie, by Rev. Albert D. Traver.

December 31, 1853

1525. Dec 22, Saugerties, Mr. Robert W. Sickler to Miss Hannah A. Bostwick, both of Unionville, by Rev. J. R. Johnson.

1526. Dec 22, Kingston, Mr. Peter Ricks to Miss Emma R. Bonesteele, both of Woodstock, by Daniel Decker.

1527. Dec 17, Lewis Schoonmaker to Jane Dubois, by Rev. H. W. Smuller.

1528. Dec 17, Lorenzo Lefever to Miss Charlotte Auchmody of Bloomingdale, by Rev. H. W. Smuller

January 7, 1854

1529. Jan 4, Town of Saugerties, Mr. Hiram Turck to Miss Ida Melissa Brower, both of Saugerties, by Rev. A. F. Selleck.

1530. Jan 2, Alonzo Low to Eliza Moor, both of Kingston, by Rev. C. Van Santvoord.

1531. Jan 7, Jacob Smidt to Julinna Blumer, of Saugerties, by Rev. C. Van Santvoord.

1532. Dec 31, Blue Mountain, John M. Hill to Angelica, daughter of John H. Place, by Rev. A. C. Hillman.

1533. Dec 26, Palenville, Mr. Gains H. Giles to Miss Emeline Crispell, both of the Town of Shandaken, by Rev. Ira Ferris, of Palenville.

1534. Dec 27, Mr. Levi B. More to Miss Mary E. Daniel, both of the Town of Catskill, by Rev. Ira Ferris, of Palenville.

1535. Dec 27, Town of Rochester, Chas. Bloom of Stone Ridge to Sarah Krom of the Town of Rochester, by Rev. Mr. Hauxhurst.

January 14, 1854

1536. Jan 8, Mr. Peter Legg to Mary L., daughter of Jacob P. Elmendorph, by Rev. H. Ostrander.

1537. Jan 10, Brunswick, Jacob S. Sharp of Greenbush to Miss Martha A. Ensign of Brunswick, by Rev. David Kline.

1538. Jan 2, Benjamin J. Moore of Middletown to Jane Rose of Kingston, by Rev. M. Smuller.

1539. Dec 31, James Krum to Catharine Merrihew, both of Olive, by Rev. S. Harlow.

January 21, 1854

1540. Jan 17, Flatbush, George Hutton to Ann Maginnis, both of Glasco, by Rev. Dr. Gosman.

1541. Jan 5, Kingston, Andrew L. Styles to Harriet S. Bonesteel, both of Kingston, by Rev. Mr. Griffen.

1542. Jan 7, Kingston, Abram Hasbrouck to Martha A. Mash, both of Kingston, by Rev. W. Loomis of Poughkeepsie.

1543. Jan 4, Marbletown, Mr. H. B. Hornbeck to Sarah Schoonmaker, both of Rochester, by Rev. C. Van Dyck.

January 28, 1854

1544. Jan 18, Esopus, Zachariah Acker of Lloyd to Lucinda Terpening of Esopus, by Rev. J. Whitaker.

1545. Jan 13, Rondout, Wm. Finley to Jane Thompson, both of Rondout, by Rev. B. T. Philips.

February 4, 1854

1546. Nov 25, Jared W. Clark of Windham Centre to Catharine Bennet of the Town of Saugerties, by Rev. Josiah Leonard.

1547. Dec 31, Peter E. Bell to Rachel Hoff, both of the Town of Saugerties, by Rev. Josiah Leonard.

1548. Jan 25, Kingston, Alfred Hudler to Delia Dubois, both of Kingston, by Rev. Dr. Hoes.

1549. Jan 21, Marbletown, Stephen Coons to Mary J. Silkworth, by Rev. N. H. Bangs.

1550. Jan 21, Marbletown, James H. Vandermark to Judith Winchel, both of Olive, by Rev. N. H. Bangs.

1551. Jan 21, Shandaken, William Lane to Sarah Slusser, both of Shandaken, by William Risely, Esq.

February 11, 1854

1552. Nov 13, John L. Elmendorf to Eliza C. Knorr, both of Hurley, by B. C. Lippincott.

1553. Jan 18, Henry Mason of Newark, New Jersey to Catharine Morris of Rosendale, by B. C. Lippincott.

February 18, 1854

1554. Feb 9, Mr. Sherwood Rowe to Miss Christina J. Falk, both of the Town of Catskill, by Rev. Ira Ferris of Palenville.

1555. Feb 13, Kingston, Robert Fleming of Rondout to Maria Waver of Kingston, by Rev. M. W. Smuller.

1556. Feb 2, Christian Winne, Jr. to Sarah Catharine Hill, both of Shandaken, by Rev. John W. Hammond.

February 25, 1854

1557. Feb 9, Mr. Seaman G. Searing to Miss Julia, daughter of John C. Welch, both of Saugerties, by Rev. Mr. Nichols.

1558. Feb 18, Alvin D. Spencer of Rochester to Yetta M. Vanaken of Saugerties, by Rev. Dr. Gosman.

1559. Jan 29, Kingston, James Hilme to Amy Jones, both of Ellenville, by Rev. Mr. Griffin.

1560. Feb 15, Kingston, at the Methodist parsonage, Robt. Noble to Miss Margaret Martin, both of Kingston, by Rev. Mr. Griffin.

1561. Feb 9, Cornelius Hotaling to Mary Ann Myer, both of Hurley, by Rev. R. C. Lippincott.

1562. Feb 12, Auguston Sutton to Deborah Sutton, both of Hurley, by Rev. R. C. Lippincott.

March 4, 1854

1563. Feb 15, St. Louis, Mr. Philip W. Hermance to Miss Mary E. Darby, niece of the Hon. John F. Darby, all of that city, by Rev. Father Duggan.

1564. Feb 17, Ellenville, Mr. Jacob M. Hendricks of New Paltz, to Miss Elizabeth Stilwell of Rochester, by Rev. Mr. Ayers.

1565. Feb 25, Kingston, Peter Ten Eyck to Eliza M. Schoonmaker, both of Kingston, by Rev. H. W. Smuller.

March 11, 1854

1566. Feb 2, Rosendale, Jonathan Deyo of Rosendale to Lucinda Constable of Olive, by Jas. H. Elmendorf.

1567. Feb 9, Olive, Isaac I. Lyons to Gitty Jane Bartholemew, both of Olive, by John Shorter, Esq.

March 18, 1854

1568. Mar 9, Kingston, Mr. Franklin Fulton of Rondout to Miss Gertrude Terry of Kingston, by Rev. Dr. Hoes.

1569. Mar 8, Woodstock, Mr. Elias Fields of Boston to Miss Sarah E. Reynolds of Woodstock, by Rev. Alex. Gulick.

1570. Mar 16, Blue Mountain, Mr. Lewis Egner to Eliza Catharine, daughter of the late Wm. Timmerman of Kiskatom, by Rev. A. C. Hillman.

March 25, 1854

1571. Mar 22, Saugerties, Mr. William H. Bullock to Miss Orilla A. Barber of Hurley, by Rev. C. Van Santvoord.

1572. Mar 21, Saugerties, Mr. Christopher Caver to Miss Jacobena Buchart, both of Saugerties, by Rev. A. F. Selleck.

1573. Mar 15, Palenville, Mr. Campbell A. Wallace of Saugerties to Miss Catharine Bassett of Catskill.

1574. Mar 13, Ellenville, Mr. John Milliken to Miss Rebecca Gorton, by Rev. S. B. Ayers.

April 1, 1854

1575. Mar 30, Saugerties, George Wells to Harriet Lewis, by Rev. C. Van Santvooord.

1576. Mar 22, Palenville, Franklin Petit to Clarissa Peck, both of Catskill, by Rev. I. Ferris.

1577. Mar 21, Kingston, at St. John's Church, John Hughes to Elizabeth Hackett, both of Kingston, by Rev. George Waters.

1578. Mar 25, Bloomingdale, Frederick J. S. Schoonmaker to Hannah L. Thompson, by Rev. S. S. Relyea.

April 8, 1854

1579. Mar 27, Saugerties, Robert H. Whitaker to Elizabeth l. Russell, both of Saugerties, by Rev. A. F. Selleck.

1580. Mar 29, Saugerties, John H. Swart to Gertrude E. Schoonmaker, both of Plattekill, by Rev. A. F. Selleck.

1581. Apr 6, George W. Dederick to Selia, daughter of Henry O. Myer, all of Saugerties, by Dr. Ostrander.

1582. Apr 4, Rondout, Nelson Van Gasbeek to Harriet Dewitt, both of Wiltwick, by Rev. S. Fitch.

1583. Apr 1, Mr. Levi Leonard to Sarah Lane, both of Shandaken, by Rev. John W. Hammond of Olive.

1584. Mar 30, James H. Merrihew to Cornelia B. Dubois, both of Beaverkill, by Rev. John W. Hammond of Olive.

1585. Mar 25, Bloomingdale, Frederick J. Schoonmaker to Hannah L. Thompson, by Rev. S. S. Relyea.

1586. Mar 16, Thomas Lenehan to Miss Catharine Haynes, both of Kingston, by Edward Davison, Esq.

April 15, 1854
1587. Apr 6, Philip Deringer to Agnes W. Abeel, both of Saugerties, by Christopher Fiero, Esq.

1588. Mar 26, Wiltwick, James Whitaker of Rondout to Eliza C. Lee of Wiltwick, by Rev. S. Fitch.

1589. Apr 6, Rondout, Wm. H. Wight to Althea M. Schultz, both of Arnoldton, by Rev. S. Fitch.

1590. Apr 1, Rosendale, Jacob B. Slater to Mary M. Lane, both of Rosendale, by Ten Eyck De Witt, Esq.

1591. Apr 1, Levi Leonard to Suson Lane, both of Shandaken, by Rev. J. W. Hammond, Esq.

1592. Apr 1, Napanoch, Peter C. Weaver of Rosendale to Margaret B. Avery of High Falls, by Rev. T. B. Smith.

April 22, 1854
1593. Apr 14, Zachariah More of Hurley to Eliza Catharine Bogart of Olive, by Rev. John W. Hammond.

1594. Mar 29, Olive, Lorenzo Fish to Maria Selbeworth, both of Olive, by Martin Schutt, Esq.

1595. Apr 13, Shokan, George Saterly to Bridget Breadstreet, both of Shandaken, by Martin Schutt, Esq.

April 29, 1854
1596. Apr 29, Peter Wynkoop of Marbletown to Miss Julia E. Jackson of Kingston, by Rev. Dr. Hoes.

1597. Apr 18, Henry Schropp of Rosendale to Hanna Roth of Lackawack, by Melford Vernooy, Esq.

1598. Apr 20, Kingston, John H. Lockwood to Sarah A. Willis, both of Woodstock, by Rev. Mr. Griffen.

1599. Apr 18, Kingston, Wm. Tieball of Williamsburgh to Hanna Ellis of Kingston, by Rev. Mr. Griffen.

May 6, 1854
1600. Apr 30, Wilbur, Nathaniel Booth of Wilbur to Dorcas A. Shaffer of Saugerties, by Rev. Jno. Madden.

1601. Apr 26, Marbletown, Rev. Lyman W. Walsworth of the New York Annual Conference to Anna Elvira, eldest daughter of Isaac Bloom, Esq., of Marbletown, by Rev. J. Burton Beach.

1602. Apr 24, Rochester, Peter Wynkoop to Harriet Parsell, both of Rochester, by John J. Snyder, Esq.

1603. Apr 26, Poughkeepsie, Wm. W. Smith to Huldah M. Gilbert, both of Poughkeepsie, by Rev. H. G. Ludlow.

May 13, 1854
1604. May 4, Rondout, Calvert Vaux, Esq. of Croydon, England to Mary S., eldest daughter of J. S. Mc Entee, of Rondout, by Rev. Dr. Sawyers of New York City.

1605. May 1, Poughkeepsie, George Nelson, Esq., of Rondout to Margaret Mortimer of Poughkeepsie, by Rev. H. G. Ludlow.

1606. May 4, Schenectady, at St. George's Church, Gilbert R. Tobey of New York to Eliza H., daughter of the late Archibald Campbell, Esq. of Schenectady, by Rev. Wm. Payne.

May 20, 1854

1607. Apr 30, Abram Craft to Mrs. Elmira Moore, by Rev. C. Van Santvoord.

1608. May 14, Calvin S. Terwilliger to Anna Maria Shumway, both of the Town of Saugerties, by Rev. Thomas Lape.

1609. May 14, West Camp, Abraham De Witt Merrit to Hannah Holden, both of the Town of Saugerties, by Rev. Thomas Lape.

1610. May 10, James Griffith to Anna Margaret, daughter of Tunis I. Houghtaling, both of Kingston, by Rev. Dr. Hoes.

1611. May 11, New York, at the home of Thomas T. Griffen, Benjamin C. Arnold of Arnoldtown to Mary J. Griffen of New York City, members of the Society of Friends.

1612. May 5, Marbletown, George Davis to Amanda Pine, both of Marbletown, by Rev. N. H. Bangs.

1613. May 6, Marbletown, Thomas Winchel of Denning to Sarah Davis of Marbletown, by Rev. N. H. Bangs.

1614. May 8, Brooklyn, James Forde of Kingston to Ellen Keefe of Brooklyn.

May 27, 1854

1615. May 8, Kingston, John Raules of Troy to Catharine Le Fever of Kingston, by Rev. H. W. Smuller.

1616. May 20, Kingston, Tunis Vandemark of Kingston to Susan Hoffman of Poughkeepsie, by Rev. H. W. Smuller.

June 3, 1854

1617. May 31, New York City, William Mauterstock of Saugerties to Miss Julia A. Schenck of Hightstown, by Rev. D. M. Graham.

1618. May 28, Kingston, Mr. Thomas J. Schoonmaker to Mariah H. Terhune, both of Rochester, by Rev. Dr. Hoes.

1619. May 21, Rondout, Augustus R. Stone to Rachel Thompson, both of Rondout, by Rev. Mr. Fitch.

June 10, 1854

1620. Jun 3, Kingston, Abram S. Schoonmaker to Mary Jane Conner, both of Kingston, by Rev. R. A. Chalker.

June 17, 1854

1621. Jun 3, Plattekill, Christopher Longendike of Saugerties to Anna Maria Stewart, by Rev. N. F. Chapman.

1622. Jun 11, Plattekill, Wm. H. Sole of Geneva to Miss Lucy A. Post of Kingston, by Rev. N. F. Chapman.

1623. Jun 8, John Salisbury Burhans to Anna Elizabeth Hoffman, both of Kingston, by Rev. Dr. Hoes.

1624. May 30, John C. Wygant to Jemima Velie, both of Marlborough, by Rev. S. H. Jagger.

1625. May 31, Tunis B. Velie to Charlotte W. Wygant, both of Marlborough, by Rev. S. H. Jagger.

June 24, 1854

1626. Jun 17, Blue Mountain, Peter Ransom to Elizabeth, daughter of David Garrison, by Rev. A. C. Hillman.

July 1, 1854

1627. Jun 23, at the house of Peter Kelder, William Davis to Nelly Smith, both of Marbletown, by T. E. De Witt Vedder, Esq.

1628. Jun 10, Henry Smith to Lavina Catharine Vandemark, both of Marbletown, by R. E. De Witt Vedder, Esq.

1629. Jun 18, Rondout, at the Methodist Episcopal Church, Samuel Dubois Deyo to Anna Matilda, eldest daughter of Elisha Brown of Rondout, by Rev. S. Fitch.

1630. Jun 21, Rondout, German Rouse of Hoboken, New Jersey to Louiza Eighmey of Woodstock, by Rev. S. Fitch.

July 8, 1854

1631. Jul 4, Kingston, Wallace Lee of Olive to Persillia Flowers of West Hurley, by Rev. John W. Hammond.

1632. Jun 24, Rondout, Adam Gunther to Ann Michaely, both of Kingston, by Johannis D. Hasbrouck, Esq.

1633. Jun 22, Coxsackie, Norman M. Welling of the steamship Nautilus to Miss Maria Louisa, daughter of Capt. F. G. Demming of that village, by Rev. J. Coe.

July 15, 1854

1634. Jun 29, New York City, John Post of Seneca, Ontario Co., to Miss Adelaide Louise, 2nd daughter of Samuel Schoonmaker of New York, by Rev. Thomas J. Sawyer.

1635. Jul 4, John Plain of Schenectady to Miss Sarah Post of Kingston, by Rev. R. A. Chalker.

1636. Jul 6, Robert Kinner to Susan Van De Bogert, both of West Hurley, by Rev. R. A. Chalker.

1637. Jul 3, Harrison Brock of New York City to Arietta Dubois of Kingston, by Rev. Dr. Hoes.

1638. Jun 29, Marbletown, Jacob H. Snyder to Mrs. Mary A Van Wagenen, by Rev. C. L. Van Dyck.

1639. Jul 3, Marbletown, Thomas H. Vandemark to Sarah Jane Bush, by Rev. C. L. Van Dyck.

July 22, 1854
1640. Jul 14, David Yerry to Cemira Catharine Shultis, both of Woodstock, by Rev. John W. Hammond of Olive.

1641. Undated, Flatbush, Derick W. Sparling to Martha W. Converse, both of Kingston, by Rev. Dr. Gosman. <July 18, 1854, Flatbush Reformed Church Records, ed.>

1642. Jun 19, Athens, Capt. John Pennington of May's Landing, New Jersey to Elizabeth Ann, oldest daughter of Byron Cook of Athens, by Rev. Thomas Lape.

July 29, 1854
1643. Jul 20, Marbletown, Mr. Abraham I. Sahler to Miss Margaretta L. Wilklow, by Rev. C. L. Van Dyck.

1644. Jul 16, Benjamin Sanford to Miss Fanny Holliday, both of Poughkeepsie, by Rev. Mr. Ferris.

August 5, 1854
1645. Jul 30, Flatbush, Garret Tymeson to Eliza Rush, both of Saugerties, by Rev. Dr. Gosman.

1646. Jun 29, Saugerties, Jacob Van Gelden of Catskill to Eliza M., daughter of William Van Etten of Saugerties, by Rev. C. Van Santvoord.

1647. Jun 29, Saugerties, Daniel T. D. York to Julia Taylor, by Rev. C. Van Santvoord.

1648. Jun 29, Wiltwyck, Society of Friends, Gabriel Contant of Dashville, Esopus to Hannah Tremper of Ponkhockie.

1649. Jul 16, Jacob A. Krom, widower to Elizabeth Coddington, widow, both of the Town of Rochester, by Rev. David Sampson.

1650. Jul 12, Robbert F. White of New York City to Jane C. Pattison of Hurley, by Rev. B. C. Lippincott.

August 12, 1854

1651. Aug 5, Peter Weaver to Jane Ann Haliwick, both of Kingston, by Rev. William Blake.

1652. Aug 5, John Hoffman to Barbara Gunn, both of Saugerties, by Rev. William Blake.

1653. Aug 6, Henry A. Viderman to Augusta Durand, both of Saugerties, by Rev. William Blake.

1654. Aug 7, Charles Cook to Margaret Sythes, both of Saugerties, by Rev. William Blake.

1655. Aug 3, New York City, Frederick Weaver, Jr. of Rondout to Catharine Willis of New York, by Rev. Mr. Geissenhimer.

August 19, 1854

1656. Jul 26, Ellenville, Peter Seis to Mrs. Catharine Seis, both of Napanoch, by Rev. S. B. Ayers.

1657. Jul 26, Sandburgh, Alfred M. Teller to Miss Hannah Terwilliger, by Rev. S. B. Ayers.

1658. Aug 9, Esopus, John E. Adams of Michigan to Miss Sarah Helen Crook of Esopus, by Rev. Mr. Fort.

1659. Aug 12, Marbletown, Levi De Puy to Rachel Krum, by Rev. C. L. Van Dyck.

1660. Aug 12, Marbletown, Mr. Henry Quick to Sophia Wagoner, both of Rochester, by Rev. C. L. Van Dyck.

1661. Jul 26, Hughsonville, Solomon Brodhead to Catharine M. Keator, both of Rosendale, by Rev. A. N. Botsford.

1662. Aug 5, Rochester, John B. Van Wagenen to Rachel A. Smith, both of Rochester, by L. B. Hasbrouck, Esq.

August 26, 1854

1663. Aug 12, Saugerties, Andrew J. Bartlett of Albany to Olive A. Craw of Durham, by Rev. William Blake.

1664. Aug 5, New Paltz, Samuel Selleck of Cold Spring to Maria Dubois of New Paltz, by Rev. C. H. Stit.

1665. Aug 12, Poughkeepsie, Amos B. Ferguson of Pleasantville, Westchester Co., NY to Louisa J. House of Esopus, by Hon. G. Dean.

September 2, 1854

1666. Aug 21, Kingston, John Kelley to Miss Mary Ann Freston, both of Creek Locks, by Rev. Geo. Waters.

1667. Aug 24, Simon Embree of Marbletown to Mary Quimby of Rochester, by John Shurter, Esq.

September 9, 1854

1668. Sep 4, Saugerties, Henry M. De Myer to Sarah, daughter of David Schoonmaker, all of Saugerties, by Rev. C. Van Santvoord.

1669. Sep 3, Kingston, at St. John's Church, Mr. Robert Finley to Miss Jane Manning, both of Port Ewen, by Rev. George Waters.

1670. Aug 21, North Newburgh, Mr. Benjamin B. York of Wawarsing to Miss Jane, daughter of Jacob Wilkes, by Rev. Thomas Edwards.

September 16, 1854

1671. Sep 6, Hyde Park, at the residence of her father, Cornelius Alexander Cole of Kingston to Phebe E., daughter of John P. Dennis, Esq., by Rev. R. A. Chalker.

1672. Sep 7, Kingston, at the residence of her father, George L. Dennis of Hyde Park to Magdelena E., daughter of Wm. P. Cole, Jr., Esq., of Kingston, by Rev. R. A. Chalker.

1673. Sep 5, Jacob Brink to Jane Van Steenburgh, both of Kingston, by Rev. Dr. Hoes.

1674. Sep 4, Bloomingdale, Francis G. Raymond to Almira P. Meade, by Rev. B. F. Snyder.

1675. Sep 2, Marbletown, at the home of Jacob Irwin, James G. Weeks to Charlotte Moore, both of Marbletown, by A. Benson, Esq.

September 23, 1854

1676. Sep 12, Red Hook, Edward J. Mc Carthy, Esq. of Saugerties, to Eliza, daughter of Henry Staats, Esq. of Red Hook, by Wm. D. Stroebel, D. D.

1677. Sep 6, Lake Hill, Woodstock, Mr. Benjamin L. Short to Gertrude M. Sagendorf, both of Woodstock, by Rev. H. C. Longyear of Shandaken.

1678. Sep 7, John Marakle of West Hurley to Catharine Winchell of Olive, by Rev. Alexander Gulick.

1679. Sep 6, Kingston, James Cagan of Kingston to Sarah Burger of Esopus, by Rev. H. W. Smuller.

September 30, 1854

1680. Sep 20, Kingston, Wm. Mickins to Mary, daughter of Martin Minor, all of Kingston, by Rev. Mr. Dubois.

1681. Sep 20, Kingston, Wm. H. Hayes to Sarah C. Mickins, both of Kingston, by Rev. Mr. Waters.

1682. Sep 16, Poughkeepsie, Jesse Steel of Old Paltz to Ann H. Brodhead of Marbletown, by Rev. A. M. Mann.

1683. Sep 16, John P. Dewitt to Elmira Roosa, both of Rochester, by John Shurter, Esq.

October 7, 1854

1684. Sep 28, John H. Scott of Denning to Louisa L. Gillet of Fallsburgh, by Rev. John W. Hammond of Olive

1685. Sep 28, Nelson March of Otsego to Emma J. Longyear of Olive, by Rev. John W. Hammond.

1686. Oct 3, West Camp, Jacob F. Bouck, Esq. of Albany to Catharine E., daughter of Wm. Adams, Esq. of West Camp, by Rev. David Kline.

1687. Sep 27, Kingston, John D. Sleight to Ann Eliza, daughter of Peter E. Hasbrouck, Esq. of Kingston, by Rev. Dr. John Gosman.

1688. Sep 27, Rondout, Charles Bailey to Nancy Roe, both of Rondout, by Rev. B. T. Phillips.

October 14, 1854

1689. Sep 20, Kingston, Mr. James Sullivan of Philadelphia to Catharine Boyle of Kingston, by Rev. R. A. Chalker.

1690. Oct 4, St. James Methodist Episcopal Church, William Beatty to Mrs. Eliza Catharine Knox, both of Kingston, by Rev. R. A. Chalker.

1691. Oct 4, Kingston, Peter Masten to Susan E., daughter of David Conklin, all of Kingston, by Rev. John F. C. Hoes, D. D.

1692. Sep 16, James Carrol to Mrs. Mary Ann Fitch, both of Stone Ridge, by T. E. De Witt Veeder, Esq.

1693. Sep 30, Abram Quick to Katy Jane Hendrickson, both of Rochester, by T. E. De Witt Veeder, Esq.

October 21, 1854

1694. Oct 12, Ellenville, James Collins of Greenfield to Mrs. Mary Waters of Wawarsing, by Rev. James W. Denton.

1695. Oct 5, near Bloomingburgh, Edward H. Leggett to Miss Mary C., daughter of Jacob Randal, Esq. of Wallkill, Orange Co, by Rev. John H. Leggett.

October 28, 1854

1696. Oct 26, Aaron Hasbrouck of Kingston to Alida J., daughter of Henry Peal of Saugerties, by Rev. C. Van Santvoord.

1697. Oct 21, Blue Mountain, Cornelius Plough to Sarah, daughter of Jas. Wines, by Rev. A. C. Hillman.

1698. Oct 26, Lewis Fratscher to Sarah Whitely, both of Saugerties.

November 4, 1854

1699. Oct 28, Christopher Teetsel to Eliza Catharine Hommel, both of Saugerties, by Rev. Thomas Lape.

1700. Oct 29, Rondout, Jacob Nestlen to Anna Knorr, both of Saugerties, by Rev. C. H. Siebke.

1701. Oct 26, Robert L. Winne of Shandaken to Elizabeth Ann Weeks of Olive, by Rev. John W. Hammond.

1702. Oct 26, Catskill, at the Church of St. Luke, Hiram Atkins, editor of the Bellows Falls, Vt., *Argus* to Maria Abeel Dewitt of Catskill, by Rev. Thomas Richley.

1703. Oct 26, Garret D. Vandemark to Maria Middaugh, both of Marbletown, by Rev. Dr. Hoes.

1704. Oct 21, Olive, George W. Jones of Portsmouth, New Hampshire to Susan Ferris of Dover, Dutchess Co., by Rev. Dr. Gosman.

November 11, 1854

1705. Nov 4, William A. Dubois of Saugerties to Louisa Phillips of Fort Plain, Montgomery Co., by Rev. C. Van Santvoord.

1706. Nov 9, at the home of Dr. W. C. Dewitt, Frederick Saam to Magdelena Glasbeener, by Rev. C. Van Santvoord.

1707. Nov 6, Kingston, Abm. F. Calkins of New York City to Elizabeth E. Avery of Kingston, by Rev. Dr. Hoes.

November 18, 1854

1708. Oct 18, John V. Winne to Eliza Catharine, daughter of John Kimball, both of Saugerties, by Dr. Ostrander.

1709. Nov 12, David Ranson to Anna Maria Wolven, both of Saugerties, by Dr. Ostrander.

1710. Nov 12, Alexander Wilson Dederick to Eugenia Shaffer, both of Saugerties, by Dr. Ostrander.

November 25, 1854

1711. Undated, Cornelius S. Decker to Mary M., daughter of Martin Wolven, all of Saugerties, by Dr. Gosman. <November 11, 1854, Flatbush Reformed Church Records, ed.>

1712. Nov 16, Esopus, Peter Delamater to Sophia H. Thompson, by Rev. Dr. Hoes.

1713. Nov 14, Kettleburgh, Solomon Van Orden to Sarah C., daughter of Cornelius Lefever, by Rev. John N. Jansen.

1714. Nov 9, Geo. Richards of Windham Centre, Greene Co., to Elizabeth L. Hubbard of West Hurley, by Rev. Alex Gulick.

1715. Nov 14, William H. Van Etten to Barbara A. Van Etten, both of Kingston, by Rev. Alex. Gulick.

December 2, 1854

1716. Dec 30, <sic> Mr. John H. Smith to Frances E. Place, both of Unionville, by Rev. C. Van Santvoord.

1717. Nov 21, Woodstock, Wm. H. Whitaker to Jane Ann Slater, by Rev. A. C. Hillman.

1718. Nov 19, Poughkeepsie, Josiah R. Wood of Gardiner to Sarah E. Agin of Poughkeepsie, by Rev. L. H. King.

December 9, 1854

1719. Nov 30, Frederick Davis to Sarah Amelia Bodley, both of Olive, by Rev. John W. Hammond.

1720. Dec 6, Saugerties, Bernherd Laran of Rondout to Elizabeth Young of Saugerties, by Samuel Merclean, Esq.

1721. Nov 28, Kingston, David N. Terhune of Rochester to Lavina M. Place of Kingston, by Rev. Dr. Hoes.

December 23, 1854

1722. Dec 17, Kingston, Mr. Cornelius Van Wey of Whiteport to Miss Maria Catharine Elting of Kingston, by Rev. Henry W. Smuller.

1723. Dec 19, Simon P. Place to Eleanor Smith, both of Unionville, by Rev. W. Blake.

1724. Dec 16, Saugerties, William W. Timmerman of Kiskatom to Miss Catharine Magee of the Town of Saugerties, by Rev. Thomas Lape.

1725. Dec 9, Ellenville, Robert W. Carley of Ellenville to Maria Lake of Lackawack, by R. B. Taylor, Esq..

January 5, 1855

1726. Dec 23, Blue Mountain, Levi Becker to Gitty Cole, by Rev. A. C. Hillman.

1727. Dec 27, Thomas Booth of Wilbur to Ann E. Kearney of Saugerties, by Rev. Michael Power, D. D.

1728. Dec 30, John Wood to Caroline Gulnick, both of Woodstock, by Rev. John W. Hammond.

1729. Dec 30, Blue Mountain, John Berry to Sarah E. Parker, by Rev. A. C. Hillman.

1730. Jan 1, Valentine Mote to Caroline Claseais, by Rev. A. C. Hillman.

1731. Dec 26, Jacob L. De Witt to Martha Jane, daughter of John H. Schryver, both of Kingston, by Rev. R. A. Chalker.

January 19, 1855

1732. Jan 10, Poughkeepsie, George S. Simions of Montreal, U. C. to Anna, daughter of N. Cantine of Wawarsing, Ulster Co., by Rev. A. M. Mann.

January 26, 1855

1733. Jan 7, Rondout, George Bennett to Adelia Tronson, both of Kingston, by Rev. S. Fitch.

1734. Jan 2, Anning Smith of Lloyd to Annie J. Carpenter of Poughkeepsie, by Rev. A. M. Mann.

February 2, 1855

1735. Jan 25, Plattekill, Mr. James D. Longendike to Miss Arrietta Maria, daughter of Sebastian Plass, by Rev. N. F. Chapman.

1736. Jan 29, Kingston, Wm. M. Clark to Julia W. Peck, both of Kingston, by Rev. G. Waters.

1737. Jan 28, Castleton, Peter B. Ransom, formerly of Saugerties to Miss C. Vandenburgh of Castleton, by Rev. E. P. Stimson.

February 9, 1855

1738. Jan 28, Geo. Rehfers to Gottleiben Klein, by Rev. C. Van Santvoord.

1739. Jan 24, Kingston, John I. Longyear of Woodstock to Abigail Lindsley of Delaware Co., by Rev. S. S. Relyea.

February 16, 1855

1740. Feb 12, Saugerties, Frederick W. Grosse to Arletta C. B. Dymond, both of Saugerties, by Rev. Mr. Blake.

1741. Feb 11, Louis W. Van Hoesen of Coxsackie to Isabella A. Maxwell of Saugerties, by Rev. Mr. Blake.

1742. Feb 11, Thomas Maxwell, Jr. to Jane A. Hommel, both of Saugerties, by Rev. Mr. Blake.

1743. Feb 4, Rondout, William Mink, printer, to Elizabeth H., only daughter of S. Reynolds of Kingston, by Rev. Mr. Phillips.

February 23, 1855
1744. Feb 14, Rondout, at the home of Stephen Abbey, Delakire Budd of New York to Charlotte Augusta Marshall of Rondout, by Rev. B. T. Phillips.

March 2, 1855
1745. Feb 17, Kingston, at Schryver's Hotel, Jeremiah Auchmoody of Esopus to Hannah Gardiner of Lloyd, by Rev. Anson Dubois.

1746. Feb 22, Marbletown, William Krum of Marbletown to Hannah Maria Vandemark of Rochester, by T. E. De Witt Veder, Esq.

March 9, 1855
1747. Feb 25, Jacob Fritz to Margaret Maines, both of Kingston, by Rev. R. A. Chalker.

1748. Mar 1, Thomas B. Ostrander of Rochester to Mary C. Davis of Marbletown, by Rev. R. A. Chalker.

1749. Mar 1, Mortimer Van Etten to Eliza Ann Ostrander, both of Kingston, by Rev. Dr. Hoes.

March 16, 1855
1750. Mar 8, Saugerties, Jacob Kaufman to Rosie Heer, both of Saugerties, by Rev. C. Van Santvoord.

1751. Mar 13, Saugerties, Henry E. Snyder to Mary Yaman, both of Saugerties, by Rev. Mr. Blake.

1752. Mar 14, Saugerties, James Y. Bates to Miss Amanda Dann, both of Colchester, Delaware Co., by Rev. Mr. Blake.

1753. Mar 1, Noah Snyder to Mrs. Hannah Myer, both of the Town of Saugerties, by Rev. N. F. Chapman.

1754. Mar 10, Silas W. Laig of West Hurley to Miss Margaret M., daughter of Hosea Wood of Woodstock, by Rev. Dr. Ostrander.

1755. Mar 12, James T. Mc Intyre to Ann P. Merritt, both of Kingston, by Rev. Anson Dubois.

1756. Mar 3, John W. Cassell to Mrs. Eliza Hanford, both of Kingston, by Rev. R. A. Chalker.

1757. Mar 8, Kingston, Edgar Elmendorf of Hurley to Mary V. Elmendorf of New York City, by Rev. Dr. Hoes.

March 23, 1855

1758. Mar 10, Blue Mountain, Jack Spealman to Margaret M. Wolven, by Rev. A. C. Hillman.

1759. Mar 7, William A. Allison, Esq., editor of the Newburgh *Gazette*, to Ellie Russell, eldest daughter of Loring L. Lombard, Esq., of New York, by Rev. Dr. Burchard.

1760. Feb 27, Marlborough, Aaron Atkins of Kingston to Florence D. Osborn of St. Petersburgh, Russia, by John Wood, Esq.

March 30, 1855

1761. Mar 21, Mr. William Taylor to Emily Lewis, both of West Hurley, by Rev. William Blake.

1762. Undated, George M. Livingston of Malden to Anna, daughter of Peter Emerick of Saugerties, by Rev. C. Van Santvoord.

April 6, 1855

1763. Mar 24, Blue Mountain, James E. Mason, Jr. to Martha D. Mason, by Rev. A. C. Hillman

1764. Mar 26, Blue Mountain, George E. Young to Lavina Snyder, by Rev. A. C. Hillman.

1765. Mar 25, Ellenville, Henry Missener of Shandaken to Mary Ware of Ellenville, by Rev. J. N. Robinson.

April 13, 1855

1766. Mar 3, Esopus, James Van Keuren to Sarah Jane Marten, both of Esopus, by John A. Bodley, Esq.

1767. Apr 5, Andrew Rosa to Jane Brodhead, both of High Falls, by Rev. C. L. Van Dyck.

1768. Apr 3, Ellenville, John H. Van Wagenen to Janette Broadhead, both of Ellenville, by Rev. E. W. Bentley.

1769. Apr 3, near Ellenville, Judson Schultz to Anna Eastgate, both of Wawarsing, by Rev. E. W. Bentley.

April 20, 1855

1770. Apr 4, David Roos to Agnes Schneider, both of Saugerties, by Rev. N. F. Chapman.

1771. Apr 16, Darius Peck of Peckville, Dutchess Co. to Maria Dennager of Saugerties, by Rev. William Blake.

1772. Apr 11, Beaverkill, West Hurley, William Moore to Lucy M. Baker, both of Hurley, by Rev. H. C. Longyear.

April 27, 1855

1773. Apr 24, Rome, Jason Gillespy of Saugerties to Mary, daughter of A. Vredenburgh, Esq. of Rome, by Rev. W. E. Knox.

1774. Apr 24, Kingston, William A. Gunn of Lexington, Ky. to Mary D., daughter of the late E. O'Neil of Kingston, by Rev. R. A. Chalker.

1775. Apr 19, Ellenville, Abel Blanshan of Napanoch to Hannah M. Terwilliger of Ellenville, by Rev. J. N. Robinson.

May 4, 1855

1776. Apr 21, Augustus Wolven to Sarah Ann Waters, both of Quarryville, by Rev. Mr. Blake.

1777. Apr 29, George Thomas to Sarah C. Love, both of Saugerties, by Rev. Mr. Blake.

1778. Apr 25, Dr. Abraham Crispell of Rondout to Jane A., daughter of P. Catlin of Kingston, by Rev. R. A. Chalker.

May 11, 1855

1779. May 8, Blue Mountain, Mr. Manasseh Newkirk to Elizabeth M., daughter of Peter Young, by Rev. A. C. Hillman.

1780. May 5, Blue Mountain, William Brown to Margaret, daughter of John E. Boise, by Rev. A. C. Hillman.

1781. May 1, Phelps, Ontario Co., Philip Snyder, Principal of Public School # 3 of Albany to Malendea Deuel of Phelps, by Rev. Charles Hawley.

1782. May 5, William M. Deits of Rosendale to Mrs. Ann E. Parsons of Kingston, by Rev. R. A. Chalker.

May 18, 1855

1783. May 17, Rondout, Mr. Mynderse Schoonmaker of Saugerties to Miss Loraine, youngest daughter of Nathan T. Anderson, Esq., of Rondout, by Rev. S. Fitch.

1784. May 8, Kingston, James Robinson of High Falls to Sarah C. Westbrook of Kingston, by Rev. H. W. Smuller.

1785. May 1, John E. Mc Pherson to Sarah, daughter of Benj. G. Newkirk, both of Hurley, by Rev. B. C. Lippincott.

1786. May 2, Rondout, Julius A. Matson to Sarah K. Spencer, both of New York, by Rev. B. T. Phillips.

1787. Apr 30, Rondout, William Van Woert to Emily, daughter of Anthony Everson, all of Rondout, by Rev. S. Fitch.

June 8, 1855

1788. May 31, Ephraim M. Bishop to Miss Eliza Ann Wood, both of Olive, by Rev. John W. Hammond.

June 15, 1855

1789. Jun 9, Flatbush, Joseph Seaman of Kingston to Lydia Ann Bell of Glenerie, by Rev. Dr. Gosman.

1790. Jun 7, Andrew Low to Harriet Seaman, both of Kingston, by Rev. Dr. Gosman.

1791. Jun 2, Town of Saugerties, Nehemiah Wolven of the Town of Woodstock to Sally Magee of the Town of Saugerties, by Rev. Thomas Lape.

1792. Jun 9, Blue Mountain, Adam Rightmyer to Jane, daughter of David Miller, by Rev. A. C. Hillman.

1793. Jun 5, Kingston, S. Franklin Forbes, MD, of Toledo, Ohio to Mary J. Deforest of Kingston, by Rev. H. W. Smuller.

1794. May 30, Kingston, John Bissell to Margaret Tateal, both of Kingston, by Richard W. Tappen, Esq.

June 22, 1855

1795. Jun 14, Joseph S. Lane to Sarah Jemema Ketch, both of Olive, by Rev. John W. Hammond.

1796. Jun 17, Glasco, George Tompkins of Plattekill to Sarah Cook of Glasco, by Rev. Mr. Blake.

1797. Jun 13, Joseph P. Ostrander to Margaret A., daughter of S. S. Hommel, all of Kingston, by Rev. C. Van Santvoord.

1798. Jun 13, F. D. Ladew of The Corner to Matilda Woodworth of Woodland, by Rev. D. J. Wright.

June 29, 1855

1799. Jun 21, James Nelson Lasher to Elizabeth, daughter of David B. Lasher, Esq., both of Woodstock, by Rev. Thomas Lape.

1800. Jun 23, David H. Waters to Sophira, daughter of Leonard S. Mower, both of the Town of Saugerties, by Rev. Thomas Lape.

1801. Jun 21, Ellenville, Wesley Budd of Mamakating to Janette Mackey of Ellenville, by Rev. W. H. Smith.

1802. Jun 13, Ellenville, Wm. H. Myers of Port Jervis to Emily Cook of Ellenville, by Rev. E. W. Bentley.

July 6, 1855

1803. Jul 3, Flatbush, at the Reformed Church parsonage, Abraham Turck, Jr. of Kingston to Mary Ann Davis of Flatbush.

1804. Jul 3, Flatbush, John H. Swart of Saugerties to Irena Cramer of Kingston.

1805. Jul 1, John Myer to Melissa Burgher, both of Kingston, by Rev. S.B. Willis.

1806. Jul 3, George Eckler to Mary H. Winchell, both of the Town of Saugerties, by Rev. Thomas Lape.

1807. Jun 28, Samuel Patterson to Ann Eliza Hamilton, by Rev. H. W. Smuller.

July 20, 1855

1808. Jul 16, at the residence of the bride's father, Garrit Van Hoesen of the Town of Catskill to Lamantha, only daughter of Capt. John Bell of the Town of Saugerties, by Rev. Josiah Leonard.

1809. Jul 4, Homer, Cortland Co., Wm. P. Burhans of Kingston to Mrs. Uretta Heald of Homer, by Elder Carson.

1810. Jul 11, New York, Hon. Gilbert Dean of Poughkeepsie to Mary, daughter of Alvan Stewart, Esq. of New York, by Rev. Dr. Adams.

1811. Jul 14, Kingston, John Dubois Van Wagenen of Rosendale to Sarah J. Salter of Rochester.

July 27, 1855

1812. Jul 19, Hiram Risedorf of Malden to Eliza A. Snyder of Quarryville, by Rev. William Blake.

1813. Jul 2, J. C. Van Buskirk to Ann E. Miller, by Rev. Wm. Blake.

1814. Jul 7, Wm. J. Turck to Maria Dederick, by Rev. Wm. Blake.

1815. Jul 17, New Brunswick, New Jersey, Wm. H. Thompson of New Brunswick to Mary E. Hamlin of Rondout, by Rev. S. V. Monroe.

August 3, 1855

1816. Jul 21, Rondout, Benjamin Franklin to Sarah Heidenheimer, both of New York, by J. Hasbrouck, Esq.

1817. Jul 22, Rondout, Thomas Thorn to Helen H. Schryver, both of Catskill, by J. Hasbrouck, Esq.

1818. Jul 23, Poughkeepsie, Morgan A. Dayton of Milton to Harriet Degroff of Poughkeepsie, by Rev. S. Fitch, Jr.

August 10, 1855

1819. Jul 31, Blue Mountain, Frederick Linik to Christina, daughter of Nicholas Conrad, by Rev. A. C. Hillman

August 17, 1855

1820. Aug 3, Samuel Mc Murray to Mary A. Mc Maken, both of Saugerties, by Rev. William Blake.

1821. Aug 2, William Shultis to Hester Mc Donald, both of Saugerties, by Rev. William Blake.

1822. Aug 14, James C. Dodge of Indiana to Harriet Terwilliger of Saugerties, by Rev. William Blake.

1823. Aug 6, Josiah Frear of Kingston to Maria L. Filkins of Poughkeepsie, by Rev. A. M. Mann.

1824. Aug 9, Jacob Greiner to Margaret E. Hutchins, both of Woodstock, by Rev. H. C. Longyear.

August 24, 1855
1825. Aug 18, Kingston, Benjamin F. Decker to Martha J. Slater, both of Eddyville, by Rev. Dr. Hoes.

August 31, 1855
1826. Aug 25, Flatbush, Augustus Van Etten of Kingston to Sybil Maria Felter of Saugerties, by Rev. Dr. Hoes.

1827. Aug 23, Alexander Marakle to Mary Dumond, both of West Hurley, by Rev. A. Gulick.

1828. Aug 6, Mr. David Whispell to Christina A., daughter of Philip Yerry, both of Woodstock, by D. P. Smith, Esq.

1829. Aug 9, Lorenzo Taylor to Emeline, daughter of Jacob Diamond, all of Woodstock, by D. P. Smith, Esq.

September 7, 1855
1830. Sep 4, Saugerties, Frederick Weidman to Hannah Lewis, both of Woodstock, by Rev. J. Elmendorf.

1831. Aug 9, New Paltz, John C. Sutton to Maria R. Freer, both of Marbletown, by Rev. C. H. Stitt.

1832. Aug 29, Reading, Schuyler Co., NY, John R. Stebbins to Sarah C. Abbey, adopted daughter of Geo. North, both of Rondout, by Rev. David A. Abbey.

1833. Aug 26, Rondout, George F. Dean to Mercy E., daughter of John B. Hoag, both of Rondout, by Rev. J. A. Edmonds.

September 14, 1855

1834. Sep 5, Montague, Sussex Co., NY, James O. Merritt of Kingston to Sarah, youngest daughter of Dr. Jacob L. Van Deusen of Montague.

1835. Aug 25, West Woodstock, William Hewson of New York City to Margaret S. Lasher of Woodstock, by Rev. H. C. Longyear.

September 21, 1855

1836. Sep 12, Kingston, Cornelius J. Townsend to Mary G. Conklin, both of Kingston, by Rev. Dr. Hoes.

1837. Sep 15, Kingston, Peter Rosepaugh to Nancy Winchell, both of Kingston, by Rev. R. A. Chalker.

September 28, 1855

1838. Sep 20, Kingston, John C. Deyo of New Paltz to Jane Atkins of Esopus, by Rev. R. A. Chalker.

1839. Sep 18, Clintondale, Jacob Roberts to Catharine L. Relyea, both of Clintondale, by Rev. Mr. Relyea of Kingston.

1840. Sep 17, Hurley, Samuel Plough to Ann Elsworth, both of Hurley, by Ten Eyck De Witt, Esq.

October 5, 1855

1841. Oct 2, Saugerties, Frederick C. Bulkley to Fannie M. Wilcox, by Rev. Edwin A. Bulkley of Groton, Mass.

1842. Oct 4, Rondout, George B. Hibbard to Maria Louisa, eldest daughter of Thos. J. Burgess, all of Rondout, by Rev. Mr. Duyea.

1843. Sep 25, Rondout, Stephen Winfield to Amanda Snyder, both of Rondout, by Rev. Mr. Relyea.

October 12, 1855

1844. Oct 3, Kingston, Charles H. Clearwater of High Falls to Margaret F., daughter of Wm. Kerr of Kingston, by Rev. Francis Donnelly.

1845. Sep 19, Esopus, George Joseph Smith to Harriet M. Rider, both of Kingston, by Rev. James Mc Farlane.

October 19, 1855
1846. Oct 11, Edgar Legg to Mary Elizabeth Snyder, both of Kingston, by Rev. Dr. Gosman.

1847. Undated, Mr. Abraham M. France of Kingston to Mrs. Eliza Osterhoudt of Saugerties, by Rev. Dr. Gosman. <October 3, 1855, Flatbush Reformed Church Records, ed.>

1848. Undated, Garrit Lewis Whitaker of Saugerties to Maria Low of Kingston, by Rev. Dr. Gosman. <October 16, 1855, Flatbush Reformed Church Records, ed.>

October 26, 1855
1849. Oct 20, Saugerties, Erastus Bartholomew to Christina C. Schoonmaker, both of Quarryville, by Rev. Wm. Blake.

November 2, 1855
1850. Sep 3, Malden, Mr. Frederick Bell to Miss Eliza Catharine Hoff, both of the Town of Saugerties, by Rev. Josiah Leonard.

1851. Sep 27, Mr. Peter Brink Short to Miss Elizabeth Hommel, both of Saugerties, by Rev. Alexander Gulick.

1852. Oct 29, Mr. Abraham Carnright to Miss Cornelia Vredenburg, both of Kingston, by Rev. Alexander Gulick.

1853. Oct 27, Blue Mountain, Wm. Mason to Sarah Jane, daughter of Nelson Post, by Rev. A. C. Hillman.

November 9, 1855
1854. Oct 25, Salem, Mass., Hon. Ambrose Wager of Rhinebeck to Miss Eliza, only daughter of T. Failess, Esq. of Salem, by Rev. S. Worcester.

November 16, 1855

1855. Oct 24, Louisville, Ky., Josiah Hasbrouck to Jenny A., only daughter of James Grandon, Esq., all of Marbletown, by Rev. M. S. Huntington.

November 23, 1855

1856. Nov 15, Poughkeepsie, David G. Craig of Olive to Helen Hardyman of Poughkeepsie, by C. K. Corliss, Esq.

November 30, 1855

1857. Nov 22, Saugerties, I. J. Rouse of Catskill to Angeline Turck of Saugerties, by Rev. G. A. Howard of Catskill.

1858. Nov 24, Blue Mountain, Egbert Wolven to Elizabeth A., daughter of Jacob R. Tetsel, by Rev. A. C. Hillman.

1859. Nov 17, Saugerties, John Hoffman to Catharine Margaret Shay, both of Plattekill, by Rev. J. Elmendorf.

1860. Nov 14, Thomas F. Meagher, Esq. to Miss Elizabeth, daughter of Peter Townsend, Esq. of Orange Co.

December 7, 1855

1861. Dec 1, New Paltz, Hacaliah P. Dolson of Gardiner to Esther Freer of New Paltz, by Rev. John N. Jansen of Guilford.

December 14, 1855

1862. Dec 6, Stone Ridge, James M. Dumond of Kingston to Laura Relyea of Marbletown, by Rev. J. L. Mc Nair.

1863. Dec 1, New Paltz, at the residence of the bride's father in Gardiner, William Johnson to Rachel Jane Schoonmaker, by Rev. John N. Jansen.

December 21, 1855

1864. Sep 12, Nelson North to Olivia Jane Davis, by Rev. John W. Hammond.

1865. Nov 1, Isaac D. P. Eckert to Sally C. Crispell, by Rev. John W. Hammond.

1866. Nov 15, Asa Butler to Catharine Dutcher, by Rev. John W. Hammond.

1867. Dec 1, James M. Degroff to Mary Ennist, by Rev. John W. Hammond.

1868. Dec 1, James Winchell to Sarah Louisa Ennist, by Rev. John W. Hammond.

1869. Dec 12, William F. Cooper to Almira Short, by Rev. John W. Hammond.

December 28, 1855

1870. Dec 22, Blue Mountain, Jacob Rightmyer to Christina E., daughter of Andrew Mower, by Rev. A. C. Hillman.

1871. Dec 20, Samsonville, S. Ralph Harlow, son of the minister, and publisher of the Ulster *Democrat* to M. Helen, daughter of the late Dr. Samuel Bowen of Thompson, Conn., by Rev. Samuel Harlow.

1872. Dec 21, Hyman F. Styles, printer and carpenter, to Miss Hannah M. Munson, both of Kingston, by Rev. R. A. Chalker.

September 5, 1856

1873. Aug 31, Saugerties, Joel Stewart to Mrs. Anna Maria Haber, both of Saugerties, by Rev. J. Elmendorf.

1874. Aug 25, Jeremiah Whitaker to Almira Baker, both of Glasco, by Rev. Dr. Gosman.

1875. Sep 1, Hurley, Lewis D. Crapser to Miss Elizabeth Sweet, both of Kingston, by Rev. C. Lippincott.

1876. Aug 30, John P. Kimble to Harriet Louise Kitell, both of the Town of Saugerties, by Rev. Thomas Lape.

September 12, 1856

1877. Sep 8, Blue Mountain, Wilbur C. Howland of Durham to Jane M., daughter of John . Ransom, by Rev. A. C. Hillman.

1878. Aug 30, New Paltz, Jacob H. Jenkins to Jane Freer, both of Gardiner, by Rev. C. H. Stitt.

September 19, 1856

1879. Sep 13, Saugerties, Isaac Rosapaugh, printer, to Angeline, daughter of Diah Turner, both of Saugerties, by Rev. Mr. Willis.

1880. Sep 3, Joel Van Keuren to Charlotte Ostrander, both of Hurley, by Rev. B. C. Lippincott.

September 26, 1856

1881. Sep 18, William C. Newkirk to Maria Sheely, both of Hurley, by Rev. J. C. F. Hoes, D. D.

1882. Sep 17, Hobart, James L. Van Deusen of Rondout to Lizzie, daughter of John K. Grant of Hobart, by Rev. Mr. Gibson.

October 3, 1856

1883. Sep 24, Saugerties, Thomas H. Morris to Sarah Ann Davis, both of Saugerties, by Rev. S. B. Goodenow.

1884. Sep 30, Saugerties, Jacob A. Shaw of Marbletown to Mary A. Snyder of Saugerties, by Rev. S. B. Goodenow.

1885. Sep 27, Aaron Vedder Mower to Lana Lasher, both of the Town of Saugerties, by Rev. Thomas Lape.

October 10, 1856

1886. Oct 4, Christian Wehrle to Margetha Schmehl, by Rev. B. M. Genung.

1887. Oct 2, Saugerties, Chas. F. Field to Rachel Anna, youngest daughter of the late J. V. L. Overbaugh, Esq. of Saugerties, by Rev. J. Elmendorf.

1888. Oct 5, Chancey Ludowig Shub to Anna Maria Mower, both of the Town of Saugerties, by Rev. Thomas Lape.

1889. Oct 1, Clark's Mills, Oneida Co., Mr. John Nairn of Yonkers, NY, to Miss Janet, daughter of Robert Clark, Esq. of Clark's Mills, by Rev. C. Van Santvoord.

October 17, 1856

1890. Sep 29, James Gardiner of Palenville to Melinda Hauver of Malden, by Rev. O. Matthews.

1891. Oct 5, Palenville, Peter V. Snyder to Margaret Kipp, by Rev. O. Matthews.

1892. Oct 9, Asbury, Alexander C. Whitney to Sarah C. Smith, by Rev. O. Matthews.

1893. Oct 11, Shandaken, John Mc Clellen of New York City to Abigail Smith of Shandaken, by Ira D. Chatfield, Esq.

October 24, 1856

1894. Oct 11, Blue Mountain, James F. Whitaker to Mary G., daughter of Edward Snyder, by Rev. A. C. Hillman.

1895. Undated, Shandaken Corners, John Mc Clenen of New York City to Miss Abby Smith of Pine Hill, by Ira D. Chatfield, Esq.

1896. Oct 15, Kingston, John Chipp, Jr. to Elizabeth Merritt, both of Saugerties, by Rev. Dr. Hoes.

October 31, 1856

1897. Oct 23, Town of Woodstock, John Reifenburgh to Margaret Rix, both of Woodstock, by Rev. W. I. Cutter.

1898. Oct 25, Blue Mountain, Abraham Van Aken to Jane M., daughter of Peter Landendyke of High Woods, by Rev. A. C. Hillman.

November 7, 1856

1899. Oct 23, Thomas Hudler of Kingston to Harriet M. Freer of Lloyd, by Rev. James Mc Farlane.

1900. Oct 25, Solomon Schoonmaker to Amanda Terpening of Esopus, by Rev. James Mc Farlane.

November 21, 1856

1901. Nov 16, Saugerties, Henry Lampman of Coxsackie to Mary Elizabeth Burhans of Saugerties, by Rev. J. Elmendorf.

1902. Nov 6, Blue Mountain, Joshua Valkenburgh to Emeline D., daughter of George Hill, by Rev. A. C. Hillman.

1903. Nov 7, Abraham Flatow of Kingston to Harriet Lodge of Rondout, by Rev. J. A. Edmonds.

1904. Nov 13, Kingston, Christopher Roosa of Rhinebeck to Catharine Deyo of New Paltz, by Rev. J. C. F. Hoes, D. D.

November 28, 1856

1905. Nov 22, Mr. Peter Van Steenbergh to Harriet Sparling, both of Saugerties, by Rev. B. M. Genung.

1906. Nov 23, Henry Otto to Elizabeth Miller, both of Saugerties, by Rev. B. M. Genung.

1907. Nov 18, Jacob A. Kiersted to Lucinda Hader, both of Woodstock, by Rev. Mr. Cutter.

December 5, 1856

1908. Nov 24, Shandaken, at the residence of the widow Barber, Charles L. Barber of Shandaken to Jane P., daughter of George L. Doll of Rockland, Sullivan Co., by Rev. H. C. Longyear.

1909. Nov 12, New York, Henry Husted of Kingston to Miss Josephene S., youngest daughter of the late Rene A. Pardessus of New York, by Rev. Mr. Weston.

December 12, 1856

1910. Nov 19, Daniel D. Gerow to Miss Melissa A. Seymour, by Rev. U. Messiter.

1911. Dec 4, Charles Morehouse to Melinda I. Masten, both of Plattekill, by Rev. U. Messiter.

December 19, 1856

1912. Dec 11, at the residence of her father, John H. Field to Mary C., youngest daughter of Ephraim P. Myer, all of Saugerties, by Rev. J. Elmendorf.

1913. Dec 14, John Epenhaut to Pheobe Hies, both of Saugerties, by Rev. B. M. Genung.

1914. Dec 11, Stone Ridge, Solomon Davenport to Hannah J. Carrier, by Rev. C. H. Stitt.

1915. Nov 29, Samsonville, Thomas C. Smith of Olive to Mary Paterson of Marbletown, by Rev. Samuel Harlow.

December 26, 1856

1916. Nov 26, Whitewater, Wisc., Mr. A. H. Van Vlierden to Miss Rosa Viola Barker, daughter of Jesse Barker, Jr., a merchant of Whitewater, by Rev. Mr. Montague.

1917. Dec 8, Sleightberg, Esopus, Isaac D. Sleight of Sleightberg to Sarah White of Pittsburgh, Pa., by Rev. James Mc Farlane.

1918. Dec 13, Edward A. Wright to Mary E. Warburton, both of Rondout, by Rev. J. A. Edmonds.

1919. Dec 18, Cornelius W. Scott of Mamakating to Rosina Kettle of Wawarsing, by Rev. Wm. H. Smith.

1920. Notice, all persons are forbid trusting my son, William D. Smith on my account, as I will pay no bills of his contracting. Signed, John Smith, Saugerties, December 28, 1856.

January 9, 1857

1921. Jan 1, Woodstock, Philip Britt to Lean Longyear, by Rev. W. L. James.

1922. Dec 20, Jas. Coutant to Catharine Carrol, both of Marbletown, by Rev. E. L. Prentice.

1923. Jan 1, Geo. M. Middaugh to Sarah P. Cassels, both of Kingston, by Rev. E. L. Prentice.

1924. Dec 31, Rondout, Peter Van Gaasbeek of Wiltwyck to Martha A. Burger of Rondout, by Rev. J. A. Edmonds.

1925. Jan 1, Kingston, John Hargrave of Rondout to Margaret C. Fisk of Kingston, by Rev. J. A. Edmonds.

1926. Dec 30, Kingston, De Witt Delamater of Port Jervis to Petronella Van Steenbergh of Kingston, by Rev. H. W. Smuller.

January 23, 1857

1927. Jan 15, Herman Stall of New York to Margaret Jane, eldest daughter of D. Livingston, by Rev. Thomas Lape.

1928. Jan 15, at the residence of the bride's father, Peter Hill to Jane Catharine, youngest daughter of Jacob P. Musier, all of the Town of Catskill, by Rev. Thomas Lape.

February 13, 1857

1929. Feb 2, Cleveland, Ohio, Edgar Decker of Dubuque, Iowa, formerly of Rondout to Julia I. English of Cleveland, by Rev. Mr.. White.

1930. Jan 28, Latin Town, Ulster Co., Philip Yawger to Eunice Wollsy, by Rev. M. F. Liebeneau.

February 20, 1857

1931. Jan 22, Plattekill, Cornelius S. Longendike of Kingston to Elizabeth Longendike of Saugerties, by Rev. N. F. Chapman.

1932. Feb 10, Peter Van Vleck of Kingston to Mrs. Jane W. Crawford, daughter of David Keys, Esq. of New York, by Rev. John W. Beach.

1933. Feb 11, Benjamin A. Kissgm of New York to Sarah A., daughter of Col. H. D. H. Snyder of Woodland, Ulster Co., by Rev. D. G. Wright of Prattsville.

1934. Jan 24, Charles A. Bond of West Hurley to Susie A. Tyler of Hurley, by Rev. A. Gulick.

February 28, 1857

1935. Feb 18, Titus Myer of Hurley to Blandina E., eldest daughter of Caleb M. Merritt of Marbletown, by Rev. B. C. Lippincott.

1936. Feb 14, Harry B. Montanye to Margaret A. Burrows, both of Ellenville, by Rev. William H. Smith.

March 6, 1857

1937. Feb 28, Saugerties, John S. Roosa to Mary Elizabeth Middaugh, both of Saugerties, by Rev. S. B. Goodenow.

1938. Feb 28, Blue Mountain, James O. Goodwin to Helen Jane, daughter of William Winne, by Rev. A. C. Hillman.

1939. Feb 19, West Hurley, Jacob M. Vandemark to Mary A. Lane, by Rev. Alexander Gulick.

1940. Feb 19, West Hurley, Thompson Eckert to Elizabeth Bodley, both of Shokan, by Rev. Alexander Gulick.

March 13, 1857

1941. Feb 26, Peter E. Hasbrouck to Phebe C. Van Wagenen of Rochester, by Rev. C. L. Van Dyck.

1942. Feb 9, Milton, Mr. Santa Paulis Vechi to Ann Eliza York, both of Marlborough, by John Woolsey, Esq.

1943. Feb 19, Shawangunk, William Cooley of Plattekill to Mary, daughter of J. D. Hasbrouck, by Rev. Mr. Schoonmaker.

March 27, 1857

1944. Mar 24, Saugerties, Aaron Henry Woodward of Kingston to Ann Frances, daughter of the late Abram Brewer of Saugerties, by Rev. S. B. Goodenow.

1945. Mar 18, Buffalo, Robert E. Best of Kingston to Emma Kitts of Buffalo, by Rev. E. W. Reynolds.

April 24, 1857

1946. Apr 9, Blue Mountain, Reuben Short to Miss Martha, daughter of John I. Carle, all of High Woods, by Rev. A. C. Hillman.

1947. Apr 12, Greenfield, George W. Swartwout of Ellenville to Catharine Denman of Greenfield, by Rev. E. W. Bentley.

1948. Apr 14, George H. Simmons of Poughkeepsie to Loretta Worden of New Paltz Landing, by Rev. D. W. C. Van Gaasbeek.

May 8, 1857

1949. Apr 22, in the manner of the Society of Friends, John A. Griswold, Esq. of Catskill to Elizabeth M., daughter of Wm. Roberts, Esq., of Clintondale.

1950. May 2, Cornelius P. Longendyke to Elizabeth Ann, daughter of David Decker, all of High Woods, by Rev. A. C. Hillman.

1951. Apr 23, Canajoharie, Hiram F. Weaver of Kingston to Minerva C., only daughter of William Watson, Esq., of Canajoharie, by Rev. W. H. Meeker.

June 19, 1857

1952. Jun 6, Ellenville, Nelson Perkins of Lackawack to Ruth Ann Hawxhurst of Ellenville, by J. K. Wardle.

1953. Jun 7, Albert E. Ingraham to Margiana Rosekrans, both of Denning, by Rev. C. Shook.

October 30, 1857

1954. Oct 15, Saugerties, Mr. Wells Myer to Miss Sarah, daughter of Col. S. M. Post, all of Saugerties, by Rev. S. B. Goodenow.

1955. Oct 24, at the residence of James Joy, Alfred Wallace to Sarah Margaret France, both of Saugerties, by Rev. Anson Dubois.

January 1, 1858

1956. Dec 19, Saugerties, Christian Myer to Miss Harriet Cole, both of Saugerties, by Dr. Ostrander.

1957. Dec 19, James P. Overbaugh of Catskill to Elizabeth Judson of Windham, Greene Co., by Dr. Ostrander.

January 8, 1858

1958. Dec 31, Saugerties, Mynders Dubois to Abbey M. Spenser, both of Saugerties, by Rev. J. Elmendorf.

1959. Jan 5, Saugerties, Geo. W. Judd of New York City to Mary E., daughter of Jesse Stone of Saugerties, by Rev. J. Elmendorf.

1960. Undated, West Camp, Mr. Jeremiah E. Whitney to Isabella C. Adams, both of West Camp, by Rev. O. P. Matthews.

1961. Dec 29, Peter Cantine of Saugerties to Sarah A. Starin of Fultonville, Montgomery Co., by Rev. Dr. Pells.

1962. Jan 4, Kingston, Tobias Blackwell of Kingston to Eliza C. Shultis of Rondout, by Rev. W. H. Evans.

January 15, 1858

1963. Dec 31, Blue Mountain, Eugene Hitchcock to Hannah Ann, daughter of the late Thomas Hallock, by Rev. A. C. Hillman.

1964. Jan 6, William K. Brink to Rachel Blandina Jansen, both of Kingston, by Rv. Dr. Hoes.

1965. Jan 1, Henry C. Hamilton to Julia A. Griffin, both of Kingston, by Rev. H. W. Smuller.

January 22, 1858

1966. Jan 7, Malden, Mr. Michael Moore, Jr. to Miss Martha Gough, both of Malden, by Rev. D. Welton Sharts.

1967. Jan 19, Malden, Mr. Edward Bigelow Bell to Miss Martha M. Tucker, both of Malden, by Rev. D. Welton Sharts.

1968. Jan 13, Sidney, Delaware Co., Mr. Don A. French of Saugerties to Miss Malvina H. Snyder of Sidney, by Rev. Wm. Church.

January 29, 1858

1969. Dec 31, Catskill, William W. Wight of Rondout to Lucretia C., daughter of Henry J. Jennings of Catskill, by Rev. Mr. Stevens.

1970. Jan 14, Ellenville, J. J. Ward of Franklin, Delaware Co. to Adaline V. Morse, by Rev. J. K. Wardle.

February 5, 1858

1971. Jan 28, Saugerties, John I. Whitaker to Eve Becker, both of Saugerties, by Rev. L. H. King.

1972. Jan 25, William E. Rogers to Rachel M. Brink, both of Kingston, by Rev. Charles C. Keys.

February 12, 1858

1973. Jan 28, Rochester, George Chambers, MD, of Marbletown to Mary E. Westbrook of Rochester, by Rev. Cornelius Wyckoff.

1974. Feb 2, Rondout, C. H. Gifford of Hudson to Mary Josephine, daughter of Maj. Geo. F. Von Beck of Rondout, by Rev. B. T. Phillips.

1975. Jan 20, Woodstock, George Roney of Cleaveland, Ohio to Electa P. Reynolds of Woodstock, by Rev. David, Heroy, Jr.

February 19, 1858

1976. Feb 10, Kingston, Abram H. Vanling of Port Ewen to Jeanette Dubois of Kingston, by Rev. Dr. Hoes.

1977. Feb 6, at the parsonage of the Reformed Dutch Church, Norman Cole to Jane Van Leuven, both of Esopus, by Rev. James Mc Farlane.

February 26, 1858

1978. Feb 15, Saugerties, Geo. H. Bradshaw to Mary A. Vandebogert, both of Kingston, by Rev. J.. Elmendorf.

1979. Feb 4, John Alliger to Sarah Krum, both of Stone Ridge, by Rev. J. L. Mc Nair.

March 5, 1858

1980. Feb 18, Malden, Jeremiah German of Malden to Jane Angeline Whitaker of Glasco, by Rev. D. Welton Sharts.

March 12, 1858

1981. Mar 4, Saugerties, William H. Snyder to Emily, daughter of E. B. Houghtaling, all of Saugerties, by Rev. Mr. King.

1982. Mar 3, Peter E. Roosa of Kingston to Jane Elizabeth Seaman of Glenerie, by Rev. Dr. Gosman.

1983. Mar 3, New York, Edgar Hudler of Rondout to Hannah, daughter of David Keys, Esq., of New York, by Rev. John Keyes.

March 19, 1858

1984. Mar 1, Timothy F. Tillson, Esq., of Rosendale to Miss Almira Sahler of Marbletown, by Rev. J. L. Mc Nair.

1985. Mar 6, Samuel Bullar to Mrs. Mary E. Contant, both of Rondout, by Rev. A. C. Fields.

1986. Mar 10, William Hutton to Jane, daughter of Robert R. Kerr, both of Rondout, by Rev. A. C. Fields.

1987. Mar 15, Kingston, George P. Davison to Mary E. Hillyer, both of Kingston, by Rev. Charles C. Keys.

April 2, 1858

1988. Notice - Whereas difficulties have lately occurred between myself and my wife Eliza, and she has left my house and domicil without my consent, I hereby forbid all persons trusting her on my account, as I shall not hold myself responsible for any debts she may contract. William Van Etten, March 18, 1858, Saugerties.

April 16, 1858

1989. Apr 3, Blue Mountain, John Garrison to Selina Ann, daughter of Andrew Hommel, by Rev. A. C. Hillman.

1990. Apr 3, Wiltwyck, James Cater to Sarah C. Barber, both of Esopus, by Rev. A. Fort.

April 23, 1858

1991. Mar 22, Rondout, Albert Baumbush of Poughkeepsie to Eliza Kautsman of Rondout, by J. D. Hasbrouck, Esq.

1992. Mar 22, Rondout, John C. Barber to Mary E. Phillips, by J. D. Hasbrouck, Esq.

April 30, 1858

1993. Apr 17, Blue Mountain, Joseph Cole to Elizabeth, daughter of the late John Max, by Rev. A. C. Hillman.

May 7, 1858

1994. Apr 26, Richmond, Va., Cornelius Battelle to Elizabeth D., daughter of the late William Finney, Esq., by Rev. J. Peterkin.

1995. Apr 28, Kingston, John E. Van Etten, Counsellor-at-Law to Addie Green, both of Kingston, by Rev. Anson Dubois.

1996. Apr 11, Napanoch, Solomon D. Terwilliger to Sarah Van Wagenen, both of Wawarsing, by . D. D. Bell, Esq.

May 14, 1858

1997. Apr 22, New Paltz, Abraham Craig to Sarah Judkins, both of New Paltz, by Rev. C. H.. Stitt.

1998. Aug 28, New Paltz, John W. Saxton of Fermington, Mich. to Julia A. Dunn of New Paltz, by Rev. C. H. Stitt.

1999. Apr 25, Jonathan Polhemus to Mary E. Hill, both of Ulster Co., by Rev. C. Shook.

May 28, 1858

2000. May 19, Saugerties, Joseph Moe to Mary Jane Minkler, both of the Town of Saugerties,
by Samuel Merclean, Esq.

2001. May 19, Kingston, at the 2nd Methodist Episcopal Church, Mr. John Dubois to Mrs. Rachel Blackwell of Kingston, by Rev. Wm. H. Evans.

2002. May 6, Newburgh, Mr. Cyrus Cook to Miss Martha J. Albertson, both of Marlborough, by Rev. David Sampson.

June 4, 1858

2003. May 15, Dr. Peter Crispell, Jr. of Hurley to Mary C. Oakley of Marbletown, by Rev. Anson Dubois.

2004. May 11, Rhinebeck, Jacob Myers to Julia K., daughter of David Norris, all of Rhinebeck, by Rev. Wm. A. Miller.

2005. May 18, Ellenville, Alfred Neafie to Ann, daughter of A. B. Preston, Esq. of Ellenville, by Rev. Mr. Bently.

2006. May 12, Skaneateles, Hardenbergh Delamater of Rosendale to Margaret Lefever of Skaneateles, by Rev. W. Ingals.

2007. May 8, New Paltz, Alexander Stanton to Amey E. Downer, both of Lloyd, by Henry Burnett, Esq.

June 11, 1858

2008. Jun 3, Rochester, Isaac Houghtaling to Maria Crum, both of Marbletown, by Rev. E. De Puy.

2009. Jun 2, Pleasant Valley, Walter Farrington, Esq. of Milton to Miss Sarah E. Kay of Poughkeepsie, by Rev. D. Lyman.

June 18, 1858
2010. Jun 3, Yonkers, Romeyn Bogardus, Esq. of New York to Julia C., only daughter of P. E. Radcliff, Esq. of Yonkers, by Rev. V. M. Hurlbut.

June 25, 1858
2011. Jun 12, Kingston, Peter W. Wiand of Whiteport to Sarah Catharine Keator of Creek Locks, by Rev. Wm. H. Evans.

2012. Jun 10, Mr. Charles Smith to Miss Elizabeth C. Griffin, both of Shandaken, by Rev. A. D. Vail.

2013. Jun 12, Poughkeepsie, James Harvey of Rondout to Mary A. Manery of New Paltz, by Rev. C. W. Smith.

July 9, 1858
2014. Jun 29, Mattewan, Dutchess Co., Mr. Isaac N. Hill of Osceola, Ill. to Miss Deborah L. Barker of Mattewan, by Rev. D. W. Sherwood.

2015. Undated, Richard Bush to Mary E. Krum, both of Stone Ridge, by Rev. D. D. Lindsley.

2016. Jun 27, Asa S. Russell to Jane Skinner, both of Ellenville, by Rev. Richard Wheatley.

2017. Jun 29, Kingston, Wm. Hammond of Grahamville to Sarah Jane Gregory of Lackawack, by Rev. Dr. Hoes.

July 23, 1858
2018. Jul 11, Mr. Francis Lewis to Miss Mary E. Cunningham, both of Saugerties, by Rev. D. W. Sherwood.

2019. Jul 15, Saugerties, Mr. John Lowther to Miss Patience Bird, both of Saugerties, by Rev. Wm. J. Lynd.

2020. Jul 15, Josiah Frieze to Mary E. Vandebeck, both of Catsbaan, by Rev. Henry Ostrander.

2021. Jul 8, Syracuse, Rev. Anson Dubois, pastor of the 2nd Dutch Church, Reformed, of Kingston to Margaret W. Wynkoop of Syracuse, by Rev. E. S. Porter, D. D.

August 13, 1858

2022. Aug 8, Saugerties, John W. Schoonmaker to Helen M. Tetter, by Rev. D. W. Sherwood.

2023. Jul 31, Port Ewen, Charles Millar to Susan Strong, both of Hudson, by Rev. C. L. Van Dyck.

August 20, 1858

2024. Aug 5, Rondout, John Hussey to Harriet M. A. Brennan, by Rev. Mr. Madden.

2025. Aug 12, Ellenville, Branson Oakley to Louisa Devoe, by Rev. E. W. Bentley.

2026. Aug 8, Shawangunk, William B. Terwilliger to Augusta Scott, by Rev. Mr. Bangs.

September 3, 1858

2027. Aug 25, Ephraim Burhans of Flatbush to Catharine Ann, daughter of Edward Burhans of Kingston, by Rev. Dr. Hoes.

2028. Aug 15, John Elmendorf to N. J. Hasbrouck, both of Ellenville, by Rev. E. W. Bentley.

2029. 5 Aug, Richard Embree to Miss Warner Vandemark, both of Olive, by John Shurter, Esq.

September 10, 1858

2030. Aug 29, Richard D. Cristle to Almira Hauxhurst, both of Ellenville, by Rev. J. K. Wardle.

2031. Aug 30, Kingston, Jeremiah Schryver to Mary Joy, both of Kingston, by Rev. Wm. H. Evans.

2032. Aug 28, Peter Dewall to Elizabeth Bresho, both of Kingston, by Rev. Anson Dubois.

September 17, 1858
2033. Sep 8, Kingston, William Lounsbery, junior editor of the Ulster *Republican* to Kate E. Kaman, by Rev. Anson Dubois.

September 24, 1858
2034. Sep 16, Saugerties, Ambrose Bradley of Newburgh to Emeline, daughter of Capt. Diah Turner of Saugerties, by Rev. J. Elmendorf.

2035. Sep 14, James Myer, Jr. to Margaret Ann Myer, both of Kingston, by Rev. Dr. Hoes.

2036. Sep 15, Kingston, John S. Albert, U. S. N. to Henrietta Nelson, by Rev. Geo. Waters.

2037. Sep 11, George Ward to Sarah Jane Lounsbery, both of Samsonville, by John Shurter, Esq.

2038. Sep 15, Rondout, Charles L. Edmonds, son of the minister, to Caroline Hayes, daughter of M. G. Hayes, Esq., all of Rondout, by Rev. J. A. Edmonds.

October 1, 1858
2039. Sep 27, Palenville, Calvin Shaffer of New York to Anna P. Pelham of Palenville.

2040. Sep 23, Kingston, Augustus Schepmoes to Laura Van Gaasbeek, by Rev. Anson Dubois.

October 8, 1858
2041. Oct 5, Saugerties, Mr. Samuel Houlihan of Hudson to Miss Alida Maria, daughter of Mr. A. S. De Myer of Saugerties, by Rev. J. Elmendorf.

2042. Oct 3, Rhinebeck, Geo. W. Clarke, editor of the *American Citizen* to Miss Jane C. Latson, both of Rhinebeck, by Rev. Wm. H. Ferris.

October 15, 1858

2043. Oct 14, Reformed Dutch Church, Mr. Jas. Balen of New York City to Miss Julia, daughter of Peter B. Myer of Saugerties, by Rev. J. Elmendorf.

2044. Oct 7, Saugerties, Mr. George W. Canine to Miss Emily J. Brink, both of New York City, by Rev. L. H. King.

2045. Oct 13, Mr. Wm. S. Faurot to Miss Temperance S. Smith, both of Fort Montgomery, by Rev. L. C. Lockwood.

2046. Oct 6, Greenbush, Thomas C. Broadhead of Kingston to Louisa Maston of Greenbush, by Rev. Mr. Rollo.

October 22, 1858

2047. Oct 12, Kingston, Rev. E. L. Prentice of the New York Annual Conference to Lila M. Rogers of Rondout, by Rev. D. L. Marks.

2048. Oct 14, Rondout, John Van Wagener to Eliza Van Aken, both of St. Remy, Esopus.

2049. Oct 17, Kingston, David Van Etten to Mary E. Ferguson, both of the Town of Kingston, by A. S. P. Snoder, Esq.

2050. Oct 21, Saugerties, Mr. Tunis M. Post to Miss Mary J. Walters, both of Saugerties, by Rev. L. C. Lockwood.

October 29, 1858

2051. Oct 19, John Halwick of Esopus to Mrs. Elizabeth Smith of Kingston, by Rev. Dr. Hoes.

2052. Oct 22, George W. Durham of Rosendale to Miss Rachel Maria Neise of Esopus, by Rev. Dr. Hoes.

2053. Oct 14, Shokan, Alonzo Vanbramer to Amelia Snyder, both of Woodstock, by Rev. P. S. Stoddard.

November 26, 1858
2054. Nov 18, Town of Saugerties, Mr. George Whiting, lately of Winsted, Conn., now of Brooklyn, N. J. <sic> to Miss Elizabeth L. Waker of the Town of Saugerties, by Rev. L. C. Lockwood.

December 3, 1858
2055. Nov 26, Newton, at her father's home, Mr. R. S. Van Keuren of Saugerties to Miss Kate E. Fairchild, by Rev. Dr. Marble.

2056. Nov 25, West Camp, Mr. Joel W. Porter of Athens to Miss Maria M. Emerick of West Camp, by Rev. D. F. Heller.

December 10, 1858
2057. Dec 2, Saugerties, Mr. William Couse to Miss Catharine Dunn, both of Saugerties village, by Rev. D. W. Sherwood.

2058. Dec 1, Kingston, Robert Hargrave of Rondout to Mrs. Frances S. Deits of Kingston, by Rev. Mr. Edmonds.

2059. Dec 4, Mr. Solomon H. Kemble of Quarryville to Miss Sarah A. Rightmyer of Blue Mountain, by Rev. C. Blauvelt.

December 17, 1858
2060. Dec 11, Saugerties, Thomas Roberts to Eliza Harrison, both of Saugerties village, by Rev. L. C. Lockwood.

December 31, 1858
2061. Dec 21, Wurtsboro, Epenetus Lounsberry to Hannah Griffin, both of Wawarsing, by Esq. Jordan.

2062. Dec 23, Saugerties, Peter W. Whitaker to Sarah A. Hendricks, both of Flatbush, by Rev. J. Elmendorf.

2063. Dec 13, Saugerties, Godfrey Frank to Iola Mackber, both of Catskill, by Rev. L. H. King.

2064. Dec 16, Saugerties, Henry Winans to Helen F. Sisson, both of Catskill, by Rev. L. H. King.

January 7, 1859
2065. Dec 16, Saugerties, Trinity Church, Peter T. Overbaugh to Caroline, eldest daughter of John Cauldwell of Saugerties, by Rev. Mr. Lind.

2066. Dec 28, Kingston, James G. Teller to Cornelia Van Etten, both of Kingston, by Rev. D. L. Marks.

2067. Dec 29, Town of Kingston, Jured Traver of Schodack to Martha Van Gaasbeek of Kingston, by Rev. Mr. Fort.

2068. Dec 25, Hurley, William Delamater to Maria Smith, both of Kingston, by Rev. B. C. Lippincott.

January 14, 1859
2069. Jan 5, New York, at the residence of P. P. Knapp, Kneeland Wright to Elizabeth Elnora Fiero, both of Saugerties, by Rev. A. M. Osborn.

January 21, 1859
2070. Jan 13, Saugerties, Edgar Blackwell to Sarah G. Newkirk, both of Saugerties, by Rev. L. C. Lockwood.

2071. Jan 16, Saugerties, at the Exchange Hotel, Conrad Hull to Eliza Bonesteel, both of West Hurley, by Rev. J. Elmendorf.

2072. Jan 18, Kingston, Charles P. Ridenour of Cincinnati, Ohio to Catharine Near of Kingston, by Rev. Dr. Harrison.

January 28, 1859
2073. Jan 22, Kingston, Peter L. Carle of Saugerties to Harriet Salpaugh of Rondout, by Rev. J. C. F. Hoes.

2074. Jan 18, Clove, Abraham Schoonmaker of New Paltz to Sarah Jane Pierce of Marbletown, by Rev. J. N. Voorhis.

2075. Jan 18, Kingston, Theodore Delilley to Eliza Newkirk, by Rev. D.L. Marks.

2076. Jan 20, Kingston, Hugh Wilson to Mary E. Payne, both of Kingston, by Rev. John Lillie.

2077. Jan 10, Prattsville, John Bivins of Middletown to Miss M. A. Turk of Prattsville, by P. K. Salisbury, Esq.

February 11, 1859

2078. Feb 3, Roxbury, Mr. Richard W. Van Dyke to Miss Eliza, only daughter of Col. Z. Preston, both of Roxbury, by L. H. King of Saugerties.

2079. Feb 1, Rondout, at the Presbyterian Church, Capt. Wm. L. Jansen of Newburgh to Miss Sarah Ann Richards of Rondout, by Rev. B. T. Phillips.

2080. Jan 29, John Stephens to Sarah M. Van Steenburgh, both of Kingston, by T. E. De Witt, Esq.

2081. Feb 3, Mathew Short to Margaret Wolven, by Rev. Alexander Gulick.

2082. Feb 3, John C. Wolven, Jr. to Charlotte Blackwell, both of Saugerties, by Rev. Alexander Gulick.

February 18, 1859

2083. Undated, Galeville Mills, Henry Alsdorf to Mary E. Goodson, both of Shawangunk, by Rev. A. F. Palmer.

February 25, 1859

2084. Feb 17, Saugerties, Wm. B. B. Dubois to Mary C., daughter of Major Eggleston, both of Saugerties village, by Rev. J. Elmendorf.

2085. Feb 10, Durham, at the Methodist Episcopal parsonage, Mr. L. P. More of Durham to Miss Mary A. Selleck, daughter of the clergyman, by Rev. A. F. Selleck.

2086. Feb 14, Gilboa, Schoharie Co., Mr. Luman Reed to Miss Martha Knapp, by Rev. W. G. F. See.

March 4, 1859

2087. Feb 23, Modena, Mr. Francis M. Doysradt to Miss Rebecca Dubois, both of Rondout, by Rev. Wm. Ostrander,

2088. Feb 26, Kingston, Christian I. Deyo of Rochester to Mrs. Mary R. Longyear of Kingston, by Rev. J. C. Harrison.

March 11, 1859

2089. Feb 17, Spuyten Duyval, Wm. H. White to Josephene Richmond, by Rev. Nathan F. Chapman.

2090. Undated, Chales Carle to Elizabeth Newkirk France, both of Saugerties, by Rev. Nathan F. Chapman.

March 18, 1859

2091. Jan 6, Saunapee, New Hampshire, Charles W. Fisk of Kingston to Sarah J. Morgan of Saunapee, by Rev. J. C. Emerson.

2092. Feb 20, John W. Smith, Esq., postmaster at Denning, to Mrs. Deborah Decker of Grahamsville, Sullivan Co., by Rev. C. Shook.

2093. Feb 27, Rhinebeck, Mr. Edward Earing of Poughkeepsie to Kate Fleming of Rondout, by Rev. Wm. H. Ferris.

2094. Mar 3, Isaac Dubois to Mary Ennest, both of Marbletown, by Rev. J. L. Mc Nair.

2095. Mar 10, Cornelius B. Sutton of Hurley to Margaret Ann Myers of Marbletown, by Rev. J. L. Mc Nair.

March 25, 1859

2096. Feb 16, at the residence of the bride's father, James W. Jones of New Paltz Landing to Miss Alice A. Clark of Poughkeepsie, by Rev. G. S. Hare.

2097. Mar 6, Rondout, Nicholas Mathews to Mary Ann Murring, both of Rondout, by Rev. Mr. Durning.

2098. Feb 24, Stone Ridge, at the parsonage, Cornelius Ostrander of Napanoch to Sarah A. Whitney of Shandaken, by Rev. D. D. Lindsley.

2099. Mar 10, John H. Ostrander of Napanoch to Ellen M. Morse of Honk Hill, by Rev. R. Wheatly.

2100. Mar 2, Poughkeepsie, Mr. Hiram B. Sutton of Marbletown to Miss Melissa Ann Slate of Poughkeepsie, by Rev. B. H. Davis.

2101. Mar 9, New Paltz, Thomas S. Kipp of Hyde Park to Hester J. Craft of New Paltz, by Rev. U. Messiter.

April 8, 1859

2102. Mar 19, Saugerties, John Warder to Catharine M. Brink, both of the Town of Saugerties, by Rev. Nathan F. Chapman. Both were 24 on that same day.

2103. Mar 26, Napanoch, R. W. Dupuy to Mrs. Sarah Ann Douglass, both of Rochester, by Rev. N. D. Williamson.

2104. Mar 31, at the home of William Rogers, Wm. Mc Elhone to Henrietta Dusenbery, both of Ellenville, by J. K. Wardle.

April 15, 1859

2105. Apr 5, Kingston, Peter Aubbell of Brooklyn to Endora Van Etten of Kingston, by Rev. Dr. Lillie.

2106. Apr 5, Kingston, Anson Morey to Miss Louisa Taylor, both of Poughkeepsie, by Rev. D. L. Marks.

April 29, 1859

2107. Apr 21, Saugerties, Daniel Lamb to Ellen Hommell, both of Saugerties, by Rev. S. B. Goodenow.

2108. Mar 3, William Lewis of High Falls to Miss Mary Beemis of Saugerties, by Rev. John W. Gorse of Kiskatom.

2109. Apr 21, Anthony Redmond to Hester Mc Clung, both of Kingston, by Rev. J. C. Harrison.

2110. Apr 20, Rondout, William Lawton, Esq. to Fannie Louisa Stevens, both of Rondout, by Rev. B. T. Phillips.

2111. Apr 20, West Roxbury, Mass., Mr. Robert Young of the firm of R. K. Chandler & Co., Rondout to Miss E. L. Standish of Roxbury.

2112. Apr 21, Rondout, James K. Holmes of New York City to Sarah Ostrander, daughter of William Ostrander, Esq., of Rondout, by Rev. A. C. Fields.

2113. Apr 14, Jacob Van Wagenen to Amanda E. Cole, both of Esopus, by Rev. A. C. Fields.

May 13, 1859

2114. May 5, Saugerties, Mr. Thomas L. Masten to Miss Mary A. Simmons of Saugerties, by Rev. D. W. Sherwood.

2115. May 7, Saugerties, Mr. Levi York to Miss Mary E. Longendyke, both of Saugerties, by Rev. D. W. Sherwood.

May 27, 1859

2116. May 18, Rondout, John Bock to Maria Kuhauht, both of Rondout, by Rev. C. K. Siebke.

June 3, 1859

2117. May 29, Kingston, Mr. Henry Budington to Sarah Martha Van Aken, both of Kingston, by Rev. Mr. Smith.

2118. May 18, High Falls, Isaac Signor to Elizabeth Rhinehart, both of High Falls, by Rev. Mr. Lindsley.

2119. May 15, Benjamin Lee of Fishkill Landing to Elizabeth White of Poughkeepsie, by Rev. Mr. Williams.

2120. May 21, Israel Low to Catharine Ann Van Keuren, both of Esopus, by Rev. Mr. Mc Farland.

June 10, 1859

2121. May 28, Kingston, Charles Yauch of Brooklyn to Annie Eliza, daughter of Wm. L. Barnes of Kingston, by Rev. Geo. Waters.

2122. Jun 2, Lloyd, Philip Le Fevre of Gardiner to Sarah M. Elting of Lloyd, by Rev. C. H. Stitt.

June 17, 1859

2123. Jun 9, Mamaroneck, Arthur G. Hoffman of New York City to Kate C., 3rd daughter of Charles Stuart, Esq., formerly of Saugerties, by Rev. John M. Ward.

June 24, 1859

2124. Jun 9, Joseph Sifts to Sarah J. Fulmer, both of Saugerties, by Rev. John M. Ward.

2125. Jun 15, Kingston, at the 1st Reformed Church, Mr. John Hess of Brooklyn to Margaret Elizabeth, only daughter of the late Wm. Cockburn, by Rev. Dr. Hoes.

2126. Jun 11, Casper Degraff to Celia Ann Van Aken, both of Esopus, by Rev. C. L. Van Dyck.

July 1, 1859

2127. Jun 26, Congregational Church, Mr. Isaac J. Suderly to Miss Anna E. Elmendorf, both of Saugerties, by Rev. L. C. Lockwood.

2128. Jun 22, Mattaewan, Dutchess Co., Mr. U. D. Gee to Miss Hannah Barker, both of Mattaewan, by Rev. D. W. Sherwood.

July 8, 1859

2129. Jul 3, Saugerties, Herman Brink of Saugerties to Henrietta Low of Kingston, by Rev. D. W. Sherwood.

2130. Jun 21, Stone Ridge, John W. Cole of Kingston to Jannet B. Treadwell of Marbletown, by Rev. J. L. Mc Nair.

2131. Jun 11, Rondout, Jonas Fitch of Whiteport to Agnes Bartz of North Haven, by J. D. Hasbrouck, Esq.

2132. Jun 23, Rondout, Robert Hutchinson to Catharine Wilson, both of the Town of Kingston, by Rev. B. T. Phillips.

July 15, 1859

2133. Jul 9, Hiram Wolven of the Town of Saugerties to Leah Van Etten of Woodstock, by Rev. Thomas Lape.

2134. Jul 4, Kingston, Howard M. Layman of Kingston to Priscilla Van Schike of New York, by Rev. J. Millard.

2135. Jul 4, Kingston, Andrew Place to Eliza C. Smith, both of Kingston, by Rev. D. L. Marks.

2136. Jul 4, Rondout, Henry Crum to Rosalie Brown of Flatbush, by Rev. Mr. Wood.

2137. Jul 2, Shokan, Chancey B. Votee to Ida L. Lenuon, both of Samsonville, by Rev. Mr. Harlow.

2138. Jul 2, Shokan, Virgil H. Bishop to Cornelia A. Lake, both of Olive, by Rev. Mr. Harlow.

July 22, 1859

2139. Jul 14, Olive, Hiram H. Everett of West Hurley to Jane Lockwood of Olive, by Rev. Mr. Hill.

July 29, 1859

2140. Jul 4, Harvey W. Hoyt of Denning to Susan Sprague of Grahamsville, by Rev. N. D. Williamson.

August 12, 1859

2141. Aug 4, Alligerville, Jacob I. Brodhead to Anna K. Davis, both of Alligerville, by Rev. D. D. Lindsley.

2142. Jul 2, Kingston, Milton A. Fowler, Esq. of Fishkill to Kate P., only surviving daughter of the late Rev. Oren Sykes of Bedford, Mass., by Rev. A. Elmendorf.

2143. Jul 31, Ellenville, Levi S. Courtright to Rachel Anna Davis of Leurenkill, by Samuel Barlow, Esq.

August 19, 1859

2144. Aug 1, Isaac Bentley to Sarah Ann Ladew, both of Mattaewan, by Rev. D. W. Sherwood.

2145. Aug 11, Kingston, Simon Pleu of Kingston to Margaret Van Keuren of Esopus, by Rev. Wm. C. Smith.

2146. Aug 11, Kingston, Wm. M. Roe to Anna Orton, both of Kingston, by Rev. Wm. C. Smith.

2147. Aug 6, Wiltwyk, David C. Woolsey to Elizabeth Eckert, both of West Hurley, by Rev. A. Fort.

August 26, 1859

2148. Aug 17, Ellenville, Rev. Wm. P. Daved of Alligerville to Miss Sarah A. Palen of Sampsonville, by Rev. Paul R. Brown.

2149. Aug 17, Napanoch, Mr. Charles S. Brigham to Miss Carrie E. Seymour, both of Napanoch, by Rev. N. D. Williamson.

2150. Aug 13, Napanoch, John Sherman to Euphemia Kettle, both of Port Jervis, by Rev. N. D. Williamson.

September 9, 1859

2151. Sep 4, Saugerties, at the Exchange Hotel, Richard E. Degraff to Rosalia Stewart, both of Kingston, by Rev. J. D. Wardle.

2152. Aug 22, Shokan, Isaac N. Gray of Woodstock to Mary L. Delong of Hurley, by Rev. William Hill.

2153. Sep 1, Rondout, Jefferson Everson to Jane M. Shaffer, both of Rondout, by Rev. Mr. Edmonds.

2154. Aug 21, Rondout, Wm. Henry Drake to Elmira Van Wagner, both of Esopus, by Rev. Mr. Edmonds.

September 30, 1859

2155. Sep 18, Plattekill, Mr. Abraham L. Myer to Miss Elizabeth Dyle, both of the Town of Saugerties, by Rev. Mr. Chapman.

2156. Sep 23, Saugerties, Giles Van Aken to Caroline Plass, both of the Town of Saugerties, by M. Osterhoudt, Esq.

2157. Sep 21, Hudson, William Boies, Esq. of New York City to Susan Rivington, eldest daughter of Hon. Henry Hogeboom of Hudson, by Rev. Mr. Demarest, D. D.

October 7, 1859

2158. Sep 22, Saugerties, at the home of James A. James, John Nelson Whitaker to Martha Myers, both of Glasco, by Rev. D. W. Sherwood.

2159. Sep 22, Saugerties, at the home of James A. James, William Thomas Young to Theresa Whitaker, both of Glasco, by Rev. D. W. Sherwood

October 14, 1859

2160. Oct 10, Kingston, William Sickles to Martha Anderson, both of Saugerties, by Rev. Geo. Waters.

2161. Sep 27, Kingston, Wilson M. Heesier to Elizabeth Elting, both of New York City, by Rev. J. C. F. Hoes.

2162. Sep 28, David Todd of Hardenbergh to Anne Barrett of Kingston, by Rev. Wm. C. Smith.

2163. Oct 1, Kingston, Isaac G. Manning of Clinton Hollow, Dutchess Co. to Rebecca Dubois of Kingston, by Rev. Dr. Hoes.

2164. Oct 2, Kingston, Thomas Caine to Margaret Hafford, both of Kingston, by Rev. Dr. Hoes.

2165. Sep 28, Chicago, Ill., Henry H. Saufeldt to Emeline, daughter of Doct. W. H. Egan of Chicago, by Rev. J. O. Barton.

October 21, 1859

2166. Oct 19, Saugerties, Mr. Ephraim Lord, Jr. of East Jewett to Miss Irena France of Hunter, by Rev. J. K. Wardle.

2167. Oct 11, Saugerties, Mr. John E. Simmons to Miss Susan Louther, both of Saugerties, by Rev. D. W. Sherwood.

2168. Oct 11, Mr. P. W. Myer to Miss T. Anna, daughter of Mr. John H. Martin, all of the Town of Saugerties, by Rev. Dr. Ostrander.

2169. Oct 12, Rondout, Ozias S. Decker of Margaretville, Delaware Co. to Harriet Newkirk of Rondout, by Rev. B. T. Phillips.

October 28, 1859

2170. Oct 20, Saugerties, at the residence of Mr. S. Fiero, Mr. Abraham H. Pangburn to Mrs. Hannah Merritt, both of Unionville, by Rev. J. K. Wardle.

2171. Oct 26, Saugerties, Mr. Peter E. Shear to Miss Margaret Ann More of Saugerties, by Rev. D. W. Sherwood.

November 4, 1859

2172. Oct 30, Kingston, William Van Keuren, editor of the Rondout *Freeman* to Jane E. Dempsey, both of Kingston, by Rev. Jno. C. F. Hoes.

November 11, 1859

2173. Nov 3, Saugerties, John Sponhaner to Catharine Garb, both of Glenerie, by Matthew Osterhoudt, Esq.

2174. Nov 2, Kingston, at the 1st Presbyterian Church, James R. Foland to Miss Mary A. Rider, both of Kingston, by Rev. John Lillie, D. D.

2175. Nov 9, Saugerties, Wm. Braby to Miss Mary Elizabeth Fiero, both of Saugerties, by Rev. L. C. Lockwood.

November 18, 1859

2176. Nov 14, Saugerties, at the residence of R. Shaler, Stephen Root of Catskill to Hannah Shaler of Saugerties, by Rev. Mr. Sherwood.

2177. Nov 14, Mr. C. R. Bascom of Durham to Miss Caroline, daughter of West Chase, Esq. of Jewett Centre, by Rev. Henry J. Fox, AM, Principal of Ashland Collegate <sic> Institute.

2178. Nov 8, Thomas H. Merritt of Kingston to Lucinda, daughter of Jacob Van Keuren of Rosendale, by Rev. B. C. Lippincott.

December 9, 1859

2179. Nov 5, Tuckahoe, Westchester Co., Edward Light to Caroline Hasbrouck, both of Kingston, by Rev. Wm. H. Evans.

2180. Nov 30, Kingston, Alvin Stone to Cornelia Morey, both of Kingston by Rev. Dr. John Lillie.

December 16, 1859

2181. Dec 3, Saugerties, John C. Neuffer to Emelie Frech, both of Saugerties, by Rev. J. K. Wardle.

2182. Dec 3, Kingston, Chauncy J. Osborn of the Town of Saugerties to Sarah M. Robinson of Kingston, by Rev. Dr. Hoes.

December 23, 1859

2183. Dec 4, Woodstock, William Lewis of Woodstock to Virginia Grant of Shandaken, by Rev. A. Brundage.

2184. Dec 10, Shokan, Thomas Maher to Angeline Delamater, both of Shandaken.

December 30, 1859

2185. Dec 20, New Hampton, Orange Co., NY, Mr. M. Lewis Clark of Chester to Miss S. Augusta Case of New Hampton, by Rev. J. K. Wardle.

2186. Dec 22, John Dourn to Eveline Hudler, both of Wilbur, by Rev. Wm. C. Smith.

2187. Dec 21, Bloomingdale, at the parsonage, Charles Kelear of Rondout to Margaret Ann Mowl of Rosendale, by Rev. J. R. Lente.

January 6, 1860

2188. Dec 28, Hartwick Seminary, New York, Rev. Reinhold Adelberg of Saugerties to Miss Julia M., daughter of the officiating clergyman, by Rev. Dr. Miller.

2189. Jan 3, Methodist Episcopal Church, Mr. John Fowkes of New York to Miss Sarah F. Featherston of Saugerties, by Rev. J. K. Wardle.

2190. Dec 31, Peter Van Vlierden, Jr. to Mrs. Ellen Field, both of Woodstock, by Rev. Thomas Lape.

2191. Jan 1, Flatbush, Mr. Karner Seeley of Dutchess Co. to Miss Sarah A., daughter of the late William W. Walbridge of Kingston, by Rev. John Minor.

2192. Jan 2, Flatbush, Mr. Cyrus Overbagh of Glenerie to Miss Lucy A. Decker of Saugerties, by Rev. John Minor.

January 13, 1860

2193. Dec 29, Kingston, 1st Methodist Episcopal Church, Styles M. Saunders to Julia A. Plough, by Rev. D. L. Marks.

2194. Jan 1, Lake Hill, Dr. Rufus Vandebogart to Miss Almira, daughter of Wm. M. Cooper, all of the Town of Woodstock, by Rev. Mr. Brundage.

January 20, 1860

2195. Jan 4, Rondout, John L. .Schultz to Rachel C. Terpening, both of Esopus, by Rev. B. T. Phillips.

2196. Jan 10, St. Remy, Sylvester Terpening, aged 84, to Mrs. Catharine Van Aken, aged 80, both of Esopus, by Rev. James Mc Farlane.

January 27, 1860
2197. Jan 16, Napanoch, James Cameron to Phebe Ann Turner, both of Wawarsing, by C. A. Vernooy, Esq.

2198. Jan 19, Kingston, John H. Raenhart to Mary O. Weeks, both of Kingston, by Rev. W. C. Smith.

February 3, 1860
2199. Feb 1, Saugerties, Benjamin Taylor to Sarah Post, both of Saugerties, by Mathew Osterhoudt, Esq.

2200. Jan 21, West Camp, Mr. Henry Shoemaker to Miss Elizabeth Mower, both of West Camp, by Rev. D. F. Heller.

2201. Jan 24, West Camp, Mr. James H. Badeau to Miss Catherine C. Van Orden, both of Catskill, by Rev. D. F. Heller.

2202. Jan 26, Mr. Eugene Gardiner to Miss Selina Elwyn, both of Glasco, by Rev. John Minor.

2203. Jan 25, South Glastenbury, at St. Luke's Church, Wm. M. Van Gelder of Catskill to Eliza, daughter of Mr. Francis Taylor of South Glastenbury, by Rev. J. B. Robinson.

2204. Jan 26, American Hotel, James Sax of Kingston to Susan Freer of New Paltz, by Rev. Dr. Hoes.

2205. Jan 16, Kingston, Herman Shador to Caroline Van Bramer, both of Kingston, by Rev. W. C. Smith.

2206. Jan 22, Kingston, Frederick Wilkie to Mrs. Margaret Greely, both of Kingston, by Rev. W. C. Smith.

2207. Jan 30, Kingston, Palmer Wiltsey of Coeymans to Almada Waters of West Hurley, by Rev. W. C. Smith.

2208. Jan 30, New Salem, Esopus, David Repsher of New York to Frances M. Eltinge of New Salem, by Rev. H. V. Jones.

February 24, 1860
2209. Feb 18, Flatbush, Shelden B. Whitaker to Margaret J. Coulter, both of Saugerties, by Rev. J. Minor.

March 2, 1860
2210. Feb 26, West Saugerties, Mr. William M. Winchel of Olive to Miss Caroline Stewart of Saugerties, by Rev. C. Blauvelt.

March 16, 1860
2211. Mar 7, West Camp, Albert Magee of West Camp to Sarah Amelia Reynolds of Jewett, by Rev. D. F. Heller.

March 23, 1860
2212. Mar 10, Shandaken Center, Jeremiah Wentworth of Woodstock to Catharine A. Eckler of Marbletown, by Rev. Wm. V. O. Brainerd.

April 6, 1860
2213. Mar 20, New York City, Joseph Smith, attorney and Counseller at law to Miss Flora, niece of John L. Butzel, Esq., all of this place, by Rev. Dr. S. Adler.

April 13, 1860
2214. Apr 10, Kingston, F. M. Nestell to Margaret A. Shultis, both of Kingston, by Rev. W. C. Smith.

2215. Mar 13, Jonathan Bogart of Olive to Rachel More of Hurley, by Rev. Samuel Harlow.

April 20, 1860
2216. Apr 3, Utica, John A. Cole of Kingston to Kittie Breeds of Utica, by Rev. Dr. Lincoln.

April 27, 1860
2217. Apr 24, Kingston, Peter E. Hommel to Margaret Joy, both of Kingston, by Rev. Dr. Hoes.

2218. Apr 18, Rondout, Austin C. Thompson of Fulton, Otsego Co. to Ann Elizabeth, daughter of Martin G. Hayes of Rondout, by Rev. J. A. Edmonds.

May 4, 1860

2219. Apr 17, Kingston, Enoch E. Carter to Sophia Van Steenbergh, both of Rondout, by Rev. J. A. Collier.

2220. Apr 24, Milton, Theodore Quick, MD to Caroline F. Townsend, by Rev. Mr. Libenau.

May 11, 1860

2221. May 7, Saugerties, H. I. Wardle to Mary E. Love, both of Saugerties, by Rev. J. K. Wardle.

May 25, 1860

2222. Mar 23, Tivoli, Edwin Risedorf of Tivoli to Penelope Ann Lasher of Clermont, Columbia Co., by Rev. D. W. Sherwood.

2223. May 21, Kingston, James T. Colligan to Jane Forsyth, both of Rondout, by Rev. Joseph A. Colher.

June 1, 1860

2224. May 29, Saugerties, John H. Coon to Mrs. Hannah Prout, both of Saugerties, by Rev. J. K. Wardle.

June 8, 1860

2225. Jun 4, Saugerties, Richard Baker of Myersville, Dutchess Co. to Miss Lydia Dean of Saugerties, by Rev. D. W. Sherwood.

2226. Jun 1, Sacramento, Calif., Amos P. Catlin, Esq., formerly of Kingston to Miss Donaldson of Sacramento.

June 15, 1860

2227. Jun 12, Kingston, Joseph Deyo Chipp to Josephine Terpenning, both of Kingston, by Rev. Joseph A. Collier.

2228. Jun 5, Poughkeepsie, Charles M. O'Neil of Kingston to Mary V. Hester of Poughkeepsie, by Rev. S. D. Brown.

June 22, 1860

2229. Jun 21, Saugerties, Capt. John Osterhoudt to Lydia A. Laflin, both of Saugerties, by Rev. J. Elmendorf.

2230. Jun 14, Newburgh, Calab M. Hotaling of Kingston to Miss Elmira Waring of Newburgh, by Rev. Charles Shelling.

2231. Jun 13, Kingston, William Van Vliet of Esopus to Miss Jeannette Acker of Hurley, by Rev. W. C. Smith.

2232. Jun 14, James E. Styles of Kingston to Amy Harnden of Alligerville, by Rev. Jacob N. Vorhis.

2233. Jun 10, Rondout, Amor Richardson of Kingston to Mary Mc Carthy of Rosendale, by Rev. Mr. Jones.

2234. Jun 7, Kingston, John J. Keas of Plattekill to Mary E. Mack of New Paltz, by Rev. Mr. Wood.

2235. Jun 12, Kingston, Columbus Van Deusen to Harriet J., daughter of David Terry, Esq., by Rev. Mr. Wood.

June 29, 1860

2236. Jun 14, Town of Saugerties, Charles D. De Witt, MD to Adeline, oldest daughter of Peter H. Freleigh, all of the Town of Saugerties, by Rev. Henry Ostrander, D. D.

2237. Jun 14, Kingston, T. Colden Goetchies of New York to Hattie H. Flemming of Kingston, by Rev. Mr. Collier.

2238. Jun 14, Kingston, John N. Littell of New York to Mary Flemming of Kingston, by Rev. Mr. Collier.

2239. Jun 13, New Paltz Landing, James A. Hyde to Mercy Ann Palmer, both of New Paltz Landing, by Rev. Mr. Keech.

2240. May 9, Port Ewen, Peter Harvey to Rebecca Ann Ostrander of Esopus, by A. Elsworth, Esq.

July 6, 1860

2241. Jul 4, Saugerties, Henry Mill to Lydia Mynders, both of West Hurley, by Rev. J. K. Wardle.

2242. Jun 24, Saugerties, Moses M. Mower of Blue Mountain to Gertrude Emma Elmendorf of Saugerties, by Rev. J. Elmendorf.

2243. Jul 3, Saugerties, Hiram S. Readon to Nelly Ann, daughter of Noah Snyder, Esq., by Rev. J. Elmendorf.

2244. Jul 3, West Camp, Ralph Myer to Miss Sarah Hovenberg, both of Saugerties.

July 13, 1860
2245. Jul 7, David Hutton to Eliza Jane Young, both of Glasco, by Rev. J. Minor.

July 20, 1860
2246. Jul 7, William R. Hill to Celia C. Keator, both of Marbletown, by Rev. U. Messiter.

2247. Jul 12, South Woodstock, A. Sagendorf to Clarissa Elting, both of South Woodstock, by Rev. H. Wood.

2248. Jul 3, Hurley, Jesse Osterhoudt of Flatbush to Sarah D. Eckert of Marbletown, by Rev. B. C. Lippincott.

July 27, 1860
2249. Jul 12, Islep, LI, at the home of John H. Miller, Ovid T. Simmons of Saugerties to Jullia Pelletreau of Islep, by Rev. Charles W. Cooper.

2250. Jul 10, Modena, John E. Cooley of Poughkeepsie to Carrie Elting of Modena, by Rev. W. Ostrander.

August 3, 1860
2251. Jul 23, John Lapolt to Nelly E. Conway, both of Lackawack, by Rev. C. Shook.

2252. Jul 14, Shandaken, Maurice Higgins to Catharine Misner, both of Shandaken, by D. C. Griffin, Esq.

August 10, 1860

2253. Aug 1, Saugerties, Joseph Fickett to Margaret E. Maines, both of Saugerties, by Rev. J. K. Wardle.

2254. Aug 6, Saugerties, at the home of Peter P. Schoonmaker, Hiram W. Keever to Temperance Merritt, both of Coeymans Hollow, NY, by Rev. J. K. Wardle.

2255. Aug 2, Elvin S. Savage to Elizabeth Smith, both of Kingston, by Rev. W. C. Smith.

2256. Aug 2, Morgan L. Harris to Margaret Fletcher, both of Kingston, by Rev. W. C. Smith.

2257. Aug 4, Peter Crook, Jr. of Kingston to Rachel Bush of Rosendale, by Rev. W. C. Smith.

2258. Aug 1, Calvin Williams to Melissa Ann Sheeley, both of Marbletown, by Rev. J. N. Voorhis.

2259. Jul 28, Newburgh, Nelson Burge to Rachel C. Rosepaugh, both of Kingston, by Rev. Mr. Hermans.

August 17, 1860

2260. Aug 4, West Camp, Paul Snyder to Jane Maria Fox, both of Blue Mountain, by Rev. D. F. Heller.

August 24, 1860

2261. Jul 17, New York, Dr. V. Sherwood of Rondout to Martha E. Paine of Kingston, by Rev. Mr. Ames.

2262. Jul 16, Saugerties, Wm. D. Hill of Rondout to Mary J. Salpaugh of Red Hook, by Rev. Charles B. Sing.

August 31, 1860

2263. Jul 22, Saugerties, William Clark to Ellen Frine, both of Glasco, by Rev. J. Elmendorf.

2264. Aug 20, Saugerties, Nathaniel Mc Daniel of Woodstock to Sarah Louisa Taylor of Saugerties, by Rev. J. Elmendorf.

September 7, 1860

2265. Aug 28, at the Reformed Dutch Church, Geo. A. Vignes to Mary Trowbridge, both of Kingston, by Rev. M. Collier.

2266. Sep 2, Kingston, Edgar Hood to Esther A. Degraw, both of Esopus, by Rev. C. B. Sing.

September 14, 1860

2267. Sep 6, at the home of James A. Simpson, Cornelius C. Winnie of Olive to Margaret K. Simpson of Shandaken, by Rev. H. C. Longyear.

September 21, 1860

2268. Sep 13, Ghent, at the Lutheran parsonage, Mr. Daniel H. Hitchcock to Miss Amanda Finger, both of Saugerties.

September 28, 1860

2269. Sep 17, Saugerties, John Van Dyck to Mary Schermerhorn, both of Catskill, by Rev. J. K. Wardle.

2270. Sep 23, Saugerties, Cambridge Coon of New York to Amelia Proctor of Saugerties, by Rev. J. K. Wardle.

2271. Sep 19, Roxbury, Delaware Co., Gilbert E. Palen, MD, of Canadensis, Monroe Co., formerly of Saugerties to Elizabeth Gould of Roxbury, by Rev. James M. Burger.

2272. Aug 22, Delhi, Delaware Co., Wm. White, A. M., former Principal of the Saugerties Academy to Harriet N. Redfield, former preceptress of the Saugerties Academy, by Rev. Mr. Doubleday.

October 5, 1860

2273. Sep 29, West Camp, Conrad Rightmyer to Ann Elizabeth Schoonmaker, by Rev. C. Blauvelt.

2274. Sep 29, West Saugerties, Edward Schoonmaker to Elizabeth Catharine Layman, by Rev. C. Blauvelt.

October 12, 1860
2275. Sep 27, Saugerties, Jerome B. Reynolds of Port Ewen to Mary N., daughter of John Robinson of Saugerties, by Rev. Dr. Gosman.

2276. Aug 9, Saugerties, Wm. M. Swart to Martha Jane Burhans, both of Flatbush, by Rev. D. W. Sherwood.

2277. Sep 4, Saugerties, at the home of David Van Aken, Isaac Post to Leah M. Van Aken, all of the Town of Saugerties, by Rev. D. W. Sherwood.

October 19, 1860
2278. Oct 11, Saugerties, Calvin E. Hull of New York City to A. Jenny, youngest daughter of Luther Laflin of Saugerties, by Rev. J. Elmendorf.

2279. Oct 10, Vernon Centre, Oneida Co., NY, Rev. George Clark of Eddyville, NY to Miss Lydia A. Barber of Vernon Centre, by Rev. J. K. Wardle.

2280. Oct 16, at the home of Mr. Wm. Dean, Robert Herald of Rhinebeck to Miss Hannah Dean of Saugerties, by Rev. J. K. Wardle.

November 16, 1860
2281. Nov 19 <sic>, Saugerties, Mr. Peter Tymeson to Miss Fanny Underhill, both of Saugerties, by Rev. J. K. Wardle. <November 10, 1860, Saugerties United Methodist Church records, ed.>

November 23, 1860
2282. Nov 20, Saugerties, at the Trinity Church, Dr. Randolph Fitzhugh Mason, USN to Lavinia Randolph, daughter of the late Fitz Allen Deas, USN, by Rev. Dr. Robertson.

2283. Undated, West Camp, at the Methodist Episcopal parsonage, Mr. Jeremiah Hommel to Catharine E. Maqwell, both of Quarryville, by Rev. J. Vandermater. <November 15, 1860 at Asbury, bride's name Kate E. Maxwell, clergy, I. R. Vanderwater, Malden-Quarryville Methodist Church records, ed.>

November 30, 1860
2284. Nov 25, Saugerties, Mr. Robert L. Young to Miss Susan A. Maines, both of Saugerties, by Rev. J. K. Wardle.

December 14, 1860
2285. Dec 6, Saugerties, Wm. H. Gorseline of Kingston to Adaline Elvira Fiero of Cairo, by Rev. J. K. Wardle.

2286. Nov 21, Rochester, Wm. U. Mason of Kingston to Mary E. Enderly of Rochester, by Rev. Mr. Wyckoff.

December 21, 1860
2287. Nov 16, Hiram Myers of the Town of Kingston to Mary Catharine, 2nd daughter of Smith Herrick of the Town of Saugerties, by Rev. Thomas Lape.

December 28, 1860
2288. Dec 25, Saugerties, George Finger to Maggy James, both of Saugerties, by Rev. Mr. Sherwood.

January 4, 1861
2289. Dec 19, Capt. Chas. Anderson of Saugerties to Letitia, daughter of the late Zachariah Hoffman of Red Hook, by Rev. Dr. De Witt.

2290. Dec 30, Saugerties, at the home of Peter G. Lasher, Thomas Way of Hudson to Gertrude Lasher of Saugerties, by Rev. J. K. Wardle.

2291. Dec 8, David Becker of West Saugerties to Susan Coviret of Cloveville, Delaware Co., by Rev. C. Blauvelt.

2292. Dec 25, George E. Carnwright to Charlotte E. A. Dibble, both of Plattekill Clove, by Rev. C. Blauvelt.

2293. Dec 29, Isaac Newkirk of Caatsban to Matilda Van Steenbergh of Greene Co., by Rev. C. Blauvelt.

2294. Dec 31, Zachariah B. Mower to Jane A. Van Steenbergh, both of West Saugerties, by Rev. C. Blauvelt.

2295. Jan 1, Samuel Rightmyer to Sarah Elizabeth Miller, both of West Saugerties, by Rev. C. Blauvelt.

January 11, 1861

2296. Jan 3, near Saugerties, at the residence of the bride's father, Geo. G. Van Hoesen of Troy, to Kate S., 2nd daughter of Wm. C. Van Hoesen, Esq., by Rev. J. Elmendorf.

2297. Jan 1, Woodstock, at the Methodist Episcopal parsonage, Lewis Huston to Almira Row, both of West Hurley, by Rev. H. Wood.

2298. Jan 5, at the home of the bride's mother, Edwin L. Comfort of Catskill to Mary Wolven of Saugerties, by Rev. H. Wood.

2299. Jan 9, Morris Burhans to Martha Plough of Kingston, by Rev. D. W. Sherwood.

January 18, 1861

2300. Jan 10, at the residence of the bride's mother, William Martin of West Hurley to Laura A. Britt of Woodstock, by Rev. H. Wood.

January 25, 1861

2301. Jan 5, Town of Saugerties, Wm. S. Low to Mary E. Moran, by Rev. Mr. Chapman.

2302. Jan 13, Rondout, Jacob H. Gildersleeve, one of the proprietors of the Rondout *Freeman*, to Maggie N. Mc Causland, both of Rondout, by Rev. B. P. Phillips.

February 1, 1861

2303. Jan 17, Saugerties, Wm. E. Ackert of Rhinebeck to Mary Frances Peck of Saugerties, by Rev. D. Sherwood.

February 8, 1861

2304. Jan 26, Paterson, New Jersey, Wm. H. Maxwell, formerly of the Town of Saugerties, to Lizzie, daughter of James Kershaw, Esq., by Rev. Mr. Cheever.

February 15, 1861

2305. Feb 10, at the Methodist Episcopal parsonage, David A. Valk of Poughkeepsie to C. Isabel Fullmer of Saugerties, by Rev. J. K. Wardle.

2306. Feb 12, Malden, Alexander Lewis of Woodstock to Mary, daughter of John Henry Valk of Malden, by Rev. Thomas Lape.

February 22, 1861

2307. Feb 7, Abm. L. Lockwood of Kingston to Emma W. Buck of Harlem, New York, by Rev. Valentine Buck.

March 8, 1861

2308. Feb 27, Pittsfield, Mass., Jacob Snyder, Jr. to Mary E., oldest daughter of John P. Foland, all of Saugerties, by Rev. J. F. Yates.

2309. Mar 2, Saugerties, Mr. Christopher Lowther to Miss Catharine M. Delanoy, by Rev. D. W. Sherwood.

2310. Mar 2, Saugerties, at the home of Peter Van Steenbergh, Mr. Louis Underhill to Miss Martha Sparling, both of Saugerties, by Rev. J. K. Wardle.

2311. Mar 5, Saugerties, at the Methodist Episcopal parsonage, Mr. Josiah Mauterstock to Miss Lucretia E. Snyder, both of Saugerties, by Rev. J. K. Wardle.

2312. Feb 4, Mr. Joseph T. Cassell of Glasco to Miss Margaret D. Towner of Malden, by Rev. E. Denniston.

March 22, 1861

2313. Feb 20, at the home of Ephraim Musier, Mr. Lamon Richardson to Miss Amy Catherine Musier, all of the Town of Catskill, by Rev. D. F. Heller.

April 5, 1861

2314. Undated, Saugerties, Mr. Henry Boght of Saugerties to Miss Jane Ann Wipple of Albany, by Rev. R. Adelberg.

2315. Undated, Malden, William Mortin to Larah E. Scales, both of the Town of Catskill, by Rev. Thomas Lape.

May 3, 1861

2316. Apr 27, Saugerties, at the Reformed Dutch Church, Harmon Carle to Susan Barrell, both of Highwoods, by Rev. J. Elmendorf.

May 31, 1861

2317. Apr 26, Blue Mountain, at the Reformed Dutch Church, Mr. Stephen O. Hagadon of Livingstonville, Schoharie Co., to Miss Sarah Jane Hill of West Saugerties, by Rev. C. Blauvelt.

2318. May 11, Mr. John O. Benn to Sarah Moose, both of West Camp, by Rev. D. F. Heller.

2319. May 15, Mr. Peter H. Hommel to Miss Elizabeth Mower, both of Saugerties, by Rev. D. F. Heller.

June 7, 1861

2320. Jun 2, Glenerie Falls, Andrew Plass of Hudson to Elsie C. Spencer of Kingston, by Rev. S. Fitch.

June 14, 1861

2321. Jun 12, Morris F. Fullmer to Delia C. Valk, both of the Town of Saugerties, by Rev. Thomas Lape.

June 28, 1861

2322. Jun 25, William S. Van Hoesen to Anna M., only daughter of Mr. Samuel F. Wolven, all of Saugerties, by Rev. J. Elmendorf.

July 12, 1861

2323. Jul 4, Saugerties, at the home of Mr. Wm. Dean, Frank Boice to Melissa Shoemaker, both of Barrytown, by Rev. S. Fitch.

2324. Jun 30, Mr. John Marriott of High Falls to Miss Sarah Catharine Kimball of Quarryville, by Rev. D. F. Heller.

August 2, 1861

2325. Jul 20, Saugerties, Lyman O'Bryon to Lida Ann Van Steenbergh, both of Malden, by Rev. J. Elmendorf.

August 9, 1861

2326. Aug 1, Brooklyn, at the South Third St. Presbyterian Church, Rev. Edward A. Collier, pastor of the Congregational Church of Saugerties to Miss Isabella G., daughter of Lewis L. James of Brooklyn, by Rev. J. D. Wells.

September 6, 1861

2327. Aug 27, West Camp, at the Lutheran parsonage, Mr. Wesley Low of Pine Bush to Miss Mary Elizabeth Ackerman of Saugerties, by Rev. D. F. Heller.

2328. Aug 26, Mr. Annason Delanoy to Miss Helen Augusta Stowe, both of Kingston, by Rev. H. V. Jones.

2329. Aug 28, Cold Spring, Joseph Delaney to Mary E. Burhans, both of Kingston, by Rev. W. C. Smith.

September 13, 1861

2330. Sep 2, Harrisburgh, Pa., T. H. Everett of Mass. to Miss Kate R., daughter of Samuel Crawford, Esq., of the village of Saugerties, by Rev. James R. Clark.

October 4, 1861

2331. Sep 24, C. D. W. Cole of Marbletown to Jane A. Snyder of Kingston, by Rev. John Minor.

October 25, 1861

2332. Oct 20, John Burnett to Hearzilla Hamlin, both of Saugerties, by Rev. J. Minor.

November 8, 1861

2333. Nov 6, Plattekill, Charles Brink to Mary Ellen, daughter of George F. Carle, Esq., all of Plattekill, by Rev. J. Elmendorf.

November 22, 1861

2334. Nov 21, Saugerties, Henry Wygant to Miss Matilda Mauterstock, both of Saugerties, by Rev. Mr. Fitch.

January 17, 1862

2335. Jan 11, Saugerties, at the Methodist Episcopal parsonage, Cornelius L. Short to Jane C. Shader, both of the Town of Saugerties, by Rev. S. Fitch.

2336. Jan 11, Saugerties, at the residence of Mr. Quimby, Charles W. Styles of Kingston to Sarah A. Edwards of Saugerties, by Rev. S. Fitch.

2337. Jan 6, Malden, James Van Slyke to Anna Hommel, both of the Town of Saugerties, by Rev. J. R. Vandewater.

January 31, 1862

2338. Jan 22, Plattekill, Abram Hommel to Angeline Brink, both of the Town of Saugerties, by Rev. Mr. Chapman.

February 28, 1862

2339. Feb 20, Kingston, at the 2nd Methodist Episcopal Church, Henry D. Brodhead of Rochester to Sarah E. Conner of Wilbur, by Rev. Wm. G. Browning.

2340. Feb 19, James Sprague of Plattekill to Adeline Summers of Gardiner, by Rev. Jacob N. Voorhis.

2341. Jan 23, Newark, New Jersey, Isaac Thomas of Rondout to Amelia Kanouse of Newark, by Rev. Mr. Williams.

2342. Feb 5, Joseph R. Gilbert of Ellenville Glass Co. to Emily, daughter of Eli D. Terwilliger, both of Ellenville, by Rev. E. W. Bently.

March 14, 1862

2343. Mar 8, Town of Woodstock, at the home of Edmund Neher, Lucas W. Bonesteel to Mary Elizabeth Salsbury of Cairo, Greene Co., by Rev. Thomas Lape.

2344. Mar 11, Saugerties, Wm. E. Van Buskirk to Mary E. Bert, both of Saugerties, by Rev. S. Fitch.

2345. Undated, Saugerties, Jared M. Guilfuss to Elizabeth E. Hommel, both of Hunter, by Rev. S. Fitch. <March 6, 1862, records of the Saugerties United Methodist Church, ed.>

April 4, 1862

2346. Apr 2, Saugerties, Rev. R. G. Williams to Miss Mary Slater, Principal of the Young Ladies Seminary, by Rev. J. Elmendorf.

April 11, 1862

2347. Apr 6, at the Methodist Episcopal Church, Harrison Blackwell to Adelaide M. daughter of the late Joseph Burhans, all of Saugerties, by Rev. S. Fitch.

May 16, 1862

2348. May 8, Mr. Clark S. Peck of Kingston to Emma Jane, only daughter of Edward Simmons, by Rev. S. Fitch.

June 6, 1862

2349. May 31, John W. Hoff of Saugerties to Elenor Lasher of Catskill, by Rev. Thomas Lape.

2350. May 20, James H. Newkirk of Caatsban to Mary E. Freligh, daughter of John H. Freligh of West Saugerties, by Rev. C. Blauvelt.

June 27, 1862

2351. Jun 25, John A. Myers to Sarah A. Russell, both of Saugerties, by Rev. S. Fitch.

July 11, 1862

2352. Undated, Saugerties, James Van De Wyngard of Brooklyn to Jane Cummings of Coxsackie, by Rev. S. Fitch. <July 5, 1862, records of the Saugerties United Methodist Church, ed.>

2353. Jul 3, Edgar Minkler to Elizabeth Schoonmaker, both of Blue Mountain, by Rev. Thomas Lape.

2354. Jul 3, Gains Van Steenberg to Sarah A. Williams, both of the Town of Saugerties, by Rev. Thomas Lape.

August 8, 1862

2355. Jun 19, Saugerties, Mr. H. J. Teter to Miss M. J. Whittaker, both of Glasco, by Rev. J. M. Ferris.

August 22, 1862

2356. Aug 16, at the Kingston Hotel, Philip H. Keater to Louisa Van Ostrander, both of Rosendale, by Rev. Dr. Hoes.

2357. Aug 16, at the Kingston Hotel, William H. Harrison to Charlotte Craig, both of Rosendale, by Rev. Dr. Hoes.

2358. Aug 14, Kingston, at the 2nd Reformed Dutch Church, George Everson of Rondout to Harriet J. Stickle of Kingston, by Rev. J. A. Collier.

September 12, 1862

2359. Sep 2, Wm. M. Everett of Malden to Leah Dederick of High Falls, by Rev. D. F. Heller.

2360. Sep 11, at the Reformed Dutch Church, John Lawrence to Miss Mary Wigram of Saugerties, by Rev. Mr. Gaston.

September 19, 1862

2361. Jul 28, Diamond Springs, Calif., Mr. G. Kaufman of Aurora to Miss Yetta Fleishman, formerly of Saugerties, by Rev. Z. Neustadt of Sacramento.

November 14, 1862

2362. Nov 12, John Henry Myer to Mrs. Maria Elmendorf, daughter of Benjamin Myer, all of Saugerties, by Rev. G. H. Coffey.

December 11, 1862

2363. Dec 6, at the residence of the bride's father, Mr. Henry A. Coon to Miss Malissa Snyder, daughter of Philo Snyder, both of the Town of Saugerties, by Rev. N. F. Chapman

2364. Dec 3, Mr. John H. Freese to Miss Jane E. Sax, both of the Town of Saugerties, by Rev. I. H. Collier.

December 19, 1862

2365. Nov 16, Kingston, Mr. Matthew Van Buren to Carrie G. Keator, both of Kingston, by Rev. Mr. Harris.

2366. Dec 16, Kingston, Mr. George Wheeler of Brooklyn to Mary, daughter of E. T. Van Nostrand of Kingston, by Rev. Dr. Hoes.

2367. Dec 16, Kingston, Alfred Van Aken to Julia, daughter of E. T. Van Nostrand, by Rev. Dr. Hoes.

December 26, 1862

2368. Dec 22, Saugerties, at the Methodist Episcopal Church, Edgar Whitaker to Eliza Simpson, both of Saugerties, by Rev. S. Fitch.

January 9, 1863

2369. Jan 8, Town of Saugerties, Sybil N. De Myer to Adam Lasher, of Glasco.

2370. Dec 25, Malden, Lafayette Mongo Dennett of New York to Leah, youngest daughter of Isaac Zeilman, Esq. of Malden, by Rev. Thomas Lape.

February 13, 1863

2371. Feb 4, at the home of Wm. H. Barber, James H. Davis to Margaret A. Barber, both of Rondout, by Rev. S. Fitch.

2372. Jan 24, John Furrnbargher to Sarah Ella Lane, both of Woodstock, by Rev. Alexander Gulick.

2373. Jan 15, Wiltwyck parsonage, Jacob Van Keuren to Ellen Post, both of Esopus, by Rev. Wm. A. Shaw.

2374. Jan 22, West Hurley, Christopher H. Warren to Sarah C. Pelham, both of West Hurley, by Rev. C. Case.

2375. Jan 22, West Hurley, Stephen A. Miller to Cynthia Warren, both of West Hurley, by Rev. C. Case.

March 13, 1863

2376. Mar 5, Catskill, Mr. Robert A. Snyder to Miss Jane S. Morgan, both of the village of Saugerties, by Rev. Geo. Webster.

2377. Mar 6, Saugerties, William Mann to Miss Christina Brown, both of Saugerties, by Rev. S. Fitch.

April 3, 1863

2378. Mar 11, Saugerties, Peter Havey to Miss Susan Post, both of Saugerties, by Rev. George H. Coffey.

April 10, 1863

2379. Apr 4, at the home of the bride, Mr. Graves to Mrs. Elizabeth L. T. Myer, both of Saugerties, by Rev. Geo. H. Coffey.

2380. Apr 4, Congregational Church, Jesse Taylor to Theresa Kerr, both of Quarryville, by Rev. Geo. H. Coffey.

May 1, 1863

2381. Apr 21, Saugerties, Alanson Osterhoudt of Flatbush to Maria C. Brink of Plattekill, by Rev. Dr. Gosman.

2382. Apr 19, Rondout, Mr. Louis Roeder of New York City to Miss Rose Meyer, sister-in-law of Mr. M. Wells, Esq., of Rondout, by Rev. Mr. Gideon.

2383. Apr 14, Earl Stone of New Milford, Conn. to Miss Sarah E. Craft, Esq. of Milton, New York, by Rev. J. W. Smith.

2384. Apr 14, New York City, William Hathaway, Esq., Agent of the Penn. Coal Co. at Port Ewen, to Lydia Mc Kibbin of New York, by Rev. Dr. Spring.

May 8, 1863
2385. Apr 21, Samuel Whitaker to Mary Elizabeth Krom, both of Marbletown, by Rev. J. L. Mc Nair.

2386. Apr 26, Rhinebeck, Geo. W. Hogan to Phebe Davis, both of Kingston, by Rev. W. H. Luckenbach.

May 15, 1863
2387. Apr 30, Wiltwyck, Edward B. Houghtaling, aged 64, to Mrs. C. Van Gaasbeek, aged 63, both of Wiltwyck, by Rev. Mr. Shaw.

2388. May 2, Joseph Zimmerman to Miss Frederika C. Kimball, both of Catskill, by Rev. William S. Chadwell.

2389. May 7, George Overbaugh to Lydiaett Abeel, both of Catskill, by Rev. J. A. Lansing.

2390. Undated, Kiskatom, Abram Van Gorden of Catskill to Mannah L. Lane of Kiskatom, by Rev. C. Rockwell. <May, 1863, records of the Kiskatom Reformed Church, ed.>

2391. May 7, Marbletown, Artemus Sahler of Kingston to Sarah C. Cole, daughter of John R. Cole, Esq., of Marbletown, by Rev. Mr. Lippincott.

2392. Apr 28, near New Paltz, Rev. John Kelly Rhinehart, minister of the Reformed Dutch Church of Roxbury, Delaware Co. to Mary I., daughter of Lefever Dubois, Esq., by Rev. C. H. Stitt, assisted by Rev. Charles Scott.

2393. Apr 27, New Paltz, Lewis W. Mansfield Semunyan, a returned soldier, to Priscilla Ann Dubois of New Paltz, by C. H. Lefever, Esq.

May 29, 1863

2394. May 14, at the 2nd Reformed Church of Kingston, Frederick F. Peters to Josephine Hess, both of Kingston, by Rev. B. C. Lippincott.

2395. May 13, at the 2nd Reformed Church of Kingston, George B. Merritt to Hilah A. Brodhead, both of Kingston, by Rev. J. A. Collier.

2396. May 20, at the 2nd Methodist Episcopal Church of Kingston, Uriah Whitaker to Miss Josephine Morey, both of Kingston, by Rev. Mr. Peck.

June 5, 1863

2397. Jun 3, Pemington, New Jersey, Mr. Wm. M. Brink to Mrs. Catharine Couse, both of Saugerties, by Rev. Mr. Chalker.

2398. May 19, Malden, at the home of Mr. Fiero, Esq., Mr. John W. Mower of West Camp to Miss Sarah C. Terpin of Malden, by Rev. D. F. Heller.

2399. Jun 1, Mr. Stuart Druse of Hornsville, Herkimer Co. to Mrs. Sarah A. Dubois of Kingston, by Rev. Dr. W. Sym.

2400. May 20, Silver Creek, Chautauqua Co., W. A. Cockburn to Miss Fanny Scoville, by Rev. E. H. Yingling.

June 12, 1863

2401. Jun 1, Mr. James Watson to Mrs. Ann Grieg, both of Rondout, by Rev. H. V. Jones.

2402. May 28, Montezuma, New York, at the home of her mother, Mrs. John B. Myer, Capt. David A. Taylor, U. S. A. to Miss Sarah Myers of Montezuma, grand daughter of Mr. Benjamin Myer of Saugerties, by Rev. T. D. Harris.

June 19, 1863

2403. Jun 17, West Camp, Mr. James F. Whitney of Catsbaan to Miss Sarah Mower of West Camp, by Rev. D. F. Heller.

2404. Jun 14, Malden, John A. Terwilliger to Miss Isabella Shafer, both of Saugerties, by Rev. Thomas Lape.

2405. Jun 4, Sherburne, New York, Congregational Church, Mr. Fort Van Keuren, MD, of New Salem (Esopus) to Miss Ellen White of Sherburne, by Rev. E. Curtis.

2406. May 4, Rosendale, Mr. John Goodsir to Miss Sarah A. Slater, both of Ellenville, by Rev. G. W. Barnes.

2407. Jun 2, Jenkintown, Ulster Co., Mr. George Adee to Miss Sarah, daughter of the late James Jenkins of Jenkintown, by Rev. C. H. Stitt.

2408. May 30, Dubois Coddington to Mary J. Summers, both of Rochester, by Rev. J. N. Voorhis.

June 26, 1863

2409. Jun 11, Bruce Mofeat, Esq. of Blooming Grove, Orange Co., to Anna Le Nettie Priest of Catskill, by Rev. C. Rockwell.

2410. Jun 17, Kingston, at the 1st Methodist Episcopal Church, Mr. Julius A. Curtis to Miss Maria Hageman, daughter of Adrian Hageman, all of Kingston, by Rev. J. G. L. Mc Kown.

2411. Jun 16, Rondout, Mr. John T. Edge of New York to Miss Agnes Bow of Rondout, by Rev. H. V. Jones.

July 3, 1863

2412. Jun 25, Catskill, Judson A. Waterbury of Saugerties to Miss Sarah Dubois of Catskill.

2413. Jun 25, Kingston, at the 2nd Methodist Episcopal Church, Eli Whitaker to Miss Jane Burhans, both of Kingston, by Rev. L. W. Peck.

2414. Jun 20, Mr. William Greves to Miss Sarah C. Harvey, both of Rondout, by Rev. Z. N. Lewis.

2415. Apr 29, Rondout, at the Presbyterian Church, Frederick Snyder to Mary L. Walter, both of Rondout, by Rev. Wm. Irwin.

July 10, 1863

2416. Jul 4, Glasco, Mr. Norman Cunyes to Miss Joanna Quick, both of the Town of Saugerties, by Rev. D. Heroy.

2417. Jun 23, George W. Bovee to Miss Mary Gaddis, both of the Town of Saugerties, by Rev. Thomas Lape.

July 17, 1863

2418. Jul 9, at the home of Mrs. Henry Teal, William P. Hommel to Lavina Teal, both of Quarryville, by Rev. Isaac H. Collier.

2419. Jul 2, Frederick L. Cazer to Melissa Osterhoudt, both of Kingston, by Rev. J. Minor.

July 24, 1863

2420. Jul 4, Saugerties, Geo. W. Cole to Fannie M. Van Steenburgh, both of Saugerties, by Rev. W. G. Browning.

2421. Jul 21 Saugerties, Wm. J. Magee of Woodstock to Helena E. Boyce of Rensslaerville, by Rev. W. G. Browning.

August 14, 1863

2422. Aug 5, Alexander Campbell to Miss Catharine Sullivan, both of Rondout, by Rev. Z. N. Lewis.

2423. Aug 4, Samuel Lundy Shotwell of Morrisania, NY to Sarah Smith Underhill of Hallock's Mills, Westchester Co., by Rev. Dr. Lillie.

2424. Aug 5, New Paltz, Jas. L. Bostwick to Mary L., eldest daughter of A. J. Story of New Paltz, both of Kingston, by Rev. O. H. P. Deyo.

August 21, 1863

2425. Aug 15, Saugerties, Wm. D. Bossard of Greenwood, Pa. to Elizabeth L. Low of Saugerties, by Rev. W. G. Browning.

September 4, 1863

2426. Sep 21, Glasco, Peter Dederick to Miss Elizabeth Wolven, daughter of Jeremiah Wolven, both of West Hurley, by Rev. Dr. Ostrander.

2427. Aug 27, Kingston, Frank Mayer of Chicago, Ill. to Jane Clinton of Saugerties.

2428. Aug 26, Geo. H. Simson of Rondout to Jane Williams of Kingston, by Rev. Dr. Hoes.

2429. Aug 20, Wm. B. Ferguson of Rondout to Miss Maria Jane Alsdorf of Newburgh, by Rev. Z. N. Lewis.

2430. Aug 25, New York City, at Calvary Church, Col. D. Tompkins Van Buren, U. S. A. to Miss Julia, daughter of James L. Morris, by Rev. A. C. Cox, D. D.

2431. Aug 9, Marbletown, Levi Terwilliger to Elizabeth Frost, by Rev. J. Markle.

2432. Aug 4, John A. Cole of Kingston to Kate B. Johnson of Albany, by Rev. Dr. Wyckoff.

2433. Aug 25, Robert J. Mc Culack to Sarah Helen Harvey, both of Rondout, by Rev. Dr. Lillie.

September 18, 1863

2434. Sep 5, Saugerties, Abram P. Phillips to Emily A. Dubois, both of Saugerties, by Rev. W. G. Browning.

2435. Sep 2, Town of Saugerties, at the home of the bride's father Samuel Freligh, Cornelius Wynkoop Carnright of West Hurley to Miss Abby Freligh of Saugerties, by Rev. Isaac H. Collier.

October 2, 1863

2436. Sep 17, Saugerties, Mm. <sic> Morgan to Jane Winne, both of Saugerties, by Rev. D. W. Sherwood. <could be Mr. or Wm, ed>

October 16, 1863

2437. Oct 14, Glasco, Mr. John Vedder, MD, of Saugerties to Mrs. Sarah M. DeLanoy of Glasco, by Rev. Mr. Sherwood.

2438. Oct 8, Andrew Simmons of Glasco to Mary Watson of Saugerties, by Rev. J. Minor.

October 23, 1863

2439. Oct 17, at the home of the bride's father, Mr. Montgomery Cunyes to Sarah A. Whitaker, both of Saugerties, by Rev. W. G. Browning.

November 6, 1863

2440. 2-th Sep, Malden, George W. Snyder, Esq. of Woodstock to Mrs. Julia Deforest of New York, by Rev. T. Lape. <date illegible>

November 20, 1863

2441. Nov 4, William H. Greenwood to Mary J., daughter of Morris C. Rushmore, both of Hudson, by Rev. Wm. A. Chipp.

December 4, 1863

2442. Nov 22, Saugerties, Fanny Bamberger, niece of John L. Butzel, Esq. to Mr. Samuel Winestock of Milwauky, Wis., by Rev. M. Winan.

December 18, 1863

2443. Dec 9, Mr. S. Ransom Backer to Miss Mary M. Fiero, both of the Town of Saugerties, by Rev. I. H. Collier.

January 1, 1864

2444. Dec 25, at the Congregational Church, Mr. Smith Wyant to Miss Lucy L. Valk, both of the Town of Saugerties, by Rev. Geo. H. Coffey.

January 8, 1864

2445. Dec 31, Glasco, Hiram D. Relyea of Kingston to Augusta Cogswill of Glasco, by Rev. D. Heroy.

2446. Dec 31, Glasco, Charles Philips to Charlotte Whitney, both of Saugerties, by Rev. D. Heroy.

January 15, 1864

2447. Dec 30, Saugerties, Mr. Edgar Davis to Miss Elizabeth Hermans, both of Saugerties, by Rev. W. G. Browning.

2448. Dec 31, Saugerties, Mr. Samuel B. Tice to Miss Cora Van Buren, both of Kingston, by Rev. W. G. Browning.

2449. Jan 9, West Camp, Mr. James Cody of Evensville, Ill. to Miss Lavina M. Mower of Saugerties, by Rev. D. F. Heller.

February 5, 1864

2450. Jan 20, Saugerties, Theodore Keys of Kingston to Maria Elizabeth Williams of Barrytown, by Rev. W. G. Browning.

February 19, 1864

2451. Feb 6, Flatbush, Lorenzo Dubois to Christina Snyder, both of Saugerties, by Rev. David Heroy.

2452. Feb 11, Flatbush, Wm. Lasher to Leah Hoyt, both of Woodstock, by Rev. David Heroy.

2453. Feb 11, Robert Robertson to Harriet Osterhoudt, both of Saugerties, by Rev. J. Minor.

2454. Feb 10, Ferris W. Eighmey of Kingston to Emeline Simmons of Saugerties, by Rev. J. Minor.

2455. Feb 9, W. J. Armstrong to Mary E. Burhans, both of Kingston, by Rev. J. Minor.

2456. Feb 11, Jonas M. Valk of the 65th New York State Volunteers to Dolly Zeilman, both of Malden, by Rev. Thomas Lape.

February 26, 1864

2457. Feb 23, Saugerties, Peter A. Smith of the 20th Regiment, New York State Militia to Mary A. Place, both of Kingston, by Rev. W. G. Browning.

2458. Feb 7, James Rouse (colored soldier) to Lucinda R. James, both of Catskill, by Rev. W. G. Browning.

March 4, 1864

2459. Feb 25, Wm. P. Low of Saugerties to Margaret A., daughter of Wm. P. Lewis of Woodstock, by Rev. Thomas Lape.

2460. Feb 15, Monroe City, Michigan, Russell H. Crosman of Kingston to Charlotte M. Calkins of Monroe City, by Rev. Mr. Fox.

March 11, 1864

2461. Whereas my wife Martha has left me without cause or provocation and taken up lodging with George Merinnis, all persons are hereby strictly forbidden to trust her on my account as I will pay no debts of her contracting, nor any liabilities for her of any kind. Signed - Lewis Underhill, Saugerties, March 9, 1864.

March 18, 1864

2462. Mar 9, Saugerties, Mr. Eliphalet P. Pollock to Miss Emily P. Mullen, both of Poughkeepsie, by Rev. W. G. Browning.

April 1, 1864

2463. Mar 23, Wm. Vanderboget to Eliza Post, both of the Town of Saugerties, by Rev. David Heroy.

2464. Dec 24, James R. Van Hoesen of the Town of Saugerties to Jane, daughter of Henry Tindall of New York City, by Rev. Mr. Searles.

April 8, 1864

2465. Apr 2, Pliny Bovee to Malissa Longadike, both of West Saugerties, by Rev. Thomas Lape.

April 15, 1864

2466. Apr 2, Saugerties, Henry Low to Anna Hillas, by Rev. Mr. Roberts.

2467. Mar 16, Mr. Moses Whitaker to Miss Anna Faller, both of the Town of Saugerties, by Rev. H. E. Fischer.

2468. Mar 17, Mr. A. S. Brink to Miss Josephine Doile, both of the Town of Saugerties, by Rev. H. E. Fischer.

April 22, 1864
2469. Apr 19, Mr. Philip J. Beare to Miss Martha L. Brink, both of the Town of Saugerties, by Rev. D. H. Heller.

2470. Apr 20, Mr. Nelson Magee to Miss Abbie H. Moose, both of theTown of Saugerties, by Rev. D. H. Heller.

April 29, 1864
2471. Apr 21, New York City, Charles Osterhoudt to Miss Hanna Shaw, both of Saugerties.

May 6, 1864
2472. Apr 27, Glasco, Wm. H. Whitiker to Emma J. Goldsmith, both of Glasco, by Rev. David Heroy.

May 13, 1864
2473. May 8, Town of Saugerties, Jeremiah Mower of Saugerties to Laura Carle of Kingston, by Rev. N. F. Chapman.

2474. May 9, Francis S. Wynkoop, Jr. to Miss Rachel Van Vleck, both of Kingston, by Rev. John Van Vleck.

May 20, 1864
2475. Undated, West Camp, Mr. Abm. A. Post to Miss Helen E. Gardner, both of Saugerties, by Rev. D. F. Heller. <April 30, 1864, records of St. Paul's Lutheran Church, West Camp, ed.>

2476. May 9, Philip Plusch to Amelia H. A. Dressel, both of Catskill, by Rev. J. A. Lansing.

2477. May 2, West Hurley, Wm. H. Cashdollar of the old 20th Regiment to Mary L. Bogardus, both of Woodstock, by Rev. C. Case.

2478. May 4, Pine Plains, Dutchess Co., Rev. Richard De Witt of Guilford, Ulster Co. to Miss Kate Hammond of Pine Plains, by Rev. Wm. Sayre.

May 27, 1864

2479. May 24, Saugerties, at Trinity Church, Mr. Guy D. Penfield of Kalamazoo, Michigan to Miss Francis H., daughter of Rev. J. J. Robertson, D. D. of Saugerties, by Rev. Daniel Henshaw of Connecticut.

June 3, 1864

2480. Jun 1, at the residence of the bride's father, Mr. John S. Post to Lavina S. Gillesby, both of the Town of Saugerties, by Rev. Geo. H. Coffey and Rev. Edward A. Collier of Kinderhook, New York.

June 17, 1864

2481. Jun 4, Town of Saugerties, Hezekiah Carle of Plattekill to Almira, daughter of David Carle of Pine Bush, Town of Kingston, by Rev. Dr. Gosman.

2482. Jun 2, Peter Van Hoesen of Coxsackie to Anna C., daughter of Jerry Hummel of Quarryville, by Rev. W. D. Buckelew of Blue Mountain.

2483. May 28, Blue Mountain, Watson Brant of Catskill to Nelly C. Hummel of the Town of Saugerties, by Rev. W. D. Buckelew.

June 24, 1864

2484. Jun 16, Coxsackie, Cyrus Burhans of Saugerties to Jane S., 3rd daughter of James Wilson, Esq. of Coxsackie, by Rev. Charles Sylvester.

July 1, 1864

2485. Jun 23, Mr. George Elmendorf to Miss Isadore Eckert, both of Saugerties, by Rev. John Gaston.

2486. Jun 28, West Camp, at the residence of the bride's father, Mr. Geo. M. Snyder to Miss Anna E. Gould, by Rev. D. F. Heller.

July 8, 1864

2487. Jun 22, Newburgh, William Augustus Gay of Saugerties to Miss Sarah Mc Gahey of Newburgh, by Rev. Dr. Brown.

2488. Jun 30, Jeremiah Pares of Malden to Christina Dederick of West Camp, by Rev. Thomas Lape.

2489. Jun 29, Yonkers, Mr. Milton S. Bradt of Oswego, New York to Miss Caroline E., daughter of Solomon W. Oakley, Esq. of Yonkers and sister of the clergyman, by Rev. J. G. Oakley of Eddyville.

July 29, 1864

2490. Jul 16, Mr. Charles H. Longyear to Mrs. Catherine Duncombe, both of Rosendale, by Rev. J. G. Oakley of Eddyville.

2491. Jul 14, Kingston, John W. Schoonmaker to Kate E. Styles, both of Kingston, by Rev. T. W. Chadwick.

September 22, 1864

2492. Sep 5, at the residence of the bride's father, Mr. Matthew Dederick to Miss Gertrude F. Magee, both of West Camp, by Rev. D. F. Heller.

September 30, 1864

2493. Sep 5, at the residence of the bride's father, Mr. Benjamin M. Coon, attorney, to Miss Mary L., youngest daughter of Col. Samuel M. Post, all of Saugerties, by Rev. George H. Coffey.

2494. Undated, at the home of the bride's father, Mr. Cyrus Osterhoudt to Miss Mary Jane Arnott, both of the Town of Saugerties, by Rev. E. Denniston.

2495. Sep 24, Saugerties, Mr. Michael Frain to Miss Euphemia Whittaker, both of Glasco, by Rev. D. W. Sherwood.

2496. Sep 24, at the home of the bride's father, William Humphrey to Susan M., eldest daughter of Wm. W. Hawley, all of Saugerties, by Rev. James M. Burger.

October 7, 1864

2497. Oct 4, Saugerties, Jefferson L. Reed to Mary A. Austin, both of Saugerties, by Rev. W. Ostrander.

October 28, 1864

2498. Oct 22, Blue Mountain, James E. Becker of High Falls to Miss Sally C. Rightmyer of the Town of Saugerties, by Rev. W. D. Buckelew.

2499. Oct 20, Saugerties, at the Congregational Church, Mr. Smith C. Rogers of Poughkeepsie to Miss Eliza E. Rogers of the Town of Saugerties, by Rev. Geo. H. Coffey.

November 4, 1864

2500. Oct 27, Mr. Benjamin Myer of Saugerties to Kate E. Cosmen of Marlboro, by Rev. J. I. Grimly.

November 18, 1864

2501. Nov 10, Candensis, Monroe Co., Pa., Mr. Edward F. Palen to Miss Elizabeth, daughter of Geo. Northrop, both of Canadensis, by Rev. Edward Townsend.

2502. Nov 15, New York City, at Trinity Chapel, Col. Jacob Sharpe to Miss Julia, daughter of Gen. P. St. Geo. Cooke, U. S. A., by Rev. Geo. Waters, Rector of St. John's Church, Kingston.

December 2, 1864

2503. Nov 16, Peter L. Parris of Malden to Sarah A. Feleans of New York City, by Rev. Thomas Lape.

December 9, 1864

2504. Dec 7, Saugerties, at the Methodist Episcopal Church, Richard Rowland, Esq. of New York City to Miss Delia Coons of Saugerties, by Rev. W. Ostrander.

December 16, 1864

2505. Dec 6, Town of Saugerties, Wm. F. Brink to Sarah A. Van Aken, both of Kingston, by Rev. Dr. Gosman.

2506. Dec 6, Town of Saugerties, John W. Van Gaasbeck to Helen C. Van Aken, both of Kingston, by Rev. Dr. Gosman.

December 23, 1864
2507. Dec 11, Westkill, Mr. Newton Whitcomb of Jewett to Miss Susie, youngest daughter of Adam Montross, Esq. of Westkill, Greene Co., by Rev. Wm. N. Allaben.

January 6, 1865
2508. Jan 5, Saugerties, at the home of the bride's father, Thomas C. Brainard, U. S. A. of Philadelphia to Miss Mari L., daughter of Joseph M. Boice, Esq., of Saugerties.

January 27, 1865
2509. Jan 21, at the residence of the bride's father, Sandford Van Leuven of Catskill to Hester Goodsell of West Camp, by Rev. Thomas Lape.

February 3, 1865
2510. Jan 26, Glasco, James W. Seaman of Glen Erie to Letitia Young of Glasco, by Rev. Dr. Gosman.

February 17, 1865
2511. Feb 11, Jesse Taylor to Eliza Post, both of Quarryville, by Rev. Thomas Lape.

2512. Feb 11, Isaac Zeilman to Julia Rock, both of Malden, by Rev. Thomas Lape.

February 24, 1865
2513. Feb 18, Washingtonville, Orange Co., Mr. Calvin Delanoy of Glasco to Miss Margaret A. Whitlock of Washingtonville, by Rev. Uriah Messister.

March 3, 1865
2514. Feb 25, Saugerties, at the residence of the bride's mother, Mr. Charles Jones to Miss Mary Amelia Youngs, by Rev. D. W. Sherwood.

2515. Feb 25, at the residence of the groom's mother, Mr. James Youngs to Miss Rachel C. Decker, both of Saugerties, by Rev. D. W. Sherwood.

2516. Feb 7, Nicholas Mauer of Kingston to Emma Brown of Saugerties, by Thomas C. Maines, Esq.

April 21, 1865

2517. Apr 18, at the home of the bride's father, George Magee to Mary Ann Dederick, both of West Camp, by Rev. Thomas Lape.

May 12, 1865

2518. May 6, Saugerties, Mr. David V. Gardner to Miss Rachael L. Haber, both of Saugerties, by Rev. D. W. Sherwood.

May 19, 1865

2519. May 9, Kingston, Mr. Philip H., son of Wm. H. Foland of Saugerties to Miss Hattie Winten of Kingston, by Rev. J. Van Keuren.

2520. Apr 26, Kingston, Gilbert Smith to Elizabeth Hogan of Kingston, by Rev. J. L. G. Mc Kown.

2521. Undated, Kingston, William Ostrander of Rondout to Miss Mary Traphagen of Kingston, by Rev. J. L. G. Mc Kown.

2522. May 3, Kingston, L. B. Van Wagenen to Kate Johnston, both of Kingston, by Rev. J. L. G. Mc Kown.

June 2, 1865

2523. May 23, at the home of the bride's father, Erastus D. Chipman, MD, of Saugerties, to Miss Aurinda, daughter of John Carn, Esq. of the Town of Saugerties, by Rev. William D. Buckalew.

June 16, 1865

2524. May 20, Saugerties, Wm. F. Kerr of Kingston to Miss Anna Wheeler of Rondout, by Rev. W. Ostrander.

2525. Jun 6, Troy, at the Church of the Holy Cross, Wm. M. Merchant of Saugerties to Miss Mary Green of Troy, by Rev. Dr. Tucker.

June 23, 1865

2526. Jun 22, North Kingston, James S. Gardner, 76, to Phebe A. Rose, a fine old lady of 13 Summers.

June 30, 1865

2527. Jun 15, Wm. H. Chalmers of Gloversville, Fulton Co. to Miss M. Augusta Reynolds of Woodstock, by Rev. D. W. C. Van Gaasbeck.

2528. Jun 15, Mr. John S. Ackert of Rhinebeck to Miss Samantha E. Thompson of Kingston, by Rev. Z. Grenell, Jr.

2529. Jun 17, Henry Dewitt to Priscilla Nobles, both of Olive, by Rev. Z. Grenell, Jr.

2530. Jun 8, Kingston, at the 1st Reformed Dutch Church, Nelson Longyear to Mary M. Decker, both of Kingston, by Rev. J. C.F. Hoes.

July 7, 1865

2531. Jun 20, Francis Wynkoop Reynolds to Mary Wynkoop Hoffman, daughter of the late Abraham Hoffman, all of Kingston, by Rev. Dr. Hoes.

2532. Jun 22, Charles L. Van Deusen to Mary E. Hencher, both of Kingston, by Rev. H. B. Rigway.

2533. Jun 15, Ferdinand Griggs of Modena to Mary Ella Lockwood of Kingston, by Rev. Jno. W. Beach.

2534. Jun 26, Adijer Dewey to Henrietta Davis, both of Kingston, by Rev. Jno. W. Beach.

August 4, 1865

2535. Jul 27, Jonas M. Smith of Saugerties to Miss Emily Burhans of Flatbush, by Rev. William Ostrander.

2536. Jul 27, Rodney Osterhoudt of Kingston to Miss Katie Davis of Flatbush, by Rev. William Ostrander.

2537. Jul 27, Alford Eldridge to Eliza M. Cantine, both of Saugerties, colored, by Rev. William Ostrander.

September 1, 1865

2538. Aug 28, at the residence of Mr. Robert Snyder, John H. Hardenberg to Miss Annie Westwood, both of Saugerties, by Rev. D. W. Sherwood.

2539. Aug 9, East Marion, LI, George C. Udell of Smithtown to Miss Libbie, youngest daughter of Deacon S. H. Tuthill of East Marion, by Rev. D. W. Sherwood.

September 15, 1865

2540. Sep 13, Saugerties, at the Reformed Dutch Church, Mr. Thomas B. Keeney to Miss Gertrude Wigram, both of this place, by Rev. John Gaston.

September 22, 1865

2541. Sep 6, Henry Felter of Kingston to Miss Mary E. Myer of Saugerties, by Rev. S. T. Cole.

2542. Sep 6, Isaac J. Van Aken to Miss Joanna M. Longendyke, both of Saugerties, by Rev. S. T. Cole.

2543. Sep 9, Henry France to Miss Eliza C. Wolven, both of Saugerties, by Rev. S. T. Cole.

2544. Sep 13, at the home of Chancey Green, Esq., Mr. Albert P. Greene to Mrs. Sarah York, both of the Town of Saugerties, by Rev. George W. Fisher.

2545. Sep 14, at the residence of the bride's mother, Mr. Robert Finger of New York City to Miss Ellen M. Russell of Saugerties, by Rev. George W. Fisher.

2546. Aug 14, Lewis N. Hermance to Harriet M. Jennings, both of Kingston, by Rev. Dr. Lillie.

2547. Sep 6, Eugene A. Jaques of Hudson City, New Jersey to Elizabeth Whitaker of Kingston, by Rev. Dr. Lillie.

2548. Sep 5, Joshua F. Snyder of Saugerties to Miss Sarah J. Dubois of Kingston, by Rev. S. T. Cole.

September 29, 1865

2549. Sep 12, New York City, at the Lexington Avenue Church, Mr. L. B. Adams of Saugerties to Miss Emily Huestid of New York City, by Rev. Joseph Sanderson.

2550. Aug 23, West Camp, Mr. Phineas Finger to Miss Christina H. Dederick, both of West Camp, by Rev. J. D. Wert.

2551. Aug 16, West Camp, Mr. William S. Vedder to Miss Mary Scutt, both of Saugerties, by Rev. J. D. Wert.

2552. Sep 17, Peter A. Hommel to Cornelia A. Teetsell, both of Quarryville, by Rev. A. Gaylord.

October 13, 1865

2553. Oct 3, Eureka, Ill., Mr. Stephen A. Hoyt, formerly of Saugerties to Miss Rutclias Gillum, all of Eureka, by Rev. J. M. Allen.

October 20, 1865

2554. Oct 14, Saugerties, John F. Coon of New York City to Mary E. Brady of Saugerties, by Rev. W. Ostrander.

October 27, 1865

2555. Undated, at the Methodist Episcopal Church, S. Marshall Knapp to Katie M. York, both of Saugerties, by Rev. William Ostrander. <October 22, 1865, records of the Saugerties United Methodist Church, ed.>

2556. Oct 14, West Camp, Mr. James A. Freeze to Miss Annice C. Rusher, both of Saugerties, by Rev. J. D. Wert.

2557. Oct 18, West Camp, J. Westley Teetsel to Miss Margaret Mower, both of Saugerties, by Rev. J. D. Wert.

2558. Oct 18, West Camp, Mr. John E. Johnston to Miss Marietta Brink, both of Saugerties, by Rev. J. D. Wert.

2559. Oct 14, West Camp, Mr. Wm. S. Valk to Miss Malissa Wolven, both of Saugerties, by Rev. J. D. Wert.

November 3, 1865

2560. Oct 25, Schuyler P. Owen, Esq. to Mrs. Rosetta W. Valentine, both of Goshen, Orange Co., by Rev. William Ostrander.

November 17, 1865

2561. Nov 8, Cattsban, George W. Reeder of Williamsburgh, LI to Maria E. Martin of Cattsban, by Rev. N. F. Chapman.

2562. Nov 9, Quarryville, Christian F. Carnwright of Catskill to Alida Miller of Quarryville, by Rev. N. F. Chapman.

November 24, 1865

2563. Nov 9, at the home of the bride's father in Phoenicia, Mr. Hiram M. Boice to Miss Emily S. Turner, both of Shandaken, by Rev. H. C. Longyear.

December 1, 1865

2564. Nov 23, Saugerties, Mr. Wm. F. Iler of Troy to Miss Sarah A. Williams of Saugerties, by Rev. D. W. Sherwood.

2565. Nov 23, Saugerties, Wm. H. Lewis of Woodstock to Cordelia White of Saugerties, by S. Merclean, Esq.

2566. Nov 29, William H. Lewis of West Camp to Julia Barringer of Germantown, Greene Co., by Rev. Thos. Lape.

December 8, 1865

2567. Nov 28, Oakhill, Greene Co., Mr. Franklin Fuller of Saugerties to Miss Arrie A. Pierce of Preston Hollow, Albany Co., by Rev. J. F. Richmond.

2568. Nov 15, Rondout Mr. John Weber, Jr. to Miss Theresa, daughter of Frederick Stephan, Esq., by Rev. M. Krug.

2569. Nov 29, at the home of the bride's father, Mr. Samuel D. Coykendall to Miss Mary Augusta, eldest daughter of Thomas Cornell, Esq., by Rev. G. W. Folwell.

December 15, 1865

2570. Dec 7, at the Flatbush parsonage, Edward Lynk of Saugerties to Sarah M. Lewis of High Falls, by Rev. Wm. B. Merritt.

December 29, 1865

2571. Dec 7, Hunter, James E. Miller of Hunter to Miss Catharine A. Quick of Saugerties, by Rev. W. S. Winans.

January 5, 1866

2572. Dec 26, Saugerties, Benjamin Hains of Hunter, Greene Co. to Lydia Ann Garrison of the Town of Saugerties, by Rev. W. Ostrander.

2573. Dec 31, Saugerties, Stephen Becker to Mary Jane Hoffman, both of Saugerties, by Rev. W. Ostrander.

2574. Undated, at the home of the bride's father, Edwin A. Shaw to Martha A. Hommel, both of Saugerties. <December 31, 1865, records of the Saugerties United Methodist Church, ed.>

2575. Dec 20, Kingston, John H. Hotaling of Hurley to Kate M. Davis of Kingston, by Rev. Dr. Lillie.

2576. Dec 26, Kingston, at the Reformed Dutch Church, Henry L. Abbey of Rondout to Mary L., daughter of Elijah Dubois, Esq. of Kingston, by Rev. Cha's H. Stitt.

January 12, 1866

2577. Dec 27, Kingston, at the Baptist Church, Mr. Richard Lattin of Marbletown to Miss Lottie Barber, daughter of Lyman Barber of Whiteport, by Rev. G. W. Folwell and Rev. J. N. Smith.

2578. Nov 8, West Camp, Mr. Charles Snyder to Miss Madora Scheffer, both of West Camp, by Rev. J. D. Wert.

2579. Jan 3, West Camp, Mr. Jonas Mower to Miss Maria Merrit, both of West Camp, by Rev. J. D. Wert.

2580. Jan 1, Quarryville, at the home of the bride's father, Mr. Joseph Teetsel to Miss Lottie Post, both of Quarryville, by Rev. Mr. Gaylar.

January 19, 1866

2581. Dec 27, Alligerville, Jacob Westbrook, Jr., Esq. of Kingston to Johanna Kerr Davis of Alligerville, by Rev. David Heroy.

2582. Jan 11, Saugerties, Joseph D. C. Hill of High Falls to Miss Ellen Mc Guill of Saugerties, by Rev. John Gaston.

2583. Jan 13, Saugerties, Nelson J. Freer to Miss E. A. Bedford, both of Rifton Glen, NY, by Rev. John Gaston.

January 26, 1866

2584. Jan 10, Kingston, at the 1st Reformed Dutch Church, Rev. O. H. Seymour of Hammondsport, NY, to Harriet S., daughter of Rev. Jno. C. F. Hoes, D. D., the officiating clergyman.

February 2, 1866

2585. Jan 25, at the residence of David Burgher, J. Davis Burgher of Woodstock to Mary E. Keator of Kingston.

February 9, 1866

2586. Feb 7, West Hurley, Benjamin Hasbrouck to Sophia Devall, both of Woodstock, by Rev. Mr. Couchman.

2587. Feb 7, West Hurley, William E. Hoyt to Marietta Hasbrouck, both of Woodstock, by Rev. Mr. Couchman.

February 16, 1866

2588. Jan 31, Kingston, Mr. Newby Barritt to Miss Sarah C. Finger, both of Saugerties, by Rev. Mr. Beach.

2589. Feb 1, New York, Erastus Y. Clark to Miss Harietta A. I. Fullmer, both of New York, by Rev. J. R. Kendrick, D. D.

2590. Feb 7, Brooklyn, Thomas T. De Witt to Louise, eldest daughter of Henry Ginnel, both of Brooklyn, by Rev. N. E. Smith.

2591. Feb 1, Brooklyn, at the home of the bride's parents, Jansen H. Anderson of Esopus to Maria N., eldest daughter of Charles L. Cornish, Esq. of Brooklyn, by Rev. William H. Bunyon and Rev. William Anderson.

2592. Jan 15, Abraham D. Whitaker to Nelly Ann Hommel, both of Quarryville, by Rev. Thomas Lape.

February 23, 1866
2593. Feb 7, Wiltwyck, Wm. J. Lennon to Miss Louisa Teetsel, both of Saugerties, by Rev. Mr. Chadwick.

March 16, 1866
2594. Feb 28, at the home of Abraham J. Longyear, Marquis D. L. Davis of Grass Lake, Mich. to Miss Delilah Short of Shandaken, by Rev. H. C. Longyear.

March 23, 1866
2595. Mar 3, Saugerties, Edward Teal of West Hurley to Mary M. Teal of Kingston, by Rev. John Gaston.

March 30, 1866
2596. Mar 28, Kingston, Mr. Abram Turck to Miss Mary E. Martin, both of Saugerties, by Rev. Jno. W. Beach.

April 6, 1866
2597. Mar 29, Saugerties, Mr. William H. Eckert to Miss Sarah E. Blackwell, both of Saugerties, by Rev. John Gaston.

2598. Apr 4, at the home of the bride's father, S. M. Hewlett, Esq. of Philadelphia to Miss Anna M., eldest daughter of Rufus Peckham, Esq. of Oneida Castle, New York, by Rev. J. Cochran.

May 4, 1866
2599. Apr 24, Gilboa, John A. G. Barker of Brooklyn to Miss Susie Reed of Gilboa, by Rev. Mr. Letson.

May 11, 1866

2600. May 3, Saugerties, at the residence of Mr. J. L. Butzel, Mr. Moses Krohn to Miss Theresa Bamberger, both of Saugerties, by Rev. E. Wolf, of Rondout.

2601. May 9, Saugerties, Mr. George Barton of Rondout to Miss Helen A. Garland of Kingston, by Rev. Mr. Sherwood.

May 18, 1866

2602. Apr 30, Shandaken Centre, Mr. James J. Norris of Middletown, Delaware Co. to Miss Susan M. Van Wagenen of Phoenicia, by Rev. J. Elliott.

2603. May 8, Kingston, Cornelius D. Roosa to Minnie F., daughter of John H. Howland, all of Kingston, by Rev. T. W. Chadwick.

May 25, 1866

2604. May 17, Town of Saugerties, Daniel Labach to Mary S. Carn, by Rev. W. D. Buckalew.

June 1, 1866

2605. May 26, Saugerties, at the home of Capt. H. L. Finger, Egbert Vosburgh, Esq. of Hartsville, Texas, formerly of Saugerties to Mrs. Mary Jane Martin of Saugerties, by Rev. W. Ostrander.

June 8, 1866

2606. Jun 6, Glasco, at the home of the bride's father, Robert L. De Lavergne of Saugerties to Kate A., only daughter of Wellington Mc Clure, Esq. of Glasco, by Rev. William B. Merrit.

June 15, 1866

2607. Jun 7, D. Alexander Valk of Malden to Alice Wolven of Saugerties, by Rev. W. Ostrander.

2608. Jun 7, Catskill, E. Mc C. Russell to Ellen H. Lusk, only daughter of Mrs. Henry Turck, both of Saugerties, by Rev. W. Chadwell.

2609. Jun 14, Saugerties, at the home of the bride's father, Frederick T. Russell to Julia, youngest daughter of John G. Mynderse, by Rev. John Gaston.

2610. May 30, Kingston, Matthew Prestley of New York to Amanda Carney of Eddyville, by Rev. T. W. Chadwick.

2611. May 2, at the home of the bride's father, Chauncey Keator of Kingston, to Josephine Winnie, daughter of Davis Winne of Shandaken, by Rev. John H. Lane.

2612. May 16, Shokan, John H. Taylor of Woodstock to Mary Everett of Hurley, by Rev. John H. Lane.

2613. May 30, Rochester, Andrew M. Green to Emma I. Sheldon, by Rev. Selah W. Strong.

June 22, 1866

2614. Jun 19, Saugerties, Jacob L. Williams to Emily B. Jones, both of Saugerties, by Rev. D. W. Sherwood.

2615. Jun 12, Glenerie, Henry A. Weideman to Caroline J. Minkler, both of the Town of Saugerties, by Rev. W. M. Merritt.

2616. Jun 6, Kingston, Henry L. Hermance to Helen L. Winchester, both of Kingston, by Rev. C. Case of West Dresden, Yates Co.

2617. Jun 10, Kingston, Sebree S. Burk to Caroline Grice, both of Rondout, by Rev. C. Case of West Dresden, Yates Co.

2618. May 31, New Hartford, Oneida Co., NY, S. M. Gallup to E. E. Sherrill, by Rev. Mr. Furbish.

2619. Jun 7, at the home of Richard Dewitt, Esq., Isaac Burhans of Rondout to Catharine Anna Dewitt of Ulster Co., NY, by Rev. H. Blauvelt.

2620. Jun 7, at the home of the bride's father, George B. Styles of Kingston to Mary E. Barbour of New York City, by Rev. John Dowling.

2621. Jun 16, Kingston, John Hamilton to Mary E. Post, both of Esopus, by Rev. John C. F. Hoes, D. D.

2622. Jun 14, at the home of the bride, Joseph Kerr to Mary Anna Sutton, widow of John J. Keator, both of Creek Locks, by Rev. A. Blauvelt.

July 6, 1866

2623. Jun 14, Jasen Van Hovenberg of Saugerties to Cordelia Burhans of Kingston, by Rev. S. T. Cole.

2624. Jun 23, James Low to Cornelia Felter, both of Kingston, by Rev. S. T. Cole.

2625. Jun 28, Alfred Anderson of New York to Catharine Dederick of Kingston, by Rev. S. T. Cole.

2626. Jun 30, Kingston, Arthur Scott to Rachael Jackson, both of Kingston, by Rev. T. W. Chadwick.

July 13, 1866

2627. Jul 3, at the Flatbush parsonage, Benj. H. Whitaker to Martha Hommel, both of Glasco, by Rev. Wm. H. Merritt.

2628. Jul 4, at the Flatbush parsonage, John Simmons to Martha Lynk, both of Glasco, by Rev. Wm. B. Merritt.

2629. Jun 26, at the home of the bride's father, Frank J. Hillebrand of Poughkeepsie to Carrie, youngest daughter of Mr. John Turner of Phoenicia, by Rev. H. C. Longyear.

2630. Undated, Kingston, at the home of James Hargraves, Esq., Charles W. Phillips to Lucia M. Bearss, all of Kingston, by Rev. T. W. Chadwick.

2631. Jul 3, Kingston, at St. John's Church, Frank Goetshuis of Rondout to Ella Frances Pruder of Kingston, by Rev. George Waters, D. D.

2632. Jul 3, Kingston, at St. John's Church, J. Rudolph Tappen to Ellen Starr Butters, 2nd daughter of the late Archibald and Mary C. Butters, of New York City, by Rev. William E. Armitage, D. D.

July 20, 1866

2633. The wife of Mr. E. Teats and a young man named Jacob Coon, of Upper Red Hook, eloped on Thursday morning of last week and have not been heard from since.

July 27, 1866

2634. Jul 3, New York City, Willis B. Whitaker to Marrietta, youngest daughter of John V. Demarest, Esq., all of New York City, by Rev. John Quincy Adams.

August 10, 1866

2635. Aug 6, Ethan Wolven to Irene Miller, both of the Town of Saugerties, by Rev. Thomas Lape.

August 31, 1866

2636. Aug 6, Chestnut Hill, Philadelphia, at the home of the bride's brother, Mr. G. A. Hart of Kingston to Miss Belle Mc Bride of Chestnut Hill, by Rev. R. Owen.

September 14, 1866

2637. Aug 22, Poughkeepsie, Mr. George Hanna to Miss Mary I., only daughter of George Mitchel, Esq., formerly of Saugerties, by Rev. J. L. Corning.

2638. Sep 3, Stone Ridge, John J. Woolsey of Kingston to Ruth A. Young of Stone Ridge, by Rev. Mr. Hall.

2639. Sep 2, Town of Rosendale, George B. Halwick to Miss Kate Butler, both of Rosendale, by Rev. J. N. Smith.

2640. Aug 22, Catskill, Mr. Jennings J. Covey to Miss Deborah Mealius, both of Catskill, by Rev. S. I. Ferguson.

2641. Aug 22, Cairo, Mr. William Flowers of Hurley to Miss Olive L. Lee of Cairo, by Rev. I. R. Vandewater.

September 21, 1866

2642. Sep 13, at the home of the bride's father, Robert Loughran, MD, formerly of Saugerties, to Mary E., daughter of E. W. Budington, Esq., both of Kingston, by Rev. Mr. Grinell.

2643. Sep 4, Leeds, Cyrenus Plank to Emeline Chandler, by Rev. S. T. Searle.

2644. Sep 5, Catskill, Charles L. Halcott of Catskill to Kittie E. Lente of Newton, Long Island, by Rev. W. S. Chadwell.

September 28, 1866

2645. Sep 24, Saugerties, Mr. Charles Turner to Miss Jennie Smith, both of Saugerties, by Rev. John Gaston.

2646. Sep 25, Saugerties, Mr. Allen Coon of Clermont, Columbia Co. to Miss Cornelia Finger of Woodstock, by Rev. John Gaston.

2647. Sep 18, Kingston, Clark B. Galton of Walden, Orange Co. to Miss Caroline Carnwright of Kingston, by Rev. Mr. Stitt.

October 5, 1866

2648. Oct 4, Saugerties, James Fowler of Rondout to Eliza Ann Decker of Saugerties, by Rev. W. Ostrander.

2649. Sep 16, Rhinebeck, John Hatten of Red Hook to Parthenia J., daughter of Mr. Wm. H. Champlin of Saugerties, by Rev. W. G. Browning.

October 12, 1866

2650. Sep 16, West Camp, Mr. John P. Baird to Miss Elsie D. Overbagh, both of Catskill, by Rev. J. D. Wert.

2651. Sep 19, at the home of the bride's father, Mr. Rowland Porter of Athens to Miss Catharine Mower of West Camp, by Rev. J. D. Wert.

2652. Oct 7, at the home of Mr. Gardener, near High Falls, Mr. George W. Pelt of Palenville to Miss Margaret C. Moon of Kiskatom, by Rev. J. D. Wert.

October 19, 1866

2653. Oct 15, Coxsackie, at the home of the bride's father, Mr. S. G. Boyd of Glens Falls, New York to Miss Kate M. Ten Eyck of Coxsackie, by Rev. J. M. Gaston.

2654. Oct 10, New York City, Edgar B. Newkirk of Rondout to Emily Tanner of New York.

2655. Oct 10, The Corner, Wm. A. Connelly of Kingston to Gertrude De La Montanye of Shandaken, by Rev. H. C. Longyear.

2656. Oct 8, Kingston, Solomon D. Niece to Josephine Kimball, both of Flatbush, by Rev. T. W. Chadwick.

2657. Oct 3, South Flatbush, Tjerck Wynkoop to Elizabeth Marquot, by Rev. B. Merritt.

2658. Oct 4, Kingston, John G. Cummings of New York to Anna R. Babcock of Kingston, by Rev. T. W. Chadwick.

2659. Oct 3, Mr. Winslow Votee to Miss Frances S. Randall, both of Shandaken, by Rev. H. C. Longyear.

2660. Oct 4, Livingston, Henry Smith of Livingston to Sarah, eldest daughter of H. S. Van Etten of Kingston, by Rev. Chas. I. Shepard.

October 26, 1866

2661. Oct 17, Rondout, at the First Baptist Church, Augustus Hasbrouck of New York City to Miss Lucy H. Winter of Rondout.

2662. Oct 17, Kingston, H. Barnard Schoonmaker to Helen M. Kiersted, daughter of C. L. Kiersted, by Rev. J. C. F. Hoes.

November 2, 1866

2663. Oct 25, Decatur, Otsego Co., Mr. Benjamin Hoff of Saugerties to Miss Anna Elizabeth Sharp of Decatur, by Rev. Mr. Wood.

2664. Oct 24, Blue Mountain, Mr. George Teal of Palenville to Miss Adaline Chiritree of High Falls, by Rev. W. D. Buckalew.

November 9, 1866

2665. Nov 5, Saugerties, Mr. John Coons of Glasco to Miss Mary Ann Delhanty of Saugerties, by Rev. D. W. Sherwood.

2666. Nov 1, at the home of the bride's father, William H. Hommel, Jr. of Catsbaan to Ann Elizabeth, daughter of Peter Hommel of Quarryville, by Rev. N. F. Chapman.

November 16, 1866

2667. Nov 13, Flatbush, Russel Myers of Saugerties to Mary E. Lown of Kingston, by Rev. Wm. Merritt.

November 23, 1866

2668. Nov 18, Saugerties, at the Exchange Hotel, Mr. Jonas Ham to Mrs. Mary E. Anthony, by Rev. D. W. Sherwood.

2669. Oct 31, Kingston, Mr. Wm. Swart to Miss Alida A. Lobdell, both of Kingston, by Rev. Mr. Beach.

2670. Nov 15, Rondout, Mr. Peter W. Myer of Kingston to Miss Minerva Perkins of Kingston, by Rev. S. T. Cole.

2671. Nov 14, Woodstock, at the Reformed Dutch Church, Rev. Cornelius Blauvelt, pastor of the Reformed Dutch Church of Closter, New Jersey to Maria E., daughter of Cornelius Risely of Woodstock, by Rev. D. B. Wycoff.

2672. Nov 15, Kingston, John A. Shultis to Sarah A. Van Keuren, both of Kingston, by Rev. Dr. Lille.

November 30, 1866
2673. Nov 13, Saugerties, Ethelbert L. Billings of Ellenville to Emma F. Hughes of Syracuse, by Rev. George Fisher.

December 7, 1866
2674. Nov 7, Hudson, Jeremiah Hommel of Malden to Miss Augusta A. Edgerly of Cairo, Greene Co., by Rev. Wm. Leavitt.

December 21, 1866
2675. Dec 19, Saugerties, at the residence of the brother of the bride, Peter Cantine, Mr. Chauncey P. Shultis to Miss Hattie E. Cantine, all of Saugerties, by Rev. J. Gaston.

December 28, 1866
2676. Dec 25, Saugerties, at the residence of Mr. Wm. M. Brink, Bruce A. Chilton to Mary Adaline Mc Chesney, both of Brooklyn, by Rev. Jno. Gaston.

2677. Dec 19, Glasco, Mr. Washington Porter to Miss Catharine Fraley, both of Bethel, by Rev. A. F. Palmer.

January 4, 1867
2678. Dec 27, Windham, Wm. H. Romeyn, Jr. of Kingston to Miss Lizzie Winfield of Windham, by Rev. Charles Kendell.

January 11, 1867
2679. Jan 1, at the residence of Wm. W. France, Malon Hanford to Miss Eliza J. France, both of Walton, Delaware Co., by Rev. S. T. Cole.

January 18, 1867
2680. Jan 10, Kingston, Mr. Chester Blackwell to Miss Sarah L. Lewis, both of Saugerties, by Rev. Mr. Beach.

January 25, 1867
2681. Jan 23, at the home of the bride, Mr. Charles Lusk to Miss Elizabeth A. Pollock, both of Saugerties, by Rev. W. Ostrander.

2682. Jan 20, Hiram R. Tappen of New York to Kate Doll of Kingston, by Rev. Dr. Lillie.

February 1, 1867

2683. Jan 20, Holyoke, Mass., at the residence of the bride's father, Mr. Wm. Bloomer Pollock of Saugerties to Miss Luie M., daughter of Henry L. Craw, formerly of Freeport, Maine, by Rev. L. R. Eastman.

2684. Jan 15, Red Hook, at the Methodist Episcopal Church, Mr. Le Grand Curtis to Miss Helen Andrews, both of Red Hook, by Rev. J. Selleck.

February 8, 1867

2685. Undated, at the residence of the bride's father, Mr. Charles A. Dunakin to Miss Elnora, daughter of John S. Winans, formerly of Saugerties, both of Avon, NY.

2686. Jan 22, Woodstock, at the Methodist Episcopal parsonage, John J. Halowick to Mary A. Brink, both of West Hurley, by Rev. J. Whitaker.

2687. Jan 24, Wiltwyck, Miss Jane M., daughter of Charles Taylor to Mr. John L. Jagger, both of Kingston, by Rev. Wm. A. Shaw.

February 22, 1867

2688. Feb 6, Catskill, at the residence of H. D. Johnson, Mr. Watson Crawford of Smith's Landing to Rachel S. Wicks of Catskill, by Rev. S. I. Ferguson.

2689. Feb 21, Kiskatom, John W. Clum to Martha J. Myers, both of Kingston, by Rev. W. T. Stilwell.

March 1, 1867

2690. Feb 13, Hudson, M. D. Perrine of Kingston to Mrs. Sara A. Oakley, oldest daughter of James Best, Esq.

2691. Feb 14, Rhinebeck, Christian Frey, formerly of Saugerties, to Mrs. Barbary Zigler, by Rev. Zeuben Hill.

March 15, 1867

2692. Mar 3, Flatbush, at the residence of D. P. Simpkins, Orange Ingraham of Denning to Mary J. Haines of Saugerties, by Rev. Wm. B. Merritt.

2693. Feb 27, Woodstock, Andrew Elting to Mary E. Hauver, of Lexington, Greene Co., by Rev. J. Whitaker.

March 22, 1867

2694. Mar 2, Blue Mountain, Rufus T. Smith to Margaret Minkler, by Rev. W. D. Buckelew.

2695. Mar 14, at the home of S. W. Ransom, N. Warren Myer of Palmyra, NY to Amelia Swart of the Town of Saugerties, by Rev. W. D. Buckelew.

March 29, 1867

2696. Mar 17, Woodstock, Everitt Wagenen to Lizzie Selzea, by Rev. J. Whitaker.

2697. Mar 19, Kingston, John C. Wolven of Saugerties to Mrs. Elizabeth Burger of Kingston, by Rev. D. B. Wyckoff.

2698. Mar 20, Woodstock, James Reed to Harriet, daughter of John C. Wolven, both of Saugerties, by Rev. D. B. Wyckoff.

2699. Mar 20, at the residence of the bride's father, Wm. H. Birkins of Saugerties, to Jane Ann, eldest daughter of Benjamin Whitaker, of the Town of Kingston, by Rev. Wm. B. Merritt.

April 5, 1867

2700. Mar 27, Catskill, Mr. George W. Dubois to Miss Amanda Staples, both of Rondout, by Rev. M. W. Staples.

April 12, 1867

2701. Apr 9, Flatbush, William P. Myer of Glasco to Jane C. Elwyn of Woodstock, by Rev. Wm. B. Merritt.

April 19, 1867

2702. Apr 13, Brazill R. Martin to Rachael A. Gay, both of the Town of Saugerties, by Rev. Thomas Lape.

2703. Apr 10, New Brunswick, New Jersey, D. M. De Witt of Rondout to Mary Antoinette Mc Donald of New Brunswick, by Rev. Wm. Beattie.

May 10, 1867

2704. Apr 28, Quarryville, at the home of Mr. Peter Teetsel, John King of Fallsburg, Sullivan Co. to Mrs. Eliza Ann Van Hoovenberg of Saugerties, by Rev. W. D. Buckelew.

2705. May 1, Riley Baldwin of Lexington to Elizabeth A. Longyear of Shandaken, by Rev. H. C. Longyear.

2706. May 4, Peter A. Richmeyer to Sarah C. Hommel, both of the Town of Saugerties, by Rev. Thomas Lape.

May 17, 1867

2707. May 9, Edwin Acker to Mary E. Hunt, both of the Town of Saugerties, by Rev. A. F. Palmer of Glasco.

May 31, 1867

2708. May 23, New York City, S. Herman Butzel, son of John L. Butzel of Saugerties to Henrietta Gans of New York City, by Rev. Mr. Seligsohn.

June 7, 1867

2709. Jun 3, Saugerties, at the home of the bride's parents, Eugene Barritt to Ella M. Russell, by Rev. B. F. Snyder.

June 14, 1867

2710. May 5, New York City, James A. Morrison of New York City to Miss Augusta Fullmer of Saugerties.

June 28, 1867

2711. Jun 20, Glasco, at the Methodist Episcopal Church, Norman F. Pierce to Margaret Lewis, both of Saugerties, by Rev. A. F. Palmer.

2712. Jun 25, Kingston, Mr. Edward Jernegan to Miss Kate E. Post, both of Saugerties, by Rev. Mr. Beach.

2713. Jun 13, Mr. Sanford Conyes to Miss Rachel J. Weeks, both of Saugerties, by Rev. S. T. Cole.

2714. May 29, San Francisco, Calif., at Grace Cathedral, Mr. Benjamin H. Brooks to Miss Mary Ella, daughter of the late Hon. John B. Steele, by Rt. Rev. William Ingham Kipp, Bishop of California.

2715. Jun 19, Red Hook, Mr. S. Miller Van Wyck of Hudson to Kate, daughter of E. J. Mc Carthy, formerly of Saugerties, by Rev. Jos. H. Barclay.

2716. Jun 5, Kingston, Peter S. Gallagher of the firm of Crosby, More & Company to Miss Catharine M., daughter of Robt. R. Kerr, Esq., all of Kingston, by Rev. Mr. Chipp.

2717. Jun 20, at the home of the bride's father, Geo. Hermance to Mary C., eldest daughter of N. De Myer Brink, all of the Town of Saugerties, by Rev. Wm. B. Merritt.

July 12, 1867

2718. Jun 12, Stone Ridge, Mr. George N. Stodderd of Rondout to Miss Louisa Perrine of Stone Ridge, by Rev. J. L. Mc Nain.

2719. Jun 22, Mr. Gordon Eckert to Miss Alvina Winchel, both of Olive, by Rev. F. K. Van Tassel.

2720. Jun 22, Mr. Henry W. Coons to Miss Mahala Eckert, both of Olive, by Rev. F. K. Van Tassel.

2721. Jul 2, Blue Mountain, Sandford Mc Gee to Mary J., daughter of Dennis Van Tassel, by Rev. W. D. Buckelew.

July 19, 1867

2722. Jul 3, Saugerties, at the Methodist Episcopal Church, Mr. James Merchant to Miss Katie Longendyke, both of Saugerties, by Rev. Mr. Barnum.

July 26, 1867

2723. Jul 20, Blue Mountain, William H. Burton to Mary E. Rick, both of the Town of Saugerties, by Rev. W. D. Buckelew.

August 30, 1867

2724. Aug 21, Cold Springs, Mr. F. Luckenback of Rondout to Miss Katie Genthner of Saugerties, by Rev. Wm. Ostrander.

September 6, 1867

2725. Aug 27, Glasco, Mr. Philander S. Wickham to Miss Marth A. Porter, both of Bethel, Ulster Co., by Rev. A. F. Palmer.

September 20, 1867

2726. Undated, Rosendale, Mr. D. C. Overbaugh of West Camp to Miss Sarah B. Cornell of Rosendale, by Rev. J. L. Bennett.

October 4, 1867

2727. Oct 2, Saugerties, Mr. Charles P. Fenwick of Poughkeepsie to Miss Esabella Edwards of Saugerties, by Rev. Mr. Barnum.

2728. Sep 18, Tivoli, Mr. Dennis Majory of Greenbush to Miss Mary Delanoy of Tivoli, by Rev. E. Tompkins.

2729. Sep 25, Tivoli, Mr. George A. Norcutt of Greenbush to Miss Cordelia Decker of Tivoli, by Rev. E. Tompkins.

2730. Sep 17, Eureka, Ill., Mr. F. M. Hoyt, formerly of Saugerties, to Miss Emma J. Hale, all of Eureka, by Rev. Mr. Everest.

2731. Sep 26, at the home of the bride's father, Mr. Zachariah B. Clumb to Miss Lavina, daughter of Mr. D. T. Hummel, all of the Town of Saugerties, by Rev. A. F. Palmer.

October 11, 1867

2732. Oct 9, Blue Mountain, Mr. Peter Mack to Miss Margaret, daughter of Joseph Teetsel of Quarryville, by Rev. W. D. Buckelew.

2733. Oct 3, at the home of the bride's father, Mr. Thomas Hanbridge to Miss Sarah A., daughter of Mr. John Lowe, all of Saugerties, by Rev. S. F. Barnum.

2734. Oct 6, Haverstraw, Mr. Richard Miley of Haverstraw to Mrs. Elizabeth Allen of Saugerties, by Rev. E. Gay, Jr.

2735. Oct 3, Saugerties, at the Methodist Episcopal Church, Mr. Cyrus Overbagh to Miss Mary E. Garling, both of Catskill, by Rev. F. S. Barnum.

2736. Sep 24, Astoria, Long Island, Rev. Wm. B. Merritt, pastor of the Reformed Dutch Church of Flatbush to Mary Pease Kingsbury of Astoria, by Rev. Wm. Ten Eyck.

2737. Sep 19, Stone Ridge, Nelson Ingram, Surgeon, U. S. Navy to Miss Nellie Sahler of High Falls, by Rev. N. H. Van Arsdale.

October 18, 1867

2738. Oct 3, South Rondout, Mr. Edgar F. Allen to Miss Emeline Lynch, both of South Rondout, by Rev. D. E. Ledyard.

2739. Oct 9, Rondout, N. L. Bouton to Harriet A. Everson, both of Rondout, by Rev. Wm. M. Chipp.

2740. Oct 7, Rondout, Mr. Anthony Reiser to Miss Kate Derrenbacher, both of Rondout, by Rev. Father Raufheisen.

2741. Oct 2, Flatbush, Hezekiah S. Burhans of Kingston to Sarah, daughter of S. M. Merritt of Kingston and sister of the clergyman, by Rev. Wm. B. Merritt.

2742. Oct 6, Wiltwyck, Charles J. Masten to Annie Avery, both of Kingston, by Rev. W. A. Shaw.

2743. Oct 3, Stone Ridge, Mr. James S. Dubois of Ohioville to Miss Donna M. Davis of Stone Ridge, by Rev. J. L. Mc Nair.

2744. Oct 6, Haverstraw, Richard Neely of Haverstraw to Mrs. Elizabeth Allen of Saugerties, by Rev. E. Gay, Jr.

October 25, 1867

2745. Oct 17, at the home of Abram Wolven, James Albert Ostrom to Anna Myer, both of Saugerties, by Rev. N. T. Chapman.

2746. Oct 23, Woodstock, Frederick Happy of South Woodstock to Miss Josephine Cooper of Lake Hill, by Rev. H. C. Longyear.

November 1, 1867

2747. Oct 21, Saugerties, at the home of Dr. Wilson, Mr. Nathan P. Morey of New York City to Miss Jane Wilson of Saugerties, by Rev. H. C. Longyear.

2748. Oct 22, Brooklyn, at the North Reformed Church on Clermont Ave., Joseph H. Clark of New York to Lillie M., daughter of Abram F. Calkin, by Rev. D. Porter.

2749. Oct 5, Kingston, George Middagh to Mary Frances Van Keuren, by Rev. Mr. Beach.

November 8, 1867

2750. Oct 24, Flatbush, Peter W. Whitaker to Sarah A. Burhans, both of Kingston, by Rev. Wm. B. Merritt.

November 15, 1867

2751. Nov 11, Saugerties, Mr. George Rogers of Tivoli, formerly of Saugerties, to Miss Johanna Mc Kenna Tuick of Saugerties, by Rev. Michael C. Powers.

2752. Nov 9, Saugerties, at the Baptist Church, Mr. Henry Miller of Madalin to Miss Eliza A. Wheeler of Tivoli, by Rev. H. C. Longyear.

2753. Nov 9, Saugerties, at the Baptist Church, Mr. Casens Wheeler to Miss Jane Shephard, both of Tivoli, by Rev. H. C. Longyear.

2754. Nov 2, Blue Mountain, Abraham Myer of Saugerties to Sarah Young of Hunter, Greene Co., by Rev. W. D. Buckelew.

2755. Nov 13, Blue Mountain, Christopher Short of Kingston to Harriet E. Finger of Woodstock, by Rev. W. D. Buckelew.

2756. Nov 13, Blue Mountain, Peter F. Short of Saugerties to Matilda Lasher of Kingston, by Rev. W. D. Buckelew.

2757. Nov 4, at the home of the bride's father, Mr. Alfred Walker, formerly of Kingston, to Miss Annie E. Kennedy of Albany, by Rev. Dr. Magoon.

2758. Oct 24, at the home of the bride's mother, Tobias Pine, formerly of Kingston, to Miss Helen M. Carr of Auburn, NY, by Rev. Dr. Hawley.

2759. Oct 9, Kingston, at St. James Methodist Episcopal Church, Henry H. B. Angell of New York to Ida C. Weeks of Kingston, by Rev. J. W. Beach.

2760. Nov 6, Rondout, Mr. Edward Breitenbeaker to Miss Mary S. Wells, both of Rondout, by Rev. E. W. Bliss.

2761. Oct 31, Rondout, Mr. Albert Burhans to Miss Carrie Dubois, both of Rondout, by Rev. E. W. Bliss.

2762. Oct 5, San Francisco, Calif., at the home of the bride's uncle, R. E. Hyde, formerly of Esopus to Rachel A. Coale of Baltimore.

November 22, 1867

2763. Nov 6, Glenerie, Elijah Felter of Saugerties to Mary C., eldest daughter of C. B. Tipp of the Town of Kingston, by Rev. W. B. Merritt.

2764. Oct 22, Kingston, Martin Snyder to Phebe Van Etten, by Rev. C. H. Stitt.

2765. Oct 31, Kingston, David H. Carle to Emily Carle, both of Plattekill, by Rev. C. H. Stitt.

2766. Nov 6, Kingston, Joseph Shellightner of Kingston to Emma Parssell of Port Ewen, by Rev. C. H. Stitt.

November 29, 1867

2767. Oct 16, West Camp, at the Lutheran Church, Mr. William C. Trumpbour to Miss S. Jennie Overbaugh, both of West Camp, by Rev. J. D. Wertz.

2768. Nov 14, Flatbush, Phillip Lynk of Saugerties to Fanny C. Yerry of Woodstock, by Rev. Wm. B. Merritt.

2769. Nov 20, Henry W. Turck to Mary E. Goldsmith, both of Glasco, by Rev. W. B. Merritt.

December 6, 1867

2770. Dec 2, Flatbush, David Sloss of Poughkeepsie to Margaret Jane, daughter of Michael Frazer of Glasco, by Rev. W. M. Merritt.

December 13, 1867

2771. Dec 5, at the home of the bride's father, John M. Layman to Ella Low, both of Blue Mountain, by Rev. S. T. Cole.

2772. Dec 4, at the home of the bride's father, John A. Longendyke of Saugerties to Mary Amelia Low of Kingston, by Rev. S. T. Cole.

December 20, 1867

2773. Dec 11, at the home of the bride's parents, Valentine Trumpbour of West Camp to Mary Antoinette Mc Chesney, daughter of James Mc Chesney of Brooklyn, by Rev. N. E. Smith.

December 27, 1867

2774. Dec 10, Mr. John W. Mower to Miss Margaret Moose, both of West Camp, by Rev. J. D. Wert.

2775. Dec 13, Mr. Edward Schoonmaker to Miss Estella Burhans, both of West Camp, by Rev. J. D. Wert.

2776. Dec 18, Malden, Charles E. Bush to Mary E. Barringer of Germantown, by Rev. Thomas Lape.

2777. Oct 23, West Hurley, Samuel P. Myer of Kingston to Ophelia, daughter of Joshua Nash of West Hurley, by Rev. Wm. H. Emrick.

2778. Dec 11, West Hurley, George H. Britt of Kingston to Lucy Parks of West Hurley, by Rev. Wm. H. Emrick.

2779. Nov 20, Watson A. Smith to Sarah Rightmyer, both of Olive, by Rev. T. R. Van Tassell.

2780. Nov 23, Hiram Bell to Emma Acker, both of Shandaken, by Rev. T. R. Van Tassell.

2781. Dec 11, Phillip C. Neher, MD, of Accord to Mary Stone of Olive, by Rev. T. R. Van Tassell.

January 3, 1868
2782. Dec 26, East Durham, William Dean of Saugerties to Christina Vincent of South Durham.

January 10, 1868
2783. Dec 30, Mr. Luke Fitzgerald of New York to Miss Lizzie Gay of Saugerties, by Rev. Michael Powers.

2784. Jan 1, Mr. Michael Fagen of New York to Miss Ellen Mc Grath of Saugerties, by Rev. Michael Powers.

2785. Dec 19, at the home of Mr. H. W. Backer, George Newkirk to Mary E. Barker, by Rev. W. D. Buckelew.

2786. Jan 2, at the home of the bride's parents, Theodore Brigham, merchant, of Napanoch to Fanny, daughter of David Terry of Rondout.

January 17, 1868
2787. Jan 1, Malden, Samuel Paradise to Miss Rachel Kisselbrack, both of Malden, by Rev. C. W. Lyon.

2788. Jan 8, Rondout, at the home of the bride's father, George K. Snyder of Saugerties to Miss Olive, daughter of O. G. Fowler, Esq. of Rondout, by Rev. Mr. Chipp.

2789. Jan 8, at the home of the bride's father, Mr. Albert A. Doxtader of Salisbury, NY to Miss Martha Longyear of Phoenicia, by Rev. H. C. Longyear.

January 24, 1868

2790. Jan 14, Mr. David W. Ostrander to Miss Mary F. Hart, both of Red Hook, by Rev. J. G. Johnson.

2791. Jan 9, Flatbush, James H. Van Aken to Mary A. Brink, both of the Town of Kingston, by Rev. Wm. B. Merritt.

2792. Jan 9, Flatbush, Jacob Keiffer to Jane R., daughter of David Carle, all of the Town of Kingston, by Rev. Wm. B. Merritt.

2793. Jan 7, Rondout, David B. Eighmey of Kingston to Agnes Watts of Rondout, by Rev. W. A. Chipp

2794. Jan 9, New York, at the home of the bride's uncle, Theodore R. Davis to Louise, daughter of Charles W. Schaffer, Esq., formerly of Saugerties.

2795. Dec 18, Woodstock, at the home of the bride's father, Judson Bishop to Rachel A. Ploss, by Rev. D. B. Wyckoff.

2796. Jan 1, Woodstock, Cornelius Hogan of Hurley to Kate Davis of Woodstock, by Rev. D. B. Wyckoff.

January 31, 1868

2797. Anniversary Jan 16, 1868 of the eleventh year of marriage of Mr. and Mrs. Cornelius Longendyke of Plattekill.

2798. Jan 26, at the residence of Edward Delanoy, Mr. Fonda Delanoy to Miss Lydia Kittell, both of Saugerties, by Rev. H. C. Longyear.

February 7, 1868

2799. Feb 1, at the residence of the bride's father, William L. Shoemaker to Elizabeth Wolven, both of the Town of Saugerties, by Rev. H. C. Longyear.

2800. Jan 30, at the home of the bride's father, Hiram W. Davis to Almira, daughter of Joel Osterhoudt, all of Flatbush, by Rev. Wm. B. Merritt.

2801. Dec 25, Abram Bell to Cornelia Bodley, both of Olive, by Rev. F. K. Van Tassel.

2802. Dec 31, Asa Jones to Sarah E. Smith, both of Olive, by Rev. F. K. Van Tassel.

February 14, 1868

2803. Feb 4, at the residence of the bride's mother, Dr. Charles W. Deyo, Ulster Co. clerk to Cornelia, daughter of the late Dr. David Wurts of New Paltz, by Rev. Mr. Peltz.

2804. Feb 5, at the home of the bride's father, J. W. Dubois, MD, of Kingston to Miss Emma H. Smith of Vorhees Station, New Brunswick, New Jersey, by Rev. J. Steele.

February 28, 1868

2805. Feb 24, Blue Mountain, Alva Wickham of Fish Creek to Anna Amelia Riefenberg, by Rev. W. D. Buckelew.

2806. Feb 18, West Saugerties, Corydon C. Olney of Rockport, Missouri to Kate M., daughter of Robert Smith of West Saugerties, by Rev. W. D. Buckelew.

2807. Feb 5, Kingston, Isaac N. Hammond of Highland to Sarah R. Winfield of Kingston, by Rev. Dr. Stitt.

March 6, 1868

2808. Feb 25, Georgetown, Indiana, Dr. Scott Woolf of Georgetown, to Miss Carrie, daughter of Dr. H. Wygant of Saugerties.

2809. Feb 25, Kingston, Mr. John H. Van Keuren, printer, of New York, to Miss Sarah Jane, daughter of Mr. Oscar Elliott of Kingston, by Rev. Mr. Holmes.

March 20, 1868

2810. Feb 12, Mr. Charles Magee to Miss Malissa Schoonmaker, both of West Camp, by Rev. J. D. Wart.

2811. Feb 13, at the home of the bride's father, Mr. Mervin Whitney to Miss Arietta Beare, both of West Camp, by Rev. J. D. Wart.

2812. Feb 19, Little Falls, NY, Mr. John J. Hardenburg of Rondout to Miss Emma Scott of Little Falls.

2813. Mar 8, John S. Barber of Rondout to Miss Mary E. Phillips of Olive, by Rev. Wm. M. Chipp.

March 27, 1868

2814. Mar 19, Saugerties, Mr. Robert Burhans of Flatbush to Miss Emeline Cooper of Saugerties, by Rev. John Gaston.

2815. Mar 9, Thomas W. Brink of Kingston to Sarah Ann, eldest daughter of Robert Fitzsimmons of Glenerie, by Rev. Wm. B. Merritt.

2816. Mar 18, Kingston, Mr. John C. Romeyn, one of the proprietors of the Kingston *Journal* to Miss Mary Frances, daughter of Seymour L. Stebbins, Esq. of Kingston, by Rev. Wm. M. Chipp.

2817. Mar 15, Kingston, Mr. Peter Dubois, Jr. of Rondout to Miss Lucinda C. Lasher of Kingston, by Rev. E. D. Ledyard.

2818. Mar 18, Kingston, Albert K. Coutant to Miss Sarah M., daughter of R. W. Smith, all of Rondout, by Rev. Wm. M. Chipp.

April 3, 1868

2819. Mar 5, at the home of the bride's father, Charles Maginnis of Saugerties to Sarah J. Eakins of New York City, by Rev. J. F. Richmond.

April 10, 1868
2820. Mar 31, Flatbush, Wm. H. Folant to Mary Darling, both of Kingston, by Rev. Wm B. Merritt.

April 17, 1868
2821. Mar 19, West Camp, Moses Overbaugh to Jane Gardener, both of West Camp, by Rev. J. D. Wert.

2822. Apr 2, at the home of the bride's father, Mr. John H. Gould to Miss Sarah Whitney, both of West Camp, by Rev. J. D. Wert.

April 24, 1868
2823. Apr 9, Saugerties, Gordon Minerly of Rondout to Helen Stoutenburgh of Kingston, by Rev. John Gaston.

May 1, 1868
2824. Apr 24, Saugerties, Wm. H. Mc Elroy to Milinda Whitaker, both of the Town of Saugerties, by S. Merclean, Esq.

2825. Feb 29, at the home of Henry Navey, Romeyn Spotts of Kingston to Margaret Navy of Saugerties, by S. Merclean, Esq.

2826. Apr 14, Hudson, Joseph S. Lane of Ulster Co. to Cornelia M. Fitch of Hudson, by Rev. S. Fitch.

May 8, 1868
2827. May 3, Blue Mountain, Harvey Delamater to Julia Ann, daughter of David Schoonmaker of the Town of Saugerties, by Rev. W. D. Buckelew.

2828. Apr 26, 2nd Methodist Episcopal Church, Henry B. Marsh to Juliet Sweet, both of Kingston, by Rev. David Buck.

May 15, 1868
2829. May 7, Saugerties, Alfred Gulnack to Maria C. Wallace, both of Woodstock, by Rev. H. C. Longyear.

May 22, 1868

2830. May 12, Glenerie, Wm. H. Kniffin of Rondout to Mary E., daughter of James Hillyer of Glenerie, by Rev. Wm. B. Merritt.

May 29, 1868

2831. May 25, Saugerties, at the home of Mr. Robert Knapp, Mr. Charles Gibbs to Miss Lizzie A. York, by Rev. F. S. Barnum.

June 5, 1868

2832. May 30, Saugerties, Alexander Underhill to Catherine Kelly, both of Saugerties, by Rev. H. C. Longyear.

2833. May 1, Saugerties, Nathan K. Whitaker of Glasco to Philena Cole of Saugerties, by Rev. F. S. Barnum.

2834. May 26, Saugerties, Ozias Brink of Malden to Sarah C. Mc Donald of Saugerties, by Rev. S. F. Barnum.

2835. May 28, at the home of the bride's parents, David Hommel of Saugerties to Catherine E., daughter of John H. Freligh, Esq., by Rev. W. D. Buckelew.

June 12, 1868

2836. Jun 2, Rondout, Rev. W. F. Basten of Leroy, NY to Miss E. M. Crosby of Rondout, by Rev. Mr. Grenelle of Kingston.

2837. Jun 1, Rondout, George E. Stevenger of New York to Miss J. Maria, daughter of Richard Brodhead of Rondout, by Rev. Wm. M. Chipp.

June 19, 1868

2838. Jun 13, Flatbush, Mr. James Fosbrook to Miss Levena J. Matthews, both of Saugerties, by Rev. Wm. B. Merritt.

2839. Jun 11, at the home of James I. Webster, Mr. Wm. H. Spencer to Miss Ensey G. Bullinger, both of Acra, NY, by Rev. H. C. Longyear.

2840. May 31, Joshua Snyder to Harriet E. Blue, both of Saugerties, by Rev. J. Whitaker.

2841. Jun 4, Eugene Shultis to Sarah C. Shultis, by Rev. J. Whitaker.

June 26, 1868
2842. Jun 25, Flatbush, Samuel D. Whitaker to Amanda Spencer, both of the Town of Saugerties, by Rev. Wm. B. Merritt.

July 10, 1868
2843. Jun 7, Saugerties, Peter J. Mower of Rondout to Miss Katy Brown of Saugerties, by Rev. H. C. Longyear.

2844. Jul 3, Saugerties, Mr. Evander Mc Elroy of Haverstraw to Miss Anney Delanoy of Glasco, by Rev. H. C. Longyear.

2845. Jul 3, Saugerties, Mr. Albert H. Kittell to Miss Sarah M. Quick, both of the Town of Saugerties, by Rev. H. C. Longyear.

2846. Jul 4, Glasco, George F. Kuhl to Dora Curdes, both of Saugerties, by Rev. Wm. B. Merritt.

2847. Undated, Flatbush, Jacob A. Sheffer of Germantown to Lillie J. Brown of Kingston, by Rev. W. B. Merritt. <July 2, 1868, records of the Flatbush Reformed Church, ed.>

2848. Jul 2, Flatbush, Irwin W. Joy to Harriett C. Mower, by Rev. W. B. Merritt.

July 24, 1868
2849. Jul 18, Blue Mountain, Jacob Cole to Melissa Burton, both of the Town of Saugerties, by Rev. W. D. Buckelew.

2850. Jul 6, James S. Depuy to Rosile Brown, both of Fish Creek, by Rev. R. L. Shurter.

2851. Jul 6, William B. Brown to Mary C. Depuy, both of Fish Creek, by Rev. R. L. Shurter.

2852. Jul 14, John W. Garrison of Catskill to Matilda Wilsen of Haverstraw, by Rev. R. L. Shurter.

2853. May 5, Rondout, Mr. Charles Gilpatrick of Orland, Maine to Miss Jennie A. Du Bois of Eddyville, by Rev. E. D. Ledyard.

August 7, 1868

2854. Jul 19, Flatbush, Mr. Henry V. B. Shader to Miss Mary E. Phiilips, both of Kingston, by Rev. William B. Merritt.

2855. Undated, Flatbush, Benjamin V. Ritte to Annie R. Traver, both of Flatbush, by Rev. Wm. B. Merritt. <July 22, 1868, records of the Flatbush Reformed Church, ed.>

August 14, 1868

2856. Jul 16, Asbury, Mr. Madison Mondore of Prattsville to Miss Mary F. Post of Quarryville, by Rev. Chas. W. Lyon.

2857. Jul 28, Malden, Mr. Maurice Steen to Miss Alida A. Brink, both of Malden, by Rev. C. W. Lyon.

August 21, 1868

2858. Aug 9, Saugerties, Harmon Mitrach to Susie Robinson, both of Saugerties, by Rev. Wm. B. Merritt.

2859. Aug 12, Kingston, Clark Davis of Marbletown to Rebecca M. Loew of Saugerties, by Rev. Dr. Hoes.

August 28, 1868

2860. Aug 9, Athens, at the Lutheran Church, James Mower of High Falls, Ulster Co. to Miss Sarah Jane Manning of Athens, by Rev. Mr. Hull.

September 4, 1868

2861. Notice - All persons are hereby notified that if they give aid to Margaret A. Mower, the wife of John H. Mower they do it on their own responsibility, as I will not be responsible for any debts that she makes against me. 25 Aug 1868, John H. Mower.

September 11, 1868

2862. Sep 8, Kingston, W. Scott Gillespie to Julia A., daughter of John H. Schryver, all of Kingston, by Rev. C. H. Stitt.

2863. Sep 1, High Falls, Ulster Co., Rev. A. H. Van Arsdale to Hattie M., youngest daughter of Calvin Hasbrouck, all of High Falls, by Rev. W. W. Jones of Bergen Point, New Jersey.

2864. Sep 2, Kingston, Francis A. Raenhart to Charlotte Blanshan, both of Kingston, by Rev. D. Buck.

2865. Aug 27, Bloomington, at the parsonage, Garret F. Krom to Jane A. Van Aken, all of Esopus, by Rev. A. Blauvelt.

September 25, 1868

2866. Wednesday, Rondout, at the Presbyterian Church, Mr. George C. Wolsey to Miss Anna C. Wolfer, both of Rondout, by Rev. E. D. Ledyard.

2867. Undated, Ellenville, Mr. Smart to Miss Libbie Brandemore, both of Ellenville, by Rev. E. S. Osbon.

2868. Sep 7, Kingston, Marinus Van Nostrand to Louise Bowen, both of Kingston, by Rev. J. Y. Bates.

October 2, 1868

2869. Sep 16, Kingston, Mr. Jesse H. Van Buren to Miss Mary E. Woodey, both of Kingston, by Rev. J. Y. Bates.

2870. Sep 27, Kingston, Edward B. Ennist to Christina C., daughter of Robert G. Bonesteel, Esq., by Rev. Dr. Hoes.

2871. Sep 27, Kingston, Mr. Robert West of Kingston to Miss Jane Sands of Poughkeepsie, by Rev. J. Y. Bates.

October 9, 1868

2872. Sep 20, Woodstock, at the home of the bride's father, John H. Schoonmaker of Saugerties to Martha Smith, by Rev. D. B. Wyckoff.

2873. Oct 1, Town of Saugerties, Marvin R. Burton to Amelia G. Morris, both of Saugerties, by Rev. H. Wheeler.

2874. Undated, at the home of the bride, Mr. David Hopkins to Mrs. Mary Ann Paries, both of Saugerties, by Rev. H. C. Longyear.

2875. Sep 29, High Falls, John A. Krom of High Falls to Libbie R. Lefevre of Rosendale, by Rev. N. H. Van Arsdale.

2876. Sep 30, Bulls Head, Dutchess Co., Mr. Alonzo De Pew of Rondout to Miss Nellie A. Palmer of Bulls Head, by Rev. E. W. Bliss.

2877. Sep 28, Jacob Miller to Miss Eliza Doyle, both of Rondout, by Rev. M. Chipp.

2878. Sep 26, Samuel Mottomy to Miss Cornelia E. Miller, both of Rondout, by Rev. Wm. M. Chipp.

2879. Sep 23, Mr. Louis Dubois Hoornbeck to Miss Catharine D. B., daughter of Henry D. B. Freer, Esq., all of New Paltz, by Rev. Richard De Witt.

2880. Sep 14, High Falls, Lambert J. Dubois of Philadelphia to Louisa J. Van Wagoner of High Falls.

October 16, 1868

2881. Oct 8, Blue Mountain, Franklin A. Hommel of Woodstock to Elizabeth, daughter of Abram Ryder of Woodstock, by Rev. W. D. Buckelew.

October 23, 1868

2882. Oct 17, Mr. Andrew Brink of Saugerties to Miss Elizabeth Bouse of High Falls, by Rev. F. S. Barnum.

2883. Oct 13, Kingston, James H. Jackson of New York to Martha, daughter of the late Prince Terry of Kingston, by Rev. Dr. Waters.

October 30, 1868

2884. Oct 21, Blue Mountain, Jeremiah Wolven to Maggie E. Bouton, both of West Hurley.

2885. Oct 14, Kingston, Robert W. Kerr of Rondout to Helen J. Legg of Kingston, by Rev. D. N. Vanderveer.

2886. Oct 8, Kingston, Samuel Martin to Josephine Dederick, both of Catskill, by Rev. C. H. Stitt.

2887. Oct 10, Kingston, William Aldrich of New York to Christina A. Deyo of Kingston, by Rev. C. H. Stitt.

2888. Oct 2, Kingston, Mr. Thomas Cal to Miss Mary A. Murray, both of Kingston.

November 6, 1868

2889. Oct 24, Kingston, Leroy Bishop of West Hurley to Melissa Krom of Marbletown, by Rev. A. E. Schepmoes.

2890. Oct 21, New Paltz, Peter Lefever to Rachel H., only daughter of Johannes J. Freer, Esq., all of New Paltz, by Rev. Dr. Peltz.

2891. Oct 21, at the home of the bride's father, Eltinge T. Deyo to Cornelia, daughter of Derrick W. Eltinge, Esq., by Rev. Dr. Peltz.

2892. Oct 21, at the home of the bride's father, Henry Weeks, Esq. to Lucinda Hudler, both of Kingston, by Rev. D. N. Vandever.

2893. Oct 2, Woodstock, at the Methodist Episcopal Church, Henry E. Wispel to Rebecca J. Sickler, both of Woodstock, by Rev. J. Whitaker.

2894. Oct 25, Woodstock, at the Methodist Episcopal Church, John B. Hit to Ireney F. Bishop, both of Woodstock, by Rev. J. Whitaker.

2895. Oct 28, Catskill, Stephen M. Bagley to Miss Ella, daughter of Andrew Bell, all of Catskill, by Rev. R. Weeks.

November 13, 1868

2896. Nov 9, Saugerties, Abram Cole to Sarah E. Van Steenburgh, both of the Town of Saugerties, by Honorable Justice C. P. Brink, in the office of Justice Samuel Merclean.

2897. Nov 4, Malden, William Watts, U. S. N. to Mary A, daughter of Edward Bigelow, Esq., by Rev. J. P. Stratton.

2898. Oct 28, Kingston, at St. John's Church, Engleber Lott, Jr. of Bath, Long Island to Amelia M., daughter of Warren Chipp of Kingston, by Rev. Geo. Waters, D.D.

2899. Oct 28, Mr. Albert Rider to Miss Jennett Cooke, both of Kingston, by Rev. J. Y. Bates.

2900. Oct 22, Albany, at St. Paul's Church, John B. Halcott of Catskill to Miss Carrie Winne of Albany, by Rev. J. Livingston Reese.

2901. Oct 27, Stone Ridge, Edwin W. Budington to Mary C. Houghtaling, both of Hurley, by Rev. Charles Palmer.

November 20, 1868

2902. Nov 18, Saugerties, at the home of the bride's parents, Dr. James A. Dean of Battle Creek, Michigan to Miss Selena Post.

2903. Nov 10, Mr. Charles R. Hoffman to Miss Girtude Shaffer, both of Red Hook, by C. Allendorf, Esq.

November 27, 1868

2904. Oct 23, Marlborough, Thomas Wygant of Marlborough to Amyetta Smith of Plattekill, by Rev. G. H. Gregory.

2905. Nov 12, Marlborough, John F. Kniffer to Mary F. Wygant, both of Marlborough, by Rev. G. H. Gregory.

2906. Nov 12, Marlborough, Philip Henesy of Newburgh to Emma F. Mc Mullen of Marlborough, by Rev. G. H. Gregory.

2907. Undated, at the home of the bride's parents, Rebecca A. Thorn to Herbert H. Purdy, both of Marlborough, by Rev. S. H. Jagger.

2908. Nov 15, Highland, Mr. Henry Fowler to Miss Cornelia Galaway, by Rev. N. H. Bangs.

2909. Nov 17, Abram's Hotel, John Everett of Kingston to Adaline Dietz of Rifton, by Rev. Dr. Peltz.

2910. Nov 11, Tyre, NY, Andrew Snyder of High Falls to Sarah A. Hasbrouck of Tyre, by Rev. J. C. Blauvelt.

2911. Nov 12, Clinton, at the home of Mr. John Fullmer, Edward Kipp to Miss Almira Stickle, both of Red Hook, by Rev. Geo. Neff.

2912. Nov 12, Kingston, Richard Mc Clung to Kate Boyd, both of Kingston, by Rev. Mr. Buck.

2913. Nov 10, Clarkstown, NY, Moses Whitbeck of Kingston to Mary E. Van Wagenen of New York, by Rev. B. C. Lippencott.

December 4, 1868
2914. Notice is hereby given that I, the undersigned, James H. Schutt and Sarah A. Schutt, my wife, have agreed to live separate and apart, and she having agreed to and received a certain sum of money in full satisfaction for her support and maintenance, now therefore all persons hare hereby forbid to harbor or trust my said wife, Sarah A., as I shall hereafter pay no debts of her contracting. Nov 30, 1868, Saugerties, James H. Schutt.

2915. Nov 26, Town of Saugerties, Morgan Lasher of Woodstock to Mary Helen Wolven of the Town of Saugerties, by Rev. H. Wheeler.

2916. Undated, Blue Mountain, Jonas L. Mower to Jane, daughter of Jacob Wolven, all of Saugerties, by Rev. W. D. Buckelew. <November 24, 1868, records of the Blue Mountain Reformed Church, ed.>

December 11, 1868

2917. Dec 5, Blue Mountain, Samuel A. Van Steenburgh to Mary A. Broderick, both of the Town of Saugerties, by Rev. W. D. Buckelew.

2918. Nov 25, West Camp, at the Lutheran Church, Mr. William Mower of Saugerties to Miss Sarah Trumpbour of West Camp, by Rev. J. D. Wert.

2919. Nov 25, Binghampton, J. B. Van Deusen of Kingston to Mrs. E. A. Scott, by Rev. Charles H. Platt.

December 18, 1868

2920. Dec 17, Saugerties, at the home of James A. James, Mr. Henry D. Van Leuven to Miss Betsy L. Westwood, both of Saugerties, by Rev. H. C. Longyear.

2921. Nov 25, at the home of the bride's father, Mr. Henry Andrus to Miss Martha E. Cartwright, both of South Durham, by Rev. H. C. Longyear.

2922. Nov 14, at the house of the bride, Neelly Bloodgood of Catskill to Emiline Whispell of Woodstock, by Rev. J. Whittaker.

2923. Dec 9, Hermon W. Dubois of Woodstock to Harriet Wolven of Saugerties, by Rev. J. Whittaker.

December 25, 1868

2924. Dec 20, Malden, at the Methodist Episcopal Church, Mr. Peter Paries to Miss Maria Rock, by Rev. C. W. Lyon.

2925. Dec 24, Saugerties, Mr. William Cooke of Salem, NY to Miss Hattie Whitaker of Saugerties, by Rev. F. S. Barnum.

January 1, 1869

2926. Dec 17, West Camp, Reuben Dederick to Ann Lavina Minkler, both of High Falls, by Rev. J. D. Wert.

2927. Dec 23, at the home of the bride's father, Mr. Hiram Lewis to Miss Catharine Mower, both of West Camp, by Rev. J. D. Wert.

2928. Dec 26, James O. Lewis to Sarah Mariah Hommel, both of the Town of Saugerties, by Rev. Thomas Lape.

2929. Dec 25, Saugerties, Mifﬁn R. Moyer of Logansville, Pa., to Eugenia Wiand of Saugerties, by Rev. F. S. Barnum. <Mifflin, records of the Saugerties United Methodist Church, ed.>

2930. Dec 20, Kingston, Theodore Webster to Sarah Frazer, both of Glasco, by Rev. Dr. Stitt.

2931. Dec 24, Flatbush, Charles H. Sutton to Sarah A. Croswell, both of the Town of Saugerties, by Rev. Wm. B. Merritt.

2932. Dec 10, Rosendale, Mr. Jacob S. Wood to Rachel A. Davis of Rosendale, by Rev. Mr. Liebenen.

January 8, 1869

2933. Jan 2, Saugerties, at the Exchange Hotel, Solomon Townsend to Elizabeth Andrews, both of Middletown, Delaware Co., by S. Merclean.

2934. Dec 31, West Camp, Mr. G. W. Slater of Saugerties to Miss Elizabeth Snyder of Woodstock, by Rev. J. D. West.

2935. Jan 5, West Camp, Mr. John Plass to Miss Eliza Turck, both of Glasco, by Rev. J. D. West.

January 15, 1869

2936. Jan 11, Saugerties, Jacob Hulsapple of Madalin to Miss Mahala Carnright of Saugerties, by Rev. F. S. Barnum.

2937. Jan 12, Saugerties, at the home of Josiah Myer, Esq., in a Friends ceremony, Mr. Benjamin C. Arnold of New York City to Miss Hattie Knapp of this place.

January 22, 1869

2938. Jan 13, Athens, at the home of the bride's father, Frederick R. Lape of Hudson to Emma G. Rouse of Athens, by Rev. Thomas Lape and Rev. Mr. Campbell.

2939. Jan 12, Flatbush, Benjamin Kidd to Julia Tracy, both of the Town of Saugerties, by Rev. Wm. B. Merritt.

January 29, 1869

2940. Undated, at the home of the bride's father, John Tucker of Malden to Belinda A. Hoff of Saugerties, by Rev. S. F. Barnum. <January 14, 1869, records of the Saugerties United Methodist Church, ed.>

2941. Jan 7, Kingston, at the 1st Methodist Episcopal Church, Mr. Rianza Lasher of Kingston to Miss Lucy Salapaugh of Red Hook, by Rev. J. Y. Bates.

2942. Undated, Shokan, Mr. Edwin Hunt to Miss Eliza Elwyn, both of Woodstock, by Rev. F. K. Van Tassel.

February 5, 1869

2943. Jan 28, Saugerties, Mr. Alfred Kearney to Miss Mary Sickles, both of this place, by Rev. F. S. Barnum.

2944. Jan 27, Saugerties, Mr. Oliver Ellsworth of Madalin to Miss Mary Carnright of Saugerties, by Rev. J. Gaston.

2945. Jan 28, Blue Mountain, Mr. Legrande Scribner to Margaret Morton, both of Catskill, by Rev. W. D. Buckelew.

February 12, 1869

2946. Feb 9, Syracuse, NY, at St. James Church, Carroll Whitaker of Saugerties to Kate M., daughter of the late Horace Sherman of Syracuse, by Rev. Dr. Clarke.

2947. Feb 2, Daniel Webster to Rosa A. Herbert, both of Brooklyn by Rev. T. L. Cuyler.

2948. Jan 30, West Camp, Mr. Charles Hanson of Catsbaan to Miss Angeline Scutt of Saugerties, by Rev. J. D. West.

February 19, 1869
2949. Jan 25, Cold Spring, NY, H. C. Smith of Brooklyn to S. Elma Eckert of Saugerties, by Rev. Wm. Ostrander.

February 26, 1869
2950. Feb 13, Blue Mountain, C. Fiero Teetsell to Martha Jane, daughter of John H. Teetsell, all of Saugerties, by Rev. W. D. Buckelew.

March 5, 1869
2951. Feb 21, Rondout, George W. Adams of Poughkeepsie to Miss Louisa Howard of Rondout, by Rev. Wm. M. Chipp.

March 12, 1869
2952. Feb 24, at the home of the bride's parents, Nehemiah D. Hulse to Miss Elma M. Palen, both of Fallsburgh, by Rev. J. N. Bryers.

2953. Feb 10, Palenville, Albert Brant of Saugerties to Miss Frances M. Landt of Catskill, by Rev. John W. Gorse.

March 19, 1869
2954. Mar 10, at the home of the bride's father, Mr. Joseph Millington to Miss Fanny Abeal, both of the Town of Catskill, by Rev. J. D. Wert.

March 26, 1869
2955. Feb 24, Mr. William H. Tice to Miss Artie Cudney, both of Phillipsport, by Rev. E. S. Osbon.

April 2, 1869
2956. Mar 31, Saugerties, Adolph Cohen of Leavenworth, Kansas to Fannie, eldest daughter of Francis S. Butzel of this place, by Rev. Dr. Goodheim of Temple Emanual, New York City.

April 9, 1869
2957. Apr 2, William Mc Elroy of Haverstraw to Eliza A. Mickle of Glasco, by Rev. H. C. Longyear.

2958. Apr 3, Mr. A.H. Dial to Miss Mary A. Dubois, both of Saugerties, by Rev. H. C. Longyear.

2959. Mar 24, Kingston, John Williams of Rondout to Mrs. Sarah Thompson of Kingston, by Rev. J. Y. Bates.

April 16, 1869

2960. Mar 31, Kingston, Sylvester Weeks to Laura Smedes, both of Kingston, by Rev. D. Buck.

2961. Mar 31, Richmond, Charles Winchel of Altord, Mass. to Elvina Henion, youngest daughter of Dewitt Henion of Kingston, by Rev. A. Coon.

May 7, 1869

2962. May 2, Blue Mountain, Albert Dile to Susan Burton, both of the Town of Saugerties, by Rev. W. D. Buckalew.

2963. Apr 26, Quarryville, Mr. Joseph Armstrong of Michigan to Miss Emma J. Maxwell of Quarryville, by Rev. Chas. W. Lyon.

May 14, 1869

2964. May 9, Silas Brink to Allie Riker, both of Brooklyn, by Rev. Mr. Ford.

2965. Apr 26, Port Richmond, at the North Baptist Church, Joseph L. Sherwood to Adelia F. Herbert, both of Port Richmond, by Rev. D. W. Sherwood.

May 21, 1869

2966. Apr 21, Kingston, Mr. Robert W. Dubois to Miss Sarah Darling, both of Kingston, by Rev. J. Y. Bates.

2967. May 9, Kingston, Mr. Hamilton Shufeldt of Rondout to Miss Lydia W. Young of Kingston, by Rev. J. Y. Bates.

May 28, 1869

2968. May 26, Saugerties, at the home of the bride's parents, Andrew F. Loomer of Birmingham, Conn. to Isabella Van Wart of Saugerties, by Rev. H. C. Longyear.

June 4, 1869

2969. May 27, Woodstock, at the home of the bride's parents, Albert H. Vosburgh to Jemima Shultis, both of Woodstock, by Rev. F. Hamblin.

June 11, 1869

2970. Jun 6, John Unger of Dutch Settlement to Mary Gibb of Saugerties, by E. Whitaker, Esq.

2971. Jun 3, De Witt Cunyes to Eunice Sitzer, both of the Town of Saugerties, by Rev. Thomas Lape.

June 18, 1869

2972. Jun 10, Blue Mountain, Jacob F. Mower to Jane C. Quick, both of the Town of Saugerties, by Rev. W. D. Buckelew.

July 2, 1869

2973. Jun 26, Flatbush, Harlan Teetsel to Anna Lacky, both of Saugerties, by Rev. Wm. B. Merritt.

2974. Jun 20, Glasco, at the home of Mrs. Irene Whitaker, Mr. John H. Baker to Miss Alice M. Fraser, both of Leeds, Greene Co., by Rev. H. C. Longyear.

2975. Jun 21, at the parsonage, Mr. Richard Plank to Miss Fannie Bows, both of Leeds, by Rev. H. C. Longyear.

July 9, 1869

2976. Jul 16, Eli Mower to Margaret Rock, both of Malden, by Rev. Thomas Lape.

2977. Jun 24, at the home of the bride's father, Mr. John B. Wands of Albany to Miss Violette L. Abby of West Camp, by Rev. J. D. Wert.

July 30, 1869

2978. Jul 12, Chester Springs, Pa., at the Lutheran parsonage, Mr. Virgil M. Staats of Columbia Co. to Miss Sarah B. Finger of Saugerties, by Rev. N.H. Cornell.

2979. Jul 17, Rondout, Abm. S. Groos of Wiltwyck to Caroline Winfield of Esopus, by Rev. W. H. Evans.

August 6, 1869

2980. Jul 31, Abraham L. Post to Sarah Hummel, both of the Town of Saugerties, by Rev. Thomas Lape.

August 13, 1869

2981. Aug 5, at the home of the bride's parents, Mr. Henry Brink of Brooklyn to Miss Sarah Houghtaling of Saugerties, by Rev. Wm. Ostrander.

August 20, 1869

2982. Aug 5, Quarryville, Mr. Wm. L. Frear of Sandburgh, NY to Miss Hannah M. Teetsel of Quarryville, by Rev. C. W. Lyon.

2983. Undated, Miss Fannie Stockton, a native of Saugerties and daughter of Dennis Stocking married Mr. Smith, a young Philadelphian.

September 3, 1869

2984. Aug 18, Town of Kingston, Eugene Traver of Rhinebeck to Lucy Traver of Kingston, by Rev. W. S. Shaw.

September 10, 1869

2985. Sep 5, Blue Mountain, John Ledger of West Saugerties to Miss Paulina Licht of Wietenburgh, Germany, by Rev. W. D. Buckelew.

2986. Aug 30, Kingston, at the 2nd Methodist Episcopal Church, Mr. Howard Joy to Miss Sibil Link, both of Saugerties, by Rev. E. W. Knapp.

September 17, 1869

2987. Sep 15, at the home of the bride's father, Benjamin M. Gillespy to Miss Maria Carnright, both of the Town of Saugerties, by Rev. F. S. Barnum.

2988. Sep 10, Saugerties, Silas R. Brownell of New York to Sarah Stoddard, daughter of J. B. Sheffield of Saugerties, by Rev. John Gaston.

2989. Sep 11, Flatbush, John Coon to Miss Elizabeth Winchester, both of Saugerties, by Rev. Wm. B. Merritt.

October 1, 1869

2990. Sep 16, Bethel, Theophilus Green of Saugerties to Miss Jane Ann Davis of Lyonville, by Rev. R. L. Shurter.

2991. Sep 29, Pine Bush, Charles Coon of Glasco to Miss Emma Weeks of Kingston, by Rev. R. L. Shurter.

October 8, 1869

2992. Sep 16, Kingston, Mr. Samuel Sampson of Shokan to Miss Sarah Jane, daughter of Daniel Bradbury of Kingston, by Rev. Z. Grenell, Jr.

2993. Sep 29, Catskill, Joseph F. Joesbury to Miss Agnes Hall, both of Catskill, by Rev. Francis A. Horton.

October 15, 1869

2994. Oct 12, at the home of the bride's father, John Gillespy to Miss Almena, only daughter of Wm. Vandebogart, all of the Town of Saugerties, by Rev. R. L. Shurter.

2995. Oct 12, at the home of the bride's father, Benjamin S. Myer to Miss Alice, only daughter of Henry Freese, Esq., all of Kingston, by Rev. H. B. Holmes.

2996. Oct 14, at the home of the bride's father, Samuel J. Adams of Saugerties to Miss Emma, only daughter of Hon. John Maxwell of Malden, by Rev. C. W. Lyon.

2997. Oct 2, Glasco, at the home of the bride's mother, Mr. Michael E. Briody to Miss Adaline M. Whitaker, both of Glasco, by Rev. H. C. Longyear.

October 22, 1869

2998. Oct 13, Yonkers, Edward Duff to Miss Hattie, daughter of the late J. P. Foland, formerly of Saugerties, by Rev. Mr. Mudge.

October 29, 1869

2999. Oct 21, Asbury, Mr. Jacob Myer to Miss Margaret A. Dederick, both of High Falls, by Rev. C. W. Lyon.

3000. Oct 16, Prattsville, Col. Zadock Pratt to Susie A. Grim of Brooklyn, by Rev. Mr. Prout. "The venerable Colonel is in his 80th year. His bride is considerably younger, but old age is creeping o'er her."

November 5, 1869

3001. Oct, Mr. Marshall Snyder to Miss Martha Arnett, both of Saugerties, by Rev. F. S. Barnum. <October 24, 1869, records of the Saugerties United Methodist Church, ed.>

3002. Oct 28, John H. Kimble to Miss Sarah A. Myers, both of Saugerties, by Rev. F. S. Barnum.

3003. Oct 16, West Camp, Gustavus Betshult of High Falls to Miss Margaret D. Wirth of Quarryville, by Rev. D. Wert.

3004. Oct 28, West Camp, John Brink to Miss Christianna Magee, both of West Camp, by Rev. D. Wert.

3005. Oct 27, at the home of the bride's father, Hiram T. Winans to Miss Leah C. Hommel, daughter of Herman Hommel, Esq., all of the Town of Saugerties, by Rev. W. D. Buckelew.

3006. Oct 31, John Ovaldorf to Mrs. Maria Cole, daughter of P. H. Rightmyer, all of the Town of Saugerties, by Rev. W. D. Buckelew.

November 12, 1869

3007. Nov 4, William Delanoy to Mrs. Catharine A. Wait, both of Saugerties, by Rev. F. S. Barnum.

November 19, 1869

3008. Aug 28, Kiskatom, Adelbert Wolven to Sarah E. Scribner, both of Woodstock, by Rev. Wm. G. E. See.

3009. Sep 11, Kiskatom, Leonard Brockett to Martha A. Falk, both of Palenville, by Rev. Wm. G. E. See.

3010. Nov 3, Egbert Post of Saugerties to Mrs. Maria T. Landt of Catskill, by Rev. John W. Gorse.

3011. Oct 23, Athens, Rev. J. K. Wardle to Emma Saunders, by Rev. R. Wheatly.

November 26, 1869

3012. Nov 23, Saugerties, at Trinity Episcopal Church, Miss Matilda C. Kearney, daughter of the late John Watts Kearney, Esq. of Saugerties to Samuel Verplanck of Fishkill, Dutchess Co., by Rev. Dr. Robinson.

3013. Nov 11, at the home of the bride's father, Theodore F. Martin to Miss Kate, youngest daughter of Henry Abeel, all of Saugerties, by Rev. E. Chapman.

December 3, 1869

3014. Nov 25, at the home of the bride's parents, Mr. James Jones to Miss Margaret Lackey, both of Saugerties, by Rev. H. C. Longyear.

3015. Nov 30, at the home of the bride's parents, Mr. Thomas Williams Ball of Saugerties to Miss Mary A. Vandevoort of Woodstock, by Rev. H. C. Longyear.

3016. Nov 14, Glasco, at the Methodist Episcopal Church, Wm. Stewart of Poughkeepsie to Miss Rachel Brink of Glasco, by Rev. R. L. Shurter.

3017. Nov 23, Glasco, Mr. Lemuel A. Smith of Woodstock to Miss Syble Simmons of Glasco, by Rev. R. L. Shurter.

3018. Nov 20, Kingston, Chauncy Whitaker of Saugerties to Anna Vandemark of Stone Ridge, by Rev. Dr. Hoes.

December 17, 1869

3019. Nov 25, Rochester, at the home of the bride's father, John B. Moule to Lybelia A., daughter of James H. Westbrook, Esq., both of Rochester, by Rev. S. W. Strong.

3020. Nov 24, Port Jackson, at the Methodist Episcopal Church, Jerome Plass to Rachel, daughter of Benjamin Moule, both of Rochester, by Rev. F. Hamblin of Woodstock and Rev. E. H. W. Barden.

3021. Nov 30, Rochester, Valentine Davis to Mrs. Sarah C. Bunton, both of Rochester, by Rev. S. W. Strong.

3022. Nov 25, Shawangunk, Daniel D. Dubois of New Paltz to Jane Peters of Shawangunk, by Rev. Mr. Spalding.

3023. Nov 24, Walden, Benjamin Manny to Emma J. Thomas, both of Shawangunk, by Rev. E. E. Pinny.

3024. Nov 17, Stone Ridge, at the Reformed Church, Joseph De Graff of Kingston to Kate, daughter of Clinton Woolsey, Esq. of Stone Ridge, by Rev. W. W. Brush.

3025. Jul 5, Plattekill, Charles Lewis to Miss Harriet H. Gardner, both of the Town of Saugerties, by Rev. M. L. Schenck.

3026. Jul 28, Plattekill, Charles Edgar Gardner to Miss Alice Lewis, both of the Town of Saugerties, by Rev. M. L. Schenck.

3027. Jul 29, Plattekill, Peter Livingston, Jr. to Miss Eliza C. Mack, both of Saugerties, by Rev. M. L. Schenck.

3028. Aug 25, Plattekill, Levi Vredenbergh of Poughkeepsie to Miss Anna M. Terwilliger of Kingston, by Rev. M. L. Schenck.

3029. Oct 13, Plattekill, Calvin Burhans to Miss Emma Lawson, both of Kingston, by Rev. M. L. Schenck.

3030. Dec 9, Plattekill, Wellington Wallace to Miss Louisa Brink, both of Kingston, by Rev. M. L. Schenck.

3031. Dec 9, Plattekill, Christopher Mower to Miss Lizzie Wallace, both of Saugerties, by Rev. M. L. Schenck.

December 24, 1869

3032. Dec 18, Saugerties, Mr. Samuel Myers to Miss Mary C. Whitaker, both of Glasco, by Rev. H. C. Longyear.

December 31, 1869

3033. Dec 22, at the home of the bride's parents, Dr. M. H. Wygant to Kate S., daughter of F. H. Davis, Esq., all of Stone Ridge, by Rev. W. W. Brush and Rev. C. Palmer.

3034. Dec 25, John Henry Wolven to Mary Catharine Valk, both of West Saugerties, by Rev. Thomas Lape.

3035. Dec 8, North Haverstraw, at the home of the bride's father, Mr. Samuel F. Goldsmith of Glasco to Lavinia Brooks, by Rev. I. W. Cole.

January 7, 1870

3036. Dec 28, Alexander J. Johnson to Miss Elizabeth Smith, both of Saugerties, by Rev. M. L. Schenck.

3037. Dec 29, Jacob H. Bovee of Saugerties to Miss Sarah A. Brink of Kingston, by Rev. M. L. Schenck.

3038. Dec 29, Judson H. Herrick to Miss Margaret Ann France, both of Saugerties, by Rev. M. L. Schenck.

3039. Jan 1, Wellington Carle to Miss Frances Burhans, both of Saugerties, by Rev. M. L. Schenck.

3040. Dec 13, at the home of the bride's father, Mr. Benjamin Bear of West Camp to Miss Mary J. Funk of High Falls, by Rev. J. D. Wert.

3041. Jan 1, Saugerties, at the home of the bride's parents, Mr. William Hover of Madalin to Miss Mary Leonora Champlin of Saugerties, by Rev. Henry C. Longyear.

3042. Dec 27, Rondout, Henry W. Thomas to Louisa Hoornbeck, both of Rondout, by Rev. William H. Evans.

3043. Dec 15, West Hurley, William Snyder to Loretta Williams, both of West Hurley, by Rev. C. Blauvelt.

3044. Dec 22, West Hurley, Eugene L. Smith of New Brunswick, New Jersey to Mary E., daughter of A. C. Hull, MD, of Olive, by Rev. C. Blauvelt.

3045. Dec 23, West Hurley, Peter Rowe to Phebe Rowe, both of West Hurley, by Rev. C. Blauvelt.

3046. Dec 22, Woodstock, Mr. Artemas W. Mitchell of Brooklyn to Miss Adelaide Davis of Woodstock, by Rev. De Witt B. Wyckoff.

January 14, 1870

3047. Jan 12, at the home of the bride's father, George W. Washburn to Alicia A., eldest daughter of Mr. Wm. Maginnis, all of Glasco, by Rev. Wm. B. Merritt.

January 21, 1870

3048. Dec 27, Hudson City, New Jersey, Jeremiah Overbagh, Jr. to Mrs. Sarah B. Lane, both of Catskill, by Rev. A. R. Arndt.

3049. Jan 6, Oak Hill, Aaron R. Van Buren of Tannersville to Miss Sate V. Graham of Oak Hill, by Rev. M. Randall.

3050. Jan 6, Catskill, John W. Sax of Saugerties to Mrs. Celia A. Perkins of Catskill, by Rev. Z. N. Lewis.

3051. Jan 6, at the home of the bride's parents, Samuel Van Steenbergh to Silena, daughter of John H. France, all of West Hurley, by Rev. H. C. Earl.

3052. Jan 15, at the home of the bride's parents, Jacob Henry France of Hunter to Christina, only daughter of Samuel Schoonmaker, Jr. of West Saugerties, by Rev. W. D. Buckelew.

3053. Jan 17, Blue Mountain, Martin Phillips of Saugerties to Sarah Angeline Ploss of Unionville, by Rev. W. D. Buckelew.

3054. Jan 12, West Camp, at the parsonage, Mr. Luman J. Benn to Miss Ella Hardick, both of Catskill, by Rev. J. D. West.

January 28, 1870

3055. Jan 23, George Winter of Rondout to Celestina, daughter of Augustus Schoonmaker, Esq. of Kingston, by Rev. Dr. Hoes.

3056. Jan 19, Kingston, Charles D. Capin to Maria E. Huyck, both of Saugerties, by Rev. Dr. Hoes.

3057. Jan 18, Hudson, Edwin Sickles of Coeymans to Miss Emma Derby of Saugerties, by Rev. Mr. Wheatley.

3058. Jan 12, Palenville, Cornelius Dubois of Shokan to Addie J. Goodwin of Palenville, by Rev. Wm. G. E. See.

February 4, 1870

3059. Jan 29, at the home of the bride's parents, Mr. Alfred J. Wilson to Miss M. Agatha Griffis, formerly of Saugerties, both of Poughkeepsie, by Rev. Wm. C. Smith.

3060. Jan 30, at the home of George W. Lasher, John R. Lasher to Miss Rebecca Ann Yerry, by Rev. H. Wheeler.

February 11, 1870

3061. Feb 3, Kingston, Nathaniel Winthrop Starr to Eliza Elmendorf Tappen, both of Kingston, by Rev. C. H. Stitt.

February 25, 1870

3062. Feb 19, Blue Mountain, at the parsonage, John K. Wolven of High Woods to Harriet E. Dewitt of New Paltz, by Rev. William D. Buckelew.

March 25, 1870

3063. Mar 16, at the home of the bride's father, Thomas Kidd to Isabella, daughter of Robert Fitzsimmons, both of Glenerie, by Rev. Wm. B. Merritt.

3064. Mar 15, Kingston, at the home of the bride's parents, John Douglas of Rondout to Annie, daughter of Daniel Rradbury, <sic> by Rev. Z. Grenell, Jr.

April 1, 1870

3065. Mar 30, New York City, at the Prescott House, Mr. Benj. Eiseman of Memphis, Tenn. to Miss Matie Butzel of Saugerties, by Rev. Dr. Einhorn.

3066. Mar 16, Salt Lake City, in the presence of the Saints, Elder Brigham Young to Mrs. J. R. Martin, Miss L. M. Pendergast, Mrs. R. M. Jenickson, Miss Susie P. Cleveland and Miss Emily P. Martin, all of the County of Berks, England. (no cards)

April 8, 1870

3067. Mar 24, Hudson, William Joesbury of Catskill to Miss Mary M. Plumb of Hudson, by Rev. J. K. Wardle, D. D.

April 15, 1870

3068. Undated, Westfield, Mass., at the home of the bride's father, Asa G. W. Smith, formerly of Kingston to Fannie L., daughter of Sidney Birge, by Rev. Mr. Hopkins.

April 22, 1870

3069. Apr 4, Catskill, Ambrose H. Gardner to Miss Nettie J. Hardwick, both of Catskill, by Rev. Z. N. Lewis.

May 20, 1870

3070. May 15, Saugerties, Marvin J. Sutton of Plattekill to Angeline Sinzepaugh of Glasco, by Justice Samuel Merclean.

May 27, 1870

3071. May 23, at the home of the bride's father, Mr. Martin Terwilliger to Miss M. Elizabeth; Mr. Ezra Carnright to Miss Clara J. and Mr. Alfred Teetsel to Miss M. Alice, daughters of John Maines, Esq., of Saugerties, by Rev. D. W. C. Van Gaasbeek.

3072. May 24, Saugerties, Mr. Wm. V. S. Beekman to Sarah M., daughter of P. T. B. Ten Eyck, Esq., by Rev. J. B. Thompson.

3073. Apr 28, Delhi, at St. John's Church, Newton Fiero, Esq. of Saugerties to Jennie Mc Call, niece of Alexander Shaw, Esq. of Delhi, by Rev. Joseph Richey.

June 3, 1870

3074. May 31, West Camp, Mr. James Hansen of Saugerties to Miss Amanda Shultus of West Camp, by Rev. Wm. W. Emerick.

3075. May 30, Saugerties, James Fiero of Malden to Miss Emma C. Stead of Acra, Greene Co., by Egbert Whitaker, Esq. at his office.

June 10, 1870

3076. May 24, Forest, Ill., T. J. Kerr to Miss Libbie Hoyt, formerly of Saugerties, by Rev. John P. Mitchell.

3077. Jun 1, Kingston, at the home of the bride's parents, Mr. Dewitt R. Myers to Miss Jennie Vernal, by Rev. Z. Grenell, Jr.

June 17, 1870

3078. Jun 9, Kingston, at St. John's Episcopal Church, Mr. John P. Bonesteel to Miss Julia, daughter of Robert I. Colfax, both of New York City, by Rev. F. M. Mc Allister.

June 24, 1870

3079. Jun 15, at the home of L. H. Osterhoudt in Flatbush, Silas A. Davis of Kingston to Mary A. Elwyn of Woodstock, by Rev. Wm. B. Merritt.

July 8, 1870

3080. Jun 9, Plattekill, Mr. Irwin Gaddis to Miss Annie Burhans, both of Plattekill, by Rev. M. L. Schenck.

July 22, 1870

3081. Jul 5, Kiskatom, at the home of Mr. Geo. Fisher, Mr. Oscar H. Morey of Catskill to Miss Matilda E. Fisher of Saugerties, by Rev. Wm. G. E. See.

August 12, 1870

3082. Aug 6, at the home of the bride's parents, Mr. Wm. H. Eggleston to Miss Emma Jane Myers, both of Saugerties, by Rev. H. C. Longyear.

August 26, 1870

3083. Aug 16, Saugerties, at the Phoenix Hotel, Mr. Egbert Humphrey of Kingston to Miss Everett of West Hurley, by Rev. John B. Thompson.

3084. Aug 11, Flatbush, at the parsonage, Hiram Brink of Pine Bush to Rachel A., daughter of Benjamin Burhans of Flatbush, by Rev. Wm. V. Merritt.

September 2, 1870

3085. Aug 21, Saugerties, at the Exchange Hotel, William Secord to Eliza Doney, both of Catskill, by Rev. D. W. C. Van Gaasbeck.

September 9, 1870

3086. Oct 21, Albany, at the Ash Grove parsonage, Mr. Edwin Nelligar to Miss Alida A., eldest daughter of Mr. Don Albert French, formerly of Saugerties, by Rev. S. M'Chesney

3087. Sep 1, at the home of the bride's parents, Alexander Hommel of Malden to Miss Sarah Alice Decker of Saugerties, by Rev. H. C. Longyear.

3088. Aug 28, Conrad Staegear to Mary C. Kugelman, both of Saugerties, by Rev. D. W. C. Van Gaasbeck.

3089. Sep 1, J. J. Bahret to Sarah T. Allard, both of Saugerties, by Rev. D. W. C. Van Gaasbeck.

September 16, 1870

3090. Aug 24, West Hurley, at the home of the bride's parents, Mr. Miles Holden of Saugerties to Eliza Sax of West Hurley, by Rev. H. C. Earl.

3091. Sep 4, Daniel R. Johnson to Miss Maria Shader, both of Kingston, by Rev. G. W. Knapp.

3092. Sep 7, at the home of the bride's father, Robert Wesley Sinsabaugh to Elizabeth Ann, daughter of Philip H. Plass, all of Glasco, by Rev. Wm. B. Merritt.

September 23, 1870

3093. Sep 15, Glasco, at the Methodist Episcopal Church, Lewis S. Hommel to Isabella Wolven, both of Glasco, by Rev. J. H. Wood.

3094. Sep 1, Blue Mountain, at the parsonage, Eugene Peck of Saugerties to Louisa J. Bishop, by Rev. W. D. Buckelew.

3095. Sep 18, Blue Mountain, at the parsonage, Elvira Brown of Williamsburg to Henry Barton of Palenville, by Rev. W. D. Buckelew.

3096. Sep 15, Howard W. Johnson to Addie H. Tompkins, both of Woodstock, by Rev. Fletcher Hamblin.

3097. Sep 17, at the home of the clergyman, Mr. Ephraim H. Newkirk of Kingston to Miss Rachel E. Delmater of Shokan, by Rev. H. C. Longyear.

September 30, 1870

3098. Sep 17, Charles H. French to Anna Bell Mack, both of Saugerties, by Rev. D. W. C. Van Gaasbeck.

3099. Sep 22, Kingston, Oliver Lacuss, about 25, eloped with Mrs. Fredrick Wilks, aged 50. She leaves a husband and two children.

3100. Sep 20, Rondout, at St. Mary's Church, Mr. John O'Reilly to Miss Cecilia Murphy.

October 7, 1870

3101. Oct 5, Saugerties, at the Reformed Church, Ezra P. Hunt, MD, of New Jersey to Miss Emma Reeves of Saugerties, by Rev. J. B. Thompson, D. D., assisted by the bridegroom's father.

3102. Sep 14, Catskill, Mr. J. W. Kelly to Miss Lorinda, daughter of Jacob Van Hoesen, by Rev. G. A. Howard, D. D.

3103. Sep 29, Woodstock, Mr. Madison H. Shultis to Miss Isabel Stone, both of Woodstock, by Rev. F. Hamblin.

3104. Sep 27, Kingston, Mr. Charles B. Mathis of Toms River, New Jersey to Amelia A., daughter of Mr. E. W. Styles of Kingston, by Rev. Z. Grenell, Jr.

October 14, 1870

3105. Oct 8, Blue Mountain, at the parsonage, Jacob Mower to Eleanor J., daughter of Peter Young, all of the Town of Saugerties, by Rev. W. D. Buckelew.

3106. Oct 5, Silver wedding anniversary of Mr. and Mrs. Nelson Brainard.

October 21, 1870

3107. Oct 16, at the home of the bride's father, Benjamin S. Teetsel to Miss Sarah Jane Hawley, both of Quarryville, by Rev. A. F. Selleck.

October 28, 1870

3108. Oct 25, Saugerties, Mr. George Van Loan to Miss Kitty Cole, both of Athens, by Rev. Joseph Danielson.

3109. Oct 19, Woodstock, Francis M. Hoyt to Miss Harriet J. Staples, both of Woodstock, by Rev. F. Hamblin.

3110. Oct 18, Catskill, Isaac P. Hendricks of Kingston to Sallie Moore of Catskill, by Rev. Francis A. Horton. <In the edition of Nov 11, the name is Moors, ed.>

3111. Oct 13, James B. Olney to Julia P., youngest daughter of the late Judge Malbone Watson, by Rev. G. A. Howard, D. D.

3112. Oct 22, Saugerties, A. J. Bartlett to C. M. Fiero, both of Quarryville, by Rev. D. W. C. Van Gaasbeek.

November 4, 1870

3113. Oct 22, Saugerties, Charles Dubois to Miss Emma J. Mc Donald, both of Saugerties, by Rev. H. C. Longyear.

3114. Oct 26, Woodstock, Ira Winne to Cornelia A. Lewis, both of Woodstock, by Rev. F. Hamblin.

November 11, 1870

3115. Nov 3, Flatbush, at the parsonage, Albert Kittell of Saugerties to Mary A. Stewart of Glenerie, by Rev. Wm. B. Merritt.

November 18, 1870

3116. Nov 13, Glasco, Wellington Porter, Esq. to Nellie, only daughter of J. S. Travis, MD, all of Glasco, by Rev. J. H. Wood.

3117. Nov 9, Blue Mountain, at the parsonage, B. Franklin Longendyke to Mary E., daughter of Benjamin Jones, all of the Town of Saugerties, by Rev. W. D. Buckelew.

3118. Nov 9, Jefferson, Joseph Cornell to Miss Ella M., daughter of A. J. Grant, Esq.

3119. Nov 9, Jefferson, Simon Wood of Rondout to Miss Ettie Cornell of Catskill.

3120. Nov 10, Kiskatom, Jeremiah Linzey to Miss Belle Winans, both of Kiskatom.

3121. Nov 3, New York City, Theodore B. Beach to Miss Ruth C. Cleveland, both of Catskill.

3122. Oct 19, F. Goodman Bellows to Miss Isabella Cobb, both of Catskill.

November 25, 1870

3123. Nov 19, Blue Mountain, Jerome A. Burger of Palenville to Lucy A. Hummel of Hunter, by Rev. W. D. Buckelew.

3124. Nov 3, William D. L. Montanye, MD, of Rondout to Miss Anna De Witt, eldest daughter of C. C. Smith, Esq. of Kingston.

3125. Nov 13, Kingston, John E. Folant to Miss Ida Houghtalin, both of Kingston.

December 2, 1870

3126. Nov 26, Saugerties, at the Baptist parsonage, Mr. John Hofmiester of Saugerties to Miss Mary Miller of Glasco, by Rev. H. C. Longyear.

3127. Nov 23, Kingston, Isaac D. L. Montanye to Miss Maria Cole, both of Kingston,

3128. Nov 23, Batavia, at the home of the bride's father, Geo. W. Russell of Albany to Adelaide E., daughter of William Dewey, by Rev. George F. Plumer.

December 9, 1870

3129. Dec 1, at the Baptist parsonage, John A. Bunt to Miss Susan Mason, both of Hunter, Greene Co., by Rev. H. C. Longyear.

3130. Dec 8, at the Baptist parsonage, Mr. George H. Morgan to Miss Viola Sickels, both of Saugerties, by Rev. H. C. Longyear.

3131. Dec 1, Poughkeepsie, at St. Paul's Church, Edmund Hall Hart of Federal Point, FL to Isabella Montaine, daughter of Darius Howland, Esq., by Rev. S. H. Synott.

3132. Nov 27, Christopher Sickler to Emma Cole, both of Rondout, by Rev. Wm. A. Shaw.

3133. Dec 3, Saugerties, Mr. Chas. H. Benner to Miss Ella Caldwell, both of Brooklyn, by Dr. J. J. Robertson.

December 16, 1870

3134. Nov 28, Glasco, David Fries to Georgianna Turck, both of Flatbush, by Rev. J. H. Wood.

3135. Nov 28, Glasco, John T. Williams of Kingston to Anna Carroll of Glasco, by Rev. J. H. Wood.

3136. Dec 3, Cohoes, James Peter Russell of Saugerties to Sarah Thomas of Cohoes.

December 23, 1870

3137. Dec 14, West Camp, at the church, Charles Bear of West Camp to Miss Emma Martin of Catskill, by Rev. J. D. Wert, former pastor.

Bibliography

Blue Mt. Reformed Church, unpublished manuscript

Flatbush Reformed Church - Ulster County Genealogical Society Publication

Kiskatom Reformed Church, unpublished manuscript

Malden-Quarryville United Methodist Church, unpublished manuscript

Plattekill Reformed Church, Mt. Marion, unpublished manuscript

Saugerties United Methodist Church - from the church, Washington Ave. & Post St., Saugerties, NY 12477

St. Paul's Lutheran Church, West Camp - Kinship Publication, Arthur C. M. Kelly

Index

The numbers after the entries are abstract numbers not page numbers.

---, Seciley 533
AARRIGUES, James 478
ABBERFIELD, Joshua 1176
ABBEY, Henry L 2576
  Sarah C 1832 Stephen 1744
ABBY, Violette L 2977
ABEAL, Fanny 2954
ABEEL, Agnes W 1587
  Henry 3013 Kate 3013
  Lydiaett 2389
ABRAMS, Catharine D 1178
ACKEN, Margaret 844
ACKER, Ann Eliza 1455
  Edwin 2707 Emma 2780
  Jeannette 2231 John 879
  Mary Ophelia 1217
  Zachariah 1544
ACKERMAN, Benson F 998
  Mary Elizabeth 2327
ACKERT, Harriet C 930
  John S 2528 Lewis Wilson
  1472 Wm E 2303
ACKLEY, Jane C 1183
ADAMS, --- 539
  Catharine E 1686
  Chas H 673 Cuyler 673
  Egbert 673 George W 2951
  H 1442 Harriet E 1442
  Henry 673 Isabella C 1960
  John B 255 John E 1658
  John Q 427 John Quincey
  438 L B 2549 Louisa
  Catherine 438 Samuel 205
  Samuel J 2996 Wm 1089
  1686
ADEE, George 2407
ADELBERG, Reinhold 2188
AGAN, P H 289
AGIN, Sarah E 1718

AIKEN, Daniel 553
AKIN, Joel 161
AKLEY, Eliza Ann 1324
ALBARTIS, Capt 79
ALBERT, Elizabeth 546
  Fanning 242 699 Frank 699
  George Percival 242
  John S 2036 Mary 242 699
ALBERTSON, Martha J 2002
ALDEN, Mrs 223
ALDER, Conrad 283
ALDRICH, William 2887
ALLARD, Sarah T 3089
ALLCORN, John 990
ALLEN, B 805 Captain 351
  Edgar F 2738 Elizabeth 2734
  2744 John W 1007
  Wm F 191
ALLENDORF, C 2903
ALLIGER, John 1979
ALLISON, William A 1759
ALSDORF, Henry 2083
  Maria Jane 2429
AMY, Louisa 955
ANDERSON, --- 178
  Alfred 2625 Charles C 703
  Chas 2289 David 637
  Jansen H 2591 Joseph B
  1043 Loraine 1783 Martha
  2160 Nathan T 1783 R
  Harrison 1338 Robert I 1451
ANDREWS, Ann 444
  Edwin R 203 Elizabeth 2933
  Helen 2684 James 1348
ANDRUS, Henry 2921
ANGELL, Henry H B 2759
ANGEVINE, Euphemia 1232
ANNA, Santa 101
ANTHONY, M H 738

ANTHONY (continued)
　Mary E 2668
APPLETON, Julia
　Webster 529 Samuel 529
ARCHER, Judge 620
ARLAND, John 347
ARMSTRONG, --- 11
　Joseph 2963 W J 2455
ARNETT, Martha 3001
ARNOLD, Benjamin C
　1611 2937
ARNOTT, Mary Jane 2494
ARNST, Catherine 1477
　John 1477
ARTMAN, Benjamin 31
　Matilda 303
ASHLEY, Chester 540
ASTOR, John Jacob 474
　Wm B 474
ATKINS, Aaron 1760
　Hiram 1702 James 1253
　Jane 1838 Jonas F 1313
ATWATER, George
　Merwin 1037
AUBBELL, Peter 2105
AUCHMODY, Charlotte 1528
AUCHMOODY, Jeremiah
　1745
AUSTIN, Mary A 2497
AVERY, Annie 2742
　Elizabeth E 1707
　Margaret B 1592
AVIS, --- 302
AXAHELM, Louis 1497
BABCOCK, Anna R 2658
　Samuel 293 316 Wm 313
BACHE, Doctor 253
　Richard 508
BACKER, H W 2785

BACKER (continued)
　S Ransom 2443
BACKUS, Charles 1231
　Henrietta 1231 Susan 1066
BACON, Mary 653 Mr 476
BADEAU, James H 2201
BADFORD, Lieut 605
BADGLEY, Henrietta 1335
BAEBEL, Elizabeth 1365
BAGGS, John 47
BAGLEY, Stephen M 2895
BAHRET, J J 3089
BAILEY, Charles 1688
　Edward J 1330 Nancy 432
BAIRD, John P 2650
BAISDEN, John J 1192
BAKER, Almira 1874
　D O 151 Daniel 804 John H
　2974 Lucy M 1772 Rachel
　846 Richard 2225
BALBERAS, Col 260
BALDRAS, John Lucas 261
BALDWIN, A S 79
　Jacob H 1153 Riley 2705
BALEN, Jas 2043
BALL, Thomas Williams 3015
　William 584
BALLINGER, Horatio P 1327
BALLMEYER, Mr 115
BALTY, --- 189
BAMBERGER, Fanny 2442
　Theresa 2600
BANIN, --- 728
BANKER, Josephine 1444
BANKS, William W 1216
BARBER, Charles L 1908
　Henry I 1257 John C 1992
　John S 2813 Lottie 2577
　Lydia A 2279 Lyman 2577

BARBER (continued)
  Margaret A 2371
  Officer 606 Orilla A 1571
  Sarah C 1990 Widow 1908
  William H 521 Wm H 2371
BARBOUR, Mary E 2620
BARCLAY, Henry 369 468
BARCULO, Judge 509
BARHYDT, Mr 576
BARKER, Deborah L 2014
  Geo P 388 Hannah 2128
  Jesse 1916 John A G 2599
  Mary E 2785
  Rosa Viola 1916
BARLOW, Samuel 1314 1435
  1436 2143
BARNARD, Alanson 397
  Mrs 397
BARNES, --- 594 Annie Eliza
  2121 Wm L 2121
BARRELL, Charlotte 774
  Susan 2316 Theodore 122
  Thomas 774
BARRETT, Anne 2162
  Calvin 718
  Catharine Elizabeth 1467
BARRINGER, Ann E 933
  Jacob C 933 Julia 2566
  Mary E 2776
BARRITT, Eugene 2709
  Newby 2588
BARRY, Catherine 973
BARTHOLEMEW, Gitty
  Jane 1567
BARTHOLOMEW, Erastus
  1849
BARTLETT, A J 3112
  Andrew J 1663 Captain 351
BARTOL, Oliver 296

BARTON, George 2601
  Henry 3095
BARTOW, Oliver 296
BARTZ, Agnes 2131
BASCOM, C R 2177
BASSETT, Catharine 1573
BASTEN, Charlotte 949
  W F 2836
BATCHELDER, Calvin 654
BATES, Dr 422 Frances 1113
  James Y 1752
BATTELLE, Catherine
  Barclay 468
  Cornelius 468 1994
BAUMBUSH, Albert 1991
BAXTER, Lieut Col 272
  Norris 1481 Whitmore 1009
BEACH, --- 739 Theodore B
  3121 William T 985
BEAN, John 716
BEAR, Ann Catharine 1317
  Benjamin 3040 Charles 3137
  David 1478 Margaret 818
  Nelly 817
BEARE, Arietta 2811
  Philip J 2469
BEARNHEART, Charles 1423
BEARSS, Lucia M 2630
BEATTY, Ann Jane 38
  William 1690
BEAULLY, Mary Jane 1446
BECKER, David 2291 Eve
  1971 James E 2498 Levi
  1726 Stephen 2573
BECKWITH, Mrs 592
BEDFORD, E A 2583
  Rachel 1268
BEEBE, G 1514
BEEKER, Henry 1069

BEEKMAN, Anna Maria 526
    Cornelius 526 Henry 500
    Thomas 1458 Wm V S 3072
BEEMIS, Mary 2108
BEERS, James 1255
    James T 1381
BELL, Abram 2801 Andrew
    2895 D D 1996
    Edward Bigelow 1967
    Ella 2895 Emeline 1434
    Frederick 1850
    Harris 217 597 Hiram 2780
    John 1808 John S 660
    Lamantha 1808 Lydia Ann
    1789 Matilda 265
    Mrs 100 Nancy 660
    Peter E 1547
BELLOWS, F Goodman 3122
BEMIS, Lewis 1303
BEMISH, Richard 291
BEN, George Alvin 818
BENJAMIN, Lovejoy 1300
    Park 411
BENN, John O 2318
    Luman J 3054
BENNER, Chas H 3133
    John William 262
BENNET, Ann Eliza 876
    Catharine 1546 Catharine L
    1113 Maria 1334 Mr 532
    Rev Mr 332 William 1113
BENNETT, George 1733
BENSON, A 1675 A W 1335
    Jane Elizabeth 1040
BENT, Gov 72
BENTLEY, Isaac 2144
BENTON, Sarah 376
    Senator 376
BERGER, Anna 1266

BERRY, John 1729
BERT, Mary E 2344
BESEMER, Lurenna 1330
BESMER, Jane 1401
BEST, Herman 1201 James
    2690 Robert E 1945
    Sara A 2690
BETCHELL, Wm 473
BETSHULT, Gustavus 3003
BETTLEHEIM, Dr 785
BETTS, Castle 484
BETZ, John 284
BEYEA, Samuel 714
    William 714
BIGELOW, Edward 2897
    John 1000 Mary A 2897
    Mr 503
BILBOA, James 360
    Washington 360
BILL, Edward D 275
BILLINGS, Ethelbert L 2673
BINGHAM, J B 1508
    Sarah A 1508 Thomas 1433
BINGLE, Eli 866
BIRCHALL, William 897
BIRD, Matthew 1187
    Patience 2019
BIRGE, Ada B 1501
    Fannie L 3068 Sidney 3068
BIRKINS, Wm H 2699
BISHOP, Ephraim M 1788
    Ireney F 2894
    James H 1127 Judson 2795
    Leroy 2889 Louisa J 3094
    Moses E 857 Virgil H 2138
BISSELL, John 1794
BIVINS, John 2077
BLACK, E F 202
    Matthew A 794

BLACKSKIN, Indian 232
BLACKWELL, Charlotte
  2082 Chester 2680
  Edgar 2070 Harrison 2347
  Rachel 2001 Sarah E 2597
  Tobias 1962
BLAKE, Capt 248
  Wealthy A 856
BLAKESLEE, I A 602
BLANCHARD, Lorenzo
  R 1059
BLANSHAN, Abel 1775
  Charlotte 2864
BLAUVELT, Cornelius 2671
  Isaac A 642 Sarah 642
BLISH, Novatus 787
BLOODGOOD, Harriet 1243
  Neelly 2922
BLOOM, Anna Elvira 1601
  Chas 1535 Isaac 1601
BLOOMER, Charles
  Emery 512 R H 512
BLUE, Harriet E 2840
BLUMER, Julinna 1531
BOCK, John 2116
BODLEY, Cornelia 2801
  Daniel 152 Elizabeth 1940
  Jane 1509 Jane E 1201
  John A 1334 1766
  Sarah Amelia 1719
BOGARDUS, Margaret
  A 1441 Mary L 2477
  Romeyn 2010
BOGART, Charlotte 946
  Eliza Catharine 1593
  Jonathan 2215
BOGHT, Henry 2314
BOICE, Frank 2323
  Hiram M 2563 John 1045

BOICE (continued)
  Joseph M 2508 Mari L 2508
  Phoebe Ann 1194
BOIES, William 2157
BOIS, Elizabeth 1013
BOISE, John E 1780
  Margaret 1780
BOND, --- 277 Charles A 1934
  Julia E 1249
BONESTEEL, Celia A 1390
  Christina C 2870
  Eliza 2071 Harriet S 1541
  John P 3078 Lucas W 2343
  Robert G 2870
BONESTEELE, Emma R 1526
BONNER, Mary 1148
BOOKSTAVER, J L 463
  Jesse F 1208
BOOTH, Nathaniel 1600
  Thomas 1727
BORTHWICK, Harvey 354
BOSSARD, Wm D 2425
BOSTWICK, C Byron 1057
  Cornelia 1381 Hannah A
  1525 Jas L 2424
BOSWORTH, Paymaster 146
BOUCK, Elizabeth 1118
  Jacob F 1686
BOUGHTON, Hester C 1495
BOURNE, Rachel 712
BOUSE, Elizabeth 2882
BOUTON, Maggie E 2884
  N L 2739
BOVEE, George W 2417
  Jacob H 3037 Pliny 2465
BOW, Agnes 2411
BOWEN, Louise 2868
  M Helen 1871 Samuel 1871
BOWMAN, Captain 251

BOWMAN (continued)
  Edward 611 Jacob 334
BOWS, Fannie 2975
BOYCE, Helena E 2421
BOYD, Kate 2912 S G 2653
  Samuel 345
BOYLE, Catharine 1689
BOZEMAN, --- 192
BRABY, Wm 2175
BRACKLE, Catharine 1247
  Mary Eva 1248
BRADBURY, Annie 3064
  Daniel 2992 3064 Harriet
  985 Margaret 127 Samuel
  176 Samuel C 158
  Sarah Jane 2992
BRADLEY, Ambrose 2034
  Clark 994
BRADSHAW, Catharine 1369
  Geo H 1978
BRADSHOW, George H 1246
BRADT, Milton S 2489
BRADY, Mary E 2554
  Patrick 806 Thomas 321
BRAIDY, John 681
BRAINARD, Nelson 3106
  Thomas C 2508
BRAMAN, Adam 865
BRANDEMORE, Libbie 2867
BRANNEN, John C 1426
BRANT, Albert 2953
  Charles 1302 Watson 2483
BREADSTREET, Bridget
  1595
BREAKEY, Eliza 939
BREEDS, Kittie 2216
BREITENBEAKER,
  Edward 2760
BREKENRIDGE, Mr 177

BREMOND, Louisa 721
  Pierre D 721
BREMOUD, P D 635
BRENNAN, Harriet M
  A 2024
BRENNEN, Thomas 758
BRESHO, Elizabeth 2032
BREWER, Abram 1944
  Ann Frances 1944
  Elizabeth 105
BRIGHAM, Charles S 2149
  Elisha M 1474
  Theodore 2786
BRINCKERHOFF,
  Nicholas 1391
BRINK, A S 2468 Abraham D
  170 Alida A 2857 Andrew
  2882 Andrew J 197 Angeline
  2338 Ann Marie 854 Arietta
  1499 C P 2896 Catharine M
  2102 Catherine Ann 882
  Charles 2333 Christina C 920
  Christopher 1288
  Cornelius P 6 Coroner 30
  Edward 1004 Elizabeth 1291
  Emily J 2044 Henry 2981
  Herman 2129 Hiram 3084
  J D 369 396 Jacob 1673
  James 266 James D 198
  John 170 3004 Louisa 3030
  Maria 1307 Maria C 2381
  Marietta 2558 Martha L
  2469 Mary A 2686 2791
  Mary C 2717
  N De Myer 2717 Ozias 2834
  Peter H 1080 Rachel 3016
  Rachel Ann 307
  Rachel M 1972 Robert H
  1238 Sarah A 3037

BRINK (continued)
 Silas 2964 Thomas W 2815
 William K 1964 Wm F 2505
 Wm M 266 2397 2676
BRIODY, Michael E 2997
BRITT, Charlotte 1130
 George H 2778 Laura A
 2300 Nelly Ann 1033
 Philip 1921
BROADHEAD, Janette 1768
 R A 1104 Thomas C 2046
BROADSTREET, Mr 326
BROAS, Almira 1286
 William H 1346
BROCK, Harrison 1637
BROCKETT, Leonard 3009
BRODERICK, Mary A 2917
BRODHEAD, Ann H 1682
 Charles 198 369 396 463
 464 Harriet Romeyn 1037
 Henry D 2339 Hilah A 2395
 J Maria 2837 Jacob I 2141
 Jane 1767 Louis D 1126
 Rev Dr 1037 Richard 2837
 Solomon 1661
BRONK, Benjamin 840
BROOKS, Benjamin H 2714
 James 588 Lavinia 3035
 Paschal B 33
BROOME, Catharine 1524
BROSNAN, Daniel 595
BROW, John Henry 1106
BROWER, Eliza 926
 Ellen 1277 Harriet 358
 Ida Melissa 1529 Sarah
 Catharine 356 William 357
BROWN, --- 330 360
 Abraham 24
 Anna Matilda 1629 B 779

BROWN (continued)
 Benjamin 779 Charles 330
 Christina 2377 Elisha 1629
 Elvira 3095 Emily H 1111
 Emma 2516 Francis 1468
 Hamilton 603 J H 351
 Jacob 531 James 24
 John W 69 Joseph 608
 Katy 2843 Lieut 256
 Lillie J 2847 Lydia 24
 Rosalie 2136 Rosile 2850
 Samuel 24 William 1780
 William B 2851
BROWNELL, Silas R 2988
BRUCE, --- 580
BRUGMAN, Francis 283
BRUNDIGE, Henry W 515
BRUNNER, Charles 202
BRYAN, Esther A 992
BUCHART, Jacobena 1572
BUCK, Emma W 2307
BUCKHOUT, John A 16
 Maria P 16
BUCKLEY, Philip 1481
BUDD, Delakire 1744
 Mary 1182 Wesley 1801
BUDINGTON, E W 2642
 Edwin W 2901 Henry 2117
 Mary E 2642
BUEGEL, Heinrich 1364
BUELL, Christian 1428
BUFFUM, William 389
BULKLEY, Frederick C 1841
BULLAR, Samuel 1985
BULLARD, Mrs 539
BULLINGER, Ensey G 2839
BULLOCK, William H 1571
BULSON, Joseph S 1511
BUMSTEAD, Doctor 791

BUNDY, Melissa 1220
BUNT, Charles H 8 Harriet 8
  John A 3129
BUNTON, Sarah C 3021
BURBANK, William 11
BURCHARDT, John M 1073
BURDEN, Miss 1082
BUREAN, Ellen 1225
BURGE, Nelson 2259
BURGER, Cornelia Ann 1241
  Elizabeth 2697 Israel 1352
  Jerome A 3123 Martha A
  1924 Sarah 1679
BURGESS, Caroline M 443
  Maria Louisa 1842
  Thos J 1842
BURGHER, David 2585
  Helen 306 J Davis 2585
  Melissa 1805
BURGOYNE, --- 486
BURHANS, Abby
  Catherine 493 Abram P 1383
  Adelaide M 2347
  Albert 2761 Alexander 788
  1107 Ann Catharine 1161
  Annie 3080 Benjamin 3084
  Calvin 3029 Catharine Ann
  2027 Charles 1029 Cordelia
  2623 Cyrus 2484 Edward
  2027 Eliza M 1389 Emily
  2535 Ephraim 2027 Estella
  2775 Frances 3039 George
  1203 Helen Mariah 788
  Hezekiah S 2741 Isaac 2619
  James 493 Jane 1224 2413
  Jane E 1121 Joel 740
  John C 797 John Salisbury
  1623 Joseph 2347 Margaret
  A 60 Martha Jane 2276

BURHANS (continued)
  Mary C 1513 Mary E 2329
  2455 Mary Elizabeth 1901
  Morris 2299 Nelson 381
  392 Nelson H 850
  Rachel A 3084 Robert 2814
  Sarah A 2750 Sarah Amelia
  1071 William S 1294
  Wm P 1809
BURK, Mary Elizabeth 1440
  Sebree S 2617
BURKE, William 1099
BURKS, --- 331
BURNET, Reuben 861
BURNETT, Catharine H 981
  Henry 2007 John 2332
  Mary C 31 Miss 111
  Sophia 911 William J 111
BURNETTE, Catharine
  M 826
BURNS, William 1405
BURROWS, Margaret A 1936
BURTON, Marvin R 2873
  Melissa 2849 Susan 2962
  William H 2723
BURTT, Helen M 1147
  William 1147
BUSH, Catharine W 993
  Charles E 2776 Hannah C
  1426 John 421 1321 1363
  Mary J 1503 Rachel 2257
  Richard 2015 Sarah Jane
  1639 Solomon E 1305
  William H 13
BUTLER, Asa 1866 Gen 64
  Kate 2639
BUTTERS, Archibald 2632
  Ellen Starr 2632
  Mary C 2632

BUTTRICK, Silas H 985
BUTTS, Daniel 49
BUTZEL, Fannie 2956
  Flora 2213 Francis S 2956
  J L 2600 John L 2213 2442
  2708 Matie 3065 S Herman
  2708
CAGAN, James 1679
CAHART, Marx 1284
CAINE, Thomas 2164
CAL, Thomas 2888
CALDWELL, Ella 3133
CALKIN, Abram F 2748
  Lillie M 2748
CALKINS, Abm F 1707
  Charlotte M 2460 Judson H
  697 Sarah Ann 697
CALLAN, James 116
CAMBELL, Mary Ann 782
CAMERON, James 2197
CAMPBELL, Alexander 2422
  Archibald 1606
  Eliza H 1606 Mr 570
CANFIELD, Almon 942
  Eliza 44
CANINE, George W 2044
CANNON, Edward 806
CANOT, Capt 145
CANTINE, Anna 1732 Eliza
  M 2537 Hattie E 2675 N
  1732 Peter 1961 2675
CAPIN, Charles D 3056
CAPON, Dwight 295
CAREY, Mr 634
CARKNERD, Peter 786
CARLE, Almira 2481
  Chales 2090 David 2481
  2792 David H 2765 Emily
  2765

CARLE (continued)
  George F 2333 Harmon 2316
  Hezekiah 2481 Jane R 2792
  John I 1946 Laura 2473
  Levi 927 Martha 1946
  Mary Ellen 2333 P 1163
  Peter A 1404 Peter L 2073
  Rachel Ann 1239 Wellington
  3039 William 894
CARLEY, Robert W 1725
CARLING, Sarah 914
CARLISLE, --- 156
  Earl of 764
CARMAN, Elmira 1301
  Stephen 475
CARMICHAEL, Mary
  Elizabeth 998
  Midshipman 422
CARN, Aurinda 2523
  Jacob 1002 John 2523
  Mary S 2604
CARNEY, Amanda 2610
CARNRIGHT, Abraham 1852
  Cornelius Wynkoop 2435
  Era 3071 Joseph F 125
  Mahala 2936 Maria 2987
  Mary 2944
CARNWRIGHT, Caroline
  2647 Christian F 2562
  George E 2292
CARPENTER, Annie J 1734
  Dr 218 Mary E 871
  William H 1320
CARR, Helen M 2758
  Phebe 1433
CARRIER, Hannah J 1914
CARROL, Catharine 1922
  James 1692 John 1406
  Patrick 338

CARROLL, Anna 3135
  Mrs 324
CARSON, Elder 1809
  Thomas H 578
CARTER, Elizabeth C 1202
  Enoch E 2219 Robert 396
CARTWRIGHT, Martha
  E 2921
CARY, Sarah Louisa 1120
CASE, S Augusta 2185
CASHDOLLAR, Louis 969
  Wm H 2477
CASSEL, Joseph T 1161
CASSELL, John W 1756
  Joseph T 2312
CASSELS, Sarah P 1923
CASTLE, Jeremiah 1373
  John M 830 Susan Ann 1292
CATER, James 1990
CATHART, J Thomas 752
CATLIN, Amos P 2226
  Jane A 1778 Margaret 1507
  P 1778 Pierce 1507
CAULDWELL, Caroline 2065
  John 2065
CAVER, Christopher 1572
CAZER, Frederick L 2419
CHALER, Frederick 1341
CHALETT, Josephine 999
CHALK, Wm Carl 1088
CHALMERS, Rev Dr 133
  Wm H 2527
CHAMBERLAIN, Theodore
  G 1252
CHAMBERS, George 1973
  Stephen B 768
CHAMPLIN, Mary
  Leonora 3041
  Parthenia J 2649

CHAMPLIN (continued)
  Wm H 2649
CHANCY, Lieutenant 422
CHANDLER, Emeline 2643
CHANNING, Robert 302
CHAPEDO, Antonio 757
CHAPEDOR, Antonio 757
CHAPMAN, --- 708 Charles
  167 Coroner 696 Joseph 499
  Wm R 1169
CHAPPELL, Mr 757
CHASE, Caroline 2177
  Fanny 479 Gilbert 479
  Hannah Kitty 442
  Samuel 442 West 2177
CHATFIELD, Ira D 1893
  1895 William 314
CHILDS, Timothy 342
CHILTON, Bruce A 2676
CHIPMAN, Erastus D 2523
CHIPP, Amelia M 2898
  Howard 1090 James 419
  Jane 404 John 1896
  Joseph 404 Joseph Deyo
  2227 Warren 2898
CHIRITREE, Adaline 2664
CHRISTIAN, Henry 424
CHRISTIANA, Jemima
  K 1261
CHRISTIE, Col 12
CHURCH, Otis 843
CHURCHILL, Kate 1311
CILLEY, Mr 735
CLAPP, Asa 518
CLARK, Alice A 2096
  David 648 Edward 601
  Erastus Y 2589
  George 2279 Janet 1889
  Jared W 1546 John P 780

CLARK (continued)
  Joseph H 2748
  M Lewis 2185 Mr 94 344
  Robert 1889 S 33
  William 2263 Wm M 1736
CLARKE, Geo W 2042
  Merryweather 12
CLASEAIS, Caroline 1730
CLAY, C Strong 287 Henry 70
  Lieut Col 70 Mr 177 496
CLEARWATER, Charles
  H 1844
CLEVELAND, Ruth C 3121
  Susie P 3066
CLINTON, Dewitt 191
  George W 191 Jane 2427
CLIPFELL, J 279
CLUM, Alexander 937
  John W 2689
CLUMB, Zachariah B 2731
CLURE, Miss 677
CLUTE, Nicholas P 1471
COALE, Rachel A 2762
COBB, Isabella 3122 J M 229
COCKBURN, Annetta 1057
  James 776 John 1057
  Margaret Elizabeth 2125
  W A 2400 William 814 2125
CODDINGTON, Dubois 2408
  Elizabeth 1649
CODINGTON, John 1052
CODY, James 2449
COE, Lewis H 39
COGAN, Patrick 510
COGGESHALL, Eliza 234
  Mr 30 Samuel P 234 878
COGGSWELL, Marcus
  C 1412
COGSERLL, Daniel 712

COGSWEL, Mary Eliza 1106
COGSWILL, Augusta 2445
COHEN, Adolph 2956 B 208
COIBYLE, William 534
COLE, Abram 53 2896
  Alexander 386 Amanda E
  2113 C D W 2331
  Cornelius Alexander 1671
  Cornelius P 386
  Emma 3132 Geo W 2420
  Gitty 1726 Harriet 1956
  Jacob 1275 2849 James 1001
  John A 2216 2432
  John B 1181 John R 2391
  John W 2130 Joseph 1993
  Kitty 3108 Magdelena E
  1672 Maria 3006 3127
  Mary 1132 Mary Ann 1222
  Mary G 1452 Nelly Cath 800
  Norman 1977 Philena 2833
  Sarah C 2391 Thomas 408
  William P 905 1452 1672
COLEMAN, Elias 413
COLFAX, Julia 3078
  Robert I 3078
COLLAMORE, Mr 11
COLLET, Joshua Wallace 431
COLLIER, Edward A 2326
COLLIGAN, James T 2223
COLLINS, James 1694
COLLYER, Caroline 267
COLMITZ, George 923
COLVILL, John 528 550
  Lucy 528 550
COMFORT, Edwin L 2298
COMMAUR, Lambert 375
CONDGON, Hannibal 463
CONKLIN, Charles 1407
  David 1691 Francis 433

CONKLIN (continued)
  Hannah 801 Henry 871
  Mary G 1836 Susan E 1691
  William H 1359
CONNELLY, Mary 931
  Wm A 2655
CONNER, Mary Jane 1620
  Sarah E 2339
CONRAD, Christina 1819
  Nicholas 1819
CONSTABLE, Lucinda 1566
CONTANT, Gabriel 1648
  Mary E 1985
CONVERSE, Martha W 1641
CONWAY, Andrew J 1259
  Nelly E 2251
CONYES, Sanford 2713
COOK, Byron 1642 Charles
  1654 Conrad 1114 Cyrus
  2002 Elizabeth Ann 1642
  Ella 925 Emily 1802 Louiza
  M 1086 Margaret Ann 944
  Sarah 1796 William 110
COOKE, Jennett 2899
  Julia 2502 P St Geo 2502
  William 702 2925
COOLEY, Anthony 1082
  John E 2250 Thomas 1139
  William 1943
COON, Allen 2646 Benjamin
  M 2493 Cambridge 2270
  Charles 2991 Henry A 2363
  Jacob 2633 John 2989
  John A 1223 John F 2554
  John H 925 2224
  Marietta 1358
COONS, Delia 2504
  Henry W 2720 John 2665
  Stephen 1549

COOPER, Almira 2194
  Cornelia C 1072 David 600
  Egbert 767 Emeline 2814
  James M 1333 John 1072
  Josephine 2746
  Mathias 1435 Samuel 600
  William F 1869 Wm M 2194
CORL, Elthea 1484
CORLISS, C K 1856
CORNELL, Edwin 843
  Ettie 3119 Joseph 3118
  Mary A 809 Mary Augusta
  2569 Moses J 350 N H 1074
  Peter 809 Sarah B 2726
  Thomas 2569
CORNISH, Charles L 2591
  Maria N 2591
CORNWELL, Charles E 1064
COSMEN, Kate E 2500
COTTON, John 25
COUCH, --- 324
COUHOUDT, Margaret
  Ann 1320
COULTER, Margaret J 2209
COUNTRYMAN, Jacob 410
COURTNEY, Robert 1096
COURTRIGHT, Levi S 2143
COUSE, Catharine 2397
  William 2057
COUTANT, Albert K 2818
  Elias G 1265 Hannah 851
  James 1261 1922 James A
  1393 1394 William H 1368
COVELL, Dr 729
COVEY, Jennings J 2640
COVIRET, Susan 2291
COYKENDALL, Samuel
  D 2569
CRAFT, Abram 1607

CRAFT (continued)
  Hester J 2101 Margaret 1388
  Mary 1488 Sarah E 2383
CRAIG, Abraham 1997
  Charlotte 2357
  David G 1856 Isaac 1503
CRAMER, Hiram A 819
  Irena 1804 Peter 335
CRANSON, Col 272
CRAPSER, Lewis D 1875
CRAW, Henry L 2683
  Luie M 2683 Olive A 1663
CRAWFORD, Christina 299
  1475 E L 286 Jane W 1932
  Kate R 2330 Lucinda 355
  Samuel 2330 W H 322
  Watson 2688
CRAWLEY, James 880
CREIGHTON, Rev Dr 720
CRIPS, Jacob 948
CRISPELL, Abraham 1778
  Emeline 1533 Martin H 1015
  Mary Ann 1045 Peter 2003
  Sally C 1865
CRISTLE, Richard D 2030
CRITTENDEN, Mr 532
CROGHAN, Edward 97
CRONK, Ann 1143
CROOK, Almira E 1392
  Catharine D 1391 Peter 2257
  Sarah Helen 1658
CROSBY, E M 2836
CROSMAN, Russell H 2460
CROSS, John 779
CROSSBURN, Mariah 1219
CROSWELL, Mackay 163
  Sarah A 2931
CROWLEY, Edward 719
CROWTHER, Martha 1122

CROZIER, Elizabeth 1411
CRUM, Henry 2136
  Maria 2008
CRUMB, Malinda 1237
CRUMP, James 1207
CUDNEY, Artie 2955
CUMMINGS, Jane 2352
  John G 2658
CUNNINGHAM, George 885
  Mary E 2018
CUNYES, De Witt 2971
  Frederick W 1443
  Montgomery 2439
  Norman 2416
CURDES, Dora 2846
CURRY, Joseph 608
CURTIS, Julius A 2410
  Le Grand 2684 Mrs 655
  Stephen 321 Zipporah M 5
CURTISS, N T 1170
CUSHMAN, John P 726
DALLAS, George M 508
DANIEL, Mary E 1534
DANN, Amanda 1752
DARBY, John F 1563
  Mary E 1563
DARKLEY, Herman 947
DARLING, Mary 2820
  Sarah 2966
DARRETT, Charles W 979
DAVED, Wm P 2148
DAVENPORT, Solomon 1914
DAVI, James 806
DAVID, Catharine 704
DAVIS, --- 148 538
  Adelaide 3046 Anna K 2141
  Aurelia 1380 Belinda 816
  Calvin D 970 Charles 45
  Clark 2859 Donna M 2743

DAVIS (continued)
E D 33 Edgar 2447
Elijah 737 Eliza Ann 1126
Elizabeth 929 F H 3033
Frederick 1719 George 1344
1612 Harriet L 33 Henrietta
2534 Hiram W 2800
Horatio G 401 Isaac W 1263
J W 423 James H 2371
James W 1229 Jane 1290
Jane Ann 2990 Johanna Kerr
2581 John W 1072 Kate
2796 Kate M 2575 Kate S
3033 Katie 2536 Marquis D
L 2594 Mary 662 Mary Ann
1425 1803 Mary C 1748
Melissa 1300 Moses H 1343
Mr 331 Nathan 610 Olivia
Jane 1864 Phebe 2386
Professor 196 Rachel A 2932
Rachel Anna 2143 Richard
1318 Samuel Francis 423
Samuel W 1356 Sarah 1613
Sarah Ann 1883 Silas A 3079
Theodore R 2794 Valentine
3021 William 1627
DAVISON, Edward 1091
1586 George P 1987
Sophronia 1517
DAWALD, Burket 1394
DAWES, Thomas S 1048
DAWSON, John 595
DAY, Solomon 955
DAYTON, Morgan A 1818
DE GRAFF, Joseph 3024
DE LA MONTANYE,
Gertrude 2655
DE LAVERGNE, Robert
L 2606

DE LEON, Don Antonio 261
DE MONPENSIER, Duke 1
DE MYER, A S 2041
Alida Maria 2041
Henry M 1668 Sybil N 2369
DE PARIS, Count 465
DE PEW, Alonzo 2876
DE PUY, Elizabeth 1099
Hannah 902 Levi 1659
Wm H 1310
DE WITT, Abraham 765
Blandina 406 Charles D 2236
D M 2703 Elizabeth 90
Francis M 1315 Jacob L
1731 Jacob S M 1125
John C 406 Lydia 452
Moses E 452 Richard 2478
T E 2080 Ten Eyck 1320
1494 15901840
Thomas T 2590
DEAN, G 1665 George F 1833
Gilbert 1810 Hannah 2280
James A 2902 Lydia 2225
William 2280 2323 2782
DEAS, Fitz Allen 2282
Lavinia Randolph 2282
DECATUR, Stephen 273
DECKER, Abraham 803
Apollas 903 Benjamin F 1825
Cordelia 2729 Cornelius S
1711 D L 1489 Daniel 1526
Daniel D 874 Daniel L 1176
David 1950 Deborah 2092
Edgar 1929 Eliza Ann 2648
Elizabeth 1137 Elizabeth Ann
1950 Isaac 126 1337 Lucy A
2192 Lucy Maria 126 Mary 7
1137 1275 Mary M 2530
Moses 1430 Ozias S 2169

DECKER (continued)
  P M G 1137 Peter 7 306
  Rachel C 2515 Sarah 1332
  Sarah Alice 3087
  Sarah M 1200
DEDERICK, Alexander
  Wilson 1710 Catharine 2625
  Charles 524 Christina 2488
  Christina H 2550 George W
  1581 Josephine 2886 Leah
  2359 Margaret A 2999 Maria
  1814 Mary Ann 2517
  Matthew 2492 Peter 2426
  Reuben 2926 Sarah
  Catharine 1166 Sarah E 381
  392 William 1165
  William H 32
DEDRICK, Catherine 934
  William 1210
DEFOREST, Julia 2440
  Mary J 1793
DEGNON, Jeremiah 155
DEGRAFF, Casper 2126
  Richard E 2151
DEGRAW, Esther A 2266
DEGROFF, Harriet 1818
  James M 1867
DEITS, Frances S 2058
  William M 1782
DEITZ, Eliza Ann 1259
DELAMATER, Angeline 2184
  De Witt 1926
  Hardenbergh 2006
  Harvey 2827 John F 1397
  Peter 1712 William 2068
DELANEY, Joseph 2329
  Patrick 745
DELANOY, Annason 2328
  Anney 2844 Calvin 2513

DELANOY (continued)
  Catharine M 2309
  Edward 2798 Elizabeth 881
  Emily B 867 Fonda 2798
  Mary 2728 Sarah M 2437
  William 3007
DELHANTY, Mary Ann
  2665
DELILLEY, Theodore 2075
DELMATER, Rachel E 3097
DELONG, Mary L 2152
DEMAREST, John V 2634
  Marrietta 2634
DEMING, Deborah Ann 1506
  Elvira 1096 F G M 1096
DEMMING, F G 1633
  Maria Louisa 1633
DEMPSEY, Jane E 2172
DENMAN, Catharine 1947
DENNAGER, Maria 1771
DENNETT, Lafayette Mongo
  2370
DENNIS, George L 1672
  John P 1671 Phebe E 1671
DEPEW, Heman 1521
DEPRE, Michael 225
DEPUY, James S 2850
  Mary C 2851
DERBY, Emma 3057
  John 574 Margaret 1515
DERINGER, Philip 1587
DERRENBACHER, Kate
  2740
DESCH, William 1335
DEUEL, Malendea 1781
DEVALL, Sophia 2586
DEVINE, --- 576
DEVLIN, Mark 1274
DEVOE, Louisa 2025

DEWALL, Peter 2032
DEWEY, Adelaide E 3128
  Adijer 2534 Susan 578
  William 3128
DEWITT, Andrew 1017
  Catharine Anna 2619
  Harriet 1582 Harriet E 3062
  Henry 2529 Jacob H 1006
  John P 1683 Maria Abeel
  1702 Mary 1006 Matthew P
  917 Moses F 1056 Richard
  2619 Simeon P 110
  Ten Eyck 45 948 W C 1706
DEYO, Catharine 1904
  Charles W 2803 Christian I
  2088 Christina A 2887 E 988
  Eltinge T 2891 John C 1838
  Jonathan 1566 Julia Eleanor
  39 Mary A 1141 Philip A
  1156 Reuben 1141 Samuel
  Dubois 1629 Sarah 988
  William 1454
DIAL, A H 2958
DIAMOND, Emeline 1829
  Jacob 1829
DIBBLE, Charlotte E A 2292
  E L 715
DICK, Henry 403
  Henry Reuben 403
DICKERSON, Mary Ann 382
  393 Miss 1039 Wm L 200
DICKINSON, Lt Col 79 272
  Wm L 219
DIECHLOOF, Louisa 997
DIER, Peter 842 Susan 841
DIETZ, Adaline 2909
  Philip Henry 1272
DILE, Albert 2962
DILKS, --- 214

DILKS (continued)
  Rebecca J 1007
DIMSEY, Sarah Jane 40
DINGER, Louisa 1314
DINGEY, William B 1112
DIVINE, Joel 566 760 789
DOBBS, Loretta 13
DODD, Caroline E 49
  Lewis 49
DODGE, James C 1822
DOILE, Josephine 2468
DOLL, George L 1908
  Jane P 1908 Kate 2682
DOLSON, Hacaliah P 1861
DONALDSON, Miss 2226
DONEY, Eliza 3085
DONIVAN, --- John 150
DORAN, William 29
DORMAN, Altamont J 1184
DORN, --- 686
DOUGERTY, Michael 11
DOUGLAS, John 3064
DOUGLASS, Sarah Ann 2103
  Thomas 746 Wm E 207
DOURN, John 2186
DOW, Jane 254
DOWLING, John C 203
DOWNER, Amey E 2007
DOXTADER, Albert A 2789
DOYLE, Eliza 2877
DOYSRADT, Francis M 2087
DRAKE, Wm Henry 2154
DRESSEL, Amelia H A 2476
  George 382 393
DREW, Mr 432
DROMGOOLE, Gen 129
DRUM, Lydia Ann 1260
DRUMMER, Mr 779
DRUMMOND, Widow 66

DRUSE, Stuart 2399
DU BOIS, Jennie A 2853
  John W 988
DU MONT, Van Gasbeck 446
DUBOIS, Abram C 1129
  Albert 268 Andrew 42
  Anson 1094 2021
  Arietta 1637 Carrie 2761
  Catharine 847 1504
  Charles 3113 Cornelia B
  1584 Cornelius 3058
  Daniel D 3022 Delia 1548
  Elijah 2576 Elizabeth L 1242
  Emily A 2434 George W
  2700 H 859 Hermon W 2923
  Isaac 2094 J W 2804 James 4
  621 James S 2743 Jane 1527
  Jane D 1129 Jeanette 1976
  John 2001 John W 42
  Judith M 1052 Lambert J
  2880 Lefever 2392 Lorenzo
  2451 Lucy A 941 Madgalen
  42 Magdalen 41 Maria 1664
  Mary A 2958 Mary I 2392
  Mary L 2576 Mrs 482
  Mynders 1958 Peter 1071
  2817 Peter D 50 Priscilla
  Ann 2393 Rebecca 2087
  2163 Richard 482 1091
  Robert W 2966 Samuel 41
  Sarah 2412 Sarah A 2399
  Sarah Ann 848 Sarah
  Elizabeth 415 Sarah J 2548
  Wilhelmus 552 William 300
  William A 1705
  Wm B B 2084
DUBOISE, Theodore 1033
DUCK, Daniel 750
DUDLEY, Enos 491

DUFF, Edward 2998
DUGGER, Mr 129
DUMOND, Elizabeth Ann
  1055 James 1273 James M
  1862 Jane A 548 Mary 1827
DUMONT, J F 1476
  Peter 1453 Rebecca 945
DUNAKIN, Charles A 2685
DUNCAN, Jane 623
DUNCKEL, Elijah 593
DUNCOMBE, Catherine 2490
DUNIGAN, Sarah Mariah
  1386
DUNN, Catharine 2057
  Edward 208 George W 1047
  James C 693 Judge 583
  Julia A 1998 Owen 693
DUNNEGAN, Michael 1421
DUNWOODIE, Rosina 866
DUPUY, R W 2103
DURAND, Augusta 1653
DURHAM, George W 2052
DUSENBERY, Henrietta 2104
DUSTAN, Captain 11
DUTCHER, Catharine 1866
  Sarah E 965
DUTEE, Augustus 652
DYLE, Cornelia Emeline 1430
  Elizabeth 2155
DYMOND, Arletta C B 1740
EAGER, Mr 173
EAKINS, Sarah J 2819
EARING, Edward 2093
EASTERLY, Edgar 18
  Martin 18
EASTGATE, Anna 1769
EBLE, David 1493
ECKED, Henry 1098
ECKERT, Daniel 945

ECKERT (continued)
  Elizabeth 2147 Frederick 1294 Gordon 2719 Hannah 977 Isaac D 848 Isaac D P 1865 Isadore 2485 Jane Eliza 1349 Mahala 2720 S Elma 2949 Sarah A 1015 Sarah Ann 1288 Sarah D 2248 Thompson 1940 William H 2597
ECKLER, Catharine A 2212
  George 1806 Mary A 962
EDGE, John T 2411
EDGERLY, Augusta A 2674
EDMONDS, Benjamin 1122
  Charles L 2038 J A 2038 Judge 760
EDMONDSON, Major 256
EDWARDS, --- 221
  Esabella 2727 H P 182 Hon Mr 182 Ogden 182 Ogden E 551 Pierpont 182 Sarah A 2336
EGAN, Emeline 2165
  W H 2165
EGENT, Catherine 1012
EGGER, Martina 852
EGGLESTON, Major 2084
  Mary C 2084 Wm H 3082
EGLESTON, Lucy 462
  Major 462
EGNER, Lewis 1570
EIGHMEY, David B 2793
  Ferris W 2454 Louiza 1630
EISEMAN, Benj 3065
ELDRIDGE, Alford 2537
  Charles S 1328
ELLIFISIN, John 1133
ELLINGER, John A 986

ELLIOT, Eliza 1142
ELLIOTT, Horace A 1296
  John 324 Oscar 2809 Sarah Jane 2809
ELLIS, Hanna 1599
ELLSWORTH, Isaac 1256
  Oliver 2944
ELMENDORF, Anna E 2127
  Cornelius 946
  Cornelius I 934 Cyrus 984 Edgar 1757 George 1311 2485 Gertrude Emma 2242 Jacob H 274 James 1244 Jas H 1566 John 443 2028 John L 1552 Maria 2362 Mary V 1757 Sarah Ann 1468 Theodore 661
ELMENDORPH, Jacob P 1536 Mary L 1536
ELSWORTH, A 2240
  Ann 1840
ELTING, Andrew 2693
  Blandina 917 Carrie 2250 Chas Brodhead 1522 Clarissa 2247 Derrick W 1387 Eliza 1032 Elizabeth 2161 Jacob B 494 John H 914 L 1276 Margaret D B 1387 Maria Catharine 1722 Phebe Jane 1415 Sarah Ann 1522 Sarah M 2122
ELTINGE, Cornelia 2891
  Derrick W 2891 Frances M 2208 Gertrude M 987 R 987
ELWYN, Alexander H 1220
  Eliza 2942 Jane C 2701 Mary A 3079 Selina 2202
EMBREE, John 647
  Maria Jane 1400

EMBREE (continued)
  Richard 2029 Simon 1667
EMERICK, Anna 1762
  Joshua 1035 Maria M 2056
  Peter 1118 1762
EMORY, Robert 569
ENDERLY, Mary E 2286
ENEST, Mary Jane 1472
ENGLISH, Charles S 906
  John D 1293 Julia I 1929
ENNEST, Mary 2094
ENNIS, Susan 1463
ENNIST, Edward B 2870
  Mary 1867 Mary E 1044
  Sarah Louisa 1868
ENOE, Charles E 1347
ENSIGN, Martha A 1537
EPENHAUT, John 1913
ERVIN, James 496
EVANS, Alexander 1523
  Edward W 1306 James S
  1006 Julia A 1417 Lieut 173
EVARLS, Maria 1436
EVERETT, A H 276
  Alexander H 657 Hiram H
  2139 John 2909 John S 356
  Mary 2612 Miss 3083 T H
  2330 Wm M 2359
EVERITT, George Joseph
  1445
EVERSON, Anthony 1787
  Emily 1787 George 2358
  Harriet A 2739
  Jefferson 2153
EVERTSON, Sylvester 1040
EVORY, Alfred J 1249
EWING, Robert 751
EYRE, Ald 208
FAGEN, Michael 2784

FAILESS, Eliza 1854 T 1854
FAIRCHILD, James H 1258
  Kate E 2055 Robert 868
FAIRFIELD, Senator 344
FALK, Christina J 1554
  Martha A 3009
FALLER, Anna 2467
FARNEY, Christian Charles
  821
FARRINGTON, Walter 2009
FAUROT, Wm S 2045
FAY, E 1157
  Susan Mary 1157
FEATHERLY, --- 477
FEATHERSTON, Sarah F
  2189
FELEANS, Sarah A 2503
FELLOWS, Lewis 630
FELTER, Ann I 266
  Anna M 1234 Cornelia 2624
  Elijah 2763 Henry 2541
  Jane M 1134 Lucinda H
  1136 Peter P 1234
  Sybil Maria 1826
FELTS, Sarah A 1412
FENWICK, Charles P 2727
  John E 907
FERGUSON, Amos B 1665
  Mary E 2049 Wm B 2429
FERRAL, J 606
FERRIS, Charles G 667
  Susan 1704
FICKETT, Joseph 2253
FIELD, Caroline E 490
  Chas F 1887
  Elizabeth 907 Ellen 2190
  John 798 907 John H 1912
  Maria 798 O 798
FIELDS, Elias 1569

FIERO, Adaline Elvira 2285
  C M 3112 Christian 892
  Christian C 908
  Christopher 1223 1587
  Elizabeth Elnora 2069
  James 3075 Jane Ann 888
  John 1024 Judson C 1076
  Mary Elizabeth 892 2175
  Mary M 2443 Mr 2398
  Newton 3073 Peter 1174
  S 2170 William 1372
FILE, Adam 1511
  Mary C 1511
FILKINS, Maria L 1823
FINGER, Adam 1074
  Amanda 2268 Bryan 1195
  Cornelia 2646 George 2288
  H L 2605 Harriet E 2755
  Henry L 884 Maria 1074
  Nelson 1416 Phineas 2550
  Robert 2545 Sarah B 2978
  Sarah C 2588
FINK, --- 68
FINKLE, George I 506
FINLEY, Jane 972
  Margaret 1199 Richard 1199
  Robert 1669 Sarah M 989
  Wm 1545
FINNEY, Elizabeth D 1994
  William 1994
FISH, Alexander 175
  Joseph 449 Lorenzo 1594
  Mary Jane 1305
FISHER, Albert C 1097
  Geo 3081 Matilda E 3081
FISK, Charles W 2091
  Frances 1272
  Margaret C 1925
FITCH, Cornelia M 2826

FITCH (continued)
  Jonas 2131 Mary Ann 1692
FITZ, Isaac 11
FITZGERALD, Luke 2783
FITZPATRICK, Florence 128
  Francis 78
FITZSIMMONS, Isabella 3063
  Robert 2815 3063
  Sarah Ann 2815
FLANNERTY, John 241
FLATOW, Abraham 1903
FLEICHMAN, Rev Mr 766
FLEISHMAN, Yetta 2361
FLEMING, Kate 2093
  Robert 1555
FLEMMING, Hattie H 2237
  Mary 2238
FLETCHER, Madison 460
  Margaret 2256
FLOOD, H C 691
FLOWERS, Persillia 1631
  William 2641
FLYNN, --- 9 Michael 309
  Sarah 309
FOLAND, Hannah 1047
  Hattie 2998
  J P 335 783 840 880 883
  923 1013 2998 James R
  2174 John P 2308 Mary E
  2308 Peter 736 Philip H
  2519 Wm H 2519
FOLANT, John E 3125
  Wm H 2820
FORBES, James 301
  S Franklin 1793
FORD, Zelotus 58
FORDE, James 1614
FORROW, Marietta 1021
FORSYTH, Jane 2223

FOSBROOK, James 2838
FOSTEN, Catharine 1406
FOSTER, Titus 489
FOULKS, Mary C 1516
FOUTH, Sibella Margaret 1341
FOWKES, John 2189
FOWLER, Henry 2908
  James 2648 Milton A 2142
  Mrs 650 O G 2788
  Olive 2788 Thomas 916
FOWLEY, Thomas 147
FOX, --- 694 Elizabeth 1018
  Jane Maria 2260 Joseph C 1243 Mr 352 William 95
FRAIN, Michael 2495
FRALEY, Catharine 2677
FRANCE, Abraham M 1847
  Adam 23 Charlotte A M 1027 Eliza J 2679 Elizabeth C 1068 Elizabeth Newkirk 2090 Henry 2543 Irena 2166 Jacob Henry 3052 John H 3051 Margaret Ann 3038 Richard 820
  Sarah Margaret 1955
  Silena 3051 Stephen J 964
  Wilhelmus 665 Wm W 2679
FRANCIS, Paul 723
FRANK, Godfrey 2063
  Henry 1413
FRANKLIN, Benjamin 508 1816 Hiram 341
FRASER, Alice M 2974
FRASIER, James 1151
FRATSCHER, Lewis 1698
FRAZER, Margaret Jane 2770
  Michael 2770 Sarah 2930
FRAZIER, A 1374

FREAR, Josiah 1823
  Wm L 2982
FRECH, Emelie 2181
FREDENBERGH, William 1084
FREDERICK, John 455
FREEMAN, William 228
FREER, Abraham L 1376
  Catharine D B 2879
  Clarrissa 1245 Dinah M 1262
  Esther 1861 Garritt 1522
  George 1504 Harriet M 1899
  Henry D B 2879 Jane 1878
  Johannes J 2890 Maria R 1831 Nelly 1344 Nelson J 2583 Rachel H 2890 Richard 904 Susan 2204
FREESE, Alice 2995
  Henry 2995 John H 2364
FREEZE, James A 2556
FRELEIGH, Henry M 563
  Peter H 2236
FRELIGH, Abby 2435
  Adeline 2236 Benjamin M 1214 Catherine E 2835
  Jane Catharine 130 Jane M 937 John H 2350 2835
  Mary E 2350 Peter H 130
  Rachel 1070
  Samuel 625 2435
FRENCH, Alida A 3086
  Charles 11 Charles H 3098
  Don A 1968
  Don Albert 1003 3086
FRESTON, Mary Ann 1666
FREY, Christian 2691
FRIAR, John 1196
FRIES, Anthony 60
  David 3134 Henry 1224

FRIEZE, Josiah 2020
FRINE, Ellen 2263
FRITZ, Jacob 1747
FROST, Elizabeth 2431
FUEHS, Emanuel 870
FULLER, Abner H 1483
  Charles 102 Franklin 2567
  Henry 913
FULLMER, Augusta 2710
  C Isabel 2305 Harietta A I
  2589 John 2911
  Morris F 2321
FULMER, Margaret 1079
  Sarah J 2124
FULTON, Franklin 1568
  Robert 294
FUNK, Mary J 3040
FURMAN, Cordelia 1331
  Harriet A 915
FURRNBARGHER, John
  2372
GADDESS, Robert 1506
GADDIS, Irwin 3080
  Mary 2417
GAFFNEY, --- 535
GAHAIN, Catharine 1140
GALAWAY, Cornelia 2908
GALLAGHER, Peter S 2716
GALLUP, S M 2618
GALTON, Clark B 2647
GANS, Henrietta 2708
GANTT, Lieut 329
GARB, Catharine 2173
GARDENER, Jane 2821
  Mr 2652
GARDINER, --- 779
  Amanda Jane 1168
  Cornelia 125 Eugene 2202
  George 562 Hannah 1745

GARDINER (continued)
  James 1890 Joseph T 935
  Susan Ann 658
GARDNER, Alida 1238
  Ambrose H 3069 Catharine
  1085 Charles Edgar 3026
  David V 2518 Harriet Eliza
  1306 Harriet H 3025 Helen E
  2475 James S 2526
GARLAND, Helen A 2601
GARLING, Mary E 2735
GARRETSON, Benager 1420
GARRISON, David 1626
  Elizabeth 1626 John 1989
  John W 2852 Lydia Ann
  2572 Stephen 554
  William H 1013
GASKINE, Anna 1485
GASKING, George 1492
GASTON, E 441 Hiram 441
GATES, Theodore B 1175
GAUL, John 732
  Mary Jane 732
GAY, Edwin D 862
  Lizzie 2783 Rachael A 2702
  William Augustus 2487
GEDNEY, Thomas 11
GEE, U D 2128
GEILFUS, Christian 739
GELEATI, Col 260
GENNINGS, Edward 257
GENTHNER, Katie 2724
  Philip A 325
GEORGE, Samuel 254
GERMAN, Jeremiah 1980
GEROW, Daniel D 1910
GIBB, Mary 2970
GIBBS, Charles 2831
  Elizabeth 1019 Ellen 1459

GIBBS (continued)
　James L 216
GIFFORD, C H 1974
　George 839
GIHON, D W 695
GILBERT, G S 1452 Huldah
　M 1603 Joseph R 2342
GILDERSLEEVE, Jacob H
　2302
GILES, Gains H 1533
　Wm V 1301
GILLEN, Montgomery G 628
GILLESBY, Lavina S 2480
GILLESPIE, Richard 430
　W Scott 2862
GILLESPY, Benjamin M 2987
　Catherine 543 Jason 1773
　Job 271 John 1024 2994
　Martha 1024
GILLET, Cyntha J 1254
　Gilbert M 1340
　Louisa L 1684
GILLUM, Rutclias 2553
GILPATRICK, Charles 2853
GINNEL, Henry 2590
　Louise 2590
GLADMAN, --- 92
GLANTON, Wm A 113
GLASBEENER, Magdelena
　1706
GLEASON, Capt 683 George
　919 John 11 Sarah C 919
GLENNEY, J G 1026
GOETCHIES, T Colden 2237
GOETSCHIUS, Maria 862
GOETSHUIS, Frank 2631
GOLDSMITH, Emma J 2472
　Mary E 2769 Samuel F 3035
GOLENGER, John 152

GOODRICH, Henry W 523
GOODSELL, Hester 2509
GOODSIR, John 2406
GOODSON, Mary E 2083
GOODWIN, Addie J 3058
　James O 1938 James R 420
GOODYEAR, Mary 244
GORDEN, John 399
GORHAM, William 245
GORMAN, Major 70
GORSELINE, Wm H 2285
GORTON, Rebecca 1574
GOSLIN, --- 154 Hannah 1456
GOSS, Doctor 477
GOUGH, Martha 1966
GOULD, Anna E 2486
　Elizabeth 2271 John H 2822
GRAHAM, Elizabeth 1312
　Ellen 1280 G G 1280
　Lieut Col 272 Sate V 3049
GRANDON, James 1855
　Jenny A 1855
GRANT, A J 3118 Ella M
　3118 John K 1882 Lillis 1278
　Lizzie 1882 Virginia 2183
GRASSFIELD, John H 824
GRAVES, J W 735 Mr 2379
GRAY, Isaac N 2152
　Jonathan 1448 Margaret
　1362 Morgan 1070
GREELY, Margaret 2206
GREEN, Addie 1995
　Andrew M 2613 Ashbel 568
　Chancey 2544 Eigith M 1403
　Jeremiah 1384 Joel 915 John
　747 Mary 2525 Nancy E
　1424 Theophilus 2990
　Van Keuren 1019
GREENE, Albert P 2544

GREENWOOD, E 534
  William H 2441
GREGG, James G 536
GREGORY, Sarah Jane 2017
GREINER, Jacob 1824
GREVES, William 2414
GRICE, Caroline 2617
GRIEG, Ann 2401
GRIFFEN, Marenus W 1513
  Mary J 1611 Thomas T 1611
GRIFFIN, Angelica 811
  Charlotte 1017 D C 2252
  David 1146 Elizabeth C 2012
  Hannah 2061 Julia A 1965
GRIFFIS, M Agatha 3059
GRIFFITH, James 1610
GRIFFITHS, Isaac L 1079
  William H 258
GRIGGS, Ferdinand 2533
GRIM, Susie A 3000
GRIMES, James 1505
GRISWOLD, John A 1949
GROABER, Anna M 1464
  William 1464
GROOS, Abm S 2979
GROSSE, Frederick W 1740
GUDTHER, Henry G 180
GUERNSEY, Alonzo 350
GUIL MORE, Mary Ann 1432
GUILFUSS, Jacob J 966
  Jared M 2345
GUION, Esther P 1370
GULNACK, Alfred 2829
GULNICK, Caroline 1728
GUNN, Barbara 1652 Vincent
  H 302 William A 1774
GUNTHER, Adam 1632
GURLEY, --- 185
HABER, Anna Maria 1873

HABER (continued)
  Francis 1010 Rachael L 2518
HACKER, William H 1370
HACKETT, Elizabeth 1577
  Hugh 1411
HACKISON, M 1065
HACKSTAFF, J Lawrence 77
HADER, Lucinda 1907
HAFFORD, Margaret 2164
HAGADON, Stephen O 2317
HAGELL, Henry 769
HAGEMAN, Adrian 2410
  Maria 2410
HAINES, Daniel 431
  Harriet A 1376 Mary J 2692
HAINS, Benjamin 2572
HALCOTT, Charles L 2644
  John B 2900
HALE, Augustus W 1349
  Emma J 2730 Marvel 215
HALIWICK, Jane Ann 1651
HALL, Agnes 2993
  Andreas 669 Caroline 645
  Lydia C 1319
HALLET, Hannah 1340
HALLOCK, Hannah Ann 1963
  Thomas 1963
HALOWICK, John J 2686
HALSEY, Oliver 1453
  Sarah H 1453
HALWICK, George B 2639
  John 2051
HAM, Jonas 2668
HAMAR, Brigadier Gen 35
HAMILTON, Ann Eliza 1807
  Henry C 1965 John 2621
HAMLIN, Charles 91
  Hearzilla 2332 Mary E 1815
HAMMEL, Daniel 1498

HAMMOND, Isaac N 2807
  Kate 2478 Wm 2017
HANBRIDGE, Thomas 2733
HANFORD, Eliza 1756
  Malon 2679
HANNA, George 2637
  William 141
HANSEN, James 522 3074
HANSON, Charles 2948
  Mr 629
HAPPY, Frederick 2746
  Mary 849
HARDELY, --- 701
HARDENBERG, John H 2538
  Margaret 1020 Richard 1020
HARDENBERGH, Andrew D
  W 991
HARDENBURG, John J 2812
HARDENBURGH, Alida 557
  Daniel 1392 Elmira 889
  John D 557
HARDICK, Ella 3054
HARDIN, Col 70 173
HARDWICK, Nettie J 3069
HARDYMAN, Helen 1856
HARGRAVE, John 1925
  Robert 2058
HARGRAVES, James 2630
HARLOW, S Ralph 1871
  Samuel 1871
HARMONY, Benjamin 1078
HARNDEN, Amy 2232
HARNEY, Col 80
HARRICK, Ira Leonard 1185
HARRINGTON, --- 341
  Knowlton 502
HARRIS, --- 136 Elizabeth
  1176 Morgan L 2256
HARRISON, Eliza 2060

HARRISON (continued)
  William H 2357
HART, Edmund Hall 3131
  G A 2636 Mary B 1221
  Mary F 2790
HARTWIG, Henry 1209
HARVEY, James 2013
  Peter 2240 Sarah C 2414
  Sarah Helen 2433
HASBROUCK, Aaron 1696
  Abram 1542 Ann Eliza 1687
  Augustus 2661 Benjamin
  2586 Calvin 1116 2863
  Caroline 2179 Catharine 968
  Daniel 1461 Dubois 1116
  Emeline 384 395 Hattie M
  2863 Howard 1289 J 1816
  1817 J D 1943 1991 1992
  2131 Jansen 896 Johannis D
  1632 Josiah 1855 L B 1662
  Marietta 2587 Mary 1116
  1943 N J 2028 P S 1440
  Peter E 1687 1941 Philip S
  1332 Reuben D 1141
  Sarah A 2910 Tobias 564
HASKELL, Pilsbury S 589
HASLIN, Dr 11
HASTINGS, J 780
HASWELL, Samuel 1188
HATCH, Philura Adeline 835
  Warren 835
HATHAWAY, Charles 1517
  Geo W 123 William 2384
HATTEN, John 2649
HAUVER, Melinda 1890
  Wyan 838 Mary E 2693
HAUXHURST, Almira 2030
HAVENS, J W Harrison 1502
  Mr 520

HAVEY, Peter 2378
HAWLEY, Sarah Jane 3107
  Susan M 2496 Wm W 2496
HAWXHURST, Ruth Ann 1952
HAYES, Ann Elizabeth 2218
  Caroline 2038 Clarissa 1210
  Coroner 709M G 2038
  Martin G 2218 Olive 1209
  Wm H 1681
HAYNES, Catharine 1586
HAYS, Coroner 588 806
  Elizabeth 575 James 796
  Thomas 575
HEALD, Uretta 1809
HEALEY, Sarah 352
HEATH, Wm W 85
HEER, Rosie 1750
HEERMANCE, Benjamin 437
  Elizabeth 598 Russel Scouten
  666 Simon P 598 666
HEERMANS, Rachel 285
HEESIER, Wilson M 2161
HEIDENHEIMER, Sarah 1816
HEINGMANN, Charles August 864
HELMS, Catharine 1337
HEMPHILL, Charlotte 350
  John 350
HEMPSTEAD, Robert A 919
HEN, Joseph 1247
HENCHER, Mary E 2532
HENDERSON, Elizabeth 1125
  Hannah Jane 808 Lieut 456
HENDREN, Archibald 1182
HENDRICKS, B 471 Eliza
  Ann 1028 Isaac P 3110
  Jacob M 1564 James 22

HENDRICKS (continued)
  John 587 Martin 1030
  Nelly 921 Nelson 1447
  Peter 62 Philip 1359
  Rachel C 1359 Rebecca 62
  Sarah A 2062
HENDRICKSON, Katy Jane 1693
HENESY, Philip 2906
HENION, Dewitt 2961
  Elvina 2961 Hiram O 627
HENNESSY, James 104
HENOLD, George 224
HENRY, Herman 455
  Mary A 1023
HENSHEW, John R 267
HEPWORTH, John 624
HERALD, Robert 2280
HERBERT, Adelia F 2965
  Rosa A 2947
HERMANCE, Catharine 1098
  Geo 2717 Henry L 2616
  Lewis N 2546 Philip W 1563
HERMANS, Elizabeth 2447
HERRICK, Judson H 3038
  Mary Catharine 2287
  Smith 2287
HERZOG, Hermina 883
  Joseph 783
HESS, John 2125
  Josephine 2394
HESTER, Mary V 2228
HEUSTIS, Ann 916
HEWLETT, S M 2598
HEWSON, William 1835
HEYER, Charles E 17
HIBBARD, Charles 206
  George B 1842 Mary A 960
HICKMAN, Gideon 351

HIES, Pheobe 1913
HIGBIE, Alfred 444
HIGGINS, Charles 155
  Maurice 2252
HILL, Andrew S 43
  Egbert 1398 Emeline D
  1902 George 1902 Isaac N
  2014 James 977 Jane Eliza
  85 John M 1532 Joseph D C
  2582 Mary E 1999 Moses
  779 Nelly Ann 1418 Peter
  1928 Sarah Catharine 1556
  Sarah Jane 2317 W 804
  William R 2246 Wm D 2262
HILLAS, Anna 2466 John 956
HILLEBRAND, Frank J 2629
HILLYER, James 2830
  Mary E 1987 2830
HILME, James 1559
HILTON, Mrs 11
HINE, Mary M 1518
HIT, John B 2894
HITCHCOCK, Daniel H 2268
  Eugene 1963
HIXON, James 1312
HOAG, John B 1833
  Mercy E 1833
HOBLEMAN, Mary 1233
HOES, Harriet S 2584
  Jno C F 2584
HOFF, Belinda A 2940
  Benjamin 2663 Eliza
  Catharine 1850 John W 2349
  Rachel 1547
HOFFMAN, Abraham 2531
  Anna Elizabeth 1623
  Antonio 243 Arthur G 2123
  Charles R 2903 John 1652
  1859 Letitia 2289

HOFFMAN (continued)
  Mary Jane 2573
  Mary Wynkoop 2531
  Michael 734 Morris 1298
  Susan 1616 Zachariah 2289
HOFMIESTER, John 3126
HOGAN, Cornelius 2796
  Elizabeth 2520 Geo W 2386
HOGEBOOM, Henry 2157
  Susan Rivington 2157
HOHNES, Ann Eliza 624
HOLDEN, Edwin 157
  Hannah 1609 Miles 3090
HOLDRIDGE, Augustus 68
HOLLAND, Charles 668
HOLLENBROOK, Hosea 609
HOLLEY, J M 467
HOLLIDAY, Fanny 1644
HOLLISTER, Emma 450 Jane
  450 Lewis 450
HOLMES, Amelia 970
  Gilbert R 519 James K 2112
  Martha L 1252
HOLT, J V 1039
HOMMEL, Abraham 886
  Abram 2338 Alexander 3087
  Andrew 464 1989 Ann
  Elizabeth 2666 Anna 2337
  Clarissa 828 Conrad 1119
  Cornelia 361 David 2835
  Eliza Catharine 1699
  Elizabeth 1851 Elizabeth E
  2345 Franklin A 2881
  Herman 3005 Jane A 1742
  Jeremiah 2283 2674
  Leah C 3005 Lewis S 3093
  Margaret A 1797 Maria 912
  Martha 2627 Martha A 2574
  Nelly 1159 Nelly Ann 2592

HOMMEL (continued)
 Peter 2666 Peter A 2552
 Peter E 2217 Peter H 2319
 Rachel Ann 1102 S S 1797
 Sarah C 2706 Sarah Mariah
 2928 Selina Ann 1989
 William H 2666
 William P 2418
HOMMELL, Ellen 2107
HONK, Theresa 877
HOOD, Edgar 2266
HOOK, Daniel 377
 Mary J 1342
HOOKER, Col 744 Thomas 25
HOOPER, --- 622
HOORNBECK, Louis Dubois
 2879 Louisa 3042
HOORNBEEK, Phebe Ann
 1127
HOOVENBURG, Julia 820
HOPKINS, David 2874
 Erastus 498
HOPPER, David B 1456
 William 1292
HOPPING, Brigadier Gen 251
HOPPS, S M 619
HORINE, Capt 256
HORNBECK, Edward 1135
 H B 1543 John 378
 John H 1270 Joseph K 1054
 Lewis D 1361
HORTON, Mr 636
HOTALING, Calab M 2230
 Cornelius 1561 David V N
 1149 John H 2575 Martin C
 899 Peter 1480
HOTCHKISS, Emily 1058
HOUGHTAILING, Evelina
 1051 Isaac 900

HOUGHTALIN, Ida 3125
HOUGHTALING, Anna
 Margaret 1610 Chancey
 1093 Cornelius 1437 E B
 1981 Edward B 2387 Eliza
 1449 Emily 1981 Isaac 2008
 Julia 799 Julia Antoinette
 1095 Mary C 2901 Melissa
 1437 Nellie 1492 Rensselaer
 1496 Sarah 1445 2981 T I
 1095 Tunis I 1610
HOUGHTON, B R 173
HOULIHAN, Samuel 2041
HOUSE, Louisa J 1665
HOVENBERG, Amelia Ann
 1188 Peter 1188 Sarah 2244
HOVER, William 3041
HOWARD, Louisa 2951
 Richard 643 Samuel R 1115
HOWLAND, Darius 3131
 Isabella Montaine 3131
 John H 2603 Minnie F 2603
 Mr 241 532 Wilbur C 1877
HOY, Alexander 88
HOYT, F M 2730 Francis M
 3109 Harvey W 2140 Justin
 429 Leah 2452 Libbie 3076
 Stephen A 2553
 William E 2587
HUBBARD, Elizabeth L 1714
 Judge 353 Moses 315
 Mrs 218 Nancy 315
 Seth N 358
HUDLER, Alfred 1548
 Edgar 1983 Elizabeth 855
 Eveline 2186 Lucinda 2892
 Margaret Jane 1354
 Thomas 1899
HUDSON, George W 119

HUERLA, Col 260
HUESTED, H D 172
HUESTID, Emily 2549
HUGHES, Anthony 458
  Emma F 2673 Henry 330
  John 1577
HUGLE, Benj 295
HULL, A C 3044 Calvin E
  2278 Catharine 1523
  Charlotte A 680 Conrad
  2071 Francis 1142 Mary E
  3044 Mr 680 William 1336
HULSAPPLE, Jacob 2936
HULSE, Nehemiah D 2952
  Oliver 139
HUMMEL, Anna C 2482
  D T 2731 Jane E 1469
  Jerry 2482 Lavina 2731
  Lucy A 3123 Nelly C 2483
  Sarah 2980
HUMPHREY, Adaline 670
  Egbert 3083 Orlando 1418
  Robert 670 William 2496
HUNT, Atkinson 579
  Edwin 2942 Ezra P 3101
  Mary E 2707
HUNTER, Augustus W 811
HUNTINGTON, Henrietta
  Amelia 918 Jos 918
HURLE, James 121
HURLEY, James 581
  Thomas 581
HUSSEY, John 2024
HUSTED, Henry 1909
HUSTON, Lewis 2297
HUTCHINS, Margaret E 1824
HUTCHINSON, Robert 2132
HUTTON, Christopher 1237
  David 2245 George 1540

HUTTON (continued)
  John W 1164 Matilda 1329
  William 1986
HUYCK, Henry 1479
  Louisa 1479 Maria E 3056
HYDE, James A 2239
  R E 2762
ILER, Wm F 2564
INGELFRITZ, Charles 595
INGRAHAM, Albert E 1953
  David 1422 Orange 2692
INGRAM, Nelson 2737
IRWIN, Jacob 1675
  Peter 1466
ISHAM, Charles 663 Flora 663
ISON, --- 651
ITERBURDE, General 124
JACK, Elizabeth 1010
JACKSON, James H 2883
  Julia E 1596 Rachael 2626
  S W 611 Sarah Jane 1318
JACOBS, George 281
JAGGER, John L 2687
JAKE, Dutch 510
JAMES, --- 9 Isabella G 2326
  James A 2158 2159 2920
  Lewis L 2326 Lucinda R
  2458 Maggy 2288
JAMISON, John 705 Mary 705
  Wm H 240
JANNSEN, Rachel 1285
JANSEN, Abraham 69
  Catharine S 1299
  Egbert 246 Egbert H 28
  Hannah 1139 James A 963
  Joseph 615 Lavinia 1255
  Rachel Blandina 1964
  Sarah Ann 246 Thomas
  1063 1299 Wm L 2079

JAQUES, Eugene A 2547
JARVER, Anthony 957
JAYCOX, Hester J 1413
JENICKSON, R M 3066
JENKINS, George A 238
 Jacob H 1878 James 2407
 Mary 611 Sarah 2407
JENNINGS, Ann M 612
 Harriet M 2546 Henry J 1969
 Joshua 111 Lucretia C 1969
 William 111
JENNINS, Eve 1065
JERNEGAN, Edward 2712
JINGLER, Michael 222
JOESBURY, Joseph F 2993
 William 3067
JOHNSON, --- 701 Alexander
 J 3036 Anne 1405 Ben 480
 Caroline 412
 Daniel R 3091 E B 424
 H D 2688 Henry 1510
 Howard W 3096 James 778
 Kate B 2432 Marshall 460
 Sarah 11 Thomas 1145
 William 1863
JOHNSTON, John E 2558
 Kate 2522
JONES, Amy 1559
 Andrew R 119 Asa 2802
 Benjamin 3117 Catherine
 1229 Charles 559 782 2514
 Cornelius T 1347 David 278
 Elijah 1500 Emily B 2614
 George W 1704 Hannah 924
 James 3014 James W 2096
 Mary E 3117 Morgan 278
 Nancy H 1150 Phebe A
 1347 Ruth 1315 Solomon
 1332 Spencer 1446

JORDAN, Esq 2061
JOY, Howard 2986
 Irwin W 2848 James 1955
 Margaret 2217 Mary 2031
 Tjerck 872
JUDD, Geo W 1959
JUDKINS, Capt 212
 Sarah 1997
JUDSON, Elizabeth 1957
KAMAN, Kate E 2033
KANOUSE, Amelia 2341
KASPER, Barbara 821
KAUFMAN, Charles 1497
 G 2361 Jacob 1750
 Theressa 1497
KAUTSMAN, Eliza 1991
KAVANAGH, Edward 745
KAY, Sarah E 2009
KEARNEY, Alfred 2943
 Ann E 1727 Doctor 253
 Dr 422 Jane 366 John 366
 John W 468 771 John Watts
 3012 Matilda C 3012
 Michael 366 Stephen W 771
KEARNY, Stephen Watts 12
KEAS, John J 2234
KEATER, Philip H 2356
KEATOR, Carrie G 2365
 Catharine M 1661 Celia C
 2246 Chauncey 2611
 Elthea 1398 John J 2622
 Mary Anna 2622
 Mary E 2585 Moses 1509
 Rosina 511 S P 851
 Sarah Catharine 2011
KEEFE, Ellen 1614
KEEGAN, Thomas 166
KEENAN, Charles R 350
KEENER, Elizabeth 887

KEENEY, Thomas B 2540
KEEVER, Hiram W 2254
KEIFFER, Jacob 2792
KEITHLEY, Mary 387
KELDER, Peter 1627
KELEAR, Charles 2187
KELLEY, John 252 1666
KELLOGG, Nathan 140
KELLY, --- 294 582
  Catherine 2832 J W 3102
  John 236 Mary 83
  Wm H 751
KELTS, Angeline 1419
KEMBLE, Solomon H 2059
KENNEDY, Annie E 2757
KENT, James 343
KEOGENS, Eliza J 1360
KERR, Catharine M 2716
  Jane 1986 Joseph 2622
  Joseph W 304 Margaret F
  1844 Robert R 1986 2716
  Robert W 2885 T J 3076
  Theresa 2380
  Wm 1844 Wm F 2524
KERSHAW, James 2304
  Lizzie 2304
KETCH, Mary E 893
  Sarah Jemema 1795
KETCHAM, Benjamin 613
KETCHUM, T Jane 1333
KETTLE, Euphemia 2150
  Rosina 1919
KEYS, David 1932 1983
  Hannah 1983 Jane W 1932
  Theodore 2450
KIDD, Benjamin 2939
  Thomas 3063 Willett 15
KIENER, John 265
KIERSTED, C L 2662

KIERSTED (continued)
  Caroline 61 Helen M 2662
  Jacob A 1907
  James 246 464 John 61 1031
  Wynkoop 1230
KIMBALL, Eliza Catharine
  1708 Frederika C 2388
  John 1708 Josephine 2656
  Mary L 1115 Mr 11
  Rachel C 1076
  Sarah Catharine 2324
KIMBLE, Anne Elizabeth 274
  John H 3002 John P 1876
  Margaret M 1174
KING, Charles M 1374
  Cordelia 661 Eunice 654
  John 2704 L H 2078
KINGMAN, Matthew 793
KINGSBURY, Mary 2736
KINGSLAND, Joseph 1041
KINNER, Robert 1636
KIPP, David 1512 Edward
  2911 James 1245 John H
  402 Margaret 1891 Sarah
  Ann 1512 Thomas S 2101
  William E 1159
KIRBY, Mr 719
KISER, Silas 1051
KISSELBRACK, Rachel 2787
KISSGM, Benjamin A 1933
KITELL, Harriet Louise 1876
KITTELL, Albert 3115
  Albert H 2845 Lydia 2798
KITTS, Emma 1945
KLEIN, Gottleiben 1738
KLINE, Ann 1476 D 1476
  Henry 887
KNAPP, David 1280
  George 1020 Hattie 2937

KNAPP (continued)
  Martha 878 2086 P P 2069
  Robert 2831 S Marshall 2555
  Susan S 304
KNICKERBOCKER, Annis A
  1466 Hannah 1422
KNIFFER, John F 2905
KNIFFIN, Wm H 2830
KNOCH, Hendrick 997
KNORR, Anna 1700
  Eliza C 1552
KNOWLES, Betsey I 793
KNOX, Bridget 1481 Eliza
  Catharine 1690 John C 264
KOONS, Catherine 963
  Philip F 680
KOWAN, Martin 501
KRAFT, John 974
KROHN, Moses 2600
KROM, Garret F 2865
  Jacob A 1649 Jemima 1461
  John A 2875 Mary Elizabeth
  2385 Melissa 2889 Nelson
  929 Sarah 1535
KROS, Mattaew 1279
KROWS, --- 57 William 198
KRUM, George 1286 James
  1539 Maria 860 Mary E
  2015 Rachel 1659 Sarah
  1979 Washington 1440
  William 1324 1746
KUGELMAN, Mary C 3088
KUGLEMAN, John 733
KUHAUHT, Maria 2116
KUHAUPT, Catharine
  Elizabeth 864
KUHL, George F 2846
KUYKENDALL, Jane Ann
  1297

LA FORGE, John D 981
LA VEGA, Gen 101
LAANDAN, John G 852
LABACH, Daniel 2604
LACKEY, Margaret 3014
LACKLAND, B F 256
  G E 256
LACKY, Anna 2973
LACUSS, Oliver 3099
LADENBERGH, Mary C 1289
LADEW, F D 1798
  Sarah Ann 2144
LAFFADAY, Charles 434
  Thomas 434
LAFLIN, A Jenny 2278
  Fordyce L 1147 Helen M
  140 Henry Dwight 1444
  Luther 2278 Lydia A 2229
  Mari L 1117 Walter 1117
LAFONTAINE, --- 114
LAIG, Silas W 1754
LAKE, Cornelia A 2138
  Isaac V 662 Maria 1725
LALLY, Major 273 280
LAMAN, Jane 1008
LAMB, Daniel 2107
LAMPHERE, Capt 218
  Caroline M 1195
  Margaret 1167
LAMPMAN, Henry 1901
LANDENDYKE, Jane M 1898
  Peter 1898
LANDPHIER, George W 1121
LANDT, Elizabeth 681
  Frances M 2953
  Maria T 3010 Matilda 807
  Montgomery 807
LANE, George 1168
  Joseph S 1795 2826

LANE (continued)
  Mannah L 2390 Mary A
  1939 Mary M 1590 Riley
  725 Sarah 1583 Sarah B
  3048 Sarah Ella 2372 Suson
  1591 William 1212 1551
LANGFELDT, Charles 572
LANGLEY, Benjamin 1236
LANMAN, J G 411 Mrs 411
LAPE, Frederick R 2938
LAPOLT, John 2251
LARAN, Bernherd 1720
LASHER, Adam 2369
  Catherine 831 David B 1799
  Elenor 2349 Eliza 873 1416
  Eliza Catharine 325
  Elizabeth 775 1799
  George W 3060 Gertrude
  2290 James Nelson 1799
  John 362 John E 1198
  John R 3060 Lana 1885
  Lavinia 928 Lucinda 824
  Lucinda C 2817 Margaret S
  1835 Matilda 2756 Morgan
  2915 Penelope Ann 2222
  Peter G 2290 Philip Henry
  1166 Rianza 2941 Rufus 361
  William 940 2452
LATHROP, H B 774
LATSAL, Sarah 335
LATSON, Jane C 2042
LATTIN, Richard 2577
LAVERTY, Edward 176 369
  Robert 369
LAWRENCE, John 2360
  Mary 1146 Mr 111
  Talmadge N 1089
  Walter P 708
LAWSON, Emma 3029

LAWSON (continued)
  Lucius 1499
LAWTON, William 2110
LAYMAN, Elizabeth Catharine
  2274 Howard M 2134
  John M 2771
LE FEVER, Catharine 1615
LE FEVRE, Philip 2122
LE ROY, William 348
LEACH, Mr 742
LEAYENFT, Judge 629
LEDGER, John 2985
LEE, Ann 899 Benjamin 2119
  Chas 350 Eliza C 1588
  Hannah 350 Joseph T 762
  Margaret Ann 1093
  Olive L 2641 Wallace 1631
LEFEVER, Abram W 1387
  C H 2393 Cornelius 1713
  Lorenzo 1528 Margaret
  2006 Peter 2890
  Sarah C 1713
LEFEVRE, Libbie R 2875
LEGG, Edgar 1846
  Helen J 2885 Peter 1536
LEGGETT, Edward H 1695
LEGROODT, James H 1414
LEIGH, William J 1424
LEMUS, General 124
LENEHAN, Thomas 1586
LENNARD, Libby 1409
LENNON, Wm J 2593
LENTE, Kittie E 2644
LENUON, Ida L 2137
LEON, Gen 260
LEONARD, Levi 1583 1591
LEOSER, John 424
LEPAREUX, Alexander 812
  Claudius 801

LEPPER, John 599
LEVERT, Joseph 319
LEWIS, Alexander 2306
　Alice 3026 Augustus 901
　Barnet A 959 Charles 3025
　Cornelia A 3114 Dixon H
　761 Elizabeth 1207 Emeline
　1029 Emily 1761 Francis
　2018 Hannah 1830 Harriet
　1575 Henrietta 1078 Hiram
　2927 Jacob Richlie 461
　James O 2928 Jane 1399
　Josephine 861 Julia 1107
　Lucretia 236 Margaret 2711
　Margaret A 2459 Mrs 11 252
　Sally Ann 1519 Sarah L 2680
　Sarah M 2570 Wesley 414
　William 2108 2183
　William H 2565 2566
　William M 1519 Wm P 2459
LICHT, Paulina 2985
LIGHT, Edward 2179
LINCOLN, Capt 70
LINDERMAN, Willett 2
LINDSLEY, Abigail 1739
LINGFELDT, --- 766
LINIK, Frederick 1819
LINK, Sibil 2986
LINZEY, Jeremiah 3120
LIPPINCOTT, Elizabeth R
　184
LITTELL, John N 2238
LITTS, John 1417
LIVINGSTON, D 1927
　Edward P 980 George M
　1762 Margaret Jane 1927
　Mary C 980 Peter 3027
　Robert L 463
LIZARDO, Anton 253

LOBDELL, Alida A 2669
LOCKS, Hugh 1362
LOCKWOOD, Abm L 2307
　Christopher S 847
　Frederick 513 514
　Jane 2139 John H 1598
　John W 1386 Maria A 1031
　Martha 513 Mary Ella 2533
　Thomas S 1031
LODGE, Harriet 1903
LOEW, Rebecca M 2859
LOFTUS, Patrick 263
LOMBARD, Ellie Russell 1759
　Loring L 1759
LONG, Capt 754 Sarah 795
LONGADIKE, Malissa 2465
LONGENDIKE, Christopher
　1621 Cornelius S 1931
　Elizabeth 1931 James D
　1735 Mary Catharine 1283
LONGENDYCK, Cornelius
　1087 Cornelius I 548
LONGENDYKE, B Franklin
　3117 Cornelius 2797
　Cornelius P 1950 Joanna M
　2542 John A 2772 Katie
　2722 Mary E 2115
　Semon P 1136
LONGGON, Ann 533
　James 533
LONGYEAR, Abraham J 2594
　Charles H 2490 Cornelius
　1351 Elizabeth A 2705
　Emma J 1685 Jacobus 978
　John I 1739 Julia 447
　Lean 1921 Manassah 855
　Martha 2789 Mary R 2088
　Nelson 2530
LOOMER, Andrew F 2968

LORD, Ephraim 2166
LOTT, Engleber 2898
LOUGHRAN, Robert 2642
LOUNSBERRY, Epenetus
 2061 Lavina 1186
LOUNSBERY, Edward 38
 Sarah Jane 2037
 William 2033
LOUTHER, Susan 2167
LOVE, Mary E 2221
 Sarah C 1777
LOW, Abram 1367 Alonzo
 1530 Andrew 1790 Christina
 1367 Elizabeth L 2425
 Ella 2771 Frederick B 307
 Henrietta 2129 Henry 2466
 Israel 2120 James 2624
 John Jay 1508 Maria 1848
 Mary Amelia 2772 Rebecca
 1510 Thomas E 1419 Wesley
 2327 Wm C 333 Wm H 1190
 Wm P 2459 Wm S 2301
LOWE, John 2733
 Sarah A 2733
LOWER, Sarah 428
 Tobias 428
LOWN, Mary E 2667
LOWRIE, Walter M 345
LOWTHER, Christopher 2309
 John 2019
LUCE, Eleazar 441
LUCKENBACK, F 2724
LUKIN, John N 211
LUMIS, Jacob 944
LUSK, Charles 2681
 Ellen H 2608 Gilbert 1067
LUTE, John 853
LYNCH, Emeline 2738
LYNK, Edward 2570

LYNK (continued)
 Martha 2628 Phillip 2768
LYONS, Isaac I 1567
 Simon P 1357
MACAR, John 351
MACAULEY, Robert F 288
MACFARLAN, John 11
MACK, Anna Bell 3098
 Eliza C 3027 Mary E 2234
 Peter 2732
MACKBER, Iola 2063
MACKELRAY, --- 631
MACKENZIE, Alexander
 Slidell 720
MACKEY, Janette 1801
MACKINSON, James A 350
 John 424
MACLINS, Mary Ann 932
MADISON, Ann 350
MAFFIT, John Newland 73
MAGEE, Albert 2211 Anna
 461 Catharine 1724 Charles
 2810 Christianna 3004
 George 2517 Gertrude F
 2492 Mary C 1379 Nelson
 2470 Sally 1791 Wm J 2421
MAGINNIS, Alicia A 3047
 Ann 1540 Charles 186 2819
 Wm 3047
MAGNES, Capt 606
MAGUIRE, --- 179
MAHAN, Lieut 131
MAHER, Thomas 2184
MAINES, Clara J 3071
 James 1515 John 3071
 M Alice 3071 M Elizabeth
 3071 Margaret 1747
 Margaret E 2253 Susan A
 2284 Thomas C 2516

MAINS, Elizabeth 614
MAIOFF, Adaline 936
MAJORY, Dennis 2728
MALLOT, Nathan 619
MANCE, John B 1482
MANCHESTER, David S
 1287 Jerome B 327
 Silas 327
MANERY, Mary A 2013
MANEY, John W 27
MANLEY, Calvin 204
MANLY, --- 753 Gov 753
MANN, William 2377
MANNAN, Johanna 1325
MANNING, Isaac G 2163
 Jane 1669 Sarah Jane 2860
MANNINGY, Samuel 779
MANNY, Benjamin 3023
MAQWELL, Catharine E 2283
MARAKLE, Alexander 1827
 John 1678
MARCH, Nelson 1685
MARKLE, Elizabeth 1353
MARQUOT, Elizabeth 2657
MARRIOTT, John 2324
MARRYATT, Capt 711
MARSH, Henry B 2828
MARSHAL, Elizabeth 1208
 Joshua 539
MARSHALL, Charlotte
 Augusta 1744 Chief Justice
 571 Henrietta 1352
 James M 571 Thomas 571
MART, Jacob 1477
MARTEN, Sarah Jane 1766
 William R 1382
MARTIN, Abram 1034
 Amanda Alvira 357
 Brazill R 2702

MARTIN (continued)
 Eleanor 900 Emily P 3066
 Emma 3137 Henry 759
 J R 3066 John H 2168
 Lieut 683 Margaret 1560
 Maria E 2561 Mary A 1371
 Mary E 1056 2596
 Mary Jane 2605 Samuel
 2886 Sarah A 1191 T Anna
 2168 Theodore F 3013
 William 2300
MASH, Martha A 1542
MASON, Capt 248 Henry
 1553 James E 1763
 Martha D 1763
 Randolph Fitzhugh 2282
 Susan 3129 Wm 1853
 Wm U 2286
MASTEN, Charles J 2742
 Daniel 44 Melinda I 1911
 Peter 1691 Thomas L 2114
 William 549
MASTON, Louisa 2046
MATEOS, Capt 260
MATHEWS, Nicholas 2097
MATHIS, Charles B 3104
MATSON, A 1378
 Julius A 1786
MATTHEWS, George B 1023
 Levena J 2838
MATTOON, John 1226
MAUER, Nicholas 2516
MAUTERSTOCK, Josiah
 2311 Matilda 2334
 William 1617
MAX, Elizabeth 1993
 John 1993
MAXSON, Daniel 1055
MAXWELL, Emma 2996

MAXWELL (continued)
  Emma J 2963 Isabella A
  1741 John 2996 Kate E 2283
  M 380 Rev M 374 Sarah J
  908 Thomas 1742 Wm H
  2304
MAYBE, James 1186
MAYBEE, Phebe Ann 617
MAYER, Frank 2427
MAYHEW, Philip 11
MAYSE, Litty C 1321
MC BRIDE, Belle 2636
MC CALL, Jennie 3073
MC CANN, Charles 76
  Mrs 655
MC CARTHY, E J 2715
  Edward J 1676 Kate 2715
  Mary 2233
MC CAUSLAND, Jefferson
  836 Maggie N 2302
MC CHESNEY, Catharine
  Jane 157 George 210 James
  2773 Mary Adaline 2676
  Mary Antoinette 2773
MC CHICKERING, Mr 727
MC CLELEN, Matthew 337
MC CLELLEN, John 1893
MC CLENAHAN, James 256
MC CLENEN, John 1895
MC CLUNG, Hester 2109
  Richard 2912
MC CLURE, Kate A 2606
  Wellington 2606
MC COMB, John 1331
MC COOL, Elizabeth 975
MC CREARY, Margaret 1295
MC CULACK, Robert J 2433
MC CULLOUGH, William 623
MC DANIEL, Nathaniel 2264

MC DERMOTT, Michael 727
MC DONALD, Emma J 3113
  Hester 1821 James 293
  Mary Antoinette 2703
  Sarah C 2834
MC ELHONE, Wm 2104
MC ELROY, Alonzo Adebbut
  363 Evander 2844 Jane 1158
  Mr 370 454 505 Thomas
  1158 William 2957 William
  H 363 2824
MC ELVY, Joseph 1291
MC ENTEE, J S 1604
  Mary S 1604
MC ENY, Elon 1038
MC EWEN, Niel Tounsley 415
MC GAHEY, Sarah 2487
MC GAVY, Jas 1385
MC GEE, Sandford 2721
MC GEORGE, Alice 1346
  Philis 827 William 827 1346
MC GHEE, Dr 331
MC GONAGEL, John 82
MC GRATH, Ellen 2784
MC GRAW, Mary Ann 880
MC GUILL, Ellen 2582
MC INTIRE, Mrs 188
MC INTOSH, Col 272
MC INTYRE, James T 1755
MC KEE, Capt 70 Isaac 1354
  Mrs 177
MC KIBBIN, Lydia 2384
MC KIEAN, Mr 160
MC KINISTREY, Floyd Smith
  987
MC KINNEY, Frances 1189
  John A 1271
MC KNIGHT, Mr 457
MC LAIN, John J 930

MC LANAHAN, T 497
MC LINDEN, Jane 958
MC MAKEN, Mary A 1820
MC MILLAN, Mary Ann 584
MC MULLEN, Emma F 2906
  James 189
MC MURRAY, Samuel 1820
MC PHERSON, John E 1785
MC QUINN, William 730
MC QUOID, Hannah J 1514
MEAD, Smith 319
MEADE, Almira P 1674
MEAGHER, Thomas F 1860
MEALIUS, Deborah 2640
MECKING, Catherine 870
MEEHAM, Jane A 865
MEEHAN, Andrew 296
MEEK, Major 567
MEIER, Christine 1428
MELICK, Mary C 1500
MELLANY, Mary Ann 1083
MELONY, Thomas 1140
MENNANY, Joseph 1083
MERCHANT, James 2722
  Thomas 383 394
  Wm M 2525
MERCLEAN, S 2565 2824 2825 2933 Samuel 799 1520 1720 2000 2896 3070
MERINNIS, George 2461
MERRIHEW, Catharine 1539
  James H 1584
MERRILL, Capt 272 Peter 98
MERRIT, Abraham De Witt 1609 Maria 2579
MERRITT, Ann P 1755
  Blandina E 1935 Caleb M 1935 Elizabeth 1896
  George B 2395

MERRITT (continued)
  Hannah 2170 James O 1834
  S M 2741 Sarah 2741
  Temperance 2254 Thomas H 2178 Wm B 2736 2741
METCALF, George C 586
MEYER, John A 355
  Rose 2382
MICHAELY, Ann 1632
MICKINS, Sarah C 1681
  Wm 1680
MICKLE, Eliza A 2957
  John Henry 882 Peter 1367
MIDAS, Jeanette 783
MIDDAGH, George 2749
  James 1463
MIDDAUGH, Alexander 841
  Geo M 1923 Jesse 889
  Joseph H 1178 Maria 1703
  Mary Elizabeth 1937
  Rachel Jane 957
MILES, John 443
MILEY, Richard 2734
MILL, Henry 2241
MILLAR, Charles 2023
MILLER, Adeline 1293
  Alida 2562 Ambrose C 1297
  Ann E 1813 Cornelia 810
  Cornelia E 2878 David 1792
  Elizabeth 1011 1906
  Ellen D 906 Francis 815
  Franklin 906 Gabert 1393
  George 931 George B 1293
  Henry 2752 Hiram 1345
  Irene 2635 Jacob 2877
  James E 2571 Jane 1792
  John 507 John F 108
  John H 2249 Julia M 2188
  Margaret 1394 Mary 3126

MILLER (continued)
  Mary Ann 27 Mr 756
  Philip B 506 Rachel M 1112
  Rev Dr 2188 Sarah Elizabeth
  2295 Stephen A 2375
  Wm 291
MILLIGAN, John L 593
MILLIGEN, Catharine J 1338
MILLIKEN, John 1574
MILLINGTON, Joseph 2954
MILLKEN, Marcus 1338
MILLS, Jacob 1473
  Stephen D 1350
MINDERS, John 1490
MINER, Mary Elizabeth 885
MINERLY, Gordon 2823
MINK, William 1743
MINKLER, Ann Lavina 2926
  Caroline J 2615
  Edgar 2353 Margaret 2694
  Mary Jane 2000
MINNERLY, Altanah 974
MINOR, Frederick 636
  Lieutenant 375 Martin 1680
  Mary 1680 Mr 636
MISNER, Catharine 2252
MISSENER, Henry 1765
MITCHEL, George 2637
  Mary I 2637
MITCHELL, Ann 1377
  Artemas W 3046 Mr 432
  Robert 989
MITRACH, Harmon 2858
MOBERG, A A 220
MOE, Joseph 2000
MOFEAT, Bruce 2409
MOHLER, John 1410
MONDORE, Madison 2856
MONELL, Robert 1524

MONELL (continued)
  Robert D 14
MONROE, Lt 237
MONTANYE, Harry B 1936
  Isaac D L 3127
  William D L 3124
MONTGOMERY, --- 486
MONTROSS, Adam 2507
  Horace W 965 Margaret 227
  Susie 2507
MOODY, Mrs 542
MOON, Eliza 935
  Margaret C 2652
MOOR, Capt 70 Eliza 1530
MOORE, Ann Adelia 117
  Benjain J 1538
  Charlotte 1675 Elmira 1607
  Frederic W 690 Henry 75
  Michael 1966 Nancy 1309
  Sallie 3110 William 1772
MOOSE, Abbie H 2470
  Adam 198 Henry Luther
  1317 Margaret 2774 Maria
  1165 Sarah 2318
MORAN, Mary E 2301
MORE, Catharine A 364
  L P 2085 Levi B 1534
  Margaret Ann 2171
  Rachel 2215 Sally 966
  Zachariah 1593
MOREHOUSE, Charles 1911
  E 537 Marilla G 1063
MOREY, Anson 2106
  Cornelia 2180 Josephine
  2396 Nathan P 2747
  Oscar H 3081
MORGAN, --- 181 George H
  3130 Jane S 2376 Mary B 26
  Mm 2436 Sarah J 2091

MORKEE, Eli 815
MORPETH, Lord 764
MORRIS, Amelia G 2873
  Catharine 1553 James A
  1235 James L 2430 Julia
  2430 Lieutenant 422
  Mary Ann 1373 Simon P
  834 Thomas H 1883
MORRISON, Elizabeth 1505
  James A 2710
MORSE, Adaline V 1970
  Ellen M 2099
  Maria E 1402 Mr 263
MORTERSTOCK, John H 817
MORTIMER, Margaret 1605
MORTIN, William 2315
MORTON, Margaret 2945
MOSHER, John 507
  Sarah E 1407
MOSIER, Henrietta 446
MOSLER, Charles 86
MOTE, Valentine 1730
MOTT, Adam 577
MOTTOMY, Samuel 2878
MOULE, Benjamin 3020
  John B 3019 Rachel 3020
MOULTON, David 1295
MOUNT, Amelia G 414
  Joseph 414
MOWER, Aaron Vedder 1885
  Andrew 1870 Anna Maria
  1888 Catharine 2651 2927
  Catherine 886 Christina E
  1870 Christopher 3031 Eli
  2976 Elizabeth 2200 2319
  Harriett C 2848
  Jacob 3105 Jacob F 2972
  James 2860 Jeremiah 2473
  John David 65

MOWER (continued)
  John H 37 2861
  John W 2398 2774
  Jonas 2579 Jonas L 2916
  Lavina M 2449 Leonard S
  1800 Margaret 840 2557
  Margaret A 2861
  Moses M 2242 Nicholas 198
  Peter 775 Peter J 2843
  Sarah 2403 Sophira 1800
  William 2918
  Zachariah B 2294
MOWL, Margaret Ann 2187
MOYER, Miffin R 2929
MULCHAY, Thomas 1325
MULL, --- 582
MULLANY, Erina A 845
  James R 845
MULLEN, Emily P 2462
  Patrick 676
MULLER, Elizabeth 1429
  Frederick 936
MUMFORD, Lieut 131
MUNDAY, John 30
MUNKSON, Sarah 1363
MUNN, --- 741
MUNSON, Hannah M 1872
MURPHY, Cecilia 3100
  John 138
MURRAY, D 174 James 539
  L M 697 Mary A 2888
MURRING, Mary Ann 2097
MURRY, Mary Ann 770
MUSIER, Amy Catherine 2313
  Ephraim 2313 Ephraim E
  1379 Jacob P 1928
  Jane Catharine 1928
MUSSIER, Jacob 953
  Sarah 953

MUTER, --- 188
MYER, Abraham 2754
  Abraham L 2155
  Abram J 833 Anna 2745
  Augustus 883 Benjamin 6
  1180 2362 2402 2500
  Benjamin S 2995 Caroline
  1410 Catharine A 1089
  Cecilia A 952 Christian 1956
  Elizabeth 197 Elizabeth L T
  2379 Ephraim P 1912
  Frances 1160 Hannah 1753
  Henry 545 975 1307
  Henry O 1581 Jacob 2999
  James 2035 John 1805
  John B 2402 John Henry
  2362 John M 407 Jonas 373
  464 770 Josiah 2937 Julia
  2043 Louisa 6 Margaret Ann
  2035 Maria 545 2362
  Mary Ann 1561 Mary C
  1912 Mary E 2541
  Mynard 407 N Warren 2695
  P W 2168 Peter B 2043
  Peter D 448 Peter W 2670
  Rachel 724 Rachel Maria
  1002 Ralph 2244 Sally 407
  Samuel P 2777 Sarah Ann
  1034 Sarah Elizabeth 373
  Selia 1581 Simeon P 1002
  Titus 1935 Tjerk 226
  Wells 1954 William 724
  William P 2701
MYERS, Catharine 830
  Dewitt R 3077
  Emma Jane 3082 Hiram
  2287 Jacob 2004 Jannette
  1383 John 137 John A 2351
  Margaret Ann 2095

MYERS (continued)
  Martha 2158 Martha J 2689
  Mary 137 Mary Ann 1193
  Russel 2667 Samuel 3032
  Sarah 2402 Sarah A 3002
  William 1233 Wm H 1802
MYNDERS, Lydia 2241
MYNDERSE, Elizabeth 1214
  John G 1214 2609
  Julia 2609
NAGLE, --- 535
NAIRN, John 1889
NARVY, Catharine 1385
NASH, Jerusha C 819
  Joshua 2777 Ophelia 2777
  Thomas 495
NAVEY, Henry 2825
NAVY, Margaret 2825
NEAFIE, Alfred 2005
NEAL, Joseph C 171
NEAR, Catharine 2072
  Sylvester 1462
NEELIS, Francis 259
NEELY, Richard 2744
NEHER, Edmund 2343
  Phillip C 2781
NEILL, Lewis 79
NEISE, Rachel Maria 2052
NELLIGAR, Edwin 3086
NELSON, George 1605
  Henrietta 2036
NESTELL, F M 2214
NESTLEN, Jacob 1700
NEUFFER, John C 2181
NEWCOMB, John H 566
NEWKIRK, Benj G 1785
  Benjamin G 400 1160
  C 1143 Edgar B 2654
  Eliza 2075 Ephraim H 3097

NEWKIRK (continued)
  George 2785 George W
  1484 Harriet 2169 Isaac
  2293 James H 2350
  Manasseh 1779 Margaret
  Ann 1160 Maria V 400
  Mariah Catherine 978
  Mary Ann 15 Mary C 1077
  Peter L 1103 Sarah 1785
  Sarah G 2070
  William C 1881
NEWMAN, Charles W 1431
NICHOLS, Alonzo 827
  Isabella 1474
  Lydia A 1414 Nancy 84
NIECE, Solomon D 2656
NOBLE, Robt 1560
NOBLES, Priscilla 2529
NODINE, Anson E 1221
NORCUTT, George A 2729
NORRIS, David 2004
  James J 2602 Julia K 2004
  Mr 622
NORTH, Catharine 401
  Geo 1832 Nelson 1864
NORTHROP, Elizabeth 2501
  Geo 2501
NORTHRUP, Amos 244
NORTON, Lieut 11
  Richard 365
NUNNALLY, Grief 542
NURSE, George W 87
NUTTING, Alfred 1403
OAKES, Ellen 652
OAKLEY, Branson 2025
  Caroline E 2489 Hiram 993
  J G 2489 Mary C 2003
  Sara A 2690
  Solomon W 2489

O'BRIEN, Edmund 888
  Smith 763
O'BRYAN, James 1075
O'BRYON, Lyman 2325
O'CONNELL, Daniel 132
  Mr 212 671
ODELL, Henry 96 Squire 1194
O'DONNELL, --- 685
  Simon Pleu 2145
O'FARREL, Joseph 556
O'FARRELL, Joseph 396
OGDEN, Elizabeth 55
  Emily M 55 Isaac 466
  Peter Sken 567 Reuben 55
O'HARA, James 590
OLIVER, Margaret B 905
  William 612
OLIVITT, Estha Eliza 829
OLNEY, Corydon C 2806
  James B 3111
O'NEIL, Charles M 2228
  E 1774 Mary D 1774
ORBANDO, Colonel 101
O'REILLY, John 3100
ORTON, Anna 2146
OSBORN, Chauncy J 2182
  Florence D 1760
OSTERHOUDT, Abraham
  1308 Alanson 2381 Almira
  2800 Charles 2471 Cyrus
  2494 Eliza 1847 Eliza
  Catharine 1181 Emeline 1138
  Gertrude 547 Harmon 585
  Harriet 2453 Jacob 875 Jesse
  2248 Joel 2800 John 2229
  John P 547 John P L 385
  L H 3079 M 2156
  Margaret 1162 Mary 492
  Matthew 2173 2199

OSTERHOUDT (continued)
  Melissa 2419 Peter I 492
  Rodney 2536 Sarah 1110
OSTERHOUSEN, Johannes K 1267
OSTERHOUT, Nelly Ann 825
OSTOWN, Abram 439
  Mrs 439
OSTRANDER, Charlotte 896 1880 Cornelius 2098
  David W 2790 Eliza Ann 1749 J D 896 Jacob R 1001
  John H 2099 Joseph P 1797
  Philip 784 Rebecca Ann 2240
  Rev Dr 765 Sarah 2112
  Thomas B 1748 William 2112 2521 William A 784
OSTROM, J S 971
  James Albert 2745
OSTRUM, J S 1439
OTIS, Harrison G 773
O'TOOL, Mrs 459
O'TOOLE, Patrick 430
OTTO, Henry 1906
OVALDORF, John 3006
OVERBAGH, Cyrus 2192 2735 Elsie D 2650
  Jeremiah 3048 Peter 292
OVERBAUGH, D C 2726
  George 2389 J V L 1175 1887 Jacob 1227 James P 1957 Jane C 1302
  Judith N 1227 Maria V L 1175 Moses 2821 Peter T 2065 Rachel Anna 1887
  S Jennie 2767 William 1469
OWEN, Schuyler P 2560
PAINE, Martha E 2261
PALACIO, Colonel 101

PALEN, Edward F 2501
  Elma M 2952
  Gilbert E 2271 John 1290
  Sarah A 2148
  Sarah Jane 947
  Zachariah 1194
PALMATEER, John P 1408
PALMER, Levi 470
  Mercy Ann 2239 Mr 748
  Nellie A 2876 Permelia 834
PANGBURN, Abraham H 2170
PARADISE, Samuel 2787
PARDEE, Adaline 1152
  Rosina 954
PARDESSUS, Josephene S 1909 Rene A 1909
PARES, Jeremiah 2488
PARIES, Mary Ann 2874
  Peter 2924
PARKE, James 731
PARKER, Amasa 288
  Doctor 791 Eliza 413 John 137 Judge 726 Margaret 842 Rebecca 288 Sarah E 1729
PARKS, Lucy 2778
  William 1254
PARRIS, Peter L 2503
PARSELL, Harriet 1602
PARSON, Cynthia 1273
  Francis 1100
PARSONS, Ann E 1782
PARSSELL, Emma 2766
PATERSON, Mary 1915
PATRICK, Dr 647
PATTERSON, Capt 398
  John H C 1319
  John V 1371 Samuel 1807
  Wm M 303

PATTISON, Jane C 1650
PAYN, --- 696
PAYNE, Mary E 2076
PEABODY, Oliver William
   Bourne 657 W B O 657
PEAL, Alida J 1696
   Henry 1696
PEASE, Mary 2736 William 81
PECK, Clarissa 1576
   Clark S 2348 Darius 1771
   Eugene 3094 Julia W 1736
   Mary Frances 2303
PECKHAM, Anna M 2598
   Rufus 2598
PELHAM, Anna P 2039
   Sarah C 2374
PELLETREAU, Jullia 2249
PELLS, Jeremiah 765
PELT, George W 2652
PELTON, Champion 21
   Ezra 19 20 Nancy 20
PEMBERTON, A H 168
PENDERGAST, L M 3066
PENFIELD, Guy D 2479
PENNINGTON, John 1642
PENROSE, Cornelius H 1442
PER LEE, Samuel R 190
PERKINS, Celia A 3050
   Minerva 2670 Nelson 1952
   Norman H 1390 Tilit 779
PERRINE, Louisa 2718
   M D 2690
PERRY, Com 517
   John C 1514
PERSE, Sarah 1228
PERSONS, Joel T 463 464
PETERS, Elizabeth 323
   Frederick F 2394
   Jane 3022 John 323

PETERS (continued)
   Wm 1191
PETERSON, Capt 772
   Charles 471
PETIT, Franklin 1576 H 447
PETTIT, John 1438
PFESTER, Anna Jane 1282
PHELPS, Mr 231 Smith 224
PHILIPS, ---685 Charles 2446
   Jane E 1105 John 543 Mary
   E 2854 Oscar 1008
PHILLIPPE, Louis 465
PHILLIPS, Abram P 2434
   Charles W 2630 Edward 633
   Edward Bromfield 633
   Louisa 1705 Martin 3053
   Mary E 1992 2813
   Robert 373
PIERCE, --- 742 Arrie A 2567
   General 398 J B 187 Norman
   F 2711 Sarah Jane 2074
PIERPONT, Austin 649
PILCH, Rev Mr 24
PINE, Amanda 1612
   James S 713 John Wesley
   379 Sarah Elizabeth 713
   Sarah M 713 Tobias 2758
   Wesley 371 509 541 565
PINKHAM, --- 561
PITTS, E 705 1046
   Elizabeth 705 Orlando 11
PLACE, Andrew 2135
   Angelica 1532 Frances E
   1716 John H 1532 Lavina M
   1721 Mary A 2457 Sarah M
   868 Simon P 1723
PLAIN, John 1635
PLANK, Cyrenus 2643
   Richard 2975

PLANTER, James 791
PLAS, Jacob 733 Sarah 733
PLASS, Andrew 2320
  Arrietta Maria 1735
  Caroline 2156 Elizabeth Ann
  3092 Jerome 3020 John 2935
  Philip H 3092 Sebastian 1735
PLATT, M E 319 Russell W
  489 Zeph C 319
PLEU, Marietta 1343
PLOSS, Rachel A 2795
  Sarah Angeline 3053
PLOUGH, Catherine 1218
  Cornelius 1697 Henry 359
  Jacob 995 John 1494
  Julia A 2193 Leah 45
  Martha 2299 Peter 1144
  Samuel 1840
PLUM, Henry 1464
PLUMB, Mary M 3067
PLUSCH, Philip 2476
POINT, Columbus 973
POLHEMUS, Jonathan 1999
POLK, James K 336
POLLOCK, Eliphalet P 2462
  Elizabeth A 2681
  Wm Bloomer 2683
POLSTON, --- 214
POND, Charles H 1026
  Maria L 1026
POOL, Frederick W 1459
PORTER, F B 247 Gertrude
  247 Joel W 2056 Louisa 579
  Lucinda 1050 Marth A 2725
  Mary 247 Rowland 2651
  Washington 2677
  Wellington 3116
POST, Abm A 2475
  Abraham L 2980 Abram 426

POST (continued)
  Abram F 710 Amelia 768
  Ann M 1372 Celia H 402
  Egbert 710 3010
  Eliza 1179 2463 2511
  Elizabeth C 1326
  Ellen 2373 Frances J 710
  Isaac 2277 Jane 823
  John 1634 John B 1038
  John H 1266 John S 2480
  Kate E 2712 Lottie 2580
  Lucy A 1622 Mary A 1151
  Mary E 2621 Mary F 2856
  Mary L 2493 Melissa 769
  Nelson 1853 Peter E 1358
  S M 1954 Samuel M 2493
  Sarah 1635 1954 2199
  Sarah Jane 1853 Selena 2902
  Susan 2378 Thomas 1189
  Tobias 1092 Tunis M 2050
  William 463 823
POULTNEY, Evan 1000
  Jane Tunis 1000
POWELL, Jane 891 Sarah 897
  Thomas 606
PRASLIN, Dutchess of 250
PRATT, Ephraim 25 John 25
  Joshua 25 Nancy E 843
  Phinehas 25 Zadock 25 3000
PRENTICE, E L 2047
PRENTISS, S S 496
PRESTLEY, Matthew 2610
PRESTON, A B 2005 Ann
  2005 Col Z 2078 Eliza 2078
  Rev Mr 324 Susan 890
  Truman J 1128
PRICE, William 112
PRIEST, Anna Le Nettie 2409
PRINDLE, John A 1486

PROCTOR, Amelia 2270
PROUT, Hannah 2224
  Ranson 962
PRUDER, Ella Frances 2631
PULTZ, Alfred 1241
  Sarah 1059
PUNCH, --- 230
PURDY, Elisha S 348
  F B 960 Harriet 54
  Herbert H 2907 Irena 682
PUTNEY, James 1068
QUICK, Abram 1693
  Catharine A 2571 Henry 1660
  Jane C 2972 Joanna 2416
  Mary 1081 Sarah M 2845
  Theodore 2220
QUIMBY, Mary 1667
  Mr 2336
QUINLAN, Alfred F 918
QUINN, Catharine 1240
QUISENBERRY, Chas 256
QUYNN, Nancy 352
RADCLIFF, Julia C 2010
  P E 2010
RADEMACHER, Catharine
  572 Mr 469
RAENHART, Francis A 2864
  John H 2198
RANDAL, Jacob 1695
  Mary C 1695
RANDALL, Frances S 2659
RANSOM, Elizabeth 350
  Henry 350 Jane M 1877
  John 1877 Mrs 350
  Peter 1626 Peter B 1737
  S W 2695 Truman B 398
RANSON, Adaline 1145
  David 1709
RAPPLEYEA, Nancy F 1448

RAREDON, Daniel 675
RATTO, --- 685
RAULES, John 1615
RAYMOND, Francis G 1674
READON, Hiram S 2243
REASE, S 331
REDFIELD, Harriet N 2272
REDICKER, Nicholas 109
REDMAN, Alexander 607
REDMOND, Anthony 2109
REED, Alexander 1231
  Augusta 1097 James 1018
  2698 Jefferson L 2497
  Joseph O 5 Luman 2086
  Mathew 555 Susie 2599
REEDER, George W 2561
REEVES, Emma 3101
REHFERS, Geo 1738
REIFENBURGH, John 1897
REIGHTMYER, Mary E 1451
REINHART, --- 103
REISER, Anthony 2740
RELYEA, Catharine L 1839
  Hiram D 2445 Laura 1862
  Maria 1498 Mr 560
REMBALDT, Louisa 869
RENISON, Thomas 1432
REPSHER, David 2208
REQUA, Sarah C 1460
REYNOLDS, Electa P 1975
  Elizabeth H 1743
  Francis Wynkoop 2531
  Gideon 632 Jane R 1114
  Jerome B 2275
  M Augusta 2527 Peter 1032
  S 1743 Sarah Amelia 2211
  Sarah E 1569
RHIND, Francis 558
  Widow 558 William 890

RHINEHART, Elizabeth 2118
  John Kelly 2392
  Mary A 1375
RHODES, Jane 858
RHODUM, --- 781
RIBEN, Don Francisco 457
RICE, Peter 94
RICH, Catharine 1101
  Hannah 901
RICHARDS, --- 472 Geo 1714
  Sarah Ann 2079
RICHARDSON, Amanda 1438
  Amor 2233 Lamon 2313
RICHEY, James 863
  Martha Ellen 863
RICHMEYER, Peter A 2706
RICHMOND, A H 369 463
  Josephene 2089
RICK, George 971 Jacob 1439
  Mary E 2723 Nelly 1439
RICKS, Peter 1526
RIDENOUR, Charles P 2072
RIDER, Albert 2899
  Harriet M 1845 Jacob 544
  Maria 875 Mary A 2174
  Parmelia 1190
RIEFENBERG, Anna Amelia
  2805
RIELL, H E 650
RIGHTMIRE, James 573
RIGHTMYER, Abram 1218
  Adam 1792 Ann 1119
  Christian O 1450
  Conrad 2273 Jacob 1870
  Maria 3006 P H 3006
  Sally C 2498 Samuel 2295
  Sarah 2779 Sarah A 2059
  Wm 198
RIKER, Allie 2964

RILEY, --- 260
RILYEA, Maria 1498
RINGGOLD, Major 36
RISEDORF, Edwin 2222
  Hiram 1812
RISELEY, William 1132 1409
RISELY, Cornelius 2671
  Maria E 2671 William 837
  1301 1351 1422 1551
RISLEY, William 874
RITCHIE, Lieutenant 64
RITTE, Benjamin V 2855
RITTER, Franklin 1429
RIX, Margaret 1897
ROBERTS, Elizabeth M 1949
  Hurley 1316 Izry 320
  Jacob 1839 Thomas 2060
  Wm 1949
ROBERTSON, Francis H 2479
  J J 2479 Robert 2453
ROBINSON, Cornelius 639
  James 1784 Jane M 1489
  John 2275 Mary N 2275
  Polly 1091 Sarah M 2182
  Susie 2858
ROCK, Julia 2512
  Margaret 2976 Maria 2924
RODEN, Mary Ann 352
ROE, B E 1264 John B 384
  John E 395 Nancy 1688
  Saloma 1060 Wm M 2146
ROEDER, Louis 2382
ROGERS, Alexander 1095
  Cornelia Jones 664
  Edwin 1132 Eliza E 2499
  George 2751 J Warren 664
  Lieutenant 422 Lila M 2047
  Lucretia 874 Smith C 2499
  William 2104 William E 1972

ROMEYN, Herman M 416
 John C 2816 John T 525
 Maria S 416 Wm H 2678
RONEY, George 1975
ROOS, David 1770
ROOSA, Ann 1053 Ann
 Catherine 1274 Christopher
 1904 Cornelius D 2603
 Derick W 1183 Elmira 1683
 Emanuel 198 1003
 Harriet 971 John S 1937
 John T 858 Martin 968
 Mary Margaret 1003
 Peter E 1982 William 976
 William H 1441
ROOT, Erastus 34
 Stephen 2176
ROSA, Andrew 1767
 Emma C 1257 Matilda 894
 William 854
ROSALAAM, Jacob 1282
ROSAPAUGH, Isaac 1879
ROSE, James 1058 Jane 1538
 Lydia Rachel 1397
 Phebe A 2526 William 1520
ROSEKRANS, Margiana 1953
ROSEPAUGH, Peter 1837
 Rachel C 2259
ROSS, John P 992
ROTH, Hanna 1597
ROUNDY, Nathaniel W 779
ROUSE, Carrie 1256
 Emma G 2938 German 1630
 I J 1857 James 2458
 Margaret 836 Robert 836
ROVES, Charles 832
ROW, Almira 2297
ROWE, Peter 3045 Phebe
 3045 Sherwood 1554

ROWLAND, Richard 2504
 Thomas 972
RUBY, Sarah 11
RUGGLES, Charles H 980
RUNYAN, David H 74
RUSH, Benjamin 644
 Eliza 1645 Julia 644
 Richard 644 Thomas 1240
RUSHER, Annice C 2556
RUSHMORE, Mary J 2441
 Morris C 2441
RUSHWORTH, --- 179
RUSSELL, --- 779 Ambrose S
 506 Asa S 2016 Benjamin
 371 Caleb 67 E Mc C 2608
 Eliza 379 Elizabeth 1048
 Elizabeth l 1579
 Ella M 2709 Ellen M 2545
 Frederick T 2609
 Geo W 3128 Henry 308
 J 800 1475 J P 1475
 James 308 802
 James Peter 3136 Jas 637
 Jeremiah 176 299 396 463
 1048 Mrs 390 509
 Phebe 637 Sarah A 2351
RYAN, Martha N 967 Mr 634
 Nancy 1025 Roger 684
RYDER, Abram 2881
 Elizabeth 2881
RYKERT, Jane Emeline 1043
RYLEY, Charles 11
RYNE, Edwin 958
SAAM, Frederick 1706
SACH, Henry 328
SAGE, Catherine 853
 Hart C 418
SAGENDORF, A 2247
 Gertrude M 1677

SAHLER, Abraham I 1643
   Almira 1984 Artemus 2391
   Nellie 2737 Solomon 1304
SALAPAUGH, Lucy 2941
SALISBURY, P K 2077
SALPAUGH, Harriet 2073
   Mary J 2262
SALSBURY, Mary Elizabeth
   2343
SALTER, Sarah J 1811
SAM, Jacob 1250
SAMMONS, George 1202
SAMPSON, Samuel 2992
SAN, Harman 1498
SANDERS, James 440
SANDS, Jane 2871
SANFORD, Aurelia 1368
   Benjamin 1644
SANGFELD, --- 469
SAPETCH, Mary 638
SATERLY, George 1595
SAUFELDT, Henry H 2165
SAUNDERS, Charles 794
   Emma 3011 Styles M 2193
SAVAGE, Elvin S 2255
SAWYER, Mr 297
SAX, Adam 1211 Eliza 3090
   James 2204 Jane E 2364
   John W 3050
   Sarah Eliza 1049
SAXTON, John W 1998
   Silas 1396 1397
SCALES, Larah E 2315
SCHAFFER, Charles W 2794
   Louise 2794
SCHALL, Wm 202
SCHECANCE, John 424
SCHEFFER, Madora 2578
SCHENCK, Julia A 1617

SCHEPMOES, Augustus 2040
   Peter B 56 Rachel 991
   Sarah 544
SCHERMERHORN, Mary
   2269
SCHMEHL, Margetha 1886
SCHMIDT, Jacob 591
SCHNEIDER, Agnes 1770
   Michael 1427
SCHOONMAKER, Abraham
   641 2074 Abram E 10
   Abram S 1620 Adelaide
   Louise 1634 Alida 63 Ann
   Elizabeth 2273 Anna
   Elizabeth 698 Anthony L
   1353 Augustus 3055 Calvin
   949 Caroline 1100 Catharine
   32 Celestina 3055 Charlott
   904 Christina 3052 Christina
   C 1849 Cornelius 876
   David 1668 2827
   Edward 2274 2775
   Eliza M 1565 Elizabeth 1155
   2353 Frances 463 Frederick J
   1585 Frederick J S 1578
   Gertrude E 1580 H Barnard
   2662 Jane 1087 Jane Ann
   1088 Jane E 1092 John H
   2872 John W 2022 2491
   Julia Ann 2827 Lewis 1527
   Lucas E 1380 Malissa 2810
   Margaret 1361 Maria 895
   Martin T 1262 Mary E 943
   1192 Matilda 1450 Mynderse
   1783 Nathan 1285 Peter 63
   Peter A 1465 Peter D 895
   Peter P 2254 Rachel 65 1357
   Rachel Jane 1863 Samuel
   1155 1634 3052

SCHOONMAKER (continued)
  Sarah 1543 1668
  Sarah I 1149 Solomon 1900
  Thomas J 1618 Tjerck 698
SCHRIVER, Martin 292
SCHROPP, Henry 1597
SCHRYVER, Amelia 938
  Helen H 1817 J H 1244
  Jeremiah 2031 John H 938
  1731 2862 Julia A 2862
  Martha Jane 1731
SCHULTZ, Althea M 1589
  John L 2195 Judson 1769
SCHUTT, Harriet 1153
  James H 2914 Mahala Jane 4
  Margaret 264 Martin 26 401
  660 847 848 857 893 946
  947 977 1063 1142 1305
  1355 1386 1468 1594 1595
  Sarah A 2914
  Sarah Christina 986
SCHWAB, Ludwig 1365
SCHWART, Catharine 1303
SCOTT, Arthur 2626
  Augusta 2026 Cornelius W
  1919 E A 2919 Emma 2812
  Gen 64 71 101 248 260 273
  John H 1684 Lieut 312
  Martin 272 398
  William J 400
SCOVILLE, Fanny 2400
SCRIBNER, John 142
  Legrande 2945 Sarah E 3008
SCUDDER, Aaron 1044
  Warren W 537
SCUTT, Abraham H 1339
  Angeline 2948 Mary 2551
SEAMAN, Harriet 1790
  James W 2510

SEAMAN (continued)
  Jane Elizabeth 1982
  Joseph 1789
SEARING, Seaman G 1557
SEARS, Elizabeth 1271
SEBASTIANA, Marshal 250
SECOR, Francis M 996
SECORD, William 3085
SEELEY, Karner 2191
SEIS, Catharine 1656
  Peter 1656
SELBEWORTH, Maria 1594
SELLECK, A F 2085
  Mary A 2085 Samuel 1664
SELZEA, Lizzie 2696
SEMMES, --- 196
SEMUNYAN, Lewis W
  Mansfield 2393
SERGEANT, John 508
SEYMOUR, Carrie E 2149
  Melissa A 1910 O H 2584
SHADER, Henry V B 2854
  Jane C 2335 Maria 3091
SHADOR, Herman 2205
SHAFER, Isabella 2404
SHAFFER, Calvin 2039
  Dorcas A 1600
  Eugenia 1710 Girtude 2903
  Jacob 658 Jane M 2153
SHALER, Hannah 2176
  R 2176
SHARP, Anna Elizabeth 2663
  Elizabeth Ann 1435
  Jacob S 1537 Mary Ann 545
  W Ten Broeck 545
  William 1436
SHARPE, Jacob 2502
SHATTUCK, Ira A 846
SHAW, Alexander 3073

SHAW (continued)
  Edwin A 2574 Hanna 2471
  Jacob A 1884 Prosper P 412
  Samuel W 1158
  William B 1495
SHAY, Catharine Margaret 1859
SHEAR, Capt A 696
  Peter E 2171
SHEARMAN, William 1143
SHEARS, Hepsabeth Ann 1203
SHEELEY, Melissa Ann 2258
  Thomas 1425
SHEELY, Maria 1881
SHEETS, Catharine 1284
SHEFFER, Jacob A 2847
  Nancy 1348
SHEFFIELD, J B 2988
  Sarah Stoddard 2988
SHELDEN, Milton 853
SHELDON, Emma I 2613
  Martin W 1355
SHELLIGHTNER, Joseph 2766
SHEPARD, Mr 430
SHEPHARD, Jane 2753
SHERMAN, Horace 2946
  John 2150 Kate M 2946
SHERRILL, E E 2618
SHERWOOD, John E 932
  Joseph L 2965 V 2261
SHICK, George R 1366
SHIELDS, Gen 101
SHOEDER, J R 350
SHOEMAKER, Henry 2200
  Melissa 2323 William L 2799
SHOOK, Ambrose 1179
SHOP, John 1277

SHORT, Almira 1869 Ann L 333 Benjamin L 1677
  Christopher 2755 Cornelius L 2335 Delilah 2594
  Elizabeth Ann 857 Henry 983 Mathew 2081 Nelly
  Catharine 1487 Peter Brink 1851 Peter F 2756 Reuben 1946 Susan Ann 983
SHORTER, John 1567
SHOTWELL, Samuel Lundy 2423
SHUB, Chancey Ludowig 1888
SHUBB, Lodowick 54
SHUBRICK, T B 79
SHUFELDT, Hamilton 2967
  William F 845
SHULTIS, Cemira Catharine 1640 Chauncey P 2675
  Eleanor 1351 Eliza C 1962
  Eugene 2841 Hiram W 837
  Irena 909 Jemima 2969
  John 362 John A 2672
  Madison H 3103 Margaret A 2214 Matilda 910 Moses 1049 Peter W 1409 Sarah C 2841 Stephen 1108
  William 1821
SHULTS, Philip 982
SHULTUS, Amanda 3074
SHULTZ, George F 298
SHUMWAY, Anna Maria 1608
SHUNK, Ex-Governor 674
  Governor 205
SHURTER, John 1363 1400 1426 1434 1486 1667 1683 2029 2037

SICKELS, Viola 3130
SICKLER, Christopher 3132
  Rebecca J 2893 Robert W
  1525 Victor S 1399
SICKLES, Edwin 3057
  Mary 2943 William 2160
SIDNEY, Rollerson 339
SIFTS, Joseph 2124
SIGNER, Jacob I 1205
  Rebecca A 1205
SIGNOR, Isaac 2118
SILKWORTH, Mary J 1549
SIMIONS, George S 1732
SIMMERMAN, Sarah A 1457
SIMMONS, Andrew 2438
  Edward 2348 Emeline 2454
  Emma Jane 2348 George H
  1948 Jane C 1173 John 2628
  John E 2167 Mary A 2114
  Ovid T 2249 Samuel 169
  Syble 3017 William H 1027
  1134
SIMPKINS, D P 2692
SIMPSON, Benjamin 678
  Eliza 2368 J A 447 James A
  2267 Margaret K 2267
SIMSON, Geo H 2428
SINGER, Paymaster Major
  790
SINSABAUGH, Robert
  Wesley 3092
SINZEPAUGH, Angeline 3070
SISSON, Helen F 2064
SITZER, Eunice 2971
SKINNER, Elizabeth 1336
  Jane 2016 Levi B 1336
SLAIGHT, John 729 Mary 729
SLATE, Melissa Ann 2100
SLATER, Almira 898

SLATER (continued)
  Cornedia M 1313
  G W 2934 Jacob B 1590
  Jane Ann 1717 Martha J
  1825 Mary 2346 Sarah A
  2406 Thomas E 1131
SLAYTER, David 639
  Sally Ann 639
SLEIGHT, Isaac D 1917
  John D 1687
SLIGHTER, Eliza L 1327
SLOAT, Martha L 1421
SLOSS, David 2770
SLUSHER, Jane E 1212
SLUSSER, Sarah 1551
SLUYTER, Alfred 863
  Lydia 948 Peter 405
SMART, Mr 2867 Mrs 11
SMEDES, Abraham W 816
  Laura 2960
SMEDIS, Catharine 1491
  Lydia 1490
SMIDT, Jacob 1531
SMITH, --- 194 A G 1232
  A J Madison 1415
  Aaron 1223 Abby 1895
  Abigail 1893 Amos 1268
  Amy 669 Amyetta 2904
  Anna De Witt 3124
  Anning 1734 Asa G W 3068
  Benjamin 317 C C 3124
  Captain 772 Catharine 1470
  Charles 2012 Cyrus 77
  D P 1828 1829
  Deputy Sheriff 507 Dr 422
  E 1395 Ekee Maria 1393
  Eleanor 1723 Elijah 1213
  Eliza C 2135 Elizabeth 640
  942 2051 2255 3036

SMITH (continued)
 Ellen 1223 Emma H 2804
 Eugene L 3044 Francis 755
 George Joseph 1845
 Gilbert 2520 Grace 1408
 H C 2949 Hannah 1396
 Henry 1628 2660 Hiram
 1235 Ira T 933 Jacob 902
 James 346 910 Jennie 2645
 John 1920 John H 506 1716
 John W 1396 2092 Jonas M
 2535 Joseph 2213 Kate M
 2806 Lanah 286 Lemuel A
 3017 Lewis 640 Lydia M 77
 Major 248 Margaret A 1520
 Maria 2068 Martha 2872
 Mary 959 Mary Ann 982
 Mary C 1235 Mr 107 2983
 Nelly 1627 Noah 632 669
 Officer 145 Peter A 2457
 R W 2818 Rachel 1486
 Rachel A 1662 Robert 2806
 Rufus T 2694 Sarah C 1892
 Sarah E 2802 Sarah M 2818
 Solomon A 1117 Sophia
 Weed 640 Temperance S
 2045 Thomas C 1915
 Thomas W 416 Uriah 1434
 Warren 11 Watson A 2779
 William 330 532 950 1101
 1267 1268 William D 1920
 Wm W 1603
 Zachariah S 1228
SMOOT, Sergeant 679
SNELLING, Elizabeth 990
SNODER, A S P 2049
SNOOK, Alanson 973
SNOWDEN, Thomas 618
SNYDER, Amanda 1843

SNYDER (continued)
 Amelia 2053 Amelia A 832
 Andrew 2910 Andrew J
 1061 Ann Christina 884
 Anna Maria 52 Catherine
 1061 Charles 524 2578
 Christina 2451 Christopher
 1234 Edward 1894 Elias 873
 Eliza A 1812 Elizabeth 2934
 Frederick 2415 Geo M 2486
 George B 1375 George K
 2788 George W 2440
 H D H 1933 Helen 524
 Henry E 1751 Horatio A 52
 Isaac H 1239 Jacob 920
 2308 Jacob H 1638 Jane A
 2331 Jeremiah 464 John J
 1467 1602 Joshua 2840
 Joshua F 2548 Lavina 1764
 Levi 511 Lorinda 1216
 Lucretia E 2311 Malissa
 2363 Malvina H 1968
 Margaret 723 Marshall 3001
 Martin 2764 Mary A 1884
 Mary Elizabeth 1846
 Mary G 1894 Nelly Ann
 2243 Noah 1753 2243 Paul
 2260 Peter 464 1110
 Peter V 1891 Philip 1781
 Philo 2363 Rachel M 300
 Rebecca 37 Robert 2538
 Robert A 2376 Sarah A
 1933 Sarah C 1454
 Susan Mariah 1036 Tjerk E
 300 William 3043 William H
 1981 Zechariah 52
SOLACE, W V 11
SOLE, Wm H 1622
SOLLINS, James 743

SOULE, Henry 826
SOUSER, Alexander 1171
   Rachel Ann 1171
SOUTHWICK, George 952
SPAHN, Michael 1012
SPAIN, Infanta of 1
SPARLING, Derick W 1641
   Elizabeth 922
   Emmeline 1473 George 860
   Harriet 1905 Martha 2310
   Morgan L 1053
SPAULDING, Maj 689
SPEALMAN, Jack 1758
SPECKMAN, Mr 594
SPENCER, Alvin D 1558
   Amanda 2842 Ambrose 453
   Elsie C 2320
   Sarah K 1786 Wm H 2839
SPENSER, Abbey M 1958
SPIELMAN, Isabella 940
SPINDLER, Daniel 869
SPONHANER, John 2173
SPOTTS, Romeyn 2825
SPRAGUE, James 2340
   Susan 2140
SPRINGSTEEN, John J 1269
SPRINGSTEIN, Uriah 792
   Urial 792
ST DENNIS, --- 319
STAATS, Eliza 1676
   Henry 1676 Rachel Ann
   1204 Virgil M 2978
STAEGEAR, Conrad 3088
STALL, Herman 1927
STANDISH, E L 2111
STANTON, Alexander 2007
STAPLES, Amanda 2700
   Harriet J 3109
STARIN, Sarah A 1961

STARKEY, Lewis F 530
STARR, Nathaniel Winthrop
   3061
STEAD, Emma C 3075
STEBBINS, John R 1832
   Mary Frances 2816
   Seymour L 2816
STEEL, Jesse 1682 O N 537
   Tom 671
STEELE, Frederick 329
   John B 2714 Mary Ella 2714
STEEN, Abram J 1244
   Maurice 2857
STEENBERGH, Elizabeth
   1109
STEPHAN, Frederick 2568
   Theresa 2568
STEPHENS, John 2080
   Lucy M 1131
STERNBERGH, W A 294
STEVENGER, George E 2837
STEVENS, Fannie Louisa
   2110 Hannah E 289 Jason
   1016 John G 779
   John L 289
STEVENSON, Martin 808
STEWARD, Budd 692
   Edward 1449 Nancy 1103
STEWART, --- 106 A L 700
   Alexander 99 Alvan 1810
   Anna Maria 1621
   Caroline 2210 Joel 1873
   Margaret Ellen 1041
   Mary 1810 Mary A 3115
   Mary Ann 635 Mr 754
   Rosalia 2151 Wm 939 3016
STICKLE, Almira 2911
   Harriet J 2358
STICKMAN, Henry 351

STILL, Charles H 844
  William 1154
STILLING, Sarah A 951
STILWELL, Cornelius S 938
  Elizabeth 1564
  Louise B 1156
STOCKER, Horatio W 1501
STOCKING, Dennis 2983
STOCKTON, Fannie 2983
  R F 644 Richard 644
STODDERD, George N 2718
STONE, Alvin 2180
  Augustus R 1619 Earl 2383
  Henry 57 Isabel 3103
  Jesse 1959 Mary 2781
  Mary E 1959
STORY, A J 2424
  Mary L 2424
STOUSE, Margaret 923
STOUTENBURGH, Harriet
  1328 Helen 2823
  Tobias L 664
STOW, Daniel B 867
STOWE, Helen Augusta 2328
STRANAHAN, Sarah S 1226
STRATTEN, John H 838
STRINGSTLER, John J 1281
STRONG, Susan 2023
STRUTZER, John L 1086
STUART, Charles 2123
  Kate C 2123
STUR, --- 487
STYLES, Amelia A 3104
  Andrew L 1541
  Charles W 2336 E W 3104
  George B 2620
  Hyman F 1872 J R 954
  James E 2232 James J 367
  Kate E 2491 Mary Delia 367

STYLES (continued)
  Prudence 1267 Robert S 835
SUDAM, Catherine 1229
  John 1229
SUDERLEY, Abram J 1326
SUDERLY, Isaac J 2127
SULLIVAN, Catharine 2422
  James 1689 John 709 Mr 345
SUMMER, John 638
SUMMERS, Adeline 2340
  Mary J 2408
SUTPHIN, John V 999
SUTTON, Auguston 1562
  Charles H 2931 Cornelius B
  2095 Deborah 1562 Henry L
  1225 Hiram B 2100 John C
  1831 Marvin J 3070
  Mary Anna 2622
SUYDAM, Coroner 166
  John Rutgus 1155
SWAN, Jane A 1230
SWART, Amelia 2695
  Arietta 961 Chancy M 831
  Charles Ody 417 Cyrus 1172
  Helena C 995 James 417
  John H 1580 1804
  Levi 1215 Rachel Ann 258
  Rosina 994 Sally Ann 1135
  Teunis 483 Wm 2669
  Wm M 2276
SWARTWART, John 893
SWARTWOUT, George W
  1947
SWEET, Benjamin 149
  Elizabeth 1875 Juliet 2828
SYKES, Kate P 2142
  Oren 2142
SYLVESTER, J R 702
SYMMES, Calvin 777

SYTHES, Margaret 1654
TABER, Martha 749
TABNER, Richard 229
TALLIS, Mr 88
TANEY, Col 391 Roger 391
TANNER, Emily 2654
  James 1102
TAPPEN, Eliza Elmendorf
  3061 Hiram R 2682
  J Rudolph 2632
  Richard W 1794
TATEAL, Margaret 1794
TAYLOR, Benjamin 2199
  Charles 2687 Cornelia 1154
  David A 2402 Eliza 2203
  Francis 2203 Gen 64 78 251
  H B 898 Jane M 2687 Jesse
  2380 2511 John H 2612 Julia
  1647 Lorenzo 1829
  Louisa 2106 R B 931 1104
  1725 Sarah 1197
  Sarah Louisa 2264
  Wesley 1437 William 1761
TEAL, Edward 2595
  George 2664 Henry 2418
  Lavina 2418 Mary M 2595
TEARNEY, Lawrence 205 340
TEATS, E 2633
TEEL, Harriet Ann 1211
  Henry 1211 1251
  Sarah 1251
TEEPLE, Emeline 1263
TEERPENNING, Solomon
  290
TEETSEL, Alfred 3071
  Benjamin S 3107
  Christopher 1699
  Hannah M 2982 Harlan
  2973 J Westley 2557

TEETSEL (continued)
  Joseph 2580 2732
  Lavina C 1075 Louisa 2593
  Margaret 2732 Peter 2704
TEETSELL, C Fiero 2950
  Cornelia A 2552 John H
  2950 Martha Jane 2950
TEISTLER, John 1005
TEITZEL, George 3 Mary 3
TELLER, Alfred M 1657
  James G 2066 John 1402
TEN BROECK, A J 537
TEN BROOK, Harmon Jay
  1516
TEN EYCK, A 673 Edward
  1457 Kate M 2653 P T B
  3072 Peter 1565
  Sarah M 3072
TENBROUCK, Eve 1069
TER BUSH John 1042
  Mary 1042
TERHUNE, David N 1721
  Mariah H 1618
TERPENING, Amanda 1900
  Lucinda 1544 Rachel C
  2195 Sylvester 2196
TERPENNING, Josephine
  2227
TERPIN, Sarah C 2398
TERRY, David 2235 2786
  Eliza Ann 1287 Fanny 2786
  Gertrude 1568 Harriet J
  2235 Martha 2883
  Prince 2883
TERWILLIGER, Anna M
  3028 Calvin S 1608 Eli D
  2342 Elizabeth 1244 Elmira
  1265 Emily 2342
  Hannah 1296 1657

TERWILLIGER (continued)
  Hannah M 1775 Harriet 1822
  Isaac 859 John A 2404 Levi
  2431 Martin 3071 Mary J
  1009 Rachael Ann 1482
  Robert 1401 Sarah Jane 950
  Solomon D 1996 Wealthy
  Ann 1308 William B 2026
TETER, H J 2355
TETSEL, Elizabeth A 1858
  Jacob R 1858
TETTER, Helen M 2022
THELLER, Dr 530
THOMAS, Captain 500
  Emma J 3023 George 1777
  Henry W 3042 Isaac 2341
  Sarah 3136 Wm 1200
THOMPSON, Adelia 1133
  Agnes W 1090 Austin C
  2218 Capt 398 Catharine
  1172 George 1395
  Hannah L 1578 1585
  Jane 1545 Julia Ann 226
  Mrs 11 Rachel 1619
  Samantha E 2528
  Sarah 2959 Sarah L 1431
  Sophia H 1712 Thomas
  1090 Thomas S 822
  Wm H 1815
THORN, Rebecca A 2907
  Thomas 1817
THORNTON, --- 331
  Capt 248
THORP, David 1137
  Sarah E 1253
TICE, Samuel B 2448
  William H 2955
TIEBALL, Wm 1599
TILDEN, Lieut 687

TILLSON, Timothy F 1984
TIMMERMAN, Eliza
  Catharine 1570 William 1570
  Wm W 1724
TINDALL, Henry 2464
  Jane 2464
TIPP, C B 2763
  Mary C 2763
TOBEY, Gilbert R 1606
TOBIAS, M T 164
TODD, David 2162
TOLMAN, Jacob 439 Mrs 439
TOMPKINS, Abram J 1521
  Addie H 3096 Angeline 613
  George 1796
TORNELL, --- 631
TOWNER, Margaret D 2312
TOWNLY, --- 111
TOWNSEND, Benj 1415
  Caroline F 2220 Cornelius J
  1836 Elizabeth 1860
  Hannah Caroline 1005
  Peter 1860 Richard G 996
  Sarah C 1384 Solomon 2933
  William 1205
TRACY, Julia 2939
TRAPHAGEN, Mary 2521
  Timothy 1455
TRAVER, Annie R 2855
  Eugene 2984 Jured 2067
  Lucy 2984 Osbon 1150
TRAVIS, George 435
  J S 3116 Nellie 3116
  Stephen 435
TREADWELL, Jannet B 2130
TREFRY, Henry 779
TRELEASE, William H 1377
TREMMELS, W C 703
TREMPER, Hannah 1648

TRIPP, Susan M H 1269
  Susan M S 1281
TRONSON, Adelia 1733
TROWBRIDGE, Mary 2265
TRUESDALL, Elizabeth 1067
TRUMPBOR, Mrs 767
TRUMPBOUR, Caroline 767
  Eliza 1022 Matthew T 961
  Mrs 828 879 Sarah 2918
  Valentine 2773
  William C 2767
TUCKER, John 2940
  Martha M 1967 Mr 282
TUICK, Johanna Mc Kenna 2751
TURCK, Abraham 1803
  Abram 2596 Angeline 1857
  Ann 481 Catharine E 1215
  Cornelia 850 Eliza 2935
  Georgianna 3134
  Henry 396 2608
  Henry W 2769 Hiram 1529
  Jacob 481 John A 1042
  William 1050 Wm J 1814
TURK, M A 2077
TURNBULL, Major 248
TURNER, --- 201 Amanda M 833 Angeline 1879 Carrie 2629 Charles 2645
  Diah 1879 2034 Dr 70
  Emeline 2034 Emily S 2563
  John 2629 Peter 744
  Phebe Ann 2197
TUTHILL, Geo W 1094
  Libbie 2539 Mary Ann 1094
  S H 2539
TUTTLE, Aunt 577
TWIGGS, Gen 273
  George Decatur 273

TWIGGS (continued)
  Major 272 273 422
TYLER, John 148
  Susie A 1934
TYMESON, Garret 1645
  Peter 2281
TYRREL, Addison 48
TYSON, Stephen 1124
UDELL, George C 2539
ULRICH, Matilda 1279
UNDERHILL, Alexander 2832
  Fanny 2281 James 372
  John Jay 943 Lewis 2461
  Louis 2310 Martha 2461
  Mary 812 Sarah M 1356
  Sarah Smith 2423
UNDERWOOD, Francis 1433
  Truman 195
UNGER, John 2970
UPTON, Edward 451
URMY, J 1322
URSERY, Nathaniel 161
VAIL, Mary E 1322
VALCK, Abraham F 912
  Betsy Adaline 872
VALENTINE, Rosetta W 2560
VALK, D Alexander 2607
  David A 2305 Delia C 2321
  John Henry 2306
  Jonas M 2456 Lucy L 2444
  Mary 2306 Mary Catharine 3034 Wm S 2559
VALKENBURGH, Joshua 1902
VALLETT, Jane 287
VAN AKEN, Abraham 1898
  Alfred 2367 Catharine 2196
  Celia Ann 2126 David 2277

VAN AKEN (continued)
  Eliza 2048 Giles 2156
  Helen C 2506 Isaac J 2542
  James H 2791 Jane A 2865
  Leah M 2277 Margaret 969
  Rachel Christina 1035
  Sarah A 2505
  Sarah Martha 2117
VAN ARSDALE, A H 2863
VAN BRAMER, Caroline
  2205
VAN BUREN, Aaron R 3049
  Augustus 120 Catharine 706
  Christina 707 Cora 2448
  Cornelius 1060 D Tompkins
  2430 Egbert 1283 Elizabeth
  814 Henry 527 604 Jesse H
  2869 John 120 John C 46
  Joseph 527 Matthew 2365
  Peter 1152 Philip 706 Sarah
  1496 Tobias 814
  William Andrew 706
VAN BUSKIRK, Evilena 144
  Henry W 967 J C 1813
  Wm E 2344
VAN CORTLAND, Pierre 616
VAN DE BOGERT, Susan
  1636
VAN DE WYNGARD, James
  2352
VAN DEBOGERT, Catherine
  522
VAN DENBERGH, Harriett K
  1169
VAN DER BECK, James J 892
VAN DERMARK, Dubois
  1217
VAN DEUSEN, Charles L
  2532 Columbus 2235

VAN DEUSEN (continued)
  J B 2919 Jacob L 1834
  James L 1882 Sarah 1834
VAN DOREN, Wm Theodore
  416
VAN DUSEN, George N 1111
VAN DYCK, John 2269
VAN DYKE, John V H 436
  Richard W 2078
VAN ETTEN, Adeline 1404
  Augustus 1826 Barbara A
  1715 Cornelia 2066 David
  2049 Eliza 1988 Eliza M
  1646 Endora 2105 H S 2660
  John E 1995 Leah 2133
  Louisa 521 Mortimer 1749
  Peter 1062 Phebe 2764
  Sarah 2660 Uriah 1162
  William 1646 1715 1988
VAN GAASBECK, John W
  2506 Sarah Ann 365
VAN GAASBEEK, C 2387
  Eve Mariah 1108
  Harriet 1177 Jno 1197
  Laura 2040 Martha 2067
  Peter 1924 Wilhelmus 1369
VAN GASBEEK, Nelson 1582
VAN GELDEN, Jacob 1646
VAN GELDER, Wm M 2203
VAN GOLDEN, Susan A 1213
VAN GORDEN, Abram 2390
VAN HOESEN, Garrit 1808
  Geo G 2296 Jacob 3102
  James R 2464 Kate S 2296
  Lorinda 3102 Louis W 1741
  Peter 2482 William S 2322
  Wm C 2296
VAN HOOVENBERG, Eliza
  Ann 2704 Hiram 951

VAN HOUVENBURGH, Abraham 922
VAN HOVENBERG, Jasen 2623
VAN KEUREN, Catharine Ann 2120 Catherine 1458 Fort 2405 Gerrit 1085 Jacob 2178 2373 James 1766 Joel 1880 John H 2809 Lucinda 2178 Margaret 2145 Mary Frances 2749 R S 2055 Sarah A 2672 William 1360 2172
VAN KLEEK, Mary Jane 1323 Rozilla 1355
VAN LEUVEN, Henry D 2920 Jane 1977 Sandford 2509
VAN LOAN, George 3108
VAN LOON, Charles 318
VAN NEST, --- 228
VAN NOSTRAND, E T 2366 2367 Julia 2367 Marinus 2868 Mary 2366
VAN OLINDA, Captain 272 646
VAN ORDEN, Catherine C 2201 Henry D 732 Solomon 1713
VAN OSTRAND, James 1242
VAN OSTRANDER, Louisa 2356
VAN RAMST, Eleanor C 839
VAN RENSSELAER, Nicholas 486
VAN SCHIKE, Priscilla 2134
VAN SLYKE, James 2337
VAN STEENBERG, Ann 1350 Gains 2354
VAN STEENBERGH, Jane A

VAN STEENBERGH (cont.) 2294 Lida Ann 2325 Matilda 2293 Miss 1180 Peter 1905 2310 Petronella 1926 Samuel 3051 Sophia 2219
VAN STEENBURGH, Fannie M 2420 Francis 1470 Gilbert 1309 Hiram 1299 Jane 1673 Leah C 1339 Samuel A 2917 Sarah E 2896 Sarah M 2080
VAN STEINBERG, Eliza Catharine 563
VAN TASSEL, Dennis 2721 Mary J 2721
VAN VALKENBERG, John 1021
VAN VALKENBURGH, Isaac 1219 John 1488
VAN VLECK, Peter 1932 Rachel 2474
VAN VLIERDEN, A H 1916 Alida 1443 Margaret 913 Peter 913 1443 2190
VAN VLIET, James 941 Jane 1001 William 2231
VAN WAGENEN, Jacob 2113 John B 1662 John Dubois 1811 John H 1768 Judith A 1244 L B 2522 Mary A 1638 Mary E 2913 Phebe C 1941 Sarah 1996 Susan M 2602
VAN WAGENER, John 2048
VAN WAGNER, Elmira 2154 Robert S 1507
VAN WAGONER, Louisa J 2880
VAN WART, Isabella 2968

VAN WEY, Cornelius 1722
VAN WOERT, William 1787
VAN WYCK, S Miller 2715
VANAKEN, Yetta M 1558
VANBRAMER, Alonzo 2053
VANCLEAF, Elijah 183
VANDEBECK, Mary E 2020
VANDEBOGART, Almena
  2994 Rufus 2194 Wm 2994
VANDEBOGERT, Mary A
  1978
VANDEMARK, Anna 3018
  Charles A 1138 Garret D
  1703 Hannah Maria 1746
  Jacob M 1939 Lavina
  Catharine 1628 Thomas H
  1639 Tunis 1616
  Warner 2029
VANDENBERGH, John H
  911
VANDENBURG, Eleanor
  1480
VANDENBURGH, C 1737
VANDERBILT, Sarah 786
VANDERBOGERT, Hannah
  1246
VANDERBOGET, Wm 2463
VANDERMARK, George N
  1193 James H 1550
VANDERPOOL, Judge 726
VANDEVOORT, Josiah 1334
  Mary A 3015
VANDOVER, Martha J 1521
  Stephen 1521
VANHOVENBURGH,
  Catherine C 964
VANLING, Abram H 1976
VANOVER, --- 538
VANTEMA, Pedro 757

VANVORMER, Mr 742
VASQUEZ, Gen 101
VAUGHN, Mrs 177
VAUX, Calvert 1604
VECHI, Santa Paulis 1942
VEDDER, Albert 349
  Andrew 926 John 2437
  R E De Witt 1628
  T E De Witt 1627
  William S 2551
VEDER, T E De Witt 1746
VEEDER, T E De Witt 1692
  1693 Ten Eyck 445
VELDEZ, Gen 80
VELIE, Jemima 1624
  Tunis B 1625
VERNAL, Jennie 3077
VERNOOY, C A 2197
  Melford 1597
VERPLANCK, Samuel 3012
VICKERS, James 51
VICTORIA, Queen 488
VIDERMAN, Henry A 1653
VIELE, Sylvester 1485
VIGNES, Geo A 2265
VINCENT, Christina 2782
VINE, Robert 11
VINTON, John R 79
VIRTUE, Henry 193
VOLK, David 812
VON BECK, Geo F 1974
  Mary Josephine 1974
VON DER LIPPE, Count 672
VOSBURGH, Albert H 2969
  Egbert 2605
VOTEE, Chancey B 2137
  Winslow 2659
VREDENBERGH, Abram
  1028 Levi 3028

VREDENBURG, Cornelia 1852
VREDENBURGH, A 1773
  Adelia C 1462 Maria 626
  Mary 1773 Wm 626
VROMAN, Rachel 879
VROOMAN, David 1123
WACOB, Eliza 11
WADE, Edward 270
  Henry 752
WAGENEN, Everitt 2696
WAGER, Ambrose 1854
  Effe Maria 976 Eliza C 1310
WAGES, --- 360
WAGNER, Louisa W 1502
WAGONER, Elizabeth 1447
  Sophia 1660
WAIT, Catharine A 3007
WAKEMAN, Benj 701
WAKER, Elizabeth L 2054
WALBRIDGE, Sarah A 2191
  William W 2191
WALCHEN, Dorotha 1250
WALES, Dr 471
WALKER, Alfred 2757
  Capt 310 311 George 1130
  Jane M 1264 Mrs 717
  Robert J 508
WALL, Garret D 431
  Richard 566 760 789
WALLACE, Alfred 1955
  Anna 1483 Campbell A 1573
  Lizzie 3031 Maria C 2829
  Wellington 3030
WALLINGFORD, Samuel D 233
WALSH, Catharine 143
  Mary Elizabeth 143
  Thomas 143

WALSWORTH, Lyman W 1601
WALTER, Alanson 1084
  John 11 Mary L 2415
  Matilda 1084 Mr 213
WALTERS, Coroner 555 606
  Mary J 2050
WALTON, Eleanor Jane 11
  Jacob 11 James 11 Jane 11
  John 11
WALWORTH, Chancellor 89
  Mrs 89
WANDS, John B 2977
WARBURTON, Mary E 1918
WARD, George 2037 J J 1970
WARDEN, Peter 750
WARDER, John 2102
WARDLE, H I 2221
  J K 3011
WARE, Mary 1765
WARING, Elmira 2230
WARNER, Andrew 1010
  Daniel S 1025
WARREN, Christopher H 2374 Cynthia 2375
  Le Grand 219
WARRING, Legrand 200
WARTERS, John I 953
WASHBURN, George W 3047
WASSIMAN, Maria 1294
WATERBURY, Deputy Sheriff 685 J A 1077
  Judson A 2412
WATERS, Almada 2207
  David H 1800
  George W 1251 John I 953
  Mary 1694 Sarah Ann 1776
WATKINS, H 1276
  Sarah E 1276

WATLEY, --- 331
WATSON, Col 422 Dr 11
  William 1951 James 2401
  Julia P 3111 Malbone 3111
  Mary 135 2438 Minerva C
  1951 Thomas 135
WATTLES, John O 350
WATTS, Agnes 2793 Talbot
  635 William 2897
WAVER, Maria 1555
WAY, Thomas 2290
WEAVER, Frederick 1655
  Hiram F 1951 Louisa 822
  Peter 1651 Peter C 1592
WEBB, Helen Lispenard 700
  James Watson 700
WEBER, Barbara 1366
  John 2568
WEBSTER, Daniel 529 2947
  E H 1512 Edward 529
  George 59 James I 2839
  Orange 1388 Sarah M 108
  Stephen 59 108
  Theodore 2930
WEED, Edward 1491
WEEKS, Elizabeth Ann 1701
  Emma 2991 Geo 506
  Henry 2892 Hoyt 1389
  Ida C 2759 James G 1675
  Mary O 2198 Rachel J 2713
  Sylvester 2960
  William H 1105
WEHRLE, Christian 1886
WEIDEMAN, Henry A 2615
WEIDMAN, Frederick 1830
WEISNER, Frederick 1011
WEISTER, Louis 877
WELCH, James 881
  John C 1557 Julia 1557

WELCH (continued)
  Mr 532 Mrs 30
WELLER, Andrew S 1270
WELLING, Norman M 1633
WELLS, Edward S 1157
  Elijah 1022 George 1575
  Henry 364 1260 J B 1342
  L 1170 M 2382 Mary 1471
  Mary E 1170 Mary S 2760
WELSH, Captain 772
  Stephen 656
WENTWORTH, Jeremiah
  2212
WERTH, Catharina 1364
WEST, Robert 2871
WESTBROOK, Hannah Van
  Wyck 979 Jacob 2581
  James H 3019 Jane 903
  Lybelia A 3019
  Mary E 1973 Rev Dr 979
  Sarah C 1784 Simon S 1278
WESTGATE, John 292
WESTWOOD, Annie 2538
  Betsy L 2920
WETHERELL, Mary Elizabeth
  368 Wm H 368
WHALING, James 744
WHEELER, Anna 2524
  Casens 2753 Conrad C 507
  Eliza A 2752 Eliza J 1298
  George 2366 Lavina 523 N
  K 537 Susan 1494
WHISPELL, David 1828
  Emiline 2922 John 421
WHITAKER, --- 1498
  Abm D 813 Abraham D 2592
  Adaline M 2997 Ann Eliza
  1382 Benj H 2627 Benjamin
  2699 Carroll 2946

WHITAKER (continued)
  Chauncy 3018 E 2970
  Edgar 2368 Egbert 3075
  Eli 2413 Elizabeth 2547
  Garrit Lewis 1848 Hattie
  2925 Irene 2974 James 1588
  James F 1894 Jane Angeline
  1980 Jane Ann 2699
  Jeremiah 1874
  John I 1206 1971
  John Nelson 2158
  Margaret 1123 Maria 1498
  Mary C 3032 Milinda 2824
  Moses 2467 Nathan K 2833
  Nelly 1206 Peter W 2062
  2750 R A 1163 Robert 829
  Robert H 1579 Samuel 2385
  Samuel D 2842 Sarah A
  2439 Shelden B 2209
  Theresa 2159 Thomas V L
  825 Uriah 2396 William H
  1173 Willis B 2634
  Wm H 1717
WHITBECK, Moses 2913
WHITCOMB, Newton 2507
WHITE, Capt 257 Cordelia
  2565 Dr 567 Edward D 93
  Elizabeth 2119 Ellen 2405
  Martin C 1489
  Robbert F 1650 Sarah 1917
  Wm 2272 Wm H 2089
WHITED, Margaret A 1046
WHITELY, Sarah 1698
WHITEMAN, John 209
WHITIKER, Wm H 2472
WHITING, Anna R 1004
  George 2054
WHITLOCK, Margaret A
  2513
WHITMORE, Robert C 249
WHITNEY, Alexander C 1892
  Charlotte 2446 James F 2403
  Jane 1345 Jeremiah E 1960
  Leonard L 26 Mervin 2811
  Sarah 2822 Sarah A 2098
WHITRIDGE, --- 118
WHITTAKER, Euphemia
  2495 M J 2355
WHITTLESEY, Samuel W
  425
WHITWELL, Mr 516
WIAND, Eugenia 2929
  Peter W 2011
WICKHAM, Alva 2805
  Philander S 2725
WICKS, Lydia C 927
  Rachel S 2688
WIEST, Abm V 856
  Debora 1128
WIGHT, William W 1969
  Wm H 1589
WIGRAM, Gertrude 2540
  Mary 2360
WILBUR, Gaston 895
  Samuel 805
WILCOX, Fannie M 1841
WILDER, Mary 984
WILDO, William H 40
WILKA, Louisa 1316
WILKES, Jacob 1670
  Jane 1670
WILKESON, Judge 688
WILKIE, Frederick 2206
WILKIN, Alexander 431
  Hon Mr 431
WILKINS, Capt 725
WILKLOW, Margaretta L
  1643

WILKS, Fredrick Mrs 3099
WILLARD, Mr 153 Simon 722
WILLETT, Marinus 692
WILLIAMS, --- 221 331
  Anna 1236 Calvin 2258
  Charles 898 Eliza 597
  Jacob L 2614 Jane 2428
  Jane Ann 1064 John 1177
  2959 John T 3135 Loretta
  3043 Maria Elizabeth 2450
  Mary E 14 Mr 134 Nathan
  1460 R G 2346 Rev G 217
  Sarah A 2354 2564
WILLIAMSON, Elizabeth
  1187 Isabella 956 James 891
  Mr 1148
WILLIS, Capt 70 Catharine
  1655 Sarah A 1598
WILLS, S M 1338
WILMOT, David 504
WILSEN, Matilda 2852
WILSON, Alfred J 3059
  Catharine 2132 Dr 2747
  Elizabeth 1198 Hugh 2076
  James 2484 James B 517
  Jane 2747 Jane S 2484
  Jno 1329 John 165
  Joseph 165 Midshipman 375
WILTSEY, Palmer 2207
WILTSIE, Harriet 1420
  Theresa 1378
WINANS, Belle 3120
  Elnora 2685 Henry 2064
  Hiram T 3005 John S 2685
WINCHEL, Alvina 2719
  Charles 2961 Judith 1550
  Thomas 1613
  William M 2210
WINCHELL, Catharine 1678

WINCHELL (continued)
  Catharine S 1478 James 1868
  Mary H 1806 Nancy 1837
WINCHESTER, Abel 199
  Elizabeth 2989
  Helen L 2616 John P 199
WINDER, Murray 280
WINES, Jas 1697 Sarah 1697
WINESTOCK, Samuel 2442
WINFIELD, Caroline 1304
  2979 Jane E 383 394
  Lizzie 2678 Sarah R 2807
  Stephen 1843
WING, Abraham 285
WINLEY, Lewis W 659
WINNE, Alfred 1487
  Benjamin 800 Carrie 2900
  Christian 1556 Davis 2611
  Helen Jane 1938 Ira 3114
  Jane 2436 John V 1708
  Margaret 1144
  Robert L 1701
  Sarah C 1258 William 1938
WINNIE, Cornelius C 2267
  Josephine 2611
WINTEN, Hattie 2519
WINTER, George 3055
  Lucy H 2661
WINTERS, Mary 1184
WIPPLE, Jane Ann 2314
WIRTH, Margaret D 3003
WISE, Daniel 159
WISELY, Edward 596
  Margaret 596
WISPEL, Henry E 2893
WITHERWACK, Elizabeth
  1164
WITHERWACKS, Serena
  1493

WOLCOTT, Louisa N 43
WOLFER, Anna C 2866
WOLFIN, Sally Ann 1062
WOLFORD, Caroline 1124
WOLLSY, Eunice 1930
WOLSEY, George C 2866
WOLVEN, Abram 1465 2745
  Adelbert 3008 Alice 2607
  Ann 1185 Anna M 2322
  Anna Maria 1709 Augustus
  1776 Egbert 1858 Eliza C
  2543 Elizabeth 2426 2799
  Ethan 2635 Harriet 2698
  2923 Hiram 2133 Isabella
  3093 Jacob 928 2916
  James E 921 Jane 2916
  Jeremiah 2426 2884
  Joel 1185 John C 305 2082
  2697 2698 John Henry 3034
  John K 3062 Malissa 2559
  Margaret 2081
  Margaret M 1758
  Martha 1080 Martin 1711
  Mary 2298 Mary Helen
  2915 Mary M 1711
  Nehemiah 1791
  Peter 1323 Sally 1465
  Samuel F 2322 Stephen 828
WOOD, Abram 1081
  Andrew S 409 Aurt 409
  Eliza Ann 1788 George
  1314 Henry 1120 Hilah 1054
  Hosea 1754 Jacob S 2932
  John 1728 1760 Josiah R
  1718 Margaret M 1754 Mr
  239 Nathaniel W 1167
  Simon 3119
WOODBURY, Judge 518
WOODEY, Mary E 2869

WOODSON, Henry 350
WOODWARD, Aaron Henry
  1944 Kate M 1073 T B
  1073 V R 1204
WOODWORTH, Matilda 1798
WOOLF, Scott 2808
WOOLLEY, Nathaniel C 810
WOOLSEY, Clinton 305 445
  3024 David C 2147
  Henrietta E 305 Jemima F
  445 John 1408 1942
  John J 2638 Kate 3024
  Phebe Jane 659
WORDEN, Loretta 1948
WORTH, Gen 64 71 248
WRIGHT, Edward A 1918
  Gilbert 162 Helen 1196
  Justus A 1066
  Kneeland 2069 Lemuel 470
  Lemuel S 1222 Silas 235
WURTS, Cornelia 2803
  David 2803
WYANT, Smith 2444
WYGANT, Carrie 2808
  Charlotte W 1625
  David M 1322 H 2808
  Henry 2334 John C 1624
  M H 3033 Mary F 2905
  Thomas 2904
WYNKOOP, Abraham 1467
  Eliza C 740 Francis S 2474
  Harriet Ann 1030 Henry De
  Witt 485 Hezekiah 1479
  Hezekiah H 485 Margaret W
  2021 Peter 1400 1596 1602
  Tjerck 2657 Tobias 1109
  William 1036
WYNN, Daniel 684
YAMAN, Mary 1751

YATES, John 390
　Sarah Maria 813
YAUCH, Charles 2121
YAWGER, Philip 1930
YELL, Col 70
YERRY, Christina A 1828
　David 1640 Elizabeth 837
　Fanny C 2768 Henry 849
　Philip 1828 Rebecca Ann
　3060 William 909
YOGT, Catharine E 1423
YORK, Ann Eliza 1942
　Anna Jane 1427
　Benjamin B 1670
　Daniel T D 1647
　Katie M 2555 Levi 2115
　Lizzie A 2831 Sarah 2544
YOUNG, Brigham 3066
　Charles W 1518 Coe F 809
　Eleanor J 3105
　Eliza Jane 2245
　Elizabeth 1720
　Elizabeth M 1779
　George E 1764
　Gov 219 454 507 John 1014
　Letitia 2510 Lydia W 2967
　Peter 1779 3105
　Robert 2111 Robert L 2284
　Ruth A 2638
　Sarah 1014 2754
　William Thomas 2159
YOUNGMAN, Thomas 1137
YOUNGS, James 2515
　Mary Amelia 2514
ZEIDDER, George C 924
ZEILMAN, Dolly 2456
　Isaac 2370 2512 Leah 2370
ZIELIFF, Rebecca C 1016
ZIGLER, Barbary 2691

ZIMMERMAN, Charles Phillip
1248 Joseph 2388

www.ingramcontent.com/pod-product-compliance
Ingram Content Group UK Ltd.
Pitfield, Milton Keynes, MK11 3LW, UK
UKHW021301180426
11947UKWH00015B/956